W9-BZV-934

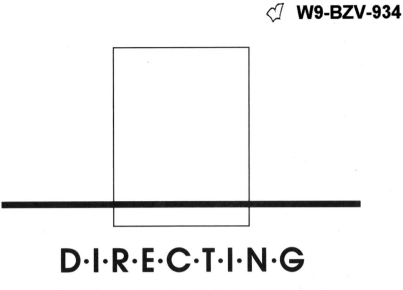

D·I·R·E·C·T·I·N·G
FILM TECHNIQUES
AND
AESTHETICS

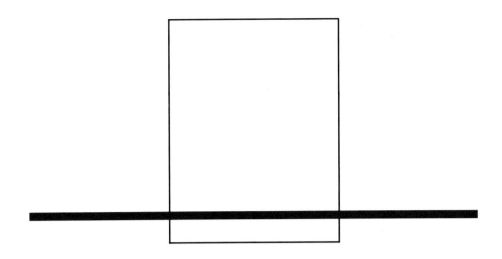

D·I·R·E·C·T·I·N·G

FILM TECHNIQUES
AND
AESTHETICS

Michael Rabiger

Focal Press
Boston   London

Focal Press is an imprint of Butterworth–Heinemann.

Library of Congress Cataloging-in-Publication Data

Rabiger, Michael.
  Directing : film techniques and aesthetics.

  Bibliography: p.
  Includes index.
  1. Motion pictures—Production and direction.
2. Motion pictures—Aesthetics. I. Title.
PN1995.9.P7R26 1989   791.43'0233   88-24543
ISBN 0-240-80011-7

British Library Cataloguing in Publication Data

Rabiger, Michael
  Directing : film techniques & aesthetics.
  1. Cinema films. Directing
  I. Title
  791.43'0233

  ISBN 0-240-80011-7

Butterworth–Heinemann
80 Montvale Avenue
Stoneham, MA 02180

10 9 8 7 6 5 4

Printed in the United States of America

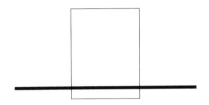

In affectionate memory of my parents

Paul Rabiger   (1912–1976)
Greta Rabiger (1913–1968)

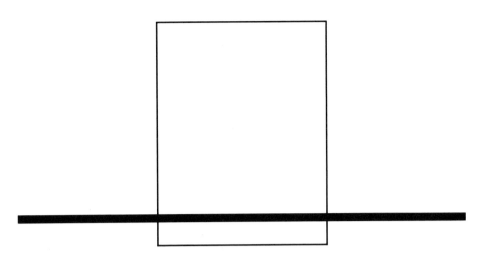

C·O·N·T·E·N·T·S

IV   AESTHETICS AND AUTHORSHIP

V   CAREER TRACK

VI   DIRECTOR AND CAST DEVELOPMENT PROJECTS

VII   FILM PROJECTS

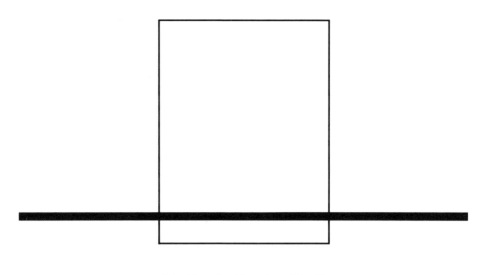

P·R·E·F·A·C·E

Here is a tried and concentrated course of development for the ambitious film-maker, whether seasoned professional or beginner. My aim throughout has been to dissolve the artificial barriers between the aesthetic and the technical, a segregation that is as rampant in film education as it is in the film industry itself. This split—a symptom, I suppose, of the way our culture divides art from technology—is particularly unreal for filmmaking since the screen is nothing if not an integrating medium. Certainly no would-be director can hide for long from the technology that makes screen utterance possible.

I believe that directors in training learn most from large quantities of practical filmmaking, so the book will lead you through the necessary technical and conceptual steps and tell you how to assess your results. Since the *why* is as important as the *how,* I have tried throughout to recommend practices and self-development procedures from within an integrated framework of theory and outlook. I have expanded this theory in Part IV: Aesthetics and Authorship.

My methods and attitudes evolved pragmatically after I began teaching sixteen years ago. At first I never questioned the logic of modeling a filmmaking education upon the professional process I had absorbed in British feature studios and at the British Broadcasting Corporation (BBC). I assumed that students, after instruction in screenwriting, basic production techniques, and the fundamentals of directing, could also form a production line and put competent cinema on the screen. How very wrong I was. Nearly always the product was that imitative and mechanical life on the screen so dismally familiar from the worst films of forty years back. I saw that other film schools were hardly doing any better.

I came to appreciate how profoundly unprepared the student is compared with any insider growing up in contact with the film industry's practices and values. I realized that an education for laymen must either substitute a set of intensive experiences for the insider's slow conditioning, or the student would never gain the requisite skills, adapt from competing to collaborating, and maintain the confidence to persist. This book represents the sum of the methods and explanations I have so far been able to devise.

It has been difficult to draw a line between what does and does not truly concern a director, but I have tried to concentrate on the creative process in all its many aspects and to outline all those matters that the director must understand or even supervise. Budgeting, fundraising, and legal matters I have left aside altogether. For this and other specialized information, consult the bibliography.

Though the book's arrangement reflects the traditional linearity of film production, this logic is mainly for the convenience of the user wanting to find information in a hurry. Throughout I stress the circularity and organic nature of filmmaking art: how important it is to respond to actors as individuals, to be ready to use improvisatory methods, to develop a creative dialogue, and to apply a holistic approach rather than the unidirectional movement of the manufacturing line. In particular I caution against treating the script as finished and immutable when, like everything else, it too is an organic entity that must either grow or die.

Recognizing that people come from different starting points and learn in different ways, the book is a resource structured around the way I have found people learn. It allows for very different skill levels and for individual methods of use. If, for instance, you are already experienced, you may want to start with the advanced considerations in Part IV: Aesthetics and Authorship. If you are a beginner wanting the basics before undertaking any production, a combination of production process chapters in Parts I through III with basic then advanced skills development exercises in Part VII might suit you best. If, like myself, you are an impatient pragmatist who prefers to learn through doing, you can jump straight into actor and filmmaking skills development through hands-on exercises and production projects in Parts VI and VII.

Each exercise or project has abbreviated conceptual instructions, technical and artistic goals, and judgment criteria to help you measure where your strengths and weaknesses lie. When production reveals specific difficulties, you can turn to the other chapters for help in analyzing and solving your particular problem.

Of course, nobody writes a book like this alone. Many of its ideas grew out of the innumerable and fruitful relationships with past and present students whose names would halfway fill this book. I have benefitted equally from interaction, advice, and criticism of my colleagues at Columbia College Film/Video Department, in particular Dr. Judd Chesler, Gina Chorak, Dan Dinello, Chap Freeman, and Tony Loeb. I owe a special debt of gratitude to Tony Loeb and Chap Freeman, whose vision, friendship, and trust during our long partnership have been of inestimable worth.

Special thanks to Tod Lending for teaching me more about dramatic form, to Ken Jacobson of Focal Press for advice on the book's organization, to Milos Stehlik of Facets Multimedia for pictorial assistance, to Gladys Mattei, and to my wife Nancy Mattei for help in developing all the phases of the manuscript. Thanks also to my cat Buford Pusser for loyal services as a paperweight.

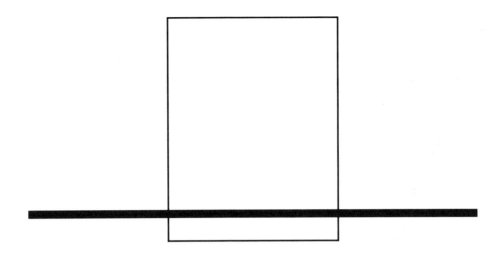

C·H·A·P·T·E·R 1

INTRODUCTION

EDUCATION FOR A CAREER

This is a good time to study filmmaking. Profound changes are taking place in the film industry, formerly closed and father-to-son like a medieval craft guild. Schools are turning out young filmmakers more experienced, more versatile, and better educated than any preceding generation. Inexpensive consumer videotape equipment is making hands-on experience a reality.

As the means of production move away from studio systems, financing and distribution should eventually become decentralized and more like publishing. Indeed, booksellers are already turning increasingly to videocassettes, and as television and videocassette machines make the moving image available upon individual demand, the need for original, contemporary screen authorship rises.

Film education and educational materials themselves need to catch up. Neither are consistent nor widely available, and though the technical skills for using camera, lighting, and sound are well documented, the conceptually based craft of directing has only been discoverable in materials pointedly intended for the theatre, or in the anecdotal material published by or about working directors. To further frustrate the aspiring director, much seemingly authoritative writing is turned out by academics lacking any experience of actual filmmaking. The depth of consciousness and range of skills that underlie even minimally competent directing are staggering, and anyone searching for a comprehensive book has been out of luck. This book aspires to fill that gap.

Developing a career is a long, uphill process, and before you commit funds to any preparatory moves you should read Part V: Career Track.

WHO CAN DIRECT?

Although mainly written for the beginner, much here will engage the media professional quietly suffocating in a technical position and wanting to break into directing. Specialization in the film industry strands many good people and leaves them segregated and in ignorance of allied crafts, above all that of directing. This book attempts to demystify the directing process for beginner and seasoned technician alike, and could even be used by a theatre director wanting to turn a play into a movie.

While I have assumed no prior knowledge of film directing or of acting, the beginner will need to acquire a good knowledge of production techniques, for which there are several good manuals (see bibliography). Even here I have tried to supply some basics so you are spared going on location carrying a library. Film technique should not be an anxiety; people who truly have something to say will figure out how to say it.

PARTICULARLY TO WOMEN AND MINORITIES

Filmmaking has long been a male preserve, but women and minorities are entering the various crafts in increasing numbers, bringing their individual talents and their different ways of seeing. This book is addressed particularly to them. My hope is that their experiences and sensibilities may eventually displace the preoccupation with power and violence that presently dominate mass culture.

THE DIRECTOR'S SKILLS

Successful screen directing relies upon the convergence of very different skills. Above all there is the need to be a down to earth doer. One must make an astute choice of subject matter, and this material—usually but not always a screenplay—needs to be thoroughly felt, comprehended, and believed in. Another skill, or perhaps instinct, lies in understanding how to fulfill the intellectual, psychological, and emotional needs of an audience. One must also understand the actor's frame of reference and the various states of consciousness the actor must control.

Good directing also means demanding much from cast and crew while making each individual feel valuable to the whole. For all this one needs the self-knowledge, humility, and toughness to be a good leader.

To find all these qualities in one human being is a tall order. Because the novice must simultaneously juggle so many untried skills, he must expect early efforts to bear the embarrassing stigma of inexpert writing, amateurish acting, and dramatic construction that is turgid and inconsistent. For these problems there has been no convenient help in print, and without access to professionals, reliable guidance is hard or impossible to find. This book is an indexed, integrated, and comprehensive approach with advice, examples, and explanations to cover most eventualities. It cannot, however, provide the patience, perseverance, and faith in self that distinguishes craftsmen and artists. That is something you supply.

WITH LOW BUDGETS IN MIND

I have assumed readers will most work with modest equipment and frugal budgets, aiming to make films of artistic reach but without elaborate settings, expensive props, costumes, equipment, or special effects. All this is both possible and desirable, for everyone respects the ability to make much out of little. Accordingly, many of the film examples come from modern low-budget cinema rather than from blockbuster Hollywood. The search for useful examples leads inevitably to resourceful, original minds working far afield in other countries and other cultures, a link that can only be good.

SHORT FILMS OR LONGER?

Anyone who has served on a festival jury knows how most films reveal their strengths and weaknesses within a few shots, or at the most in two or three minutes. The maker's sophistication (or lack of it) is immediately apparent, particularly where the troubles are basic. The trapped jury wishes ardently that the filmmaker had sought an audience after three minutes of screen time instead of a mind-numbing forty-five. The message is important: short films still require their makers to conquer the full range of production, authorship, and stylistic problems—but in a small compass and at small cost. The saving is in shooting costs and editing time, not in brainwork, for like poetry in relation to the novel, one must establish characters, time, place, and situation economically, and set appropriate limits on the subject. These are the toughest skills to learn.

Because most film schools employ feature films as examples, students generally receive inadequate guidance over how to frame short subjects. Consequently, many student films are like zeppelins, all size with no substance or agility. There is a special section in Chapter 28 on short subjects.

FILM OR VIDEO

Directing methods for screen drama remain the same for both film and video. In professional production, costs may also come out relatively equal, so film is often the preferred camera medium, although postproduction increasingly uses videotape. Currently film records a much more sophisticated image and permits a higher fidelity sound track, but this superiority will increasingly be challenged.

Videotape editing uses an electronically controlled transcription process, and although it is physically easier for the beginner, in the long run it is more arduous to control because additions and subtractions to a linear assembly are unlike the easy business of snipping into a film workprint. Film is currently easier to edit because one handles the separate pieces of sound and picture, and can see and feel what one is doing. Film editing can be likened to making a chain; it can always be broken into and links added or subtracted. Videotape compilation is like a spinning operation producing a continuous filament whose middle cannot be retrospectively altered.

Videotape is, however, a boon for people learning basic skills. For the beginner with or without access to sophisticated videotape editing, the modern consumer camcorder is a matchless learning tool. Ten years ago, shooting two hours of color sync sound rushes with a five-dollar cassette in a consumer camera was an opium dream. Now the reality is with us, and the beginner should waste no time seizing the opportunity.

With some experience and a lot of drive, you can use small-format tape to produce sophisticated work that argues persuasively for your readiness to use the more expensive formats. Since my technical discussion sometimes refers to both mediums, and sometimes either to one or the other, specialist sections are boldtyped as **film** or **video** to help the reader find particular information rapidly.

WHY THE HOLLYWOOD MODEL DOESN'T WORK FOR BEGINNERS

To appreciate which educational approaches function best, one must first compare the process of the professional feature team with that of the struggling independent group. Differences show up dramatically in production schedules alone.

PROFESSIONALS

Typically the production cycle for a feature includes

1. long, intensive script development period (six months to several years),
2. moderate preproduction period, (maybe four to twelve weeks),
3. usually no rehearsal time,
4. a very concentrated period of shooting (six to ten weeks), and
5. lengthy postproduction (four to six months).

Priorities in feature films are often determined more by dollar economics than artistic requirements: scriptwriting is relatively cheap, while tying up stars, equipment, or crew is very costly. Reliable performance is valued and experiment feared. Among actors, the ability to produce something usable, immediate, and repeatable is at a premium, while the director is under pressure to shoot a safe, all-purpose camera coverage that can be "sorted out in the cutting room" afterwards.

Locked into such a production system, the director has little option but to fight narrowly for what he (only rarely she) thinks achievable. Hollywood-style films, too profitable to change from within, are often as packaged and formulaic as supermarket novels, and look like it. A box office success is still one way for speculators to make millions overnight.

We also must consider how craft skills arise. In the industry feature film perhaps a hundred specialists carry forward their particular part of the communal task, each having begun as an apprentice in a lowly position and working half a lifetime to earn a senior level of responsibility. Many, like myself, come from film families and have had years to absorb both the job and more importantly, the mind-set that goes with filmmaking. The significance of this heritage cannot be overestimated.

Though apprenticeship is a vital factor in the continuity of skills, it is also a conditioning force that deeply discourages self evaluation and change.

INDEPENDENTS AND STUDENTS

Little of the above is apparent to the outsider, whose inclination is to climb into the shell of the professional system and try to make it work, often with the misplaced encouragement of professionals. A typical early film of, say, thirty minutes, would take roughly the following time:

1. Script (two to six months, probably one or two drafts only)
2. Preproduction (two weeks to a month)
3. Rehearsal (maybe a week, though sometimes almost none)
4. Shooting (seven to fourteen days)
5. Postproduction (six to fourteen months)

The big giveaway here is the postproduction period. Enormous time and effort is spent in the cutting room trying to recover from the problems embedded in the script (beyond the writer/director's experience), inadequate acting (poor casting, insufficient rehearsal), and shooting (hasty, too much early coverage, too little later).

I do not mean to discourage or disparage. The number of variables to be brought under control is enormous, and the newcomer cannot help but underestimate the process.

DIFFERENCES FOR THE LOW-BUDGET BEGINNER

Because the low-budget (or no budget) director seldom has a wide choice of crew or actors, he needs a method to shape nonprofessionals into a well-knit, accomplished team. Nonprofessional actors need an extended rehearsal period in which to develop empathy with their characters and the confidence that alone gives their performances conviction and authority.

Obviously the director cannot afford an immovable idea of the script's potential, because cast limitations require it to be responsive to the actor rather than vice versa. In any case a script is always a literary blueprint that by its nature is unfulfillable except through intelligent (which means flexible) translation. One can cure some of these shortcomings by choosing a subject and a treatment that need no elaborate events and environments. One can schedule more time for rehearsal (if one knows how to use it), and so on. But setting the whole low-budget situation alongside big-industry norms, it becomes very apparent that all low-budget films must set different priorities and proceed differently.

ALTERNATIVE ROUTES

It is not unrealistic to attempt professional-level results but you must travel by a road that uses trial and error as a developmental process, and makes of it a strength. As we shall see, a convincing human presence on the screen is only achieved (by amateur and professional actor alike) if the director sees and removes blocks to the actor's conviction and emotional fluidity. Left undisturbed, these obstacles will sabotage the entire film, no matter how accomplished the technical work.

The evolutionary process offered in this book creates and cements bonds between members of the ensemble, and gives the director and writer (if they are indeed two people rather than one) a positive exposure to the singularities of each cast member. The director must in turn be ready to adapt and transform the script to capitalize on cast members' individual potential.

In sum, what the Hollywood filmmaking army does with its marines and machines can be matched only if the low-budget filmmaker enters the fray as a guerrilla combatant using cautious, oblique, and experimental tactics. Once this principle of organic, mutual accommodation is accepted, the rest of the process follows logically and naturally.

Nothing in this strategy is radical or untried. A little reading will show how similar tactics have been consistently used by such diverse and accomplished talents as Allen, Altman, Bergman, Bresson, Cassavetes, Fassbinder, Fellini, Herzog, Resnais, Tanner, and many others who give primacy to the contribution by actors.

ON CINEMA AND THE HISTORY OF DRAMATIC PRESENTATION

The film director's main and often misunderstood task is not to make each actor do something extraordinary, but rather to remove a myriad of psychological obstacles. Effective screen acting lies not in the actor having a range of arcane techniques but in being relaxed, honest to his emotions, and able to jettison common misconceptions. A misconceived self-image, for instance, puts the actor's attention in the wrong place and makes him behave unnaturally. Even common psychological defenses are a major obstacle to naturalness, and more so are stereotyped ideas about acting itself. The novice feels he must produce something heightened to deserve attention and to entertain the audience. This kind of player, instead of simply being, tries to discharge his responsibility onscreen by signifying, or telegraphing thought and emotion, an activity so thought-laden and artificial that it precludes any true experiencing. He becomes a self-conscious and disunited being; one part of him performing and another anxiously watching and planning the next phase of the performance. Pitilessly, the camera reveals this unnatural and divided state of affairs.

When actors signify it is not solely inexperience or misguided effort. The impulse to stylize dramatic material actually has a long and respectable history in dramatic performance. Until modern staging and lighting methods became possible in the nineteenth century, the stage made little attempt to be naturalistic.

Greek drama was played in masks concealing the actors' psychological identity and intended to project archetypal human qualities like nobility, wisdom, or greed. Japanese Kabuki theatre used elaborate, ritualized costumes and a strange, stylized verbal delivery which, like western opera, encourages the audience to abandon surface realism for the groundswell of human passions beneath. Likewise, medieval Christian mystery plays, mime, mummers, and the Italian *commedia del arte* all used traditional characters, gestures, and episodes and all employed a stylized presentation that was deliberately nonrealistic and nonindividualisitic.

Why should the person of the actor be concealed, yet the interpretation of a stock character be so prized by audiences? Prior to the Renaissance the very idea of individual worth was a vanity amounting to blasphemy against God's purpose. The transience and bleakness of life, and the religious values rationalizing this state of affairs, made people see themselves as ephemera in a God-determined whole. Their lives were just brief threads in God's great tapestry, each individual destined to carry out a role allotted by accident of birth and patterned by such constants as ambition, compassion, love, and jealousy. Although realistic presentation to small audiences was never impossible, one sees how verisimilitude and psychological accuracy were irrelevant to the predicament audiences knew as their own.

With the new focus on individual potential that began during the Renaissance, and particularly after the impact of Darwin in the 19th century, audiences were increasingly ready to accept the significance of the individual life and to see it as a struggle for survival, rather than as a temporary stay in which to earn merit for the afterlife. Writers increasingly reflected ideas about the individual's inner life and individually wrought destiny, but acting styles seem to have been slower to change, remaining declamatory and stylized into the early days of the movies. The advent of sound cinema brought audiences eyeball to eyeball with feigned naturalism, and both actors and dramatists were forced to give new attention to what was realistic.

Just after the Russian Revolution, at a time of bold rethinking in the arts and in the wake of advances in psychology, Stanislavski in Russia developed the modern theoretical explanation for the actor's consciousness underlying any distinctive performance.

Modern audiences now expect screen characters to be no less natural than their realistically photographed settings. Unless a film strives for a subjective environment (as in German expressionistic cinema of the 1920s and 1930s, or modern genres such as horror), we have come to expect real people on the screen in real settings behaving realistically.

Given the screen's bias towards verisimilitude, realistic performances should be the student director's first goal. This is by no means easy since the process of filmmaking compels a circuitous artifice to achieve this. Cinema, with its fragmented shooting, is not even a good training ground for actors. The best seem to come from strong theatre backgrounds, where the continuity of performance and the closed loop of communication with an audience guide and instill confidence in the actor's instincts. The film actor on the other hand must perform in fits and starts; no such audience feedback is possible since during filming the only audience is the director and crew, who must be dismissed from consciousness while the camera is rolling. Acting for the camera is like being watched by a voyeur. The camera sees everything, spying at close range upon characters in their most private and intense moments, and demanding that actors live their characters' lives openly and with no lapse in experiencing their characters' inmost thoughts and feelings. Such a lapse, called "losing focus," is recognized immediately by today's audience.

Forced by the camera's realism to use realistic portrayal, the actor can seldom wear either an actual or a psychological mask, but must go maskless to merge with the part—whether that character is good or bad, attractive or ugly, intelligent or stupid. In addition, there is always a problem, particularly acute in love scenes, of behaving spontaneously before camera and crew in take after take. This throws formidable demands upon the actor's concentration, ego, and self-assurance, for it is unacceptable to merely signify villainy, or to impersonate weakness. The actor must dig deeply into his or her own emotional range in order to uncover whatever is demanded. Searching within for an "unpopular" emotion, the actor may confront an aspect of himself he finds hateful. A further threat to the actor's ego may be that of accepting and building upon critical feedback from an undemocratic audience of one: the director.

A far-ranging, "effortless" performance onscreen will be the result of an extraordinarily disciplined mind drawing widely upon its owner's emotional experience. If actor and director are to achieve such a performance, they must walk a minefield of problems together.

ON MASKS AND THE FUNCTION OF DRAMA

In various ways throughout this book I shall seek to demonstrate a curious and little appreciated fact: A cinema audience does not really go to see the film, it goes to see into itself, or more precisely, to imagine. This is no different from the reader of a novel, who reads not to see language or print, but to participate in that structured, waking, and intensely personal dream we call reading. Film at its best, with its hypnotic appeal to the senses, has also been constantly likened to dreams and dreaming.

Now we discover another purpose behind the traditional actor's masks and stock characterizations. By denying us the psychological realism of the actors, they encourage us to fill in our own mental images, just as the literary phrase "her beauty was legendary" does for a reader. Theatrical reality is masked, blurred, and held at a distance so we experience not mere human attractiveness, but the immeasurably richer beauty and terror of our own beholding mind. Ancient dramatists knew something the infant cinema is having to learn; that to fulfill its potential, an art form must not just give us sight and sound, it must evoke our imaginative cocreation.

Here we run up against the cinema's limitation: the prosaic realism of the camera, showing literally and to the last open pore whatever is placed before it. Used unintelligently it purveys a surfeit of the real and leaves nothing to the imagination. This is a severe handicap for an art medium. How can you ever show "incomparable beauty?" Films that break out of this imprisonment always, in some way, seem to connect us to the mythological, to human traditions con-

FIGURE 1–1

Carné's *Children of Paradise,* a story of unattainable love based on the Pierrot and Columbine archetypes (courtesy Museum of Modern Art/Film Stills Archive).

structed over time that unfailingly stir us at the deepest levels. The character of Garance in Marcel Carne's *The Children of Paradise* (1945) will be undyingly beautiful while one print survives and one audience member lives to see it. She is beautiful not just because the actress Arletty is beautiful, or because the black and white cinematography and the lighting are unearthly, but because her enigmatic character hides so much. She is the legendary character of Columbine reborn, the fickle, unattainable, free spirit whom poor Pierrot can never hold because he's too sincere and earthbound. In short, she raises up the poignancy of our own lost loves.

DEVELOPING CINEMA ART

Any progressive cinema form must work to activate the audience's imagination, opening up interior spaces to be filled from the hearts and minds of the viewers.

Here we are talking about richness and ambiguity in character and theme, and of a cinematic language that must further develop to show less and imply more so it can direct the audience toward something of greater worth than the superficial and the sensational. We are talking about looks, glances, averted profiles, turned backs, enigmatic silences, the suggestive voices of nature, and of primeval landscapes inhabited or abandoned by humans. We are talking of a cinema with the power to make us conscious of what exists at the dim edges of our perception, or beyond.

The more the cinema encourages the audience to bring its own experience and its own buried culture to what is on the screen, the more it will offer the emotional release of music and match the intellectual power of literature. One day it may even be able to justify robbing literature of its fans.

P·A·R·T I

PREPRODUCTION

CHAPTER 8
Final Rehearsal and Planning
Coverage   77

CHAPTER 9
Developing a Crew   81

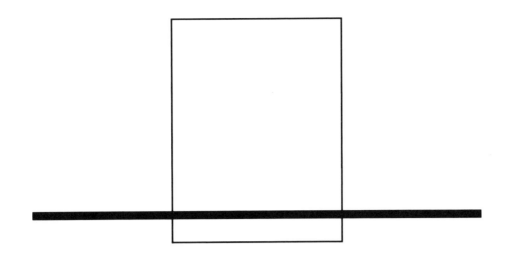

C·H·A·P·T·E·R 2

ON THE SCREENPLAY

This chapter is mainly for anyone planning to approach filmmaking with a completed script. It offers some practical guidelines on how to assess scripts and script ideas, and how to request changes and development of the scriptwriter during the script development stages.

If, however, you intend to write your own screenplay, you should carefully study the basics in this chapter and then turn to Part IV: Aesthetics and Authorship. That part of the book examines more advanced concepts and treats the authorship of a film from a more holistic angle. There you will find extensive coverage of idea development and of the aesthetic elements to be brought under control. It also considers how to find subject matter of personal significance and what is cinematic rather than imitative of other forms. Part IV also surveys the alternatives in point of view, genre, realism, and stylization, as well as in plot, structure, form, and style.

WHY NOT YOUR OWN SCREENPLAY?

The very attractive *auteur* theory of film authorship, emphasizing the integrity and control of one person's vision in filmmaking, influences many beginners to believe they should direct only from their own writing. This should certainly be a goal, but at the outset one needs the division of labor that is the strength of film as a collaborative medium, and one needs to avoid spreading oneself too thin.

By writing, directing, and editing oneself, an individual is left vulnerable to some nasty traps. Most such films are written from autobiographical sources, and by trying to reanimate remembered situations and characters, the director encounters a troublesome disparity between the developing fictional world and the purity and force of the original experience. Actors sense the restrictiveness of this situation most; fulfilling the director's exacting expectations is impossible. The resulting film is tackling too many frontiers at once and probably contains neither the subjective truthfulness of a diary nor the more objective truths of evolved dramatic vision. As a result, the director's precious self-esteem may evaporate. Another hazard is that if anyone, particularly an actor, questions the credibility or quality of the script, it becomes a disabling criticism of yourself.

This is too much to handle in your first work. You can avoid these imponderables by making your debut using a good script written by a collaborator, or by adapting an existing story (see Chapter 23). When you don't have to worry if the script is good, you will not be immobilized by self-doubt when (as is inevitable) you come under duress from the cast.

Trying to be a writer-director (or *hyphenate*) prematurely is like learning to be a juggler while learning to ride a bike across a high wire. It is simply best to learn the skills separately before combining them.

WHEN YOU DIRECT FROM YOUR OWN WRITING

If you must write and direct your own film, make it a short one. You will learn a lot, but be ready to learn from some negative experiences. Expect to have difficulty telling whether it is your directing or your screenwriting that was responsible for any failure.

In a story of your own that you strongly believe in, allow much time and effort for the writing process, and repeatedly seek out tough criticism. This is really exposing your hypothetical film to an audience for its reactions.

DECIDING ON SUBJECTS

The director should take great care in choosing a script, or a subject for a script. Unless it is a very short film indeed, you will live with your choice and its ramifications personified in the actors for a long time. Also involved are other people's time and considerable funds, so the choice needs to be wise. Once taken, it should become a commitment to completion, no matter what.

If such a commitment sounds scary, it can at least be explored with the option of retreat all through the rewriting stages. Writing and rewriting, particularly when it involves moving between the three dimensions of screenplay, step outline, and concept (explained in detail later), all allow the director to *inhabit* a text, something virtually impossible from one or two detached readings. As always when translating from one mode of presentation to another, one discovers aspects hidden from the more casual reader, no matter how expert.

Whether your film is to be comedy, tragedy, horror, fantasy, or a film for children, it must embody some issue with which you identify. Everyone bears scars from living, and everyone with any self-knowledge has an intimation of what issues smolder within awaiting attention. These can be connected with anything that has caused you very strong emotions: racial or class alienation; a childhood reputation for clumsiness; fear of the dark (horror films!), rejection by a family member, an obsession of any kind, a period of intense happiness, or a brief affair you had with someone very beautiful; a stigma such as illegitimacy, or being foreign or unjustly favored; or anything at all that has moved you to powerful feelings. Start keeping a list, and you will be surprised at how many subjects are already your own.

The object, I feel, is to produce a film that is neither a confessional nor a lesson, but a film dealing in a suitably displaced way with something you really care about and through which you can express concern for others. This is the key to communicating with an audience.

We have all come through some war zones, and one's validity as a storyteller lies with the resulting scars rather than with ideas untethered to the bedrock of experience. The emphasis should not be upon finding or writing scripts about major problems and weighty solutions, but on some corner of existence that reflects what it feels like to be alive and alive now, what it is perhaps that afflicts us or binds us in compassion and empathy for each other. That surely permits a broad choice.

Ideally you should find a film subject that is inviting because you want to learn more about it—a certainty if you commit yourself to making it into a film. Writers write to discover what they truly think, feel, and know. Filmmakers likewise make films for the joy of practicing a craft well and to better discover life's patterns and currents. Filmmaking, like other narrative arts, demands both creation and contemplation, an outward doing, and an inner growth.

WHY READING A SCRIPT IS DIFFICULT

Whether trying to raise funds or to tell actors about your intentions, much of the problem in communicating the nature of your film may arise from the difficulty of saying in advance what a film will really be like. It seems simple—you just hand someone a script, don't you? But this may accomplish nothing useful.

Scripts are very demanding to read. A well written script is purposely a minimal blueprint. Because actors, director, camera crew, and even the weather all make unforeseeable contributions, the astute scriptwriter leaves a great deal unspecified. A screenplay therefore consists of dialogue, very sparse stage directions, and equally brief remarks on character, locations, and behavior. Initially there will be no directions for camerawork or editing.

The reader must supply what is missing from his imagination, something each technician, actor, and the director contributes as a prelude to practicing his or her craft. The lay reader, wanting the detailed evocations of a short story or novel, finds that inordinate mental efforts are required to decompress the writing. This, more arduous than for reading poetry, is why nobody reads scripts for pleasure.

Inside the film industry and out, most people resist the labor of reading any script, or will read it only superficially. Since the screenplay is a verbal blueprint designed to seed a nonliterary, organic, and experiential process, it rarely gives more than a sketchy impression of what the film will really be like. A screenplay also gives no ready access to the thematic intentions behind the writing. These too must be inferred by the reader, again at considerable cost in effort. Most production companies receive several hundred dreadful film scripts a week. They give the unsolicited ones no more than a cursory glance, perhaps reading every tenth page. Because the likelihood of finding anything usable is so small, professionals often will not even look at work that has not been forwarded by a reputable agent. If you expect to be a screenwriter, you will need a good agent. If you are looking for a script, expect hard work and read very carefully.

STANDARD SCRIPT FORMS

The industry standard for layouts is simple and effective and has evolved as the ultimate in convenience. Do not invent your own.

SCREENPLAY FORMAT

Notice how in Figure 2–1 the specimen page illustrates these rules in scriptwriting.

1. Each scene begins with a full page-width capitalized scene heading that lists
    - number of the scene (once all rewrites are complete),
    - interior or exterior,
    - location,
    - main characters involved, and
    - time of day or night.
2. Body copy (action description, mood setting, stage directions) is double-spaced away from scene headings and dialogue, and runs the width of the page.
3. All character names outside dialogue are capitalized.
4. Dialogue sections are
    - within narrow margins,
    - preceded and followed by a double space,
    - headed by the speaker's name in capitals and centered, and
    - accompanied when strictly necessary by stage direction inside brackets.
5. Shot transitions like "Cut to," "Dissolve to," etc., used only when strictly necessary, placed either flush left or flush right.

Figure 2–1 is an example of pure screenplay with no camera or editing directions. Industry practice varies, many commercial scripts being hybrid creatures that try to dramatize their contents by breaking each scene into shots and making it closer to a shooting script. Done without knowledge of chosen locations, this may help sell the script but has little practical value to the director. We shall delay this phase until later.

The apprentice screenwriter's most treacherous friend is the script form itself, for its appearance and proportions reinforce the impression that films are

14. INT. LIBRARY CAFETERIA — NOON — DANA & ED

DANA places a mug of coffee on her tray next to her red helmet. She slides the
tray in sync with the quick pace of the line crowded with impatient students.
She stops at the heat lamp glowing over several small cartons of french fries.
She picks up a carton and contemplates the soggy, yellow potatoes. DANA sighs
and places the fries on her tray.

                          ED'S VOICE
              You can't live on french fries alone.

DANA, startled, turns to Ed who is chomping on a huge banana.

                            DANA
              Do you always sneak up on people?

ED moves alongside Dana as she progresses to the grill.

                             ED
              You were up and out early...

DANA reads the menu above the grill.

                            DANA
              I've got classes, remember?

                             ED
              Try the Varsity Burger, it's not bad.

                            DANA
              Whose lunch is this?

ED touches DANA on the arm with his banana hand.

                             ED
              Tired...?

DANA glares at the menu

                            DANA
                          (hissing)
              Do not touch me.

She slides the tray away. ED is momentarily stunned, then catches up with
DANA, standing close.

                             ED
              Dana... everybody cries.

FIGURE 2–1

Specimen page of screenplay format (from *A Night So Long* by Lynise Pion).

built theatrically around dialogue. While this is wretchedly true for TV soap
opera, it is quite wrong for good screen drama, which is primarily behavioral.

The screenplay format is also a danger to unwary actors and directors who
assume the primacy of the spoken over the behavioral. By cautioning in this way,
I do not mean to undercut the importance of the screenplay in the genesis of
successful screen drama. Nobody has yet demonstrated that you can effectively
coordinate actors and crew without a central structure, but that structure must
be cinematic, not literary or theatrical.

SPLIT PAGE FORMAT

This format (Figure 2–2) is frequently used in television, where multicamera studio shooting allows a whole complicated script concept to be created simultaneously. In cinema-style shooting, where each shot is created discretely and the sound "composed" afterwards in the cutting room, this density of detail is irrelevant. Split page format is, however, the only adequate layout for logging and

```
                    T.B. Sanatorium Sequence

ACTION                              SOUND
F/I L.S. Ruins of sanitorium. Camera    Birdsong, distant jet, sounds of
pans left around buildings, stops with  softball players more distant still
two small figures walking slowly

Cut to CS two pairs of feet walking     F/I sound of elderly man coughing, F/O
on brick path, weeds growing up

2S SILVIA and AARON in profile          YOUNG MAN's voice: "Dad?  Dad?"

POV shot of residential building, many  AARON: "This was his last home.  Where
windows broken                                 I saw him...

Telephoto shot of gutter with ferns            ...last.  You know what he
growing against skyline                        missed the most?"

                                        SILVIA: "Your mother?"

LS through ruined greenhouse, SILVIA    AARON: "No.  His garden.  His damned
and AARON in B/G                               garden!"

POV shot sapling growing up through     AARON: "Why did they let this place go?
broken glass roof                              It used to be so beautiful"

CS AARON's hand opening creaky gate     SILVIA: "How long did you come here?"

                                        AARON: "Just over a year.  He had a
WS enclosure with vegetable plots, one         vegetable plot here.  Towards
old man working in B/G.  SILVIA and            the end I had to do everything
AARON enter shot from camera right.            for him."

                                        SILVIA: "That's how you became such a
                                               gardener?

2S, AARON looks off camera left,        AARON: "I used to see that thing all
SILVIA follows his gaze                        the time while I was
                                               digging...

POV shot, electricity generator                ... it seemed to be waiting
building with high chimney                     for him to die".

Neglected rock garden, pond dry with    AARON: "When I was a kid and Dad had
weeds growing out of cracks                    left us, I used to try and
                                               hate him, but I never could.
                                               It was a mistake to come back
                                               here."

Frontal 2S.  SILVIA puts arm around
AARON who is disconsolate.
```

FIGURE 2–2 ————————————————————————

Example of split-page format.

analyzing a finished movie (see Chapter 33, Project 2: Editing Analysis). Unlike the screenplay format, it allows one to clearly represent the counterpoint between picture and all the various sound elements. Notice that the left hand column contains only what you would see, and the right hand column contains only what you would hear.

SCRIPTFORM CONFUSIONS

Publishers have contributed to the confusion about the true nature of the screenplay by publishing as the script of a popular film a "continuity script" or "reader's script," both transcriptions from the resulting film and not the all-important writing that initiated it. (The Glossary explains the differences.)

PREPARING TO INTERPRET A TEXT

After first reading a screenplay, examine the imprint it left on you.

- What did it make you feel?
- Who did you care about?
- Who did you find interesting?
- What does the piece seem to be dealing with under the surface events?

Note down these impressions and read the screenplay once or twice again looking for evidence of what you picked up. Next ask

- What is the screenplay trying to accomplish?
- How is it accomplishing its intentions?

Again, note these thoughts down. Now leaf through the screenplay and make a list of scenes, giving each a brief, functional description (example: "Scene 15: Ricky again sees Angelo's car: realizes he's being watched"). Using this method you transform the script into something like a flow chart, which should give you a much clearer idea of the intended film's dramatic logic. Having got an initial idea of the screenplay's structure and development, we can now look at significant detail.

GOOD SCREENPLAY ESSENTIALS

NOT OVERWRITTEN

Because a screenplay is a blueprint, not a literary narrative, it is important to exclude embellishment. A good screenplay

- doesn't include any author's direct thoughts, instructions, or comments,
- avoids qualifying comments and adjectives that will too precisely condition what the reader imagines,

- leaves most behavior to the reader's imagination and instead describes its effect (for example, "he looks nervous" instead of "he nervously runs a forefinger round the inside of his collar and then flicks dust off his dark serge pants"),
- never gives instructions to actors unless a line or an action would be unintelligible without them, and
- contains little or no camera or editing instructions.

The experienced screenwriter is an architect supplying the shell for a building knowing that the occupant will build his own walls and interiors, and select his own colors and furnishings. The inexperienced screenwriter feels compelled to specify everything down to the doorknobs and the pictures on the wall. This makes the building uninhabitable to everyone but himself.

The writer-director might seem a different case. Being in a position to know exactly what is to be shot, even where and how, it seems logical to write very specifically. But this overlooks the concessions to reality that everyone must make during filming. Without unlimited time and money, nothing ever really works out much as you envision.

OVERWRITING IS DANGEROUS

Overwriting is not just impractical, it is dangerous. Very detailed descriptions condition your readers (money sources, actors, crew) to anticipate particular, hard-edged results. The director of such a script is locked into trying to fulfill a vision that disallows all variables, even those that would contribute positively.

LEAVE THINGS OPEN

An open script challenges cast members to create their own input. The closed framework signals to the actors that they must somehow mimic the actions and mannerisms minutely specified in the text, however alien. To challenge actors means getting each to work from his own, different, and distinct personal identity rather than taking it from the script's common pool.

The good screenplay leaves the director and players to work out how things will be said and done. These should be greatly influenced by the personal qualities of the cast members and the chemistry between them and their director.

BEHAVIOR INSTEAD OF DIALOGUE

The first cowboy films made their impact because the early American cinema recognized the power of behavioral melodrama. The good screenplay is still predominantly concerned with behavior, action, and reaction. It avoids static scenes where people talk about what they feel.

PERSONAL EXPERIENCE NEEDS TO BE RECAST

A writer needs to draw a conscious line between the intensity of life as lived and what is moving or exciting in the cinema. In a moving personal experience, one is actively involved and acted upon, feeling the stresses subjectively. Screen drama must, however, be structured so that characters' inner thoughts and emotions communicate to outsiders through the characters' outwardly visible behavior. Drama is doing. What matters on the screen is what people do.

TESTING FOR CINEMATIC QUALITIES

A simple but deadly test of a script's screen potential is to ask how much of it the audience would understand with the sound turned off. Examining each sequence like this produces a relief map showing how much of a script is cinematic and how much is really radio drama with pictures. This is not to deny that people talk to each other or even that many transactions of lifelong importance take place through conversation. But dialogue should be used when it is necessary, not as a substitute for action.

CHARACTER

We judge an unknown person's character on the screen as we do in life, by looking first at physical appearance, body language, clothes, and how the person wears them. We look at the person's belongings and surroundings, and watch how he or she handles common situations. We begin to see background, formative pressures, assumptions, and associates. We learn which among these the person chose and which he or she must unwillingly accept. How the person interacts, in particular with the unfamiliar or threatening, will tell us much, as do the reactions of friends and intimates. Such interaction helps in turn to establish the relative temperaments and histories of the other characters.

Most of all we draw conclusions about character from the moral quality of a person's deeds. Unexpected actions often modify or even subvert what has hitherto appeared to be true, perhaps totally contradicting what the person says and believes.

Personal character is not just a product of personal history; it also is an active component in shaping a person's destiny. Knowing this, the astute dramatist is selective, showing only those acts, situations, and environments that will power the protagonists' forward movement in the plot.

STATIC CHARACTER DEFINITION

When looking for a screenplay's potential, assess the characters by more than their eccentricities. Useful as a character's "givens" are age, sex, appearance, situation, etc., and these can easily give rise to a static summation, something like a photograph that typifies a person by freezing him or her in one attitude. Here prior information is released and change is shown retrospectively as a series of steps already completed. Watching this kind of film is analogous to viewing the panels of a medieval fresco where each character is fixed in a typical role and attitude. The same constriction afflicts the TV commercial. Because of its propagandistic purpose and its brevity it sets character rapidly by one dominant, unchanging characteristic. People in commercials are typical: a typical mother, a typical washing machine repairman, a typical holiday couple on a typical romantic beach. Homes, streets, meals, and happy families are all stultifyingly typical. In a dramatic piece conceived like this, players put great effort into bringing the static conception to life, but everything their characters do, everything that happens to them, converges back into that dominant and static conception. This denies and paralyzes all the willpower, tensions, and adjustments present in even the most quiescent human being, and prohibits the very growth and change that is the lifeblood of true drama.

DYNAMIC CHARACTER DEFINITION

What we need is a dynamic conception of character, one concerned with flux, movement, and mobilizing the potential for development. A simple alternative way of regarding character, useful alike to writers and actors, focuses upon a character's will. To uncover this, we must keep asking at every turn

- What is this character moving toward?
- What is this character moving away from?
- What does this character want to get or do?
- What specifically is stopping him/her?
- How does he/she adapt to this obstacle in order to overcome it?

While these action-oriented questions can be applied in a general way to the phases of a character's whole career, their most vital function is in defining the phases of development in a single scene, moment by moment. When you asses a script's potential, you should be able to extemporize on each main character's volition and know every step of the way what he or she is trying to accomplish. This will only be true of a well constructed script. In a poor example, where the writer does not understand the importance of volition, trying to answer these questions will quickly reveal both its handicap and some of the solutions.

CONFLICT, GROWTH, AND CHANGE

Vital to any story is that at least one character grows and changes. This development can happen with even minor characters if each has an agenda; that is, things to struggle for and conflicts to face. In fact each of these character-defining questions above seeks evidence of conflict and movement. If they are answered creatively by director and cast, each character assumes an exciting potential for change. Most important is that the main or "point of view" character goes through significant changes that add up to a growth in awareness. This is the cardinal sign of a good script.

PLANNING ACTION

At its most eloquent the screen is a behavioral medium, one that shows rather than tells. With this in mind, look at the list of sequences you made and rate each by how readily it could be understood by a deaf person. In some sequences you will see that the film's narrative is evident through action. In others the issues reach only a verbal level and will need translating by the screenwriter into action if at all possible. For example, in a breakfast scene when a father gives his young son a sermon about homework, you could work out some "business" in which the boy tries to rearrange and balance the cutlery and cereal boxes, and the father, trying to get his full attention, keeps stopping him. Though we do not see the precise subject in dispute, we have found a way to externalize as action the conflict between the two. Whether this is best kept for the actors to work on or whether it calls for script revision is a matter of judging whether it will encourage or inhibit your actors' creativity. Too little margin for imagination is stultifying; but too open, static, and empty a text may demand an undue level of inventiveness from them.

Another way to handle the scene might be to have the boy come home and find his father waiting for him with the schoolbooks in front of him. Reluctantly, the boy sees what is at issue and silently takes the books into his room. Later his father looks in and finds his son sprawled out listening to music through headphones. At breakfast the boy avoids his father's eye, but, unasked, goes out to get his father a paper, signifying that he feels guilty and remorseful. Now the need for confrontation and interaction has been turned entirely into a series of situations and actions, completely avoiding the theatrical set-piece conversation.

However you solve the problem, every issue must find its counterpart in action of some kind. It may be minimal facial action, it may be movement and activities of a revealing metaphorical nature, or it may be movement that the character thinks will cover rather than reveal his true feelings.

Action is the manifestation of will. Notice, however, that it is frequently in conflict with what a character actually says. Through contradictory speech or action a person reveals both his inner and outer dimensions, the conscious and the unconscious, the public and the private.

The antithesis of this principle is the soap opera script, where a tide of verbiage drowns whatever might be alive and at issue.

ROSE
Uncle, I thought I'd just look in and see how you are. It's so miserable to be bedridden. You're Dad's only brother and I want to look after you if only for his sake.

UNCLE
You're such a good girl, I always feel better when you look in. I thought I heard your footsteps, but I wasn't sure it was you. It must be cold outside—you're wearing your heavy coat.

ROSE
You are looking better, but I see you still aren't finishing your meals. It makes me sad to see you leave an apple as good as this when you normally like them so much.

UNCLE
I know dear, and it makes me feel almost guilty. But I'm just not myself.

I wrote this to show the worst abominations. The writing keeps the characters static, there is no behavior to signify feelings, and no private thought going on behind the public utterances. Neither character signifies any private feelings or any of the hidden agenda that gives the family relations their undercurrents. Even between people who like each other there is always tension and conflict. Here the writing grips the audience in a vice of literalness, allowing no unspoken understandings between uncle and niece for the observer to infer. Most damning, nothing would be missed by listening with eyes closed.

By rewriting this scene to include behavior, action, and interaction, one could prune the dialogue by 80 percent and end up with something animated by a lot more tensions. If, for instance, one of the scene's functions is to reveal that the old man is the brother of Rose's father, there must be a more natural way for this to emerge. Here information issues from her mouth like ticker tape. Perhaps one could write a version where she stops in her tracks to stare at him. When he asks what the matter is, she can answer, "It must be the light. Sometimes you look so much like Dad." His reaction—whether of amusement, irritation, or nostalgia—can even give us clues as to what kind of relationship existed between the brothers.

DIALOGUE

In the cinema, dialogue follows the vernacular speech of the type of person depicted. According to whether this is a young hood, an immigrant waitress, or an academic philosopher, you might expect the person to speak street slang, broken English, or in strings of qualified, jargon-laden abstractions.

Dialogue in movies is different from dialogue in life. It is more succinct though just as informal and authentically "incorrect." It must also be written to allow for what the camera and the microphone make clear, to avoid getting redundant information ("You're wearing your heavy coat," as above).

Each character should have his or her own dialogue characteristics; vocabulary, syntax, and verbal rhythms should be special and unlike another's. Good dialogue is hard to write, an art in itself. Eavesdropping with a cassette recorder will give you superb models by which to judge movie lines. If you transcribe everything you hear, complete with "um," "er," laughs, grunts, and pauses, you will see that normal conversation is not normal at all. People converse elliptically and at cross purposes, not in the tidy ping-pong dialogue of the stereotypical drama. In real life silences are often the real "action" during which extraordinary currents are flowing between the speakers.

Good dialogue is really a form of action because each line aims to accomplish something. It is pressure applied even when it seeks to deflect pressure experienced. It is active and structurally indispensable to the scene, never a verbal arabesque or explanation of what is visible.

The best way to assess dialogue is to repeat lines aloud. Listen to the sound. Is there a better balance of words or sounds? Can it be briefer? Is what it hides interesting? Does it carry a compelling subtext (that is, a deeper underlying connotation)? Does it promote calculation or emotional response in the listener? Is it in character with the speaker? If you are used to writing poetry all these questions will be familiar.

PLOT

The plot of a drama is the logic and energy that drives the story forward, taking the audience's interest with it. Because it is unavoidably complex and closely allied to a film's structure, I have dealt with it later in Chapter 27: Plot and Structural Alternatives.

METAPHORS AND SYMBOLS

What makes the cinema so powerful is that the settings, moods, objects, and actions often function as metaphors for the hidden inner experiences of the main characters, or as a revealing arena for a particular issue. The parched, bleached settings in *Paris, Texas* (1984) are emblematic of the emotional aridity of a man compulsively searching for his lost his wife and child. In John Boorman's *Hope and Glory* (1987), the beleaguered suburb and the lush riverside haven dramatize the two inimical halves of wartime England, and also suggest the boy's split loyalties to the different world and social class of each of his parents. The film is full of symbolic events and moments, a powerful one being when the boy disinters a toy box from the ruins of the family's bombed house. Inside are lead soldiers charred and melted in eerie mimicry of the Auschwitz dead. The image is only on the screen a few seconds, yet it lives on in one's memory. It represents war and loss for the boy, who is the son of a soldier, but also for humanity immolated in warfare and particularly for the victims of the Nazi holocaust. It also suggests the poignant irreversibility of change itself.

Symbols and symbolic action have to be artfully chosen because advertising has equipped audiences to reject the manipulative symbol or the over-earnest metaphor even before it has fully taken shape. Most importantly, metaphoric settings, acts, and objects need to be organic, that is, drawn from the world in which the characters live. They must not be imposed from outside or they can easily look contrived.

INVISIBLE FOUNDATIONS: THE STEP OUTLINE AND THE TREATMENT

Though a screenplay shows the quality of the dialogue writing, it offers little about point of view, that is, what subjective attitudes and inferences remain to be conveyed through acting, camerawork, and editing. It explains still less the ideas and authorial vantage point motivating the writing in the first place.

If you are starting production work from a completed script, you will need to make (or obtain from the writer) some short-form writing that will help you gain a dramatic oversight of the piece in view.

STEP OUTLINE

Writing methods vary considerably, but most writers produce a step outline first. Here the writer summarizes in short story, third-person, present tense form only what the audience will see and hear from the screen, allowing one numbered paragraph per sequence. It should read as a stream-of-consciousness summation that never digresses into production details or into the author's philosophy. If you make the step outline, remember to set down only what the audience sees and hears, and stick to essentials. Write no dialogue, just summarize in a few words each conversation's subject and development.

Each numbered sequence is a step in the story's progression. The step outline is a concession to the busy reader who wants a compact, narrative overview before deciding whether to go further and read the full screenplay, and it is also an extremely effective way of getting a bird's eye view of the balance and progression of the material.

TREATMENT

The step outline is often called a treatment, but this term is used interchangeably for the puff piece a writer must generate to get a script considered by a production company. Geared towards establishing the commercial potential of the film, these function like a trailer advertising a coming attraction, and often present the screenplay idiosyncratically according to who is the target.

PREMISE OR CONCEPT

Neither the screenplay, treatment, or step outline articulates the ideas underpinning the film's dramatic structure and development. This is directly defined in the dramatic premise. This expresses the dramatic idea behind the scene, or even behind the whole movie. For *Don't Look Now* (1973) it might be, "A rational man who denies both the paranormal and his own repeated instances of clairvoyance must eventually be destroyed by the fate of which he was repeatedly warned." If you and your writer are rewriting, you will find that examining and reexamining the concept will yield the paradigm to your latest labors and let you know if your work is still thematically focused. Like everything else in an organic process, the premise can change as writer and director journey deeper into the material.

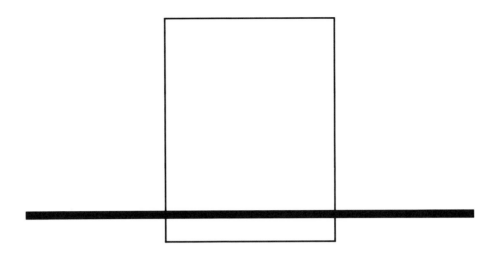

C·H·A·P·T·E·R 3

THE DIRECTOR PREPARES
THE SCRIPT

THE SCRIPT

If you have already made the step outline and concept described in the last chapter, you are on your way to becoming thoroughly conversant with its inner workings and practical implications. Since the screenplay is skeletal and open to a wide spectrum of interpretation, you will need to further assess your script's potential and to build upon it methodically and thoroughly.

FIRST IMPRESSIONS

If the screenplay is new to you, read it quickly and without interruption, noting your random first impressions. These can be a vital resource later when essentials become blurred through overfamiliarity with detail. First impressions are intuitive and, like those about a new acquaintance, become increasingly significant with greater familiarity. Make a step outline showing each sequence's function and define the film's concept.

DETERMINE THE GIVENS

Reread the script slowly and carefully, and determine what is a given, that is, what is directly specified in the screenplay. This is your hard information, which includes locations, time of day, character details, and words used by characters. All these givens are fixed and serve as the foundations determining everything else. Much is deliberately and wisely left unspecified, such as the movements and physical nature of the characters and the treatment to be given the story in camerawork, sound, and editing. The givens must be interpreted by director, cast, and crew, and the inferences each draws must eventually harmonize to be consistent. To each actor, for instance, the script provides everything known about his character's past and future. A character, after all, is like the proverbial iceberg—four-fifths being out of sight. What is visible (that is, in the script) allows the actor to infer and develop what is "below the water line" (the character's biography, motives, volition, fears, ambitions, vulnerabilities, and so on).

BREAK INTO MANAGEABLE UNITS

Next, divide the script or treatment into workable units by location and scene. This helps you to plan how each unit of the story must function and initiates the process of assembling a shooting script. If, for example, you have three scenes in the same day-care center, you will shoot them consecutively to conserve time and energy, even though they are widely spaced in the film. When production begins, everyone must be well aware of the discontinuity between the three scenes or actors may inadvertently adopt the same tone, and camera crew shoot and light in the same way. In storytelling, one is always looking for ways to create a sense of contrast, change, and development.

PLAN TO TELL THE STORY THROUGH ACTION

As mentioned in the previous chapter, cinematic films remain largely comprehensible and dynamic even with the sound turned off, so you should devise your screen presentation as if for a silent film. This way you will tell your story cinematically rather than theatrically—through action, setting, and behavior rather than through dialogue exchanges. This may require rewriting.

DEFINING SUBTEXTS

The notion that every good text is a lifelike surface hiding deeper layers of meaning or "subtext" is invaluable. It reminds us that as dramatists we must always search out the submerged stream of heightened significance flowing beneath life's surface.

THE DISPLACEMENT PRINCIPLE

In life, people very rarely deal directly with the true source of their tensions. Instead, what takes place is a displacement. Two elderly men may be talking gloomily about the weather, but from what has gone before, or from telltale hints, we learn that one is adjusting to the death of a family member and the other is trying to bring up the subject of some money owed to him. Although what they say is that the heat and humidity might lead to a storm, what we infer as the subtext is that Ted is enclosed by feelings of guilt and loss, while Harry is realizing that once again he cannot ask for the money he badly needs.

The scene's subtext can be defined as "Harry realizes he cannot bring himself to intrude his needs upon Ted at this moment, and that his situation is now desperate." We cannot interpret the subtext here without knowledge gained from earlier scenes, and this demonstrates how drama that is well conceived builds and interconnects.

AMBIVALENCE, OR BEHAVIORAL CONTRADICTIONS

Intelligent drama exploits the way each character consciously or otherwise tries to control the situation, either to hide his underlying intentions and concerns or, should the occasion demand it, draw attention to them. Once we know the subtext, we can contrive behaviors for each character to indicate the contradictions between his inner world and his outward self-presentation.

Ambivalency in the characters is the cinema audience's main evidence of a character's hidden and underlying tensions. When actors begin to act upon (not merely think about) their character's conflicts and locked energies, scenes move beyond the linear, superficial notion of human interaction and we begin to truly feel the characters' emotions. The dramatic work now begins to imply the pressurized water table of human emotion below the aridly logical top surface.

DEFINING A THEMATIC PURPOSE

Another concept vitally important to the director is that of the thematic purpose, or "superobjective," to use Stanislavski's word. This describes the authorial objectives powering the work as a whole. One might say that the superobjective to Orson Welles' *Citizen Kane* (1941) is "to show that the child is father to the man, that the power-obsessed man's course through life is the consequence of childhood deprivation that no one around him ever understands."

It is mandatory that you define a thematic purpose for a work in script form if you are to truly capitalize upon the script's potential. Usually one has a strong intuition about what it is, but it should emerge when you link up each scene's subtext as described above. A script's thematic purpose is to some degree a subjective entity derived from the author's outlook and vision. In a work of some depth, neither the subtexts nor the thematic purpose are so fixed and limited that interpretive choices for the director and cast are fixed and limited. Indeed, these choices are built into the way the reader reads and the audience reacts to a finished film, because everyone interprets selectively what they see from a background of particular experiences. These are individual but they are also cultural and specific to the mood of the times.

Kafka's disturbing story "Metamorphosis"—about a sick man who discovers he is turning into a huge beetle—might be read as a parable about the changes people go through when dealing with the incurably sick, or it might be read more from a science fiction perspective as a grisly "what if" experiment in locking a human sensibility into the body of an insect. In the first example, the thematic purpose might be to show how utter dependency robs the subject of love and respect, while the second shows how compassion goes out to a suffering heart only when it beats inside a palatable body.

Whatever you choose as your thematic purpose, it must be articulated, consistent with the text, and eventually acceptable to your creative collaborators.

Divergent, unexamined readings produce contradictory interpretations, so finding a shared understanding of the story's purpose is a prime requisite for integrated storytelling.

GRAPHICS TO HELP REVEAL DRAMATIC DYNAMICS

Below are a couple of ways to expose the heart and soul of each scene. These methods for exposing what would otherwise remain undisturbed and unexamined are consciousness-raising techniques that allow the director to confront the implications of the material. They take time and energy to implement, but will richly repay your effort.

BLOCK DIAGRAM

Make a flow chart of the movie's content, with each sequence as a block. To do this conveniently, photocopy the Story Line/Editing Analysis Form (Figure 3–1). In the box name the scene, and under "Contributes" write two or three lines to describe each scene's dramatic contribution to the story line, as in Figure 3–2. This goes further than the step outline because it is predominantly concerned with dramatic function rather than content. What you write might be predominantly factual (information that is part of a larger exposition), character defining, or the building of mood and atmosphere. Having to write so briefly makes one find the paradigm for each—a brain-strain exercise of the utmost value.

Soon you will have the whole screenplay diagrammed as a flow chart and you will be surprised by how much more you learn about its structure and its strengths. Among weaknesses look for

- expository scenes that are flat and static releases of information,
- the repetition or delayed appearance of important factual information,
- confusions in time progression,
- bunching of similar events or actions,
- disappearances of important characters for long periods,
- characters suddenly appearing to serve a limited dramatic purpose,
- a lack of alternation in mood or environment,
- excitement too early leading to anticlimax,
- similarity (and therefore redundancy) in what some scenes contribute, and
- multiple endings because of indecision over what (and therefore how) the story must resolve.

GRAPH

Another way to dig below a script's surface is to graph out the changing emotional pressures or temperatures of each scene. It can be done straight after rereading the script, but with a problematical scene it is a good exercise to do collaboratively with the actors after some initial rehearsal. I do it by making time the graph's baseline and the vertical according to prevailing tension, either

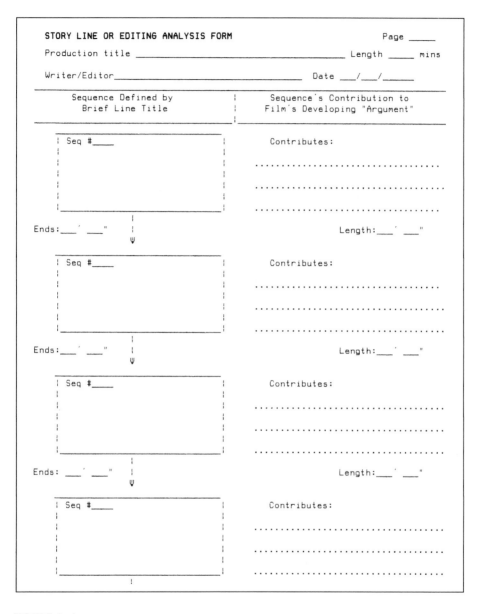

FIGURE 3–1

Form for script or editing analysis.

for the scene itself or for each main character. If, for instance, you have a comedy scene between a dentist and a frightened patient, you could graph out the rise and fall of the patient's anxiety, and then rehearse the action to progressively escalate the patient's fear and link to it the rising irritation of the dentist. Each dramatic unit within the scene culminates with a moment of realization for one

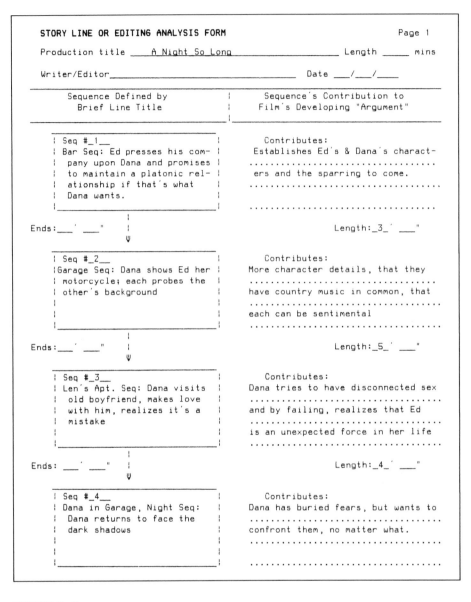

FIGURE 3–2

Specimen of block diagram analysis of a script.

or other of the characters, called a "beat" (see "Finding the Beats" in Chapter 7 for a fuller explanation).

Before you begin shooting, make a "barometric" chart for your whole film's emotional dynamics. It will not be easy because you will have to invent graphing coordinates to reflect the issues in your particular film, but again you will be surprised at how much your homework reveals. I discovered the utility of this exercise the hard way; I found I had directed a film in which many scenes had surreptitiously adopted a uniform shape and were restating the same emotional information.

To put the graphing method into action, here is a scene based on an experience of my father's in wartime London, when food was scarce and often acquired on the black market. Note that for a film treatment we put it into the present tense.

> Paul is a sailor from the docks setting out for home across London. On board ship he has acquired a sack of brown sugar and is taking it home to his family. Food of all kinds is rationed, and what he is doing is very risky. He has the sugar inside a battered old suitcase. The sugar is as heavy as a corpse, but he contrives to walk lightly as though carrying only his service clothing. In a busy street one lock of the suitcase bursts, and the green canvas sack comes sagging into view. Dropping the suitcase hastily on the sidewalk he grips it between his knees in a panic while thinking what to do. To his horror, a grim-faced policeman approaches. Paul realizes that the policeman will check what's inside the suitcase, and Paul will go to prison. He's all ready to run away, but the policeman pulls some string out of his pocket and gets down on his knees, his nose within inches of the contraband, to help Paul tie it together. Paul keeps talking until the job's done, then thanking him profusely, picks up the suitcase as if it contained feathers, and hurries away feeling the cop is going to sadistically call him back. Two streets later he realizes he is free.

The graph in Figure 3–3 plots the intensity of each character's dominant emotion against the advance of time. Paul's emotions change, while the unaware policeman's are simple and placid by contrast. Paul's stages of development roughly are

- trying to walk normally to conceal weighty contraband,
- sense of catastrophe as suitcase bursts,
- assuming policeman is coming to arrest him,

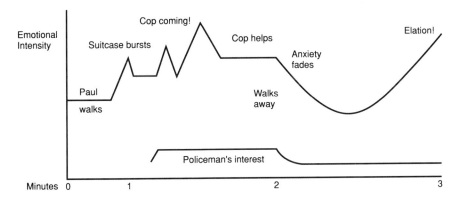

FIGURE 3–3

Graph expressing changes of emotional intensity in two characters.

- realizing his guilt is not yet apparent - all is not yet lost,
- tension while trying to keep policeman's attention off contents,
- making escape under policeman's ambiguous gaze, and
- realizing he's got away with it - sense of joyous release.

A visual of this kind is useful for the clarity it brings to changes in the dominant emotions. It shows the need to create distinct rising and falling emotional pressures within the characters, pinpoints where characters undergo major transitions, and focuses director and actor on the need to externalize these through action.

In the scene above, the policeman feels only a mild, benign interest, which falls away as the sailor with the successfully mended suitcase goes on his way. It is a very different situation for Paul. He must conceal his feelings, assuming the facade of an innocent man troubled only with a luggage problem. Knowing something the policeman does not know, the audience empathizes with the sailor's anxiety and appreciates his efforts to project petty concerns. What is missing from the scene is the knowledge of (1) the nature of the contraband, (2) where he is going with it, and (3) what he risks if he is caught. For the scene to yield its full potential, all these plotting points would need to be established earlier.

POINT OF VIEW

We could add a dimension to our scene by underscoring Paul's subjectivity. By having the policeman appear threatening as he approaches, we could make him seem to be testing Paul's guilt by offering to help. Only late in the scene would we reveal his benign motives. Camerawork, emphasizing the bulging, insecure suitcase with the policeman approaching close to it, would suggest visually the thoughts uppermost in Paul's mind.

Here we are revealing one character's point of view, which means relaying evidence that makes us identify with a particular character. This allows us to investigate the experience of unsympathetic characters as well as those of a spotlessly heroic stature. This is an important departure from the good/evil dichotomy of the simple morality play where only a main character is a rounded portrait and all the subsidiary characters remain flat.

The concept of subjective and objective points of view is enormously important to sophisticated storytelling. Unlike literature, which can easily move the reader from one person's consciousness to another, or pull away to the storyteller's bird's-eye view of human life, point of view is harder to shift in film because the camera records so impersonally and objectively. However, in my example the audience has been led to participate in Paul's inner experience while seeing all the time how he conceals what he is feeling. Actors and directors of long experience carry out this duality intuitively and it is the clarity and force of subjectivity revealed in this way that contributes so much to a satisfying performance. For the beginner lacking unfailing instincts in this direction, nothing less than a detailed, moment-to-moment analysis will yield the insight to mold the scene effectively.

Sc	Location	Script pages	Catherine	Isabella	John Thorpe	Henry Tilney	James Morland	Eleanor	Mrs. Allen	General Tilney	Mrs Thorpe
							NORTHANGER ABBEY				
1	The Dance	1-2	*						*		
2	Lower Rooms	2-6	*			*					
3	Pump Room	6-7		*							*
4	Mrs. Allen's	7-13	*	*	*		*				
5	Pump Room	13-20	*	*		*	*	*			
6	Mrs. Allen's	20-24	*	*	*		*			*	
7	On the Journey	24-25	*		*		*				
8	At the Theatre	25-27	*			*				*	
9	Mrs. Allen's	27-30	*	*	*		*	*		*	
10	Out Walking	30-35	*			*		*			
11	Mrs. Allen's	35-37	*	*							
12	In the Street	37-40	*		*						
13	At the Tilneys'	40-41	*					*		*	
14	Mrs. Allen's	41-43	*	*							

FIGURE 3—4

Typical scene and character breakdown table shows which characters, locations, and script pages are necessary for each scene.

A complex and fascinating topic, point of view receives more advanced coverage in Part IV, particularly Chapter 24.

GENERALIZED INTERPRETATION IS THE MOST COMMON FAILURE

Inexperienced players will approach a scene with a correct but generalized attitude gained from a reading or discussion. Applied like a color wash and without regard to localized detail, the unspecific, monolithic interpretation produces a scene that is fuzzy and muted where it should be sharp and forceful. Acting to a series of clear specific goals within a scene is effective acting while acting to a generalized average is its enemy. Ways to achieve this clarity are discussed in Chapters 5 through 8.

SCRIPT BREAKDOWN IN PREPARATION FOR REHEARSAL

Take the script and make a breakdown of characters appearing in each scene, like the one in Figure 3–4 made for a treatment of *Northanger Abbey*. A breakdown like this, allowing one to see at a glance which scenes require which location and what combination of actors, will be essential for planning the rehearsal schedule and the eventual shoot. It also indicates the film's inherent pattern of interactions and is yet another aid to discovering the work's underlying structures.

FIRST TIMING

A film's length absolutely determines the markets it can enter. Television has strict length requirements, so keeping control over length can be vital. Already you need to know how long the script will run. You can get a ballpark figure by allowing a minute of screen time per screenplay page. This should average out across many pages but will not necessarily work for specific passages such as a rapid dialogue exchange, or a succession of highly detailed images with long, slow camera movements. You can get a more reliable figure by reading over each scene aloud, acting all the lines, and going through the actions, either in the imagination, or for real. Using a stopwatch, make a notation for each sequence, then add up the total.

Be aware that rehearsal and development invariably slows material by adding business not specified in the script. This kind of action, described in detail in Chapters 5 and 7, must be present if the characters are to be credible and the film cinematic rather than theatrical.

If rewriting makes a scene too long, reexamine every line of dialogue to see if newly developed action makes any of it redundant.

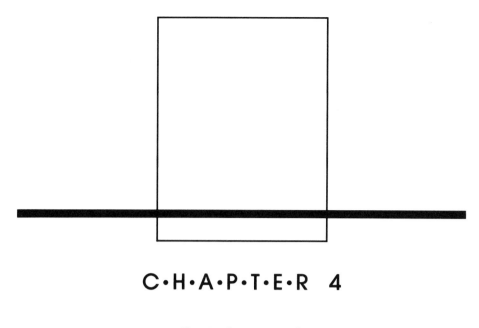

C·H·A·P·T·E·R 4

CASTING

Good casting contributes massively to the success of any film, but it is a process that beginning directors often do poorly. Many settle uncritically for the first person who seems right, or who has already proved reliable.

The object of auditioning is to find out as much as you can about the physical, psychological, and emotional makeup of each potential cast member so you can commit yourself confidently to the best choice. Doing this means initially putting many actors through a brief procedure that reveals the character of each, and indicates how he or she handles a representative situation. Later there will be semifinal and final rounds of auditioning. While procedures can be adjusted for actors with little or no training, the first aim is to identify the individual behind the facade. The director is therefore concerned with a potential actor's

- physical self (features, body language, movements, voice),
- innate character (confidence, outlook, reflexes, rhythm, energy, sociability, imprint made by life),
- intelligence (sensitivity to others, perceptiveness of environment, degree of self-exploration, and cultivation of tastes),
- grasp of acting (experience, concepts of the actor's role in drama, craft knowledge),
- directability (interaction with others, flexibility, defenses, self-image), and
- commitment (work habits, motivation to act, reliability).

THE DANGERS IN IDEALS

There are two ways to think of casting. One is to question, naturally enough, whether this particular man in front of you is right for the character of the father in the script. There is, however, a hidden bias in this attitude. The actor is being held up to an ideal of the character, as though the character were already formed, and the actor either right or wrong. This puts emphasis upon a premeditated image of the character and unconsciously you are viewing your actor through a cookie cutter. The actor, under this measurement, must always fail. Casting a film from a mental master plan is like marriage for the man knowing what his Miss Right must be before he has even met her.

Much better is to ask yourself, "What kind of father would my film have if I cast this actor?" By this you acknowledge that the role is capable of many possible character shadings. Casting becomes developmental rather than merely reproductive. Very importantly, you are already treating the actor's physical and mental being as an active collaborator in the process of making drama.

ATTRACTING APPLICANTS

An essential principle running throughout every aspect of filmmaking is that of supplying yourself with an overabundance of choice. More than anywhere else this must be applied to casting, because the human presence on the screen is what most directly and continuously commands the audience's attention. Unlike any of the film techniques you might use, the human presence is the subject of universal expertise and an area in which the director can easily be more naive than the audience.

In spite of this, casting among beginners is often the least rigorous part of the whole film process. Feeling uncomfortable with the power to choose among fellow aspirants, the embarrassed newcomer settles too early and too easily for actors who look right. An appropriate age and appearance matter, of course, but this is only the beginning. All forty-year-old men are not alike, and to uncritically presume that one can take the right face and make its owner into the script's sentimental, spendthrift father is asking for trouble.

Inadequate casting arises from two main sources: lack of confidence in one's right to search far and wide, and lack of knowledge about how to put actors through their paces in order to discover underlying potential. Learning how to audition helps to remove the crippling sense of inadequacy and embarrassment about making human choices. Knowledge and confidence are thus closely linked.

DEVELOPING CHARACTER DESCRIPTIONS

Before you can search for possible actors, you will need basic character descriptions either to post in appropriate places (newspapers, theatre or acting school billboards) or to give over the phone. A typical list might look like this:

Ken, 15, tall and thin, nervous, curious, intelligent, overcritical, obsessed with science fiction.

George, late 20s, medium height, medical equipment salesman, lives carefully and calls his parents each Friday. Husband of Kathy.

Kathy, early 30s, but has successfully lied about her age. Small-town beauty queen gone to seed after a steamy divorce. Met George through a dating service.

Ted, 60s, bus inspector, patriot, grower of prize chrysanthemums, disapproving father of George.

Eddie, 40s, washing machine repairman, part-time conjuror and clown at children's parties. Too boring to be married. Likes to philosophize.

Angela, 70s, cheerful, resourceful, a veneer of respectability that breaks down raucously after a couple of drinks. In early life made a fortune in something illicit. Determined to live forever.

Thumbnail sketches like these compress a lot into a few words and allow the reader to infer possible physical appearances. Finding people to fill these roles now becomes an attractive challenge.

ACTIVE SEARCH FOR ACTORS

With the exception of the oldest and youngest in the sample cast above, the rest are drawn from an age bracket normally kept busy with daily responsibilities. Three of the adults are blue-collar parts, a social class least likely to have done any acting, and liable to feel inadequate and self-conscious. These are generalizations whose only function is to help focus the search and indicate what kind of inventiveness is needed to locate the exceptions with the necessary qualities and spare time.

Lacking a liberal budget, you must be resourceful in finding likely people to try out. Wherever possible, save time and frustration by actively seeking out likely participants. First contact key people in theatre groups. Locate the casting director and ask if you can pay a brief visit. Whoever handles casting will be a mine of information about local talent. The next most knowledgeable people are the producers (who direct in the theatre) and committed theatre workers. Knowledgeable members will often respond enthusiastically with names you can contact and invite to try out. When a theatre group is successful enough to use only professional (union) actors, the response is likely to be more cautious, or even unfriendly. Theatres don't like their best cast members seduced away by screen parts, and may equally want to avoid prejudicing their relationship with the actors' union. You will probably be referred to the actors' union for advice.

If your budget is rock bottom, you will have to work hard. Actors well suited to specific parts can always be found, but it takes ingenuity and diligence. Never forget that your film's credibility comes not from your film technique, but from how believable the human presence is upon the screen. Good film technique simply provides a seamless storytelling medium. The better it is, the less anyone sees it, and the more the audience dwells upon that all-important human presence.

For the character of the fifteen-year-old Ken I would track down teachers producing drama in local schools and ask them to suggest boys who could play the character well. The teacher can ask the kid, or the kid's parents, to get in touch. This allays the nightmare that their child is being hunted down by a coven of hollow-eyed pornographers.

Elderly people are more of a problem. Since our culture encourages the old to rest, many become physically and mentally inactive. Your first task in casting Ted and Angela will be to locate older people who keep mentally and physically active. You may be lucky and find there is a senior citizen's theatre group to draw upon, or you may have to track down individuals.

For Ted I would look among older blue-collar men who have taken an active and extroverted role in life, perhaps in local politics, union organizing, entertainment, or salesmanship. All these occupations require some flair for interaction with other people, and a relish for the fray.

Angela is a hard person to cast, but try looking among retired actresses or vocal women's group members such as citizen's and neighborhood pressure groups—anywhere you could expect to find an elderly woman secure in her life's accomplishments and adventurous enough to play a boozy, earthy woman with a past.

Periodically when casting remind yourself that hidden among the gray armies of the conforming there are always a few individuals in any age group whose lives have been lived with wit, intelligence, and individuality. Such people rise to prominence in the often unlikely worlds to which exigency or eccentricity has taken them. Angela, for instance, might be found as the president of the Standard Poodle Fanciers Club, and Ted might be discovered in an amateur comedian contest.

Werner Herzog's actors, for instance, include nonprofessionals drawn from around him. The central figure in *The Mystery of Kasper Hauser* (1974) and *Stroszek* (1977) is played by the endearing Bruno S---, a street singer and Berlin transport manager whose surname has remained undisclosed to protect his job. In *The Trial of Joan of Arc* (1962), Bresson, who refuses to cast anyone trained to act, used lawyers to play Joan's inquisitors. A lifetime spent defining details gave them just the right punctiliousness in their cross-examining. Bresson, in *Notes on Cinematography* (New York: Urizen Books, 1975) has an interesting and elaborate rationale, akin to a documentary-making attitude, for using "models" (his word for players) who have never performed before.

PASSIVE SEARCH FOR ACTORS

If you live in a city, you can spread a large net simply by putting an advertisement in the appropriate papers. If there is a fair amount of theatre in your area, there may also be a monthly auditions broadsheet, or other professional periodical. In it, describe the project and give the number, sex and age of the characters in a few words, and a phone number to contact.

SETTING UP THE FIRST AUDITION

FIELDING PHONE APPLICANTS

As each person calls up, you will need to amplify upon the role he or she fits, specify what the audition will demand, and, if the person sounds appropriate, agree upon an audition session on one of your audition days. Schedule people into slots so that they arrive at, say, ten-minute intervals and can be individually received by someone who can answer questions.

Be direct and realistic about the project and about the unit's level of expertise. If you are a student group, say so, and above all be truthful about the time commitment you will need for rehearsal and shooting. A cool response to the time commitment is a danger bell indicating the applicant's low level of interest. Many calling themselves actors are minimally experienced, or not experienced at all. The world is full of dreamers looking for a quick path to stardom; these should be avoided except for very brief, undemanding parts. A rigorous audition helps to weed out the half-hearted. You may want to add the obviously unskilled to a waiting list so that you can audition those claiming experience first.

A first call might ask actors to perform two contrasting three-minute monologues of their own choosing, or in addition, take part in a cold reading.

THE AUDITION CALL

This session aims to net as many people as possible so later you can make callbacks for those deemed suitable. Many responding, in spite of what they said on the phone, will be devoid of everything you require, or quite unrealistic about their abilities and commitment. Expect a lot of chaff for very little wheat in this winnowing operation.

GATHERING INFORMATION

Have actors wait in a separate area from the audition space, and give each a form to complete, so later you have on file

1. name and address,
2. home and work phone numbers,
3. acting experience,
4. role for which actor is trying out, and
5. special interests and skills.

The last is purely to get a sense of what attributes the actor may have that indicate special energy and initiative. You might also have a further section asking actors to write a few lines on what attracts them to acting. This can reveal values and how serious and realistic the person is.

An excellent procedure is to have assistants in the holding area who chat informally with incoming actors about what they have written on their forms. This helps calm actors' fears, and your assistants' impressions, particularly about how punctual and organized the actor seems, can be most valuable later.

INITIAL AUDITION

The actor can now be shown into the audition space where he or she will perform. You may want to videotape the performances to help review your choices later and make comparisons, especially if you see a lot of actors for one part.

Most people are extremely nervous and apprehensive at auditions, but this is not necessarily negative since it shows they attach importance to being accepted. The presence of a camera increases the pressure.

MONOLOGUE

It is good to require two brief monologues very different in character. These can tell you whether an actor habitually acts just with his face or with his whole body, what kind of physical presence, rhythm, and energy level he has, what his voice is like, and what kind of emotional range he can produce. Whether they are well or badly performed and whether you "see" the characters are very important, but the actor's choice and handling of material also indicate what he thinks he does best. The choice may reflect intelligent research based on what the actor has found out about your production, or it may indicate an enduring self-image. A man trying out for a brash salesman who chooses the monologue of an endearing wimp has probably already cast himself in life as a loser whose best hope is to be funny. This will hardly do for, say, a part requiring him to act upon instincts of revenge. Here you may sense a quality of acquiescence that makes the actor psychologically and emotionally unsuitable for this part, though perhaps interesting for another.

COLD READING

For this you will need several copies of several different scenes. Depending upon who is in your waiting room, you might want to try combining two men, two women, a man and a woman, or an old person with someone young, and so on. It is a good idea *not* to use scenes from your film, but instead to find something from theatrical repertory that is analogous in mood and characters. Your assistant can decide from who is waiting which piece to read next, and give each actor a copy of the scene in advance.

Here you will see actors thinking on their feet and trying to give life to their character. You will probably see the same scene with more than one set of actors, and so have the opportunity to see different levels of quickness, intelligence, and creativity brought to the bare words on the page. You will also discover how each uses his voice, how some will inject movement, and how others ask questions about their character or about the piece from which the scene is drawn. Performances and behavior will affect you differently and often in ways that pose interesting and complex questions. In a reading with two characters of the same sex, you can switch the actors and ask them to read again, to see if the actors can produce appropriate and different qualities at short notice.

After actors have auditioned, always thank them and give them a date by which to expect news of the outcome.

DECISIONS AFTER FIRST AUDITIONS

If you have promising applicants, run the tapes of their contributions and brainstorm with your project coworkers. Discussing each actor's strengths and weaknesses usually reveals further dimensions, not to mention insights into your crew members and their values.

Now comes the agonizing part. Call everyone who auditioned and tell them whether they were selected for callback auditions. Telling them the bad news to those not selected is hard on both parties, but you can mitigate the disappointment by finding something positive and encouraging to say about each person's performance. With the people you want to see again, set a callback date for further auditioning.

DANGERS OF TYPECASTING

Be careful about casting characters with prominently negative traits. It can, for instance, be disastrous during shooting to have an actor slowly become aware that he has been cast for his own negative qualities. If a very boring person were cast to play Eddie, the director would have difficulty calling out his boringness because it is patently reprehensible to exploit someone's weaknesses for an audience's amusement.

In varying degrees, all actors go through difficulties playing negative characteristics because of the lurking fear that these characteristics are really within their own makeup and will become visible. The less secure the individual is, the more likely such self-doubts will become acute. A sure sign of this insecurity is when an actor makes a personal issue of his or her character's qualities and attempts to upgrade them.

To protect yourself, get the actors in view to each discuss their ideas about their character's negative traits. Their underlying attitudes may influence your choice.

LONG- OR SHORT-TERM CHOICES

One of the great temptations is to cast the person who is ahead of the pack because of an ability to give something quick and attractive during auditions. This actor may be brilliant or he may later emerge as glib and inflexible, developing less than a partner whose audition seemed less accomplished. Caution dictates that you investigate not only what an actor can do, but also how open that actor is to the unfamiliar, and how willing and interested to push beyond the boundaries of present security. All sophisticated actors are fervently committed in principle, but practice can be utterly different. It involves the whole person, not just his ideas, and one may find that a genially accomplished personality coming under the threat of the unexpected suddenly manifests bizarre forms of self-defense and resistance (See "Forms of Resistance by Actors" in Chapter 7).

THE DEMANDING PART OF THE CHARACTER WHO DEVELOPS

Not all parts require a high degree of adaptability to direction. To cast a surly gas station attendant for one short scene requires little in growth potential, whereas casting a young wife who slowly comes to recognize that her new husband is dominated by his absent mother calls for extended and subtle development. Brief character parts usually require no great changes or special depths. But if a character must go through a spectrum of emotions during which he or she changes and develops, the director must find an actor with the openness and emotional reach to undertake a grueling rehearsal and performance process.

FIRST CALLBACK

When you are ready to call back the most promising actors who auditioned, you will need to prepare some additional testing procedures.

A READING FROM YOUR SCRIPT

Give some background to the scene, which should be demanding but only a few minutes in duration.

1. Ask each actor to play his/her character in a specified way. After the readings, give the actors critical feedback and directions to further develop the scene.
2. Ask them to play the scene again. You want to see how, using your directions, the actors build upon their initial performances, holding what was praised but altering the specified areas.
3. For a further run-through, give each actor a different mood or characteristic to see what he or she produces from a radically different premise.

IMPROVISATION

Give two actors brief outlines of characters in the script, and outline one of the script's situations that involve them.

1. Ask your players to improvise their own scene upon the situation in the (unseen) script. The goal is not to see how close they get to the scripted original, but how they handle themselves when much of the creation is expected to be spontaneous.
2. After they have done a version, give them directorial guidance about aspects you see developing in their version, and ask for a further version, specifying some change in behavior and mood. Now you will be able to see not only what they can produce from themselves, but how well they respond to direction.

SECOND CALLBACK

INTERVIEW

Give your best candidates a script to read, and tell them not to learn any lines. After they have read it, spend time informally with each of them encouraging them to ask questions and to talk about both the script and themselves. By now you have formed ideas about the individual, which you try to confirm. Look for realism, sincerity, honesty, and a genuine interest in drama itself. Be wary of people who use flattery, who try to impress by name-dropping, whose readings are superficial, who are rigidly opinionated, or who want you to know they are doing you a good turn. These are danger signs that foreshadow ego and commitment problems. On the positive side, it is a good sign if an actor is sincerely excited by a part because the script explores issues central to his or her own life.

MIX AND MATCH ACTORS

When you have multiple contenders for a lead part, try them out in different permutations so you can assess the personal chemistry each has with the others. In part, this is to see how they will strike an audience. I once had to cast a short story film about a man in his thirties who becomes involved with a rebellious teenage girl. We rejected a more accomplished actor because there was something indefinable in his manner that made the relationship seem sinister. Another actor paired with the same actress changed the balance to give the girl the upper hand, as the story demanded.

It is extremely important that actors who are cast to play lovers be tried out extensively with each other because antipathy could spell disaster.

Another and equally important reason to mix and match is to try for the most dynamic chemistry between the actors themselves. Sometimes one can see early that two actors simply do not communicate well. This may be due to temperamental or philosophical differences, but whatever the cause, the result will be a wariness and stiffness in their playing that disables your film. One tries to cast players who are interested and responsive to each other. Even when this is accomplished, you may encounter a common problem, such as Alain Tanner did in *The Middle of the World* (1974). The male lead usually produced his best work in an early take while the woman playing opposite him worked to her peak over a number of takes.

FIGURE 4–1

Actors have different development rates. Philippe Leotard in Tanner's *The Middle of the World* (courtesy New Yorker Films).

FINAL CHOICES

In addition to the obvious question of body type and physical appearance, the director must, before making a final choice, review the overall advantages each actor offers, taking into account the actor's

- impact,
- imprint on the part,
- rhythms of speech and movement,
- quickness of mind,
- mimicry ability, especially if he is to maintain a regional or foreign accent,
- voice quality (extremely important!),
- capacity to hold on to both new and old instructions,
- pattern of development, whether intuitive and immediate or slower and reflective,
- commitment to the project and to acting as a profession,
- patience with filming's slow and disjunctive progress,
- ability to enter and reenter an emotional condition for several takes and camera angles, and
- compatibility with the other actors.

CAMERA TEST

To confirm that you are making the right choices, shoot a short scene with the principal actors. Even then, you will probably remain somewhat uncertain and feel you have to make difficult decisions.

If you have an overwhelming urge to cast someone that your intuition says is risky, you should tactfully but directly communicate your reservations. You might, for instance, feel uncertain of the actor's commitment, or that the actor has a resistance to authority figures and will have problems in being directed. Confrontation at this early point shows you how the actor handles uncomfortable criticism, and paves the way should that perception later become an issue or, God forbid, should replacement become a necessity. An actor who seems arrogant and egocentric will sometimes admit, when faced with a frank reaction to his characteristics, that he has an unfortunate way of masking uncertainty.

More than anything, people in all walks of life crave recognition. If the director is able to comment on the potential and the deficiencies masking it, the serious actor will respond with warmth and loyalty. Sharing and honesty is a goal in all director/actor and actor/actor relationships. It is the basis for trust and a truly creative working relationship.

When you make your final decisions, notify and thank all who have taken part. This signals your professionalism and maintains your good standing in the acting community. Needless to say, rejection is painful, and more so for those not chosen in the final round.

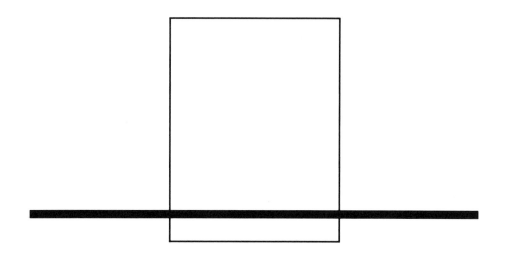

C·H·A·P·T·E·R 5

REHEARSAL AND DEVELOPMENT

Rehearsal is a much misunderstood activity. The difficulties begin with the word itself, and its unfortunate associations with repetition and drilling. A much better word would be *development*. To forgo rehearsal prior to film performances is to forgo development and therefore depth. Because movies are shot piecemeal it is often assumed that film performances, unlike theatre, need little or no rehearsal; indeed, that rehearsal damages spontaneity. This belief may be a rationalization for minimizing costs (rehearsal greatly increases costs) or perhaps people think that theatre plays rehearse to overcome the problems of a continuous performance, such as mastering lines and movements.

In truth, every piece of good theatre grows out of a radical and organic rehearsal process, even improvisatory theatre. So why not film? The argument goes that since film actors learn lines the night before shooting, and since final movements depend on the logistics of the set and even of lighting, lengthy rehearsal is a waste of time and money. A good director, given the greater degree of control, should be able to produce just what he envisions. Such myths do not arise unaided and this one is fed by publicity centering on actors famed for personality and sex appeal rather than the ability to create character and dramatic resonance.

Actors who create original character do in fact study and rehearse as intensely as concert pianists practice. This preparation—both private and collaborative—seldom makes it into the movie gossip columns. But anyone who inquires how much Dustin Hoffman and Meryl Streep—to mention only two exceptionally versatile talents—prepare themselves cannot doubt that acting is an exceptionally demanding craft and that natural and versatile talent is nearly always the outcome of dedicated work.

If top-notch professional film actors find it necessary to prepare, novices must be ready to work even harder. Few beginning filmmakers seem aware of this and the acting in student films is usually appalling. Too often student directors believe editing is an alchemy that will magically produce gold from lead.

Before something good can emerge from the rehearsal process, the director must understand the importance of tapping into the actors' creativity, and not to think of them, however privately, as puppets. They must also have the opportunity to become comfortable and interested in each other. To see the implications of this, we must examine an analogous life situation. Imagine an office birthday party where a group of people naturally integrate with each other and their environment. The outsider sees their familiarity and interdependence in everything they say and do. One could not bring in an impostor, however well briefed, without everyone knowing he was spurious.

Now think of a scene with a new cast developed from a text. Initially, at least, it is a convocation of such impostors whose pretensions to familiarity and interdependence show up painfully to every observer. Every piece of drama starts out cold in this way.

However, make the actors into an ensemble, with its own dynamic of relationships and its own history that makes up in intensity what it might lack in duration, and the company can begin to absorb dramatic situations into its own authentic reality. Fiction and actors' relationships become indistinguishably real.

That is our aim in this developmental work. The following stages aim to produce a disciplined, creative quest, the expressive results of which are channeled through the sensibility of the director, the piece's first audience.

ALLOW TIME

As soon as parts are cast, your assistant director (AD) should make a log of everyone's availability and work out possible rehearsal times. Warn actors new to the process that filming is very slow, and also warn them again of the temptations to deny the negative aspects of their characters. All human beings are made up of emotions that actors should see as neither positive or negative but, more importantly, as true. Truth has a value that transcends popularity.

Most people find it easier to work to a predetermined schedule, which also signals your professionalism. It is vital to allot enough time for the film's performances to evolve. A good rule of thumb is to invest at least one hour of developmental rehearsal for every minute of screen time. An easy three-minute scene thus needs a minimum of three one-hour rehearsals. Make rehearsals brief and frequent rather than long and comprehensive, as people doing unfamiliar work tire rapidly and lose the ability to concentrate.

FIRST READ-THROUGH

After everyone has had time to study the script, the first read-through will show how each actor interprets the piece and how well the characters are fitting together. You should also expect to get first glimpses of where your biggest problems lie, in particular scenes, particular actors, or both.

Encourage actors to use as much natural movement as they can both during the read-through and subsequently, even though the primary focus is upon the meaning of words. Holding a script will inhibit movement, but the emphasis upon doing reminds the cast that it is vital to act with the whole body, not just the voice or the face.

Depending on the length and complexity of the screenplay, read it through in sections, or all at one go if possible. Have a list of fundamental questions ready for the actors. Give little or no direction; you want to see what ideas and individuality each spontaneously brings to his role and to the piece. Show that you expect actors to be partners in seeking answers to problems, for problem-solving is at the heart of creativity. This also discourages actors from passively depending upon minute instructions, not usually a problem if your casting is good.

Although you may have strong ideas of your own, be receptive to your actors' input and individuality. It shows you expect them to dig into the piece and thoroughly explore what kind of people the characters are. They will have to judge what motivates each to do what he or she does, and to define what purposes lie behind the script as a whole. Any serious actor will find this approach attractive and challenging because it acknowledges his intelligence.

KEEP NOTES

A tough part of directing is holding on to important impressions during a rehearsal. Because you must monitor so many things simultaneously, early impressions can be erased by later ones, and you can easily turn to the actors with a mind drained of everything except the last set of impressions. Avoid this humiliation by carrying a large scratch pad and without taking your eyes off the performance, scribble a key word or two. Then glance down and place your pen at a starting point ready for the next note. Afterwards you will have several pages of large wobbly prompts. These should trigger the necessary recall.

DIRECT BY ASKING QUESTIONS

Through probing questions you can guide the cast to discover what you may already know (it also gives you time to think). Because of the energy and diversity a group brings to any enterprise, this process flushes out aspects that may never have occurred to you. Learning becomes a two-way street. Throughout production, even when everyone feels there can be nothing left to discover, the piece will continue to deepen, growing stronger as you and your cast stumble upon even more meanings and interconnections. Here lies much of the exhilarating sense of shared discovery and closeness that can develop between cast and crew, something everyone will recall nostalgically for years afterwards.

Asking challenging questions is always a more effective way of briefing and coordinating a group than simply reeling off instructions. Orders, not least because of their authoritarian nature, are easily resisted or misunderstood, especially when they prove inadequate and must be modified or superceded. But people seldom forget what they discover for themselves. That is the philosophy underlying the exercises and projects at the end of this book.

NO LEARNING OF LINES YET!

At this stage, be absolutely clear that you want nobody to learn lines yet. Committing lines to memory also means transfixing whatever action and level of interpretation has been reached. Making changes becomes immeasurably harder after the initial memorization. At this early stage there is insufficient knowledge of the piece to risk this.

SCHEDULING

Remind the actors before they leave of the next rehearsal and make sure each has a typed schedule. For the next meeting, ask the actors to set down notes on their character and develop a detailed biography to substantiate their conceptions.

FIRST DISCUSSIONS: FOCUSING THE THEMATIC PURPOSE

A theme represents an authorial system of values or beliefs that lies within the director's interpretation of the screenplay. To communicate yours on the screen, you will have to effectively argue it. Stating the thematic purpose of one's piece really means defining the steps and focus of this argument.

A story represents a limited but intense vision. Such a vision is made coherent and integrated, however subtly, by an underlying philosophy of cause and effect. Many, and perhaps most, stories are experimental in the sense that telling a story is really a way of constructing a working model of one's beliefs. If others are moved to conviction, the principles behind the model have been shared, acclaimed, and they may have merit. That is the best anyone can do.

A thematic purpose for your work need not try to encompass universal truth ("in our Western way of life the rich get richer while the poor get poorer") or be morally uplifting ("if people would just vent their real feelings, everyone could be free"). Audiences will feel they are being preached at especially when the scope of the film falls short of the global nature of its message.

Modest, solid, specific, and deeply felt aims are the most practical. Your thematic statement may focus the motivation for telling the tale onto a simple principle with profound consequences ("sometimes marriage between two good people is not practical and everyone suffers," or "though this idealogue is honest and sincere, he is dangerous to those that love him"). By taking a small truth and deeply investigating it, you can invest it with life and indicate larger truths of wider resonance. Put another way, a thoroughly absorbing and convincing microcosm will effectively create the macrocosm.

Your notion of the piece's thematic purpose will come from your study of the text but that does not guarantee that it will be shared by those who matter most: your cast. Regrettably, with small parts it may be expedient to simply tell players what the piece is about. But giving such instructions to anyone with a major role will be counterproductive since it suggests that that actor must discard any original or contrary impressions. In any case, limiting creative participation creates trouble down the road with all but the most passive actor.

A wiser approach is to form your own ideas and then either parlay your cast into accepting them, or into forming alternatives that are as acceptable or (do not tell anyone) even superior. Again, make it very plain that actors must learn no lines until interpretations, meanings, and characters have been explored and agreed.

Now that the cast has had time to study the script:

1.   Ask the players to discuss the purpose of the whole story. This reveals what spectrum of opinion exists. Encourage all points of view and impose none of your own at this time. You want the cast to reason things out for themselves. Not only will this bring them closer, but you will acquire additional insights, since each is an advocate for a single character.

2.   Ask the cast to formulate the "backstory" (what may permissibly have happened before the film begins).

3.   Ask each actor to describe his character and to prepare a brief character biography.

4.   Turn the cast's attention to successive key scenes and ask the players to develop the subtext for each.

5.   Ask the cast to review the main themes of the piece; say what you think is their hierarchy. During this process you should try to unify the body of opinion into a coherent thematic purpose for the piece.

If you cannot achieve agreement at this stage, at least agree to differ and let it go. Such disagreements often provide a creative tension that spurs closer examination during the next phases of work. Actors will probably be too busy with more immediate concerns to turn it into a running fight, and everyone will eventually arrive at a tacit agreement through shared problem-solving.

You are now ready to begin developing the piece and to test your ideas through rehearsals. You have designed your plane and now you want to see if it flies.

ENCOURAGE ACTORS TO DEVELOP THEIR CHARACTERS' BACKGROUNDS

An essential resource for any conscientious actor is his character's biography, which he writes himself. Without an explicit request some may not make the effort, especially if they have yet to learn its benefit. Others do the job inadequately or go off on a tangent through misreading the piece. This is a good time to meet alone with each actor to go over his or her ideas and to encourage, develop, or redirect.

VALUES AND HAZARDS OF WORKING ONE-ON-ONE WITH ACTORS

Much of a part's future direction will develop from one-on-one exploratory sessions. Inevitably, the larger the cast, the less the director's undivided attention can be available to individual cast members. Since feedback is so vital to actors, most feel inadequately recognized most of the time. If the actor sees another actor alone with the director, he tends to resent the special attention unless the session is evidently remedial. Because of this unavoidable pressure, the beginning director is well advised to work with a small cast, and to capitalize on relationships with good actors by using them again in subsequent productions.

A good solution to the demand for individual attention is to see everyone alone, even minor parts, at the outset. You will want to check the actor's ideas and approach, and establish a personal and supportive relationship. From then on try to rehearse openly, reserving private discussion for special support and ideas or suggestions about problem areas. Just before shooting remember to tell each actor something personal and supportive.

REHEARSING ONE SCENE AT A TIME

Initially, try to rehearse scenes in script order. Later, as the piece becomes thoroughly familiar, adopt a plan of convenience and work around people's schedules or give priority to key scenes and those still presenting special problems.

At this stage the cast is still working with "the book." Actors are searching for their characters' full range of motivations, and developing a knowledge of how each scene functions in the piece as a whole.

DEAL ONLY WITH TOP LEVEL PROBLEMS

At each of the initial run-throughs, deal only with a scene's most major problems or you risk burdening actors with too much information and blurring priorities. A rehearsal spirals backwards and forwards, oscillating between particular details and the more abstract areas of meaning and philosophy. As major problems get solved, others of secondary significance, such as single lines that lack conviction, will move to the top of the heap and claim everyone's attention. The rehearsal process is thus one of continuous discovery and refinement.

Once a scene's major difficulties are brought under control, you may now want to go over everything within each beat, one beat at a time. This system may be the only practicable one if circumstances dictate that most rehearsal takes place immediately before each day's shooting.

C·H·A·P·T·E·R 6

ON ACTING

The most useful knowledge any director can acquire apart from basic filmmaking is of acting. You can and should read about it, but more important is to take classes and actually do it. Acting is a well documented craft, so what follows is a brief digest of ideas and practices I find particularly useful.

IN SEARCH OF NATURALNESS

REALISM IS YOUR FIRST GOAL

While an animator creates a complete world according to a mental vision, live-action cinema must fashion its tales from real objects and real people. Not surprisingly, most cinema demands realism of actors rather than the more stylized playing of the theatre. Audiences expect screen characters no less credible than those in a documentary. This is no easy task and the problem is serious for the low-budget director unable to afford experienced talent. You will need some of the skills of actor and drama coach to raise your performers to the required level of credibility.

DIRECTING IS REMOVING OBSTACLES

In general, neither experienced or inexperienced actors need specialized technique or information from the director; they need help casting off layers of human insecurity. A thorough rehearsal process is the best assault on the obstacles that prevent an actor from relaxing. Freedom from tension is what permits an actor to be instead of perform. In film acting, the actor should have virtually no sense of audience and therefore no sense of performing unless for the director. The camera should capture life taking place just as it does in a documentary.

Here the difference between theatre and film acting is great, because theatre actors need the audience's belief to sustain their own beliefs in their roles. Robbed of this support, the theatre actor suffers crises of doubt concerning ability and worth. The director is the only audience and must wean the actor to a new, more internalized way of sustaining belief.

MAINTAINING FOCUS

It is vital to maintaining focus for the actor to have a continuous flow of action, things to do. An unoccupied actor is unprotected from sliding into self-awareness and becomes aware of "being." This is a vicious circle: the actor becomes self-consciously aware of how unnatural it is to be thinking about such a thing. Actions are the escape from this because doing is the gateway to being. It naturally deflects the actor's consciousness away from the self. If the actor ever ceases the character's physical or mental tasks, he or she inevitably falls victim to crippling self-awareness and becomes a divided being, one half behaving like an audience, judging the other acting half.

FOCUS AND RELAXATION

The paradox is that focus leads to relaxation, the kind that accompanies complete mental involvement. This relaxation of mind and body in turn assists the actor to find and maintain the character's mental focus.

Make a habit of looking at your actors' bodies for signs of tension—their shoulders, face muscles, hands, and walk in particular. It is usually within your power to undo this tension by reassuring actors that their work is effective and by directing their attention outwards. Have some improv games ready as a refresher to solve extreme cases.

EMOTIONAL MEMORY

The actor avoids paralyzing self-judgment by maintaining a flow of physical tasks (think of all that compulsive house cleaning in the suburbs). The experienced actor works hard to invent just the right action or task that resonates the character's present state of mind. Not only is the actor freed from self-contemplation but the truest actions also release powerful, authentic emotion during performance. Stanislavski called this curious psychic reflex emotional memory. Of his many discoveries about acting psychology, this is the most frequently misunderstood. To do it justice we must look at how the human mind works when an actor is *being* rather than *signifying*.

THE MIND-BODY CONNECTION

A person's body invariably expresses his or her state of mind to anyone who can read it. A brother knows what kind of day his sister has had from the way she gets off her bicycle. A knowledge of body language is present in us from our earliest years. Young children react intuitively to what adults express nonverbally and only become confused when the adult uses contradictory words. In later life we learn to value the cerebral over the intuitive and emotional, and begin to assume that intuitions are indefensible, childish, and not to be trusted. This is especially true for boys.

But remember our article of faith, that no inner state exists without outward evidence. We show what we feel. In the realm of acting this means that when an actor's mind is correctly occupied, when his actions are appropriate, his body will unconsciously express all his character feels. Directing should therefore be concerned with arriving at a character's true state of mind, and helping the actor develop the actions that truly accompany it.

Conversely, when an actor's action feels false, it is either poorly chosen or he has lost focus. The actor who loses focus (that is, stops experiencing his character's thoughts and emotions), shows it in his whole physical being, in everything he says and does.

Far from being peculiar to acting, being focused underpins everyone's sense of normality. In everyday life we carry on actions and relationships upon a foundation of assumptions about who we are and how we appear to others. These assumptions are only challenged under exceptional circumstances. When someone we respect watches us, or we must speak to a group, we become suddenly self-aware and stop functioning automatically and harmoniously. We cease, in fact, to behave normally. The implications are major for the film director, whose work so often centers on reproducing the processes and feel of real life.

BUSINESS

Actor and director must generate plenty of "business" or appropriate action while preparing each role. Instead of moving on when an actor has correctly described what the character feels, you must immediately develop what the character would do in the circumstance. Doing might mean giving a scream, but it is more likely to be a small but significant action, like dropping the eyes, turning to glance out of a window, feeling for change in one's pocket, or recalling the image of an indulgent aunt. Many actions will be interior as well as exterior.

STAY BUSY IN CHARACTER

As an actor, the key to maintaining your character's flow of consciousness is not solely to keep busy, but to keep busy in character. To realistically be, you must have your attention fully occupied by your character's thoughts, memories, inner visions, and outward actions. Any opportunity to indulge unstructured thought will permit your ever-anxious mind to see yourself as you must appear to those watching (foolish, undignified, heroic, handsome, deeply moving, etc.). This, of course, is disabling and leads immediately to the black hole called loss of focus.

LOSING AND REGAINING FOCUS

Insecurity of all kinds, even the fear of losing focus, leads to loss of focus. In a moment, the audience sees a believable character crumble into a beleaguered actor. Unless the actor has learned how to recover, he feels completely exposed.

An effective way for the actor to regain focus is to look narrowly at something nearby, such as a prop or the texture of his sleeve. Because it is real, something in his character's here and now, his attention is stabilized. Now he can broaden his attention to include the character's whole sphere of awareness.

USING THE ACTOR'S EMOTIONS AS THE CHARACTER'S

What should the actor do when an irrelevant emotion intrudes itself, such as pain from a headache, or surprise over an unexpected move by a partner, or confusion from a misplaced prop? Part of any good actor's training is learning to employ every genuine emotion as part of the character's present. This means, in effect, embracing and coopting the invader instead of struggling to repress it. Since every real emotion is visible, struggling to put a lid on the inappropriate will also be visible. The tactic of incorporating external emotion is thus inevitable.

By using every facet of an actor's self to maintain the character's physical and mental action, and by allowing the character to be affected by every nuance of other characters' behavior every time the scene is played, an actor stays so busy on so many levels that he or she no longer worries about lines or whether anyone is watching. Everything in the intense, subjective sphere of the character's reality recedes from consciousness. In rehearsal I have used documentary style coverage, bringing the camera within a yard of the players, and afterwards they had no memory of the camera's presence.

This intense state of focus is readily available for beginners to experience in improvisation work (which makes improv so valuable), but it is more difficult to maintain within the discipline of a text.

NEVER DEMONSTRATE

As we have often said, the director should always encourage the actor to find his own solution to a problem. Unless desperate, the director should never step forward and demonstrate what she wants. This implies you are an actor and want a mimicry of yourself, when actually you need something unique to the actor.

NEVER SAY, "BE YOURSELF"

This innocent request can set actors worrying: What did he really mean? How does he see me? Which me does he really want? Give your actor an external focus.

SET SPECIFIC, POSITIVE GOALS

Avoid negative instruction of all kinds ("Could you not be so noisy opening the closet?") You can get what you want by saying, "See if you can open the door softly this time."

Convey your wishes through redirecting attention to a particular kind of action ("I'd like to see you turn away from her in an irresolute way"). Less effective would be to say, "Be irresolute" without locating the character's doubt in particular moments of the scene. The actor may not agree but you can negotiate another, specific place. Another way of effecting a change is through suggesting a different subtext to a particular action or line ("Try giving that line an ironic undertone" or "Try closing the door on him with finality instead of regret").

ACT AS IF NOBODY'S PRESENT

Instruct actors never to look at the camera, to ignore the crew's presence, and to act as if they were alone in real life. This prevents them from falling into the trap of playing to an audience.

OBSTACLES: HABITS OF BEING

MANNERISMS

Unfamiliar circumstances cause people to fall back on their conditioning, and many ingrained behaviors are hard or even impossible to change. Certain jobs attract a certain kind of person, and among nonactors some jobs seem to generate mannerisms and self-awarenesses that are a liability in filmmaking. Lecturers and politicians tend to address invisible multitudes, instead of talking one-to-one as they did in rehearsal, firemen talk in clipped official voices, and so on. The positive aspect here is that many of the qualities for which you cast a particular person will survive the unnatural procedure of filming, to appear just as you wanted them on the screen.

Most actors have particular mannerisms that you have to live with. To eliminate them would mean changing something so basic to the person that you would disable their talents. Here the director must exert careful judgment before speaking up. As always, try to divert the actor's attention to something positive, rather than asking him to suppress the negative.

LIMITING AN ACTOR'S SPHERE OF ATTENTION

When an actor's misconception of his relationship to the camera must be altered, try to guess what is ingrained habit and what is only a misperception about filming. The latter you can probably correct. For instance, the theatre-trained actor who addresses an audience can usually be redirected by simply saying, "Imagine there is a small bubble of space only big enough to enclose you and your partner. There is only one person, him, listening to you. Talk only to him, there is no one else, no camera present, just you two". Usually reminding them of this limitation of space does the trick and keeps theatrically trained actors using authentic, unmagnified voices and actions. Interestingly, the scene intensity usually rises noticeably. Projection can also be a retreat from real feelings.

TACKLING SERIOUS PROBLEMS OF UNNATURAL ACTING

With an incurable voice projecter or anyone who is habitually artificial, the best solution is to recast. If that is impossible, some selected video playback to the actor may forcibly communicate that he has a problem. Be aware, however, that most people are so shocked and depressed when they first see themselves on the screen that showing an unsatisfactory performance should be a last resort, to be done privately and supportively.

Sometimes you will cast someone to play a small part and this person's concept of acting comes from TV commercials. Valiantly your housewife in the short scene projects a wacky personality. If she is playing a stage mom this could be just what you wanted, but in most other circumstances it would be a disaster. Take her aside and get her to talk through the character, perhaps getting the actor to recall someone similar whom she knows and upon whose image she can model herself. Trying to become an idea of the part is what is phony. Get your actor to develop her character's interior process through improvising an interior monologue or "thoughts voice" (see Chapter 32, Exercise 23: "Improvising an Interior Monologue"). Once she learns to maintain her character's interior processes, the actor can no longer stand outside herself and make a presentation, which is the root of the problem. Fully inhabiting her character, that character speaks and acts out of genuine consciousness. This at the very least takes care of realism.

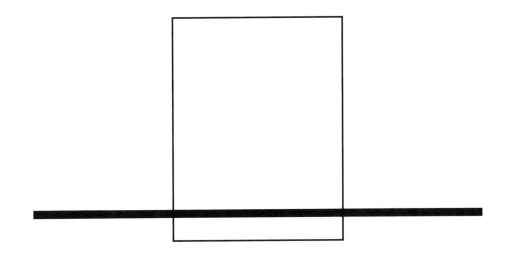

DIRECTOR AND ACTOR PREPARE A SCENE

Before trying out a scene together, director and actors should each work alone on the text if forthcoming collaborative work is to be truly effective. Their preparatory work will overlap, creating a situation of checks and balances in which action, motivations and meanings are examined from multiple perspectives. This helps avoid omissions, but it also draws valuably individual perceptions from the actors. Each tends to see his or her character, other characters, and the piece itself from the partisan perspective of the character being played. These viewpoints will not necessarily be compatible. In early group discussions the director leads the process of coordinating and reconciling them, making them a creative dialogue rather than a battle of wills. The director's vision should be nonpartisan, more embracing, and holistic, a surrogate for the future audience.

Following are the responsibilities that director and actor bear at the outset of rehearsal. Description may make them seem like an intellectual exercise, but much becomes instinctive after you have gained some initial experience.

DIRECTOR

GIVEN CIRCUMSTANCES

Know the script so you're quite certain what locations, time frame, character details, acts, etc., are exactly specified, and what other detail is only implied or must be supplied by director and cast.

BACK-STORY

Using your intimate knowledge of the script, infer what took place prior to the script's action. This is the back-story. The remaining biographical details that substantiate back-story fall into the domain of the individual character's biography. This is best created by the actor playing the part. The director, however, needs to be ahead of the game to be considered authoritative by the cast.

NATURE OF CHARACTERS: WHAT EACH WANTS

It is vital to go beyond what a character "is" and to know what he or she wants. This conception gives the character not just a fixed, static identity worn like a monogrammed t-shirt, but an active, evolving quest that mobilizes willpower to gain each new end, moment to moment. For instance, there is a great difference between saying that "Paul is afraid" and saying "here Paul wants to deflect the policeman's attention away from his suitcase." In the static example the actor playing Paul is expected to play generalized fear, while in the active example his character has a series of definite ends to gain, each one specific to the moment. A succession of such small, precise goals utterly transforms a person's acting by releasing his character's inner life into visibility.

NATURE OF ACTS

Since behavior is so important in the cinema, it helps to create a unique identity for each act under discussion, even the tiny ones. These labels or similes function as a potent directive when briefing or redirecting actors. To say that a man leaves the table during a family feud is not enough, for it provides an instruction lacking any special identity. But naming his action "the tactical retreat" or "the first step in leaving home" gives it a quality and meaning immediately assimilated by the players, something memorable, specific, and valuable. A possessive mother's behavior receiving her son's fiancee for the first time might be called "the snake dance" and a boy entering the funeral parlor where his father lies dead might be named "crossing the threshold of the underworld." In each case, the nature of the act is given a precise and imaginative coloration.

NATURE OF EACH CONFLICT

Because drama is powered by conflict, the director must know where and how each situation of conflict develops. It can appear as

- tension within each character of interest,
- conflict between characters, and
- conflict between characters and their situations.

For any conflict to exist, a pattern of oppositions must emerge, build tension in stages (rising action), climax, and then resolve (falling action). When a scene's resolution leads to harmony, this is usually only a temporary lull before a fresh set of tensions develops, starting a new cycle. This cyclical movement, taking place within the scene as beats, and true for the scene as a whole, has been likened to the cycles of an internal combustion engine (John Howard Lawson, *Theory and Technique of Playwriting* [New York: Hill & Wang, 1960] Chap. 4). The piston's compression stage is the gradual building of pressure inside the dramatic combustion chamber. At the moment of maximum pressure comes ignition and explosion, and this forces the motor forward into a new cycle of intake, compression, and explosion. One such explosion in the scene will be its "obligatory moment."

FINDING THE BEATS

A scene of tension between individuals is like a fencing match—much strategic footwork and mutual adaptation punctuated by strikes. Each moment of impact alters the balance of power and puts the match's outcome into a new light. In drama, likewise, a scene's nature and apparent premise change at each impact moment, or *beat*. Each moment of yielding to an emotional strike is one where change is irrevocable. It is a moment of high significance for at least one character and it is shared by the audience. This is the beat, the heightened moment or "crisis adaptation" for which the scene has been working. There may be several such cycles in a scene.

The space between one beat and the next contains the winding down from the last beat and the rising action leading to the crisis of the next. It can be minutes or seconds long.

Mark the beat points in your script, and see how the scene's forward movement becomes a waveform charting a series of dramatic onslaughts upon the audience's emotions.

CHANGES IN A CHARACTER'S RHYTHM

Every character has his own rhythms for speech and action. These vary according to his mood (for instance, whether he is excited or tired). It is an actor's responsibility to keep the character's rhythms distinctive and varying according to the character's inner state, which is likely to change at a beat point. Monotony is an invariable indicator of performing by rote, so know where to expect rhythmic changes.

OBLIGATORY MOMENT

This is the fulcrum point of the whole scene, the moment of change for which the whole scene exists. Subtract it and the scene is disabled or redundant.

FUNCTION OF EACH SCENE

Like a single cog in the gear train of a clock, each scene in a well constructed drama has its correct place and function. Defining this early enables one to interpret the scene confidently and to make it feed impetus into the larger pattern. Giving a name to the scene helps transfer this information rapidly and forcefully to someone else. Dickens' chapter titles from *Bleak House* make good examples: "Covering a Multitude of Sins," "Signs and Tokens," "A Turn of the Screw," "Closing In," "Dutiful Friendship," and "Beginning the World."

THEMATIC PURPOSE OF THE WHOLE WORK

It is the director's prerogative to decide and to shape the authorial thrust of the whole work. This interpretation must remain consonant with the screenplay's content and be accepted as realistic by the cast. Unlike a published play, a screenplay is not a hallowed document and directors will take considerable liberties after it has been acquired—a cause of much bitterness among screenwriters. Whatever changes you make, you alter the thematic purpose at your peril, unless you define one that is more embracing.

ACTORS

Following are the concepts most important for an actor's work. Several of the director's appear here again in abbreviated form.

BACK-STORY

Know the events that brought the characters to the script's present.

YOUR CHARACTER'S GIVEN CIRCUMSTANCES

Know at every point what circumstances, time, place, pressures, and other people are contributing to your character's physical and mental state.

BIOGRAPHY

Make up a full life story for your character, one that supports the back-story details implied by the script. This ensures that you know a great deal about the character you are creating and that everything your character says or does is rooted in the patterns created by his or her past. Without this integrity of experience and motivation, your character will lack depth and credibility. The director will often question you during rehearsal about your character's background, always centering on those aspects that are not coming across well.

BE ABLE TO JUSTIFY EVERYTHING YOUR CHARACTER SAYS AND DOES

You must know the pressures motivating your character's every action and every line. This process of justification has already been used to build your character's biography, and the biography in turn governs your character's choices and decisions. The script usually contains the relevant clues, but occasionally your character's action must be completely defined by yourself and your director.

DEFINE EACH ACTION WITH AN ACTIVE VERB

Actions are the most eloquent expression your character ever makes, so the linguistic tags by which you plan them matter a great deal. Take this example: "A woman is seen stepping away from her tipsy husband in embarrassment at a party when an indiscretion passes his lips." This description is in the commonly used passive voice, flat and only minimally informative. An actress might describe the action for herself as, "she sidesteps the landmine," "she absorbs a punch in the gut," "she springs towards the bar," or "she reels aside after stepping in filth." All these descriptions use active verbs and serve to illuminate the behavior and its motivation.

What about common actions, like opening a closet door? To perform the action in general, that is, without a specific motivation, is false to life. Giving them tags is a way of investing each action with specific meaning. For instance, "he eases the door open" shows caution and perhaps apprehension. Substitute either *jerks, rips, shoves, barges, slides, elbows, flings, dashes, heaves,* or *hurls* and you have a veritable catalogue of relationships between man and door, each example coloring and particularizing the action to great effect.

It also helps in another area peculiar to film, which expects actors to remain consistent over many takes and many angles. A single scene can take a whole day. Consistency becomes a major problem, especially for the untrained actor lacking technique. Using a tag to give each action a clear quality and motivation will help an actor remain emotionally consistent.

WHAT IS MY CHARACTER TRYING TO GET?

Answering this commonplace little question is a key to real acting. In everyday life most of us are unaware of how unceasingly inventive we are in getting what we want. Instead, we see ourselves as civilized, long-suffering victims sacrificing happiness and fulfillment to the voracious demands of others. But the word *actor* tells the whole tale: for your character to get what he or she wants (a smile, a cup of coffee, a sympathetic reaction, a rejection, a sign of guilt, a glimpse of doubt) he or she must actively adopt a strategy characteristic of your character alone, as he or she tries to realize the desire of the moment. As circumstances alter, the character's needs change and adapt. Incidentally, for an actor to be active like this is the only viable method to portray a passive person, who differs only in strategy.

WHAT ARE OTHER CHARACTERS TRYING TO DO TO ME OR GET FROM ME?

If your character constantly searches the other actors' characters for signs of will and intention, it means that your character is constantly and spontaneously moving between the defensive and offensive roles demanded by your character's ever-changing situation. In real life this happens within us automatically and unconsciously, but to master a role these reflexes must be deliberately patterned until you have fully internalized your character's spontaneous actions and reactions. This means that your character is alive to the real and unpredictable chemistry of the acted moment.

KNOW WHERE THE BEATS ARE

An actor, sustaining a single consciousness, sometimes sees peaks of consciousness in his or her character that have been overlooked by the director. See "Finding the Beats" under "Director" above.

HOW AND WHERE DOES MY CHARACTER ADAPT?

A character who has goals to pursue or defend perceives changes that signal either victory or defeat, to which he or she must make strategic adaptation. Spotting where and how these adaptations can be made helps build a dense texture for your character's consciousness. Maintaining this will help you stay in focus throughout many takes.

KEEP YOUR CHARACTER'S INTERIOR VOICE AND MIND'S EYE GOING

In real life, people are enclosed in their own ongoing thoughts, hopes, fears, memories, and visions. The good actor keeps up his or her character's stream of consciousness or "interior action." In your mind, hear or even speak your character's conflicting thoughts, summon up mental images from your character's past, remember and imagine in character, and you will be continuously convincing and interesting to an audience. Additionally, the pacing of your actions and reactions will automatically be consistent and true. The actor's art is really that of developing a disciplined consciousness, which is why acting is so difficult and so psychically demanding.

KNOW THE FUNCTION OF EACH SCENE

Not only must you know your character's objectives but you must know on a larger scale what the scene is supposed to accomplish and what your character contributes to the piece as a whole.

KNOW THE THEMATIC PURPOSE OF THE WHOLE WORK

An intelligent actor wants to grasp not just the character and the character's purview, for that leads surely to an adversarial relationship with other actors, but also to understand the meaning of the whole, so that his or her characterization can merge effectively with the thrust of the whole work.

REHEARSING WITH THE BOOK

WHICH SCENES FIRST?

At the first rehearsal you will probably cover one or two scenes that have been chosen for their centrality to the piece as a whole. Your dramatic breakdown and definition of thematic purpose should clearly indicate the turning points in the piece. Work on these will provide a sure framework for other scenes that link them by developing the issues that come to a head in the key scenes.

REHEARSAL SPACE

It is a great advantage to rehearse in the actual locations to be used, but this is often impractical. Make still photos to show actors what the space for each scene is like. This helps them imagine the proportions in which the scene is to take place and feeds the overall image of their characters' lives. Often rehearsal takes place in a borrowed or rented space that is large and bare. Indicate approximate placement of walls, key pieces of furniture, doors, and windows with tape on the rehearsal room floor.

The advantage of this sort of minimalist rehearsal is that there is nothing to distract from attention to the characters; the disadvantage is that its abstract quality can lead to performing and theatrical projection toward an imagined audience.

EARLY WORK WITH THE BOOK

By now the actors should have done their homework. So far they have still not been given the go-ahead to learn their lines. The danger, we have said, is that they would internalize an undeveloped interpretation. There is another hazard: learning lines fixes an actor's attention prematurely upon words when, in the cinema, behavior (of which language is only a part) should receive the most attention. Your cast will probably be bursting with questions and ideas. Running through each scene from the book (actors reading from the script), you should concentrate on each actor's conception of his or her character and of the nature of the scene itself. Learning the scene is much more important than learning lines. Early rehearsal work will mainly be geared toward acquiring the focus and interpretation you believe is correct. Character consistency is slow to evolve, because it requires reconciling something a character does in one scene with other actions in other scenes. Expect discussion and disagreement over nuances of motivation behind the action and dialogue.

MOVEMENT AND ACTION

Though reading from a text prevents actors from moving with any consistency or freedom, it is important to get each cast member developing the kind of action that reflects the character's internal, psychological movement. This is particularly important at the beats.

For example, a man being questioned one evening in the kitchen by his possessive mother eventually decides to confess he is engaged to marry. We know what he eventually does from the text, but how does he occupy himself during these stressful minutes, so we can learn what he feels? The screenplay does not specify. Perhaps he starts drying up the dishes, and repeatedly hands items to his mother to put away so her hands are never empty. When she becomes especially probing, he goes silent, and lets the water out of the sink, watching it drain away. As the last of it gurgles down the drain he turns and blurts out his secret. The domestic scene, the way he purges himself of the family china, the water running away like sand in an hourglass, all combine both as credible action and as metaphors for the pressure he feels to act on a "now or never" decision. Spontaneous invention usually first produces a dramatic cliche, so the director will need to be demanding in order to get something fresh and unexpected from the cast.

Without the ability to move and to truly interact with each other, actors' readings will remain inadequate, so content yourself with rough sketchwork at this stage. As soon as you are satisfied that character, motivation, and the right kind of ideas for action are agreed in outline, instruct the actors to learn their lines for a scene.

REHEARSING WITHOUT THE BOOK

Actors now freed from the constraint of carrying a script can begin to move freely. You have studied the text closely in search of meaning, but character development involves more than just intellectual understanding. It requires the surrender of the actor's whole body to the character's internal and external movements. Much of what must be done next lies in developing specific, telling actions.

VERBAL AND PHYSICAL ACTION

The common approach—learning lines and superimposing movement afterwards—is wrong because it assumes that behavior will follow if actors know what to say. Actually this violates the natural order, for in life words arise out of ongoing action, either interior (that is, within the mind) or exterior, physical action. In a work situation, for instance, we are thinking and doing and only speak when we have decided to act upon someone present.

I cannot emphasize too strongly that speech should be seen as the outcome of purposeful inner action and is therefore itself a form of action. In the hands of unsophisticated actors this truism is often turned on its head. They learn words because they are immediately available and then apply action as a decorative veneer afterwards.

Actors who learn lines in immobility will unconsciously keep returning to immobility, however much they have conscientiously rehearsed actions afterwards. They will pause, or lean, or sit when speaking, or take refuge by locking into the eyeline of the other character. Actions that manage to accompany lines will have that curiously superimposed quality so dismally familiar in amateur dramatics.

WORDS SIGNIFY MORE THAN THEY MEAN

Hollow acting usually results from the players and their director treating the dialogue as the body of the scene. Words are only the surface outcome of something happening deeper inside the speaker. As we have said, there is a displacement principle at work impelling each character to mask his vulnerability by using conversation and action that is deliberately more trivial.

An example: A man and wife arguing bitterly over who should get the plumber to mend a dripping tap are not really fighting over the tap at all, but moving perilously near to a breakdown in their marriage. Intelligent drama recognizes that, as in life itself, people almost never deal directly with what really matters to them. Instead, they tackle their problems obliquely or analogously and very seldom in direct terms. Both the man and wife in my example would know that their marriage relationship is under stress. Only the outsider lacking all insight would wonder how anyone could get so worked up over plumbing.

Actors and director developing this scene would be grossly superficial to center upon the dialogue over the tap, but this is what will happen if nobody is alert to the subtext. Here again we must stress the importance of thoroughly understanding a scene and its subtexts before anyone commits lines to memory.

When work begins without the book, do not let the increased meaningfulness of the lines usurp the development of physical action. Encourage the actors to approach the scene from a behavioral rather than textual standpoint. This confirms the importance of having a clear idea of the setting—what it is, what it contains, and what it represents to the characters themselves. It also means that you insist on the meaning and spirit of lines, not their strict accuracy. You can tighten the readings later. You'll find Chapter 31, Exercise 9: "Gibberish" a useful resource here.

TURNING THOUGHT AND WILL INTO ACTION

Only a few significant actions are specified in the average script, and unless the director and actors approach the script as an extremely spare blueprint requiring extensive development, characters will move into position, deliver their speeches in an overwrought manner, and be done. This will produce an extremely hollow, unconvincing movie.

The true power behind both speech and action is will. Imagine that you have a domestic scene between a middle-aged couple under development. It might well develop as follows.

When Lyn tells her son Jon that the car bumper is twisted, she is willing her son to feel shocked and guilty. You and your cast know this from the rest of the script, but how do you translate this into action? At the beginning of the scene, Jon hears his mother walk to the garage, but instead of driving away, her footsteps return. How does she force her angry state of mind upon her son? Your actor playing the mother slows down her entry and makes it wordless, accusatory. She stands in the door looking at him.

How does he repel or subvert the pressure she is applying? The actor tells you he feels that his character wants to be busy. You decide he is building a model car and painting the kit parts, keeping this up so he can avoid his mother's accusing gaze.

How does she command his attention? From intuition you suggest to her, "Try throwing the car keys next to the box of parts." This interrupts the evasive activity to which he resorted and creates a charged moment culminating in a beat as their eyes meet.

You and your actors are elated because you feel instinctively that you have created a strong moment. Now when the mother says, "The front bumper's all twisted," she is no longer supplying information but pushing home an accusation that began with her silent reentry. In effect, we no longer have words as neutral information, or words initiating action. We now have action culminating in words that themselves seek an effect. Driven by conscious needs, words are themselves a kind of action seeking the gratification of a reaction. This is why a line loaded in this way is called a verbal action. In good writing, all dialogue is specific and has this potential for acting upon the person addressed. Good actors, good directors try to develop pressures in the characters, pressures that produce dialogue. Then the dialogue itself becomes a further applied pressure energizing further action in the person addressed.

Developing a scene therefore means not just knowing the words and where to walk at such and such a line, but working out a detailed flow of action that evidences the internal ebb and flow of each character's being. Primarily this is each actor's responsibility, but final choice and coordination is the director's job. Proof of success is when an audience knows what is going on without hearing a word.

SIGNIFICANCE OF SPACE

How characters use space in this flow of action becomes highly significant. Continuing our scene above, the mother and son are half the room apart when she enters but she walks up to him in silence. The pressure from her proximity causes him to make a painting error, and he lays down the work, looking up at her blamingly. "It's not my fault; you parked it too close to the wall," he says, continuing to look up. She turns away in frustration and turns on the TV. Both stare at the silent picture for a moment or two, hypnotized and taking refuge in habit before they return to the divisive issue of how the car got damaged.

It is now the action rather than the dialogue that is eloquent of their distress, yet in the script only a few bald lines of dialogue appear on the page. All the action has been created to turn implication into behavior—behavior being the ebb and flow of will. In an overwritten scene you will find that some dialogue now becomes redundant and can be cut. So much the better.

A CHARACTER'S INNER MOVEMENT

A single moment of inner movement in a character can be broken down into four definite steps.

1. **Feels Impact:** Words or an action enter his consciousness.
2. **Sees Demand:** This perception, filtered through his temperament, mood, and current assumptions, is seen as a demand ("She wants. . . .")
3. **New Need Arises:** Feels a new need form ("Now I must get. . . .")
4. **Makes Counter-Demand:** The new need is expressed through an action (physical or verbal) that he expects will get fulfilling results.

In the following example we have a discussion going on between a woman and a man about an outing they have planned.

> It is early Friday evening. There is disagreement between Brian and Ann about which movie they should go to see. She wants them to drive out to the farther cinema and see a new comedy. Not really wanting to go out, he says the comedy was not well reviewed, so they might as well go to one of the nearer films. She produces a newspaper and says that on the contrary the movie got three stars in both the papers. Looking at him, seeing he is not changing his mind, she turns abruptly and moodily kicks her shoes into the closet, saying that he never wants to go out with her any more. He looks concerned and protests that it is not true. They end up going to the movie and he enjoys it more than she does.

Let us analyze a single moment of change. When Ann suggests the film at the faraway cinema, Brian, whose job requires him to drive daily far from home and who wants to watch TV and relax, goes through interior changes as follows.

1. **Feels Impact:** "Drive ten miles to see a movie when I could settle down and watch the news! Oh boy, this is really something to come home to."

2. **Sees Demand:** "It's her day off and she wants us to do something together. The old complaint that I never consider her situation, but that's not true. . . ."

3. **New Need Arises:** "I really can't get back into that traffic again for forty minutes, I've really got to put this off somehow. . . . It's not even a decent movie."

4. **Makes Counter-Demand:** (Speaking to Ann while looking ineffectually through the accumulation of newspapers) "You know, I seem to remember that David Whats-his-name in the *Times* only gave it one star."

Brian does not signal his feelings, but instead makes a direct, action-oriented leap between what he perceives to be happening and what he must do to cope with it.

In general our feelings are internalized and only require conscious examination when we are in internal conflict. Brian is not divided in himself until he realizes that Ann is nearly crying with disappointment and frustration. It is here that he is moved to an action.

Of course, not all human interaction is of overt disagreement, but it often happens in drama because drama centers on conflict, no matter whether it is comedy, tragedy, horror, or any other genre. Even when characters appear to be in harmony, one may be buying time, that is, going along verbally while turning the whole matter over in his or her mind. Since inner states always find outward expression, it is important to find a fresh, subtle action to accompany what the character is experiencing inside.

ADAPTATION

Here we have something like two characters trying to stand up in a small boat. There are and must be constant changes for which they must both compensate, each according to what one judges to be the other's strategy. In this movement there are many feints, experiments, surprises, and mistakes.

KEEPING UP AN INTERIOR MONOLOGUE

So that actors maintain their characters' inner lives, you may need to demand inner monologues; that is, the conscious internal enunciation of the characters' thoughts and perceptions. A well trained actor will have internalized this habit but the signs of its absence are clear. The character seems to lack a thought process and the actor drops into an expression of trance between lines. The character comes to life when he or she has something to say, and promptly goes dead while the actor waits for the next cue. Sometimes actors are actually visualizing the script page. This spells certain death for a movie, and the best way to shift an actor out of this mode is to ask him or her to improvise a thoughts voice between lines, as in Chapter 32, Exercise 23: "Improvising an Interior Monologue." This is also a superb strategy for examining a place in a scene where an actor repeatedly loses focus or when you suspect that the actor has a skewed understanding of a certain passage. That characters remain internally active is the only way to capture reactions that are alive. Another benefit is that having reliable interior action to carry out, an actor is more likely to stay in focus and carry out actions at a consistent rate from take to take.

USING MISPERCEPTIONS

In both comedy and tragedy, subjective errors of perception arise out of a wide range of causes. There are emotional obstacles—such as fear, misplaced confidence, wrong expectation—any of which cause a character to read a protagonist wrongly. Other misapprehensions may arise out of being unfamiliar with the culture or personality of the antagonist, inattention, preoccupation, partial or distorted information, or habit, to name just a few. Misperception is a fertile source for comedy (think of John Cleese's Basil Fawlty in the *Fawlty Towers* series) and it is equally productive of dramatic tension, provoking actions that instead of neutralizing a situation drive it forward to new developments revealing of differences and the inner lives of the characters.

The work of Harold Pinter, like that of many modern dramatists, exploits the tensions between the characters' surface conformity and the dark, groping, private worlds existing beneath. In *The Dumb-Waiter,* for instance, two hired assassins wait interminably in a disused kitchen for further instructions. The lengthening wait, punctuated with bizarre, unfulfillable requests sent down in the dumbwaiter, acts upon the two men's private fears and distrust. While trying to maintain the normality of their working partnership, an increasingly dark fear gnaws at each, and we see them regress out of sheer insecurity.

The subtext of the piece deals with masters and servants, order and chaos, security and insecurity. It presents the characters as an analogy for man waiting nervously to learn God's will. But without a response from director and actors to the possibilities of this quite grandiose subtext, the piece comes off as a light comedy of manners.

EXPRESSING THE SUBTEXT

An actor must develop not just an idea of subtext, but the physical expression of it, entering an intensive, created world where he or she lives the thoughts and feelings of the character. The actor creates the character, yet also is the character and can speak for the character and be guided by a growing sense of intuition about what works—what action (given and received) is sustaining the flux of the character's emotions or what conversely is going against the grain and needs to be examined and changed.

FORMS OF RESISTANCE BY ACTORS

ACTORS AND STRESS

The public, seeing accomplished performances as a matter of course, assumes that acting must be easy and pleasant. But actors are by the nature of their work placed under a physical and psychic scrutiny that is very rare in ordinary life. This attention is the profession's allure but it also means the actor is vulnerable and sometimes has nowhere to hide. Faced with a demanding part and a demanding director, even the experienced actor will doubt his or her competence, or, confronting an unfamiliar and unwelcome self-image, feel that it threatens his or her very ability to function. Under such conditions it is regrettably human to deny, to evade, and to blame others.

The accomplished actor is ready for these trials and does not need to be constantly on the defense. This is someone who maintains emotional and intellectual flexibility during criticism, and does not try to hide the nature or degree of problems. Such individuals are as rare in acting as they are everywhere else, and there is no one walking the face of the earth who does not have lapses. A thorough acting training seeks with painful and religious fervor to evoke self-knowledge and self-discipline. This compels an actor to stand still and confront the worst rather than find ways to resist the director's demands.

Resistance to the work at hand is remarkably constant and takes many forms. However frustrating, it must be treated with understanding and respect, since it almost always arises from insecurity rather than ill will.

LINES AND INSECURITY

Sometimes actors claim to need the book long after they should have learned the lines. This is a common insecurity symptom and it completely blocks a scene's development. If at a subsequent rehearsal and after due warning, the same individual still claims to need the book, simply take it and have a prompter supply whatever is missing. The difficulty and embarrassment of floundering through a scene in this way normally motivates the actor to come thoroughly prepared the next time. Insecure actors usually find it is liberating to deal with the substance of the scene in this way instead of its letter.

If an actor again claims not to know a scene well enough to work without a script, I say, "Well, you know what it's about, just make something up." The actor may first look appalled, but the results are usually good. The actor either knows the scene better than he or she thought, or, compelled to improvise from a general idea, takes a heightened interest in what is written. This exercise should not be undertaken punitively, but as a necessary way of getting on with business.

CLINGING TO THE LETTER OF THE SCRIPT

Conversely, being overreliant on keeping to the text or to "what we already decided" is also a resistance. The actor who is afraid to think, feel, and explore in character will often take refuge behind a structure of perceived "rules."

FEAR OF CHANGES

Sometimes the request to alter the performance in some way, or to change something previously set, triggers an irrational unwillingness to adapt.

ACTING IN ISOLATION

An actor who doggedly carries out what he or she has prepared regardless of the nuances of other performances is too unrelaxed to listen, watch, and work from life going on around. This actor will not feel the cup in his or her hand, smell the morning air, or feel the touch of his or her lover's lips. Since this actor is holed up inside a set of mental constructs, it will be through physical detail that he or she best finds his way to the piece's here and now.

OVER-INTELLECTUALIZING

The tendency to intellectualize is another way an actor puts off the fearsome task of experiencing the character's (and his or her own) emotions. The actor who wants to debate every point feels safer discussing than doing, and may try to involve the whole cast in arguments about niceties of interpretation. These are really delaying tactics, or a bid to wrest control from the director, or both.

THE ANTI-INTELLECT ACTOR

This actor scorns discussion and the search for underlying structures, and may be someone intellectually insecure (lacking formal education, for instance) or someone unusually intuitive. Results will reveal which.

CONTROL BATTLES

The actor who tries to control scenes, manipulate other actors, or resist directorial criticism is probably afraid to place trust in working partnerships of any kind. If you do not set limits this person may absorb a disproportionate share of everyone's energies. This actor often tries to direct other actors or to challenge the director's authority in public. Such challenge need not be without its creative contribution, depending on its underlying spirit. Genuinely creative personalities sometimes overflow their territory and may need a firm hand to contain them.

PLAYWRITING

This behavior plays against the flow of either a scripted or improvised scene, manipulates other actors, introduces inappropriate material, or in other ways undermines the validity of what others are doing.

INAPPROPRIATE HUMOR

Jokes or other diversions that disrupt the working atmosphere are often a means of delaying and diffusing a situation the actor finds threatening (like working without the book).

WITHDRAWAL

The actor who often deals with problems by withdrawing may be asking for special consideration, or may habitually evade the responsibility for solving problems.

UNPUNCTUALITY AND COMMITMENT PROBLEMS

These are of the utmost seriousness, and conditions for retaining the actor should be spelled out early and without compromise. An unreliable person who remains in the company gains increasing leverage daily as he or she gets more difficult to replace.

THE ADVANTAGES OF VIDEOTAPING REHEARSALS

Once your cast is off the book and beginning to be reasonably confident, try regularly covering the rehearsals with a video camera. The most useful coverage is the documentary style called direct cinema. This is a continuous take by a handheld camera, moving close for close ups, and backing away and panning as the action requires. This treats the rehearsal as a happening to be recorded without any intervention on behalf of the camera. Because it tries to be in the right place at the right time, the camera coverage needs no editing. Taping rehearsals in fact produces a fascinating range of advantages.

1. You see a dramatically complete version of the scene within minutes of calling "Cut!"
2. You learn in advance of final shooting which camera placements and movements are most likely to show the scene to advantage.
3. The mobile camera gives priority to the actors' freedom of movement.
4. The camera is choreographed into the process, rather than appearing later as an inhibiting newcomer.
5. The cast gets over its camera neuroses early, and will soon neither see nor think about the camera, resulting in natural and unstrained performances.
6. The director, able to privately run and rerun rehearsals, gets an early warning of mannerisms, cliches, trends, and subtleties that would otherwise only make themselves known in postproduction.
7. The camera crew goes to work early, looking for each scene's appropriate form in terms of camera angles, movement, lenses, and lighting.
8. Not only do they get to know each scene intimately, but the operators become familiar with the little physical indications each actor gives when he or she is going to move, and with the sightlines and movements to be expected.
9. Repetition suggests ways to cover stretches of action using fewer angles and longer takes.
10. The crew is in a position early on to tell the director what compromises an actor must make in speed or destination to overcome a camera or microphone problem.
11. By the time formal shooting arrives, everyone is an old hand and there is little of the regression that normally accompanies the first shooting.
12. Your first shooting is the dynamic version from a living reality, instead of something based on the static, heroic concepts of the storyboard approach.

Newcomers to directing often delay evolving a *mise-en-scène* (camera treatment) for their scenes until the last moment. This means that the material suffers a late and highly theoretical fragmentation that probably errs on the side of caution to ensure against all possible editing problems.

Never using a camera during rehearsals leads inevitably to performances developed in a live-performance mode that become unavoidably theatrical. This is hard or impossible to shake off when you start filming, since repetition has fixed habits immutably.

Tape can be a constant feedback source, and is a marvelous way for a director to develop an acting company. It takes dedication on the part of everyone, and may slow the process of arriving at minimally acceptable results. In an accelerated schedule, there may not be time for this lengthy process, and feedback that disturbs the player's mindset can be harmful. However, if a group intends to function as a repertory company (like Fassbinder's early group) the cycle of performance and critical viewing is a superb way of getting people to accept who and what they are, and seeing where their obstacles lie.

WHEN TO SHOW ACTORS THEIR PERFORMANCES

Taping rehearsals is thus not without risks. Cast members naturally clamor for a showing, and if unused to seeing themselves onscreen, are invariably appalled and may thereafter attempt to handle themselves differently, indeed so differently that you have a new problem. Inexperienced actors, seeing their development onscreen during production, become their own audience, and will relate to that experience while acting, instead of remaining inside their characters' thoughts and experience. At some point well before shooting, the actor must therefore relinquish monitoring and judging his or her own performance and pass that responsibility over to the director, whom we have often said represents the first audience. The actor who fails to do this becomes locked in an attitude of defensiveness and mistrust.

If you do not have a long enough schedule to take your cast through a full evolutionary process, warn everyone at the outset that it is normal to hate the way one looks on the screen, so you will make a little footage of rehearsals available for the curious, but none of the shoot. If there is any protest, explain this is normal practice in the feature film industry.

Under the usual pressured shooting schedule, show footage only to make a point that cannot be made any other way. I once convinced a player that he was acting instead of being by showing him some surreptitiously shot footage of himself in spontaneous conversation, and then contrasted it with footage of him performing a scripted conversation. The difference was so overwhelming that he abandoned his resistance to my judgment. This kind of revelation is risky because it is a negative approach. Use it cautiously and supportively only if you cannot get through any other way. The same procedure can be used with the actor of fragile ego who insists on projecting a rich and unnatural acting voice instead of his or her natural range.

Another hazard of indiscriminately showing footage is that you may end up with five cast members and six directors. With familiarity, actors come to more or less accept how they appear onscreen, but the journey to equanimity can be rough. Blame for feelings of humiliation tend to alight on other cast members or the director, and become the reason to seek control. None of this need happen if the actors work from what you communicate rather than what their over-critical eyes read from the screen.

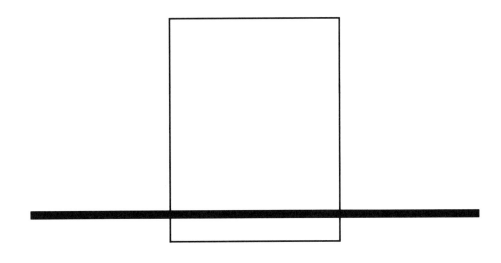

C·H·A·P·T·E·R 8

FINAL REHEARSAL AND PLANNING COVERAGE

THE DIRECTOR AS ACTIVE OBSERVER

So far, our rehearsal priorities have given primacy to the actors' sense of what their characters must do, moment to moment, with the director observing and steering the results through critical feedback. Soon the director must turn from interpreting the characters and text to planning their presentation on the screen.

Though it is natural for the director to sit while observing and taking notes, remaining static means experiencing the action like a theatregoer, and leads to choreographing the action for a static camera placement. Clearly this is uncinematic and arises largely out of the director's immobility.

As the action unfolds, it is best to move around, adjusting your position to gain the most involved and privileged view, either of the whole or of the significant parts. This leads naturally to your deciding a point of view for the scene itself and the camera angles to reveal it. Your mobility also prevents actors from relating to one flat plane, that of the audience. Now the action becomes inturned and enclosed as they play to and for each other, just like people do in real life.

When you need to fine-tune the blocking of actors and camera in relation to each other and break the action down into separate shots, it should now proceed with few conceptual problems.

FORM: SEEING IN AN UNFAMILIAR WAY

We tend to think of stories as subjects, but actually what often makes them fresh or memorable is not what is told, but how it is told. This is form as opposed to content. Storytelling is always in search of language that uniquely serves the tale in hand. Cinema form is influenced by many determinants such as photography, lighting, set and costume design, choice of location, story construction, and editing style.

Originality in form can be visual, such as the look of eighteenth century English painting in Kubrick's *Barry Lyndon* (1976), the innovative deep focus photography in Welles's *Citizen Kane* (1941), or the long lens compression and muted colors in Visconti's *Death in Venice* (1971); or it can be in narrative style, such as the single take per scene of Tanner's *The Middle of the World* (1974), the edgy, compressed, and rapid movement of Roeg's *Don't Look Now* (1973), or the predominance of stills in Marker's *La Jetée* (1963). Renewal through form can reside elsewhere in charismatic acting, as in Bertolucci's *Last Tango in Paris* (1972) or Rafelson's *Five Easy Pieces* (1970); in a musical sensibility, as in Losey's *The Go-Between* (1971) or Godard's *Pierrot le Fou* (1965); or more intangibly in a nontraditional approach to narrative itself, as in Tanner's *In the White City* (1985) or Yvonne Rainer's *Kristina Talking Pictures* (1977).

The question of form—what options exist for best presenting a story's particular world—is at the very heart of original cinema, indeed of art itself. Form, seldom uppermost in the beginner's mind, is a difficult and elusive subject upon which to make generalizations. Even professionals tend to choose unconsciously and from what is normal. But the best and most enduring work evolves from a deeper awareness of how the arts, of which cinema is the most advanced synthesis, really function.

Here I merely want to draw attention to form's importance. In Chapter 28: Form and Style, there is a detailed account for you to consider.

BLOCKING

This ugly word suggesting as it does the building of Stonehenge refers to positioning actors and camera in relationship to each other. In my outline of a scene's development the director encourages the actors to freely develop movement and action without initial regard to filming restrictions. Where each character moves and why comes from what is in the script, what each actor feels the character needs, and what the director sees as necessary. With repeated rehearsal this organic and experimental development will eventually settle into a tacitly agreed pattern of actions that express the flow of the characters' internal movements (perceptions, thoughts, feelings, will).

However, what emerges is by no means the only pattern possible. Indeed, the exigencies of filming inevitably impose changes on the action developed. By altering a walk from one side of a table to the other, for instance, an additional camera angle and a lighting change can be saved. Discoveries like this require the cast to make changes that seem to yield only inconvenience to themselves.

Rehearsing beforehand in the scene's actual location and involving the camera crew early can both keep blocking changes to a minimum. But blocking is still from first to last a process of mutual accommodation, any part of which may change at a moment's notice. Actors, geared up for a big moment and then put on hold for a lighting change, are apt to become frustrated unless thoroughly forewarned of the changeable and sporadic nature of filmmaking itself.

For this and other reasons it is good to videotape rehearsals and to maintain an open attitude about how the scene may eventually be presented. This way you will not forfeit time and morale when shooting begins.

BENEFITS OF REHEARSING AT ACTUAL LOCATION

The script will often specify locations that can be generally visualized in advance. Everyone knows what a laundromat is like, or what it is like to wait in a typical train station, eat at a typical hot dog stand, or cook in a typical suburban kitchen. But wait, all kitchens are not equal. Each in some way portrays its owners, and a messy, greasy, dark kitchen imposes different physical and emotional conditions on the user than a light, airy, modern one.

A scene rehearsed to a hazy, generalized idea of the location and then hastily transplanted into an actual kitchen for shooting will have characters who barely connect with their surroundings, a serious deficiency. If rehearsals take place in the chosen location from the beginning, then actors can interact with their physical surroundings in a highly specific way.

When multiple on-site rehearsals are not practicable, take the actors for a research exploration, or at least show them photographs, so they have a distinct mental image. Director and actor alike can benefit from research. Here one might observe or videotape someone in a kitchen and note how the character and mood are subtly reflected in the actor's actions. Notice how often action is focussed and purposeful, compared with the vagueness and gesturing of someone who only signifies living in a kitchen.

Your aim in filming should be to make each location as expressive as the characters and not a mere container for words and action. Try to see each setting as a character, worthy in itself of loving portrayal. This way you will set up an environment that makes the spectator imaginatively inhabit the movie, and maybe leaves him haunted by it long after.

HOW MUCH REHEARSAL IS ENOUGH?

Actors often express the fear that a scene will be overrehearsed. If rehearsal is drilling to a master plan, this is a real enough threat. But if it means digging down into deeper and deeper layers of meaning within the scene, of developing perceptions and restrictions that flow back and forth between the characters, of creating links and resonances with other parts of the script, then it can be unendingly productive.

Not all scenes merit such intensive work since some exist merely to supply an uncomplicated story point—that a letter is delivered to the wrong address, for instance. Such a scene may require little or no rehearsal. Others are a goldmine of possibilities that richly repay persistent exploration. Which scenes are key scenes needing special work is decided during the director's preparation and by the ensemble's growing ability to focus upon problem areas and discover solutions. This aspect, really a consequence of good leadership and good casting, can be the most rewarding aspect of collaborative work.

When an actor is convinced that developmental work cannot improve an impromptu performance, you as director must prove otherwise. Do not, however, try to push rehearsal beyond the point where you yourself can see the way ahead. When you reach your threshold switch to another scene. One can seldom fully develop a scene on its own because of its dramatic dependency upon others. Give time, therefore, to related scenes in rotation rather than concentrating exhaustively upon one. This strategy keeps up actors' energies and gives proper attention to the integrity of the whole piece.

ONSCREEN LENGTH, REHEARSALS, AND MAINTAINING A TIMING

Films intended for commercial showing have an optimum length related to their content. For television, length is also determined by the size of the slot and will be precise to the second.

Most student films are limited by budget rather than by overall timing, but the tendency is to shoot overlong scenes with too little coverage and far too much dialogue padding. Afterwards it becomes apparent how much compression must somehow be accomplished in the cutting room.

Unsuccessful films usually look as if they are trying to milk the longest possible film from available money and story content. How long, though, should a film be? A good way to arrive at screen length is to decide on the basis of a bare story outline what is the shortest screen time in which the story can adequately be told, and to budget time for each sequence accordingly. This requires a professional economy in the writing. It also means that if you add anything to one sequence you must make savings in another. Lengthening your film beyond the original plan has consequences anyway on stock requirements and scheduling, so monitoring rehearsals for the eventual screen time is important.

As rehearsals proceed, the assistant director should time each scene with a stopwatch. By adding all the latest timings together you can establish an overall timing all through the process. This keeps you alert to consequences when scenes inevitably get longer. As further business is developed for a scene, as the characters increasingly adopt realistic thinking and behavioral rhythms, individual scenes becomes shorter to watch but longer in real time. Collectively they may not hold up. Be careful. A thirty-minute script can imperceptibly turn into a forty-seven-minute epic.

As work proceeds, check new timings against earlier ones so you can make necessary decisions affecting length prior to shooting. While cutting material is a difficult or even traumatic solution with a tightly written piece, another is to review, edit, or tighten pacing as you go.

Though miracles can be wrought in the cutting room, it is unwise to rely on them for more than minor savings, and certainly not unless you have provided sufficient coverage and cutaways. Resolve now that you will never leave a scene without shooting all valid cutaways.

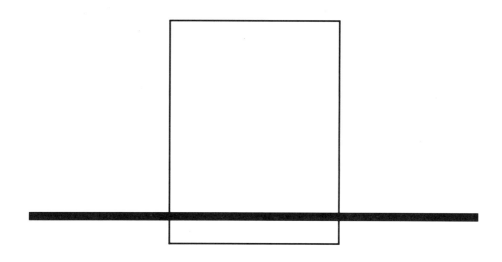

DEVELOPING A CREW

ON CREW AND ACTORS

Not only will your choice of crew affect your actors, but the crew should also be cast just as carefully for their technical and personal characteristics. In fact, many of the same personal criteria apply to both.

USING PEOPLE WITH EXPERIENCE

I have titled this chapter "developing" rather than "choosing" a crew because even when experienced crew members are available you will need to do some experimental shooting with them before the main shoot. Expect to continue developing standards and communication all through the production.

Videotaping rehearsals, using a documentary style of spontaneous coverage, is an ideal way to find out ahead of time what developments or changes are required in the crew. It lets you know how equipment is functioning and how well you understand each other. A brief and unambiguous language of communication is always important, but if you are shooting material that takes advantage of transient location conditions, such as a brief crowd condition in a city or a sunset behind a flock of birds, then camera-position changes must be made rapidly and there is little margin for misunderstanding between director and crew.

Even in highly controllable shooting circumstances, you will often discover that one operator's close-up is another's medium shot, depending on the work he or she has done before. Filmmaking is relativistic; framing, composition, speed of camera movements, and microphone positioning all come about through mutual values and compromise, something that can only happen if crew members grasp each other's terminology and assumptions. From shooting rehearsals and test or exercise footage, you must expect to unearth wide variance of skill levels, differing interpretations of standard jargon, and incompatible assumptions about solving technical problems. These impediments confirm the need for formal, clearly understood lines of responsibility and a common language, something everyone must work out ahead of the shooting, which brings enough problems of its own.

DEVELOPING YOUR OWN CREW

Let us take the most daunting situation, that you live in a place remote from centers of filmmaking, that you must start from scratch, work up your own standards, and find and train your own crew. We will assume you have access to a videotape rig comprising a camera, recorder, microphone, and a monitor. How many and what kind of people will you need? What are their responsibilities?

First and foremost, everyone you recruit must appreciate your values and commitment to the importance of drama and to the project. Ideally they should share them. Naturally this is more important in a director of photography than it is in a grip or a cutting room assistant, but the small, low-budget enterprise needs to avoid all schisms of temperament and purpose, since so much of the groundbreaking work is sustained on belief and morale.

Before taking on a crew member, examine not only his technical expertise and experience, but make an informal inquiry into his ideas and values. You might ask about favorite films, books, plays, hobbies, and interests. Technical acumen is important, but under stress a person's maturity and values are more so. Technical deficiencies can be remedied, but you might ultimately be unable to work with someone lacking positive responses to your choices of subject and treatment.

CREW MEMBERS' TEMPERAMENTS

A low-budget film crew is very small, perhaps six to ten persons. A good crew is immensely supportive not only of the project, but also of the individuals in front of the camera, who may be acting for the first time. That crew's aura of ability and optimism is easily grounded by a single misfit with a bad attitude. Such people in important positions are like black holes, swallowing up all the energy, enthusiasm, and morale.

Crew problems vary; maybe a member needs some pressure to maintain focus on the job in hand. More seriously, others far from home at a location and under pressure may to some degree become unbalanced and regress into displaying bizarre hostilities. You may therefore find yourself dealing with someone emotionally out of control and actively subversive. This is not easy to foresee, but such people are an appalling liability in an activity so dependent for its success on good relationships. Although Truffaut's *Day for Night* (1973) shows these human tendencies at work in the cast, the problem can just as easily hit the crew. The united crew makes a huge contribution to morale, for their interest and implied approval is a vital supplement to that of the director. Conversely, any crew member's detachment or disapproval may be taken to heart by actors, whose work naturally makes them hypersensitive to reactions of any kind.

When recruiting, therefore, find out if a potential crew member has done film or other teamwork, and speak with people who worked with him or her. Filming is very intense, so former colleagues soon know a person's strengths and weaknesses. If you are unable to verify a potential crew member's teamwork record, you may just have to rely on your intuition about how he or she bears up under stress.

In all crew positions, beware of the personality with only one working speed (it can be frenetic but it is usually medium slow). Faced with a need to accelerate, this insecure personality usually either slows up in confusion or, if it is a crisis, goes to pieces. Beware particularly of people who forget or modify verbal commitments, or who repeatedly fail to deliver what they promise on time. Another liability is the person who habitually overestimates his own abilities or whose attention spreads detrimentally beyond his own field of responsibility. Look for humor, low-key realism, and reliability in each crew member, as well as the ability to sustain effort and concentration for long periods. You want people who will love the work you will do together, not those for whom your work is a stepping stone to something better.

ORGANIZE AREAS OF RESPONSIBILITY CLEARLY

No crew functions well unless roles and responsibilities are clearly defined and a chain of command is established, especially to deal with contingencies. When the director is occupied with the cast, the director of photography leads the crew and makes necessary decisions. In most cases, crew members should take queries first to the director of photography rather than to the director. The production manager, assistant director, and director of photography are there to take all possible burdens from the director, whose entire energies are needed for his or her craft, not to decide whether someone should put another coin in a parking meter.

When first working together and for a long time after, it is wise to stick to a formal working structure (see Figure 9–1). Everyone should take care of his or her own responsibilities, and refrain from action or comment in all other areas. As people come to know and trust each other, the formality can by mutual consent be relaxed. In time, the members of a small film crew fall into roles. These may include such archetypes as prophet, diplomat, visionary, navigator, earth-mother, scribe, nurse, strong man, and fixer. Someone will always assume the role of jester or clown, for each crew develops its own special humor.

The feeling that comes from working effectively as a group is important: it can be the most exhilarating and energizing experience imaginable, and seems to be especially strong during times of crisis. Careful selection of the right partners makes anything in the world possible. A team of determined friends is unstoppable.

CREW ROLES AND RESPONSIBILITIES

Judging from the end credits, a feature film unit has a bewildering number of roles and an army of people. One paradox is the enormous size of low-budget film crews, until one realizes that many individuals have given only a day or two of service. A "genealogical chart" of a small film unit, showing customary lines of responsibility, is included in Figure 9–1.

The role descriptions that follow are confined to the modest core likely to carry out the low-budget film or video shoot. I have assigned desirable personality types and backgrounds to the different crew positions, but, of course, in real life some of the best practitioners will be the exceptions. This list outlines each crew member's responsibilities and the strengths and weaknesses you can expect to find. To make it complete, I have included a summary of the director's role.

PRODUCER

Answerable to: Investors or studio heads.

Responsibilities: The producer of a film assembles and administers the necessary funds, and oversees the project as a whole. Traditionally, the producer also

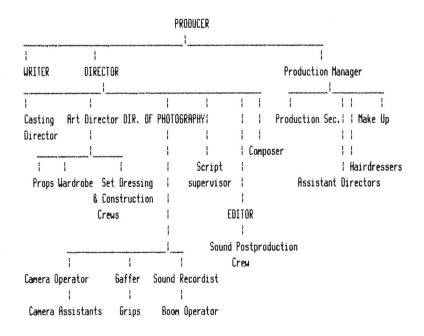

FIGURE 9–1

Lines of responsibility in a small-feature crew. Relationships may vary according to actual unit. Main creative positions are capitalized.

has ultimate say in an artistic dispute between, say, a principal actor and the director. Since status is defined by a number of factors, relative influence may be unconventional and the producer must arbitrate such problems. Since the producer's role is primarily fiscal and logistical, he has under him the production department, consisting of assistant producer, production manager, production secretary, and assistant directors.

Producers sometimes have assistants called *Associate Producers* or *Assistant Producers*.

Personal Traits: The ideal producer concentrates upon his or her own job as enabler, supplier, and rationer of vital resources. To this end, planning, scheduling and accounting should be a producer's strengths, but, if he or she is a person of taste, the producer can also be a useful arbiter of the film's artistic progress. The ideal producer is a cultivated, intelligent, and sensitive business-person whose goal in life is to nourish good work by unobtrusively supporting the artists and craftspeople hired to produce it.

Here is where it can all go wrong. Because they control money, producers have a great deal of power, and some, especially the inexperienced, assume that because artists and technicians are subordinates, their work and values are subordinate, too. Experienced filmmakers are wearily familiar with the crass philistine who has made money in insurance and now wants to express his or her artistic side by producing a film. In the end, much energy is wasted in diplomatically trying to educate such a person into trusting the experts he or she hired, but usually the film suffers as well as its makers.

Probably all producers want to control the artistic identity of the work, but the wise ones sublimate this impulse and retain respect for those whose artistry has taken many years to mature. Too many assume that the creative and organic process of filmmaking can be rationalized like a construction project or Popsicle factory.

Producers of some experience have a track record like anyone else, and you can find out from the grapevine what his or her reputation is. Never believe you will somehow be treated better than your predecessors.

With the amateur producer, you should look out for these danger signs: automatic distrust of everyone's motives, a drive to personally control everything, and an inability to listen and learn from experts' explanations. Filmmakers usually lack a flair for capitalism, and are only too aware of their dependency upon financial operators. It is in their interest to educate a producer, but this is often frustrated by the financial operator's common compulsions: trying to play people off against each other, the need to look aggressive and competent when he or she is not, a willingness to trash anybody or anything that looks as if it can be bettered, the desire to replace anyone who has seen the producer's ignorance show, and a willingness to take personal credit for other people's work whenever possible. These may all be part of the dirty tricks that won the producer ascendancy in the financial arena.

Anyone with access to money can call himself or herself a movie producer, for access to money is the prime qualification. In the last three decades I recall working for producers who were, variously, an insurance man, a real-estate developer, a gentlemanly hood, and a playboy draft-dodger. While the funds assembled by these people made production possible, their congenital distrust, crassness, and megalomania made the crews' lives into a tragi-comic rollercoaster ride. Using threats, sudden dismissal, and humiliation, such people survive only because filmmakers depend on financing to survive.

I also worked under producers who were principled, educated, restrained, and a source of support and discriminating encouragement to everyone. These men and women were the professionals—true leaders with a long history of deserving survivorship.

DIRECTOR

Answerable to: The producer.

Responsibilities: The director is responsible for nothing less than the quality and meaning of the final film. This means writing or working with writers, researching locations, auditioning actors, and assembling a cast and crew. The director develops both cast and script through rehearsals, supervises the shooting schedule, directs actors and crew during shooting, and later supervises the editing and finalization of the project. If there are no profits in view, the film may have no separate producer, so the director must additionally assemble funding before the making of the film and hustle distribution afterwards.

Personal Traits: A good director is a person broadly educated in the arts with a lively, inquiring mind, who likes delving into people's lives in search of the hypothetical links and explanations. Even when outwardly informal and easygoing, the director is usually highly methodical and organized, but able to throw away prior work if assumptions have become obsolete.

Good directors have endless patience in searching out good ideas and good performances to which they can do justice in cinematic terms. Directors need to be articulate and succinct, and to know their own minds and get the best without being dictatorial. A good director knows enough about each craft to speak on terms of respectful equality with any of the technicians, and can understand their problems and co-opt their efforts in realizing his or her intentions.

If this sounds too idealistic, here are some of the negative traits that make even good directors decidedly human. Many are obstinate, private, even awkward beings who work in idiosyncratic ways. They find difficulty in giving appropriate time and attention each to crew and actors, tending to desert one for the other. During shooting, sensory overload may sink them into a condition of acute doubt and anxiety in which each choice becomes a painful effort. During production most show signs of acute insecurity (depression, manic energy, low flashpoint, panic, irresolution). If that is not enough to puzzle crew members, the director's mental state often generates superhuman energy and endurance that test crew members' patience to the limit.

The truth is that directing a reflection of life is a heady business. The person responsible for making this happen is living existentially; that is, fully and completely in the moment as if it were his or her last. The pressures of directing a movie usually ensure that this happens whether you like it or not. This is especially true after an initial success: thereafter you face failure and artistic/professional death every step of the way. Like stage fright, the dread and exhilaration of the chase may never go away. But surely the portent of any worthwhile experience is that it makes you more than a little afraid.

CAMERA CREW GENERALITIES

Personality traits: The camera crew members should, of course, be image-conscious, preferably with a background in photography and fine art. Out of this you should hope for a sense of composition and design, and an eye for the telling details found in people's surroundings. They also need to be decisive, practical, methodical, and dexterous. Depending on the weight of the equipment, they may also need to be robust. Handholding a twenty-pound camera for most of an eight-hour day is not for the delicate, nor is loading equipment boxes in and out of transportation. The job is dirty, gruelling, and at times intoxicatingly wonderful. The best camera people seem to be calm individuals who do not ruffle easily in crises. They are knowledgeable and resourceful and take pride in improvising solutions to intransigent technical and logistical problems. What you hope to find is the perfectionist who still aims for the best and simplest solution when time is short.

Rather alarmingly, quite a number of experienced camera personnel isolate themselves in the mechanics of their craft at the expense of the director's deeper quest for themes and meanings. While it can be disastrous to have a crew of would-be directors, it can be nearly as frustrating to find you have a crew of isolated operatives. The best crew members comprehend both the details and the totality of a project and can see how to make the best contribution to it. This is why a narrow technical education is seldom good enough for anyone in a film crew.

DIRECTOR OF PHOTOGRAPHY

Answerable to: The director.

Responsibilities: Also known as lighting cameraperson, the director of photograph (DP) is the most important person in the crew after the director and is responsible for the look of the film. That is, he or she collaborates closely with the director and takes all decisions about camera, lighting, and equipment that contribute to the camerawork. The DP is also the leader of the whole crew and will often direct their work while the director concentrates on the actors. In the minimal crew the DP is responsible for specifying the lighting and camera equipment, lenses, filmstock, or their video equivalents. He or she is responsible for testing and adjusting that equipment and for being thoroughly conversant with its working principles. No important work should ever be done without running tests as early as possible in order to forestall Murphy's Law, which is inexorable in filmmaking. The DP decides and supervises the placement of lighting instruments and on a small crew reconnoiters each location in advance with the gaffer to assess electrical supplies and lighting design.

CAMERA OPERATOR

Answerable to: The director of photography.

Responsibilities: The operator is responsible for the handling of the camera, which means he or she takes an active role in deciding camera positioning (in collaboration with the director), and physically controls the camera movements such as panning, tilting, zooming in and out, and dollying. (Technical terms and their significance are explained in the Glossary.)

It is also an advantage if your operator is alert to the many behavioral nuances that reveal character. In improvisation work or in documentary, the camera work is often "grab-shooting" so the operator must decide moment to moment what to shoot in a busy scene.

While the director sees content happening three-dimensionally in front of (or sometimes behind) the camera, the operator sees the action in its framed, cinematic form. The director may redirect the camera to a different area, but much of the time the operator alone knows exactly what the action will look like on the screen. The director must therefore be able to place considerable reliance upon the operator's discrimination, and this is also true for very controlled framing and composition, since movement within the frame often requires immediate and spontaneous adjustment of the camera's framing.

CAMERA ASSISTANTS

Answerable to: The camera operator.

Responsibilities: On a feature film there may be more than one assistant cinematographer (AC). Division of labor makes one a clapper operator and magazine loader, and another whose job it is to manually follow focus when the distance changes between subject and camera.

ACs keep the camera optics and film gate clean and manhandle the camera equipment from place to place. Their main requirements are to be highly organized, reliable, and zealous at maintaining the camera in prime condition, whether it is film or videotape. Because their responsibilities are almost wholly technical, it is more important they be good and diligent technicians. On a small unit, one camera assistant often does all the ancilliary work, though this can lead to costly holdups.

GAFFER AND GRIPS

Answerable to: The director of photography.

Responsibilities: The job of the gaffer is to rig lighting and to know how to go about doing anything that needs to be fixed, mounted, moved, pushed, lifted, or lowered. The gaffer must have a good grasp of mechanical and electrical principles in order to improvise solutions for which there is no available piece of equipment. A good gaffer also understands not only the lighting instruments but the principles and practice of lighting itself, because he or she must be able to quickly grasp the meaning of the DP's lighting instructions.

The job of the grip is to fetch and carry, and to rig lighting according to the gaffer's instructions. He or she also has the highly skilled and coordinated job of moving the camera support (dolly, crane, truck, etc.) from mark to mark as the camera takes mobile shots. Grips should be strong, practical, organized, and willing. On the minimal crew they may double up to help with sound equipment, camera assisting, turning on and off the videotape deck, and may leave the crew to fetch or deliver while shooting is in progress. A skilled grip knows something about everyone's job and is capable of standing in for some technicians in an emergency.

Personality traits: Gaffers and grips need lots of patience, as their work means they must carry and maintain large varieties of equipment, of which there never seems enough for the job at hand. While they work, production waits; while production is in progress, it is they who wait. When everyone else is finished, they go to work tearing down their masses of equipment and stow it, haul it away, then set it up again for the next day's shoot. All this must be good for the soul, for they are often highly resourceful and very funny. *Gaffer* is old English for grandfather, singularly appropriate for one who must know every imaginable way to skin the proverbial cat.

SOUND RECORDIST AND BOOM OPERATOR

Answerable to: The director of photography.

Responsibilities: In the inexperienced crew the unfailing casualty is sound quality. Capturing clear, clean, and consistent sound is either deceptively skilled, or sound recording does not have the glamour to induce people to try. Probably both are true. Another obstacle is that even quite expensive videorecorders have a propensity for picking up every known electrical interference, allied to a sound quality that would embarrass the humblest sound cassette recorders. Improvements are in the pipeline, but many older machines will survive to bring tears of rage to the low-budget filmmaker.

It is the sound recordist's responsibility to check sound and videotape equipment in advance, and to solve malfunction problems as they arise. The boom operator's job is to place the mike as close to sound sources as possible, without getting the mike in shot or creating shadows. In a complicated dialogue scene this means moving the mike around to catch each new speaker.

Personality traits: The sound crew person needs to have patience, a good ear, and the maturity to be low man on the totem pole. In an interior setup, lighting and camera position are determined first, and the sound recordist is expected to somehow position the mikes without them being seen, without causing shadows, and without losing sound quality. A shoot therefore turns into a series of aggravating compromises that the recordist is all too inclined to take personally. A significant number of professionals turn into frustrated mutterers who feel that standards are routinely trampled. But it is the disconnected craftsman more than the whole filmmaker who fails to see the necessity and priority of compromise. Sound can be reconstituted in the sound studio later, but camerawork and actors' performances are immutable once on film.

The recordist is often kept inactive for long periods and then suddenly expected to "fix up the mike" in short order, so it helps to have someone who habitually thinks ahead. The unsatisfactory recordist is the one whose mind only begins to work when his setup time comes, and who then asks for a lighting change.

The sound recordist listens not to words but to sound quality, so it is essential to have someone who listens analytically, and actually hears the buzz, rumble, or edginess that the novice will unconsciously screen out. The art of recording has very little to do with recorders, and everything to do with the selection and placement of mikes, and being able to hear the difference. There is no independent assessment possible apart from the discerning ear. Only musical interests and, better still, a musical training seem to instill this critical discipline.

Sound recording is often brushed aside as easy and unglamorous among the uninitiated, and left uncritically to anyone who says he or she can do it. But poor sound disconnects the audience even more fatally than a poor story. Too many student films sound like studies of characters talking through blankets in a bathroom.

Handheld shooting is done with a mobile unit. Without benefit of a conclusive rehearsal, the sound crew must keep the mike on the edge of the camera's field of view and close to the sound source without casting shadows or letting the mike creep into frame. With a camera on the move, this takes both skill and agile, quiet footwork. Nobody can wear construction boots or creaky leather jackets when shooting sound.

There are usually several solutions to any one sound problem, so a knowledge of available equipment and an interest in up-to-date techniques is a tremendous advantage.

PRODUCTION MANAGER

Answerable to: The producer.

Responsibilities: The production manager (PM) might be considered a hard-to-find luxury on a minimal crew, but there are many people whose business background equips them to do this vital job surpassingly well.

The PM is the producer's delegate and closely concerned with preproduction and production. He or she is a business manager who is based in an office and takes care of all the arrangements for the shoot. These might include finding overnight accommodations, booking rented equipment to the specifications of camera and sound people, making up (with the director) a shooting schedule, negotiating travel arrangements, and locating restaurants near the shoot. The PM will watch cash flow and incubate contingency plans in case bad weather stymies exterior shooting. He or she will hustle to prepare the way ahead. All this lightens the load on the director for whom such things are a distraction from controlling the performances and visualizing the film as it evolves.

Personality traits: The good PM is organized, a compulsive list-keeper, socially adept and businesslike, and able to scan and correlate a number of activities. He or she should be able to juggle priorities, make decisions involving time, effort, and money, and be the kind of person who is unintimidated by officialdom.

ASSISTANT DIRECTOR

Answerable to: The production manager.

Responsibilities: On a feature shoot there may be a first, second, and third AD. ADs seldom become directors since their skills are organizational rather than artistic and lean toward production management. Their job is to do all the leg-work and take care of all the logistical needs of the production. Scheduling, arranging, contacting, reminding, acquiring information, calling artists, herding crowds, and doing the director's barking all come within the AD's purview. Sometimes in a director's absence an AD will rehearse actors, but only if he or she has a strong grasp of the director's intentions. The experienced AD may direct the second unit, but this more often falls to the editor.

Personality traits: The main requirements for an assistant director are to be organized, have a good business mind, and to be both firm and diplomatic.

SCRIPT SUPERVISOR

Answerable to: The director.

Responsibilities: The script supervisor (also called *continuity supervisor*) must understand how the film will be edited together, and during shooting must continuously monitor what words, actions, props, and costumes are in use from shot to shot. Shooting on videotape makes checking a relatively simple (though time-consuming) matter, but with film no such record is visible until the rushes have been processed. An eagle-eyed observer who keeps a record of every significant variable is therefore the only safeguard that one shot will match another.

The script supervisor also assists the director by ensuring there is adequate coverage of each scene, and when time or resources must be saved, is able to define what can be omitted or shortened.

Personality traits: The script supervisor needs to understand the principles of editing, must know the script inside out, and have fierce powers of concentration. On a feature film, continuity's records are used extensively by the cutting rooms, so fast accurate typing is also a necessity. On films with subsistence level budgets that could not afford a script supervisor, I have seen the editor do the job. The motivation is certainly there.

ART DIRECTOR

Answerable to: The director.

Responsibilities: To design everything possible in the film's environment to effectively interpret the script. This means overseeing props and costumes, as well as managing the interior design of sets and locations. If the film is a period production, the art director will research the epoch and its social customs to ensure that costumes and decor are accurate and make an impact. On a low-budget movie the art director will do his or her own set dressing, while on a larger production there is a special person, the set dresser, to take care of this responsibility.

Personality traits: A good art director should have a fine arts background and be able to sketch or paint fluently. He or she should have a lively eye for fashion and social distinctions, and a strong interest in the historical background of these phenomena. The art director should also have a strong grasp of the emotional potential of different color and color combinations, and be able to translate the script into a series of settings with costumes, all of which heighten and intensify the underlying intentions of the script.

WARDROBE AND PROPS

Answerable to: The art director.

Responsibilities: Wardrobe and props' jobs are to locate, store, and maintain costumes and properties (objects such as ashtrays, baby toys, or grand pianos that dress the set), keep master lists, and produce the right thing in good order at the right time. When no wardrobe person is available, each actor becomes responsible for his own costumes. The AD should doublecheck beforehand what clothes each actor must bring for the next scene, so today's costume is not still in the actor's laundry basket.

Personality traits: Wardrobe and props people are highly resourceful and good at developing large numbers of contacts among antique, resale, theatrical, and junk shop owners. They must be practical, since things borrowed or rented must often be carefully operated and maintained. Costumes, especially ones that are elaborate or antique, take great expertise to keep clean and functional and may need temporary alterations to fit a particular actor. Props and wardrobe departments must be completely organized: each scene has its special requirements and the right props and costumes must appear on time and in the right place or shooting turns into a nightmare.

MAKEUP AND HAIRDRESSING

Answerable to: The production manager.

Responsibilities: The people in makeup and hairdressing produce the appropriate physical appearance in face and hair, often with careful attention to period details. A hidden part of the job is catering to actors' insecurities by helping them believe in the way they look. Where the character demands negative traits, the makeup artist may have to work against an actor's resistance. Makeup is particularly tricky; directors should shoot tests to make sure the makeup looks credible and is compatible with color stock and any special lighting.

Personality traits: Diplomacy and endurance. My father was a makeup man and got to work before anyone else, preparing artists hours ahead of shooting when elaborate beards and whiskers were required. Apart from the usual kind of character or glamor preparation, his work included the bizarre, such as putting a black patch over the eye of Fagin's dog in David Lean's *Oliver Twist* (1948), applying the gold paint on the naked girl in *Goldfinger* (1964), and inventing ghoulish effects for Hammer horror films like flesh melting from a face to leave eyeballs staring out of bony eye-sockets. Needless to say, it helps to be inventive and have a relish for the unusual, but he also spoke of the miseries of trying to make up foul-tempered alcoholics in the early morning. After the dawn rush, makeup and hairdressing must often sit idle, keeping watch for when their handiwork needs repair.

EDITOR

A complete description of the editor's role and responsibilities is to be found in Chapter 15: Preparing to Edit.

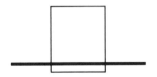

PREPRODUCTION SUMMARY

The points summarized here are only those most salient. Some are commonly overlooked. To find them or anything else relating to preproduction, go to the table of contents at the beginning of this part.

DECIDING ON SUBJECTS

- Choose your subject carefully; you are going to live with it for a long time.
- Through your film, be concerned for others.
- Choose a subject and issues you would love to learn more about.

ASSESSING A SCRIPT

- Who did you care about and find interesting?
- Is the plot credible, or can it be made so?
- What is the screenplay trying to do, and how is it going about it?
- Make a step outline.
- Extract the screenplay's premise.
- Make a flow chart for the proposed film, with the function for each scene.
- Make an oral summary to a listener and hear the problems emerge.

SCRIPT EDITING

- Convert discussion into behavior and drop lines wherever possible.
- What does each character want?
- What stops the character and how does he/she adapt to this obstacle?
- Who grows and develops in the script and who remains only "typical?"
- Make scene/character/location breakdown and a first timing.

CASTING

Organizing the Audition:
- Write brief character descriptions; advertise appropriately.
- Actively search out likely participants for audition.
- Preinterview on phone before giving an audition slot.
- Thoroughly explain time and energy commitment.
- Ask actor to come with two contrasting monologues learned by heart.

First Audition:
- Receptionist chats informally with actors, has them fill out information form.
- See actor's monologues and characterize his or her self-image.
- Look for acting with whole body and assess voice.
- Ask "what kind of _____ (character) would I get from this actor?"
- Thank actors and give date by which decision will be communicated.

Decisions Before Callback:
- Call each actor and inform whether he or she is suitable and wanted for callback.

- If you are rejecting, tell each something positive about his or her performance.
- Avoid casting people for their real-life negative traits.

Callback:
- Combine promising actors in different permutations.
- Have actors play parts in different ways to assess capacity for change.
- Test spontaneous creativity with improvisations based on the piece's issues.
- Redirect second version of improv to see how actors handle changes.
- Review each actor's
  impact,
  rhythm and movements,
  patterns of development,
  imprint on part,
  quickness of mind,
  compatibility with other actors,
  ability for mimicry (accents, character specialties, etc.),
  capacity to hold on to both new and old instructions,
  intelligence, temperament, and type of mind,
  commitment to acting and to this particular project, and
  concentration and attention span.
- Shoot camera test on principals.
- Consider confronting actors with your reservations before casting.
- Thank all for taking part and arrange date for notification.

DEVELOPING THE CREW

- Cast crew carefully, since they create the work environment.
- Test even experienced members by shooting tests.
- Inquire into crew members' interests and values.
- Check reputation in previous collaborations.
- Assess flexibility, dependability, realism, commitment to project.
- Delineate areas of responsibility and begin with formal relationships.

SCRIPT INTERPRETATION

- Determine the givens.
- Convert conversation into action that a deaf viewer could follow.
- Make sure screenplay establishes facts and necessary values for audience.
- Define point of view, subtexts, and characters' hidden pressures for each scene.
- Graph dramatic pressure changes for each scene, then string them together to graph out dramatic development for the film as a whole.

REHEARSAL

- Actors study the piece, make character biography, but do not yet learn lines.
- Director encourages the search for action and movement at every stage.
- Meet principal actors singly to discuss his or her character.
- Expect actors to problem-solve.
- Keep notes during each run-through.

Focusing Thematic Purpose with the Players:
- Discuss back-story and purpose of the piece with cast.
- Discuss subtext for key scenes and what it reveals about the characters.
- Develop a hierarchy of themes so you know what is most important.

Rehearsal with the Book:
- Work on motivations; find and characterize the beats.
- Deal only with top level of problems at each pass.
- Tackle key scenes first, link scenes thereafter.
- Rehearse in location or thoroughly brief actors on particularity of location.
- Rough out movement and develop possible actions.
- Find special actions for the beat points.
- Actors may now learn their lines.

Rehearsal without the Book:
- The film actor has no audience except the director.
- Where an actor keeps losing focus, figure out the obstacle.
- Staying in character comes from staying appropriately busy in mind and body.
- Focus leads to relaxation.
- Watch your actors' bodies for signs of tension.
- Authentic physical action liberates authentic emotion during performance.
- Use improv to set level of focus to be matched in work from text.
- Give specific, positive goals for actors to reach toward.
- Characters' actions should generally seek an effect in other characters.
- Dialogue should be a verbal action also seeking effect.
- Does the scene communicate effectively as a silent film?
- Are your actors effectively using the available space?
- Do actors see their characters' inner visions and memories?
- Does each character pursue his or her own agenda?

THINKING AHEAD ABOUT COVERAGE

- Set a timing limit for the scene and keep tabs on rehearsal timings.
- Prepare cast for blocking changes should exigency so require (it often does).
- Cut dialogue or action to stay within timing goals.

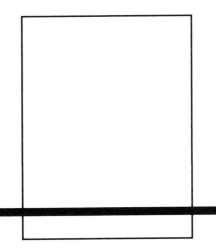

P·A·R·T I·I

PRODUCTION

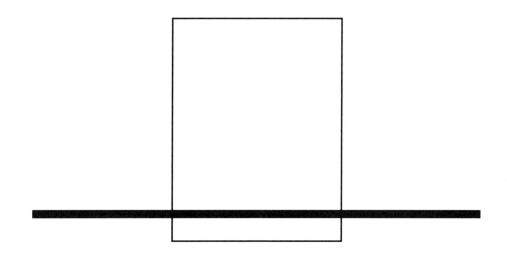

MISE-EN-SCÈNE BASICS

The French expression *mise-en-scène* (literally, putting in the scene) is a usefully holistic term describing those aspects of directing that take place during shooting. It covers such things as the directing of actors, camera placement and movement, lens choice, and composition. Planning to shoot a scene involves carefully considering the dramatic intentions, whose consciousness the audience should identify with, and how to carry out one's intentions in practical terms. While the DP takes responsibility for everything concerning camera and lighting, the director must be aware of what options exist and how to discuss them with the DP, the director's most important collaborator.

SCREENPLAY TO SHOOTING SCRIPT

Planning how to shoot a scene means first of all amplifying upon the screenplay, which so far contains no camera directions. You cannot specify anything that would be impractical either for financial or pragmatic reasons, so the shooting script is a plan to make the most of known resources, human and material. It is the last stage after considerable rehearsal, location reconnaissance, conferring with the director of photography, checking whether financial resources allow special lighting or camera equipment, and so on.

While simple poverty may make it difficult to impose an elaborately professional look upon a scene (dollying or craning shots, freeze frames, special titling, and optical work), this is slick packaging and its absence should never debilitate a worthwhile film. Decades of classic cinema shot with limited equipment shows that you can function well by astute dramatic analysis of your material and by keeping to the simplest techniques that serve the film's artistic intentions.

The screenplay must now be turned into a shooting script. Scenes that were previously headed by titles alone (to avoid confusion from draft to draft) must now receive scene numbers. Necessary camera directions and transitions must be specified. From rehearsals you should have a firm sense of the camera coverage required, but final codification with your DP will be dealt with later in this chapter.

In consultation with your DP, decide what coverage is desirable for a scene, and then in consultation with your script supervisor, pencil in lines to bracket portions of the scene. Each represents a camera angle and each has a brief identifying description, as in Figure 10–1. This shows at a glance what editing al-

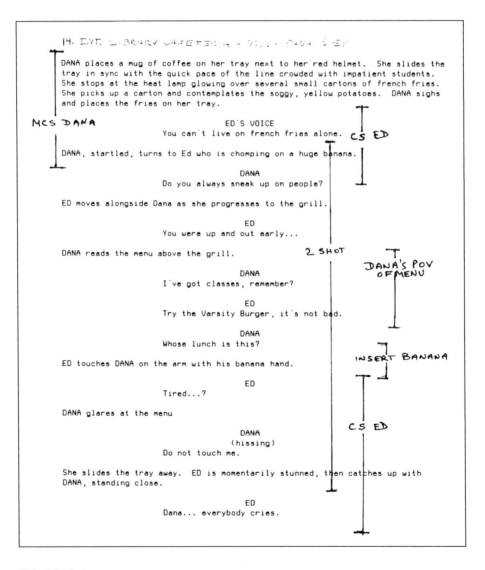

FIGURE 10–1

Script page marked up for shooting.

ternatives will exist. To make editing possible, remember that there must be an overlap from shot to shot. To make editing look smooth and seamless, the best place to make a cut to another angle is always on a physical movement. You will understand this best by analyzing a well made scene and from practical experiment. Exercises and projects to help you do this are all in Part VII: Film Projects. In Chapter 33 there is a discussion of principles in Project 1: Picture Composition Analysis, and a sequence examination exercise in Project 2: Editing Analysis. Shooting exercises and further conceptual discussion follow in Chapter 34, beginning with Project 5: "Basic Techniques: Going and Returning".

SCRIPT, CONCEPT, AND SCENE DESIGN

The design for a scene, while it must compromise with the limitations of cinematography, really proceeds from the scene's underlying function in the script. How, for instance, would you show a man who is being watched by the police get into his car and try to start it?

Basic questions about function need to be asked, such as

- What is the scene's function in the script?
- What does the audience need to know about the scene's geographical layout at the outset of the scene? What later?
- What are the relationships in terms of physical space?
- What are each character's expectations in the scene?
- How much does each character know about his predicament?
- What is the relationship between the watchers and the watched?
- Is there anything the audience but not the characters should learn?

The questions will vary with the scene, and depend on its contents, complexity, and what it contributes to the film as a whole. Defining what the audience should notice and feel helps you decide the means of revelation and makes them seem much less arbitrary.

POINT OF VIEW

WHOSE POINT OF VIEW

Point of view is for many people a baffling notion. It is not literally "what so-and-so sees," though this may comprise one shot. Rather it attempts to relay to the audience how a character in the film is experiencing particular events. We might for instance experience the trial of Joan of Arc from Joan's angle, or we could tell the story from the perspective of a compassionate judge who wants her to admit she has made up her visions so he can let her go. For a heightened effect we might participate in a number of perspectives so we can feel with Joan how the inquisitors, the faithful, the crowd, and God, must be judging her.

Top priority will always be to ask, whose point of view is this scene to favor? A great many of your decisions about composition, camera placement, and editing flow from this. Are we, for instance, to see the man getting into his car from the attitude of the policeman, or from a more omniscient (that is, story teller's) point of view in which we (but not the man) notice the cop? Surely this is easily decided on plot grounds.

Imagine a more complex scene in which a child witnesses a sustained argument between his divorced parents. How should point of view be handled here? We must determine what the argument represents. Is it "child realizing he is a pawn," or is it "parents make bitter accusations, not caring that their child can hear?" Are we mainly interested in what the child sees or how the dispute acts upon him? Does new information come from the parents or are we focusing on the child's presence and reactions? Questions like these determine whose scene it really is; the boy's, the father's, or the mother's. The scene can be shot and edited to polarize our sympathetic interest in any of these directions.

There remains an additional and more detached way of observing the events, that of the omniscient storyteller. This point of view is a resource you will want to use to relieve pressure on the audience before renewing it again. Sustained and unvarying pressure would be self-defeating because the audience either adapts or opts out. Notice how Shakespeare uses scenes of comic relief in his tragedies.

POINT OF VIEW CAN CHANGE

Imagine now a scene in a clinic starting on a young, unhappy-looking doctor telling a patient that he has incurable cancer. As the patient begins to understand his predicament we abandon the patient's point of view and adopt that of the doctor, keeping him only as a voice and dwelling exclusively on the sick man hearing his death sentence. This example illustrates how point of view is an entity that naturally migrates from person to person, although finally the whole film may be about the patient. Paradoxically, to understand and feel for the doctor, we need to share those moments when he empathizes with our central character, vacating his own protected reality to enter that of the man facing death. A character who never loses his own identity in this way would be someone alienated or possibly inhuman. Even if that is true (let us say we are making a biographical film about a Nazi despot), we might still move the point of view to the Nazi's victim simply to allow the audience a vehicle for its pent-up feelings, and to force a comparison between the feeling and the unfeeling persons.

The only guide to deciding point of view is asking what makes dramatic sense. This can be decided only within the complex pattern of the entire script. There may be no overriding determinant, in which case it is the editor who decides later, based on the nuances of the acting.

Sometimes a film will make us experience a situation from an intentionally detached (though no less interesting) perspective, such as in Tanner's *Jonah Who Will be Twenty-Five in the Year 2000* (1976). Here Tanner tells the story of six couples, survivors from the turbulent 1960s, each of whom is trying to live out earlier ideals even though the social revolution he fought for has failed. Quite deliberately Tanner avoids aligning us with any couple or any individual so we shall see them in broad social terms and not as rebel individualists.

As a rough and ready guide, a subjective point of view is one that tends to use closeups and tends to be shot with the camera close to the axis or "line of tension" between characters. An objective point of view tends to be a wider shot and further from that line (Figure 10–2). We will look at examples later in the discussion on camera placement. My approach is no more than a rule of thumb; point of view is something subtle that impinges on the audience through a unique combination of action, characters, lighting, mood, events, and context. For this reason multiangle coverage can only be finely adjusted in the cutting room after shooting.

COMPOSITIONAL OPTIONS

SHOW RELATEDNESS

Returning to the boy and divorced parents scene: how are the protagonists to be spatially related? Showing the couple arguing in the same frame but the boy separated in a closeup reinforces his separation from both of them. Relating boy and mother in one frame to father alone in another suggests a different config-uration of alliances or antipathies. There could be other factors—using fore-ground and background, the sides of the frame, different camera heights and different levels of lighting—any combination of which might predispose the au-dience toward interpreting the scene in a particular way or from a particular point of view.

It would be misleading and simplistic to suggest there are any rules here, since human judgment is made upon a multiplicity of nuances. What matters is the sensibility and rationale by which each shot is composed, lit, and blocked. Your sensibility and the eyes and ears of your audience are the final arbiters. Because in filmmaking everything is relativistic, there are almost no formulae: compositionally you are always showing the specifics of relationship between one object and another, one person and another, and implying the relationship of one idea, principle, or judgment to another. To do this you may also use

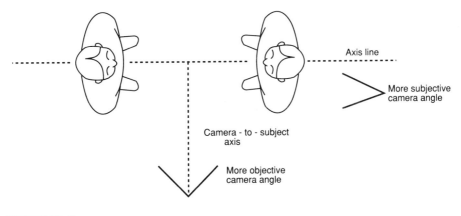

FIGURE 10–2

Camera-to-subject axis can be close or at right angles to the scene axis; this controls how subjective or objective the angle feels to the audience.

editing or story construction (parallel storytelling, for instance, where you inter-cut a boxing match with a lover's feud). Whatever works, works through sug-gestion and implied comparison.

CAMERA PLACEMENT

USING LINES OF TENSION

Here are some helpful guidelines concerning the camera's relationship to what I call a scene's lines of tension. These invisible connections are the lines you would draw between the most important people and objects in a scene. Often they are also sightlines. They have great dramatic potential (changes of eyeline, for in-stance) and they often dominate the composition. To understand the latter, read the notes for Chapter 33, Project 1: Picture Composition Analysis. Better yet, do the project itself. Lines of tension legitimize particular camera angles but also imply the emotional connections (and therefore points of view) associated with particular characters. This is not an easy concept to describe, and you will un-derstand best if you do the next exercise, Project 2: Editing Analysis.

SUBJECTIVE AND OBJECTIVE

No matter whose point of view your film favors, point of view itself will move, and changes in lines of tension are your prime clue as to how and where this happens. This needs some more exploration. Let us look at the way the con-sciousness of an onlooker moves around when observing the archetypal scene of two people in conversation.

The concept of the involved observer is important, for his or her impulses are the model for how the camera or the editing moves us from angle to angle. The combination of camera work and editing in fact always mimics the way an observer's eyes and psychological focus moves around an environment, following stimuli and pursuing a line of logical inquiry based on predisposition and the unfolding events. This observer, whether a character within the film or a story-teller directing our attention, tends to vary in intensity; the observer's detached attention is objective, while a more involved, identifying intensity leads him or her to become subjective. A film will "breathe" between these two extremes, but the difference itself needs further explanation.

Imagine you are watching two tennis players. The ball flies along the line of tension or axis between them. You can observe from the umpire's position near the net and see the game from a detached, objective position at ninety degrees to the axis, or one can walk in an arc around one corner of the court until you are looking over one player's shoulder. Here you become subjectively involved with the game, since you are now aligned with the predicament of one of the players by virtually standing in his or her shoes. This is also an angle where you make no choice; you are always seeing both players, though one from behind.

This principle, where the observer moves from being at right angles to the scene's axis to being almost on the axis itself, looking down the "firing line," applies to all situations of verbal, physical, or psychological interaction. It may be complicated by there being more than two protagonists, but coverage is always predicated upon the lines of tension that can be drawn. These lines are usually between major characters, but someone waiting anxiously might be connected by an invisible line of tension to an object like a clock, a phone, or a finger on the trigger of a gun.

The closer the camera is to a line of tension, the more subjectively involved the audience will feel. When complementary angles are used the audience is switched rapidly between each protagonist's subjective experience, so the aggregate effect may be to enter the fray without necessarily identifying with one contestant over the other. This depends on the balance of editing as well as, less measurably, the power in each actor's characterization.

SIGHTLINES AND LINES OF TENSION

Look at the floorplan for the argument between the mother and father who are being observed by the child (Figure 10–3A). The various psychic connections or

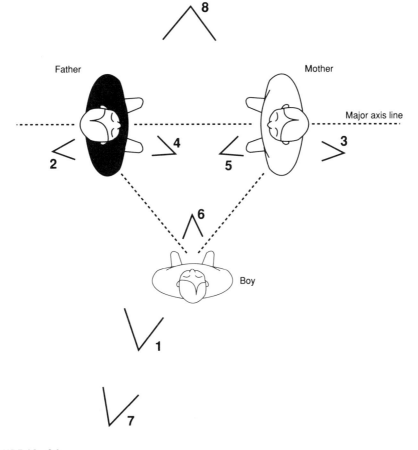

FIGURE 10–3A ————————————————————————————

Camera positions to cover a child's view of an argument between his parents. Lines of tension are indicated between characters.

possible lines of tension are in fact duplicated by the dotted-in sightlines. The major axis is between the parents, but others exist between each parent and the silent child. Each sightline suggests a camera position. What each camera angle covers is shown in the storyboard sequence (Figure 10–3B). Some angles are close (as in 4, 5, and 6), some in medium two-shot (1, 2, and 3), and there are two master shots, further angles that take in everything (7 and 8). Positions 1, 2, and 3 are all to some degree omniscient because they are an outsider's view of the characters; that is, in pairs and related to each other. Position 7 is even more comprehensive, taking in all three. Positions 4, 5, and 6 are, however, close and subjectively involved, as if viewed by one of the other characters. Position 6 would be useful to show the child's eyeline shifts.

DO NOT CROSS THE AXIS!

Because the child remains in a fixed position, camera coverage that replicates his vision of his parents must stay one side of the A to B axis line. The camera must not cross the axis if screen direction is to be maintained. If you cross this axis with your camera, as in position 8, your characters begin to look in the wrong screen direction, as you see in the storyboard sequence. In positions 1 through 7, the father always looks screen left to screen right, and the mother right to left. Even in the big closeups (4 and 5) the eyelines still show the characters maintaining the same screen direction. However, in camera position 8 that consistency disappears because the camera has strayed across the major axis line.

Many people find blocking the camera to maintain screen direction a confusing matter. Chapter 34, Project 5: "Basic Techniques: Going and Returning" is a hands-on exercise to help you figure out the rules, learn how to change screen direction, and also handle moving characters who end up in different places and therefore require changes of screen direction. From this project you will learn that there are no unredeemable sins. In fact you can cross the line halfway through that street parade or during that conversation, but you would have to dolly the camera sideways during the shot from position 3 to position 8 so the audience sees the camera move to the new position on the other side of the axis. From here onwards, you must shoot everything from the new side of the axis to preserve the revised logic of screen direction in which characters now face in the opposite screen direction. Everything has its dramatic use. A change of screen direction might be the way to handle a beat point where contestants each adopt the other's position, something that happens often in situations of argument.

MOVEMENTS THAT LEAD TO REGROUPING MUST BE SHOWN

In an interior scene where the characters move around, they themselves will regroup to face in new screen directions during the scene. This means that early and late reaction shots cannot be interchanged, and the scene cannot easily be restructured in the cutting room if so desired. Movements that lead to regrouping must be shown onscreen. They are the transitions that precede new compositional phases of the scene. Movements should also be dramatically significant, so you will want to show them anyway. Plan carefully so that the scene cuts together effortlessly on the screen.

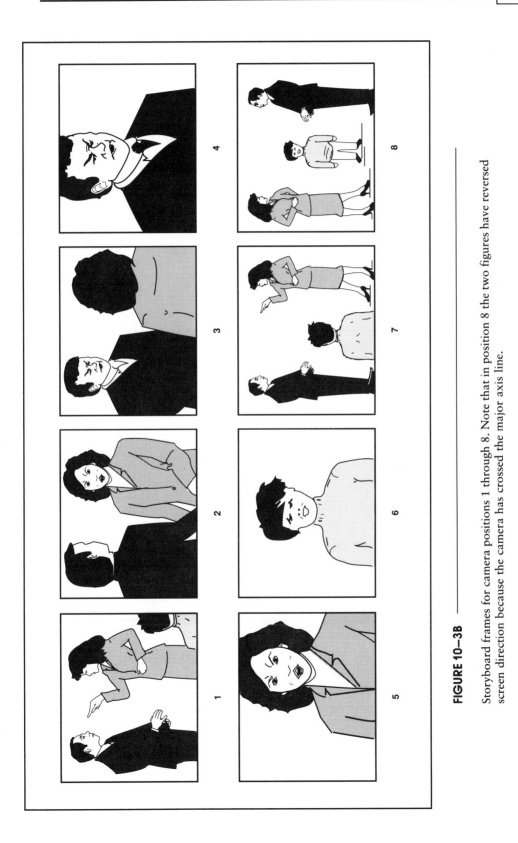

FIGURE 10–3B

Storyboard frames for camera positions 1 through 8. Note that in position 8 the two figures have reversed screen direction because the camera has crossed the major axis line.

MOVEMENT IS THE BEST EDITING POINT

As we have said, plan to use any definite movement in the scene as the cutting point between angles. This is called an action match cut. The best guide is to initiate a little of the movement in the outgoing scene, and to complete the bulk of it in the incoming shot. Fast movements need two or three frames of repeated action on the incoming shot since the eye does not register the first two or three frames of any new image.

PLANNING COVERAGE

To "cover" a scene means shooting varied enough footage to show it to advantage on the screen. Depending on the nature of the film this can mean long, intricately choreographed takes as used by Hitchcock in *Rope* (1948) and by Tanner in *The Middle of the World* (1974), or it might call for a flow of rapidly edited images as favored by such disparate filmmakers as Eisenstein in *The Battleship Potemkin* (1925) and Nicholas Roeg in *Don't Look Now* (1973). The advantages and disadvantages of each are further discussed in Chapter 28 under "Form." Briefly, the long-take method requires either a mobile camera or careful blocking of camera and actors to avoid a flat, stagey appearance, while the short-take method is inherently more likely to look manipulated because at the extreme it barrages the spectator with fragments from which he must infer the whole.

EDITING AS REFRESHMENT

Cutting between different angles is a way of renewing the perspective of the spectator, showing different points of view, and invoking different kinds of experiencing. If the angles stayed close to the axis we should remain subjectively involved, so for variation we cut to a more objective angle, causing us to step out of the firing line and see more from an outside perspective. In a political meeting scene this might suggest a stepping away from the intensely personal to take a historical or sociological perspective. This, too, is a refreshment, a juxtaposition of impressions that interrupts what has become normal and pushes us to interpret from another intellectual or emotional angle.

QUESTIONS TO ASK YOURSELF

Whichever combination of aspects you choose to show, in the scene, try to consider these factors:

Geography:
- What must the scene show to establish the environment satisfactorily?
- Does this orientation come early, or is it delayed for dramatic reasons?
- What combination of distance and lens will you need for the widest angle?
- Will you have enough lighting to shoot the most comprehensive shot?

Movements by Characters:
- At which points do characters physically move from one point to another?
- How will you show it? (Drop back to a wide angle? Move the camera with a character? Show another character's eyeline changing and hearing the moving character's footsteps?)
- What axis does the character move along at each stage of his movements?

Point of View:
- At each significant moment, whose point of view are we sharing?
- Whose point of view overall?
- When and why does point of view change?
- Is it subjective or objective?
- What emotion, thought, or preoccupation might the point of view convey?

Eyelines:
- What are the significant eyelines in the scene? (These significantly motivate what the audience wants to see, and therefore motivate where the camera may be placed from shot to shot.)
- Where do eyelines change?
- Where should the camera look along an eyeline?

Camera Movement:
- When and why should the camera move?
- What feeling does its movement create? (In Robert Enrico's *Occurrence at Owl Creek Bridge* [1962] the tendency of the camera to slide sideways creates a sense of stalking, peering unease. A camera movement can suggest a retreat, a glance, a searching gaze, a running forward—a myriad of subjective sensations.)
- At what speed should the movement be? (Movements must be paced appropriately if they are to integrate with other aural or visual rhythms in a scene. Be careful of strobing when panning over repetitive patterns such as railings. See camerawork manual for further information.)

Compositional Relationship:
- At what significant moments will it be necessary to show relationship? (One might frame a sleeping character supposed to be catching a plane with a clock in the background—more effective than laboriously intercutting the clock. Or one might play a whole mother-daughter argument in tight single shots to emphasize the adversarial, disconnected feel of their relationship.)

Isolation:
- What or who might legitimately be isolated from surroundings? (A misfit boy might frequently be shown alone, while the gang who try to recruit him always appear as a pack. A phone silently refusing to ring for someone waiting on tenterhooks for a call might also be shown as a single shot. In

112   PRODUCTION

each case this isolation complements a dominant perception, either of someone within the film, or that of the storyteller.)

Space:
- What is the significance of space between characters? (The changing distance between two characters having a conversation is highly indicative of who is gaining control, who is retreating or hiding. Camera position and the choice of lens can alter the audience's perception of space. For instance, a crowded street is often shot with a telescopic lens in order to compress cars and people into a bobbing sea, while someone reaching imploringly through prison bars might be shot with a wide-angle lens so his hand comes across a void and becomes enormous in the foreground.)

CRIB SHEETS

When directing your first films, work hard to brief yourself and make copious, organized reminder lists so you forget nothing in the hurly-burly of the set. As fatigue, the director's occupational hazard, sets in, your memory and imagination will shut down, and those notes (see Figure 10–4) will be a lifesaver.

```
             Scene 15: TONY RETURNS HOME AFTER 5 YEARS' SILENCE.

Metaphor: Return of the prodigal son

Timing:    2 mins 25 secs

     Tony wants to:   avoid showing the love he feels for his father
                      evade specifics of the past
                      signify apology but evade admissions
                      make his father think he's returned out of duty
                      make contact with his childhood again
                      move his father to affection and thus forgiveness
                      retrieve mother's photo
                      convince Dad he's not a failure
                      ask for forgiveness

     Dad wants to:    keep Tony at an emotional distance
                      deny to himself that he's very moved by the boy's return
                      get him to think he's washed his hands of him
                      let him know the whole family disapproves of him
                      not act in the authoritarian way that alienated the boy
                      not let him know his bedroom has been kept unchanged
                      deny that he used the boy to get at his mother
                      signify that he loves him
                      ask for forgiveness

     Scene must convey that:   Tony has grown in confidence through travel
                               Dad has been ill and sees his own mortality
                               House is still as Mother left it
```

FIGURE 10–4

Example of director's crib notes.

When you have defined the story points to be made, and have nailed down what you need from each sequence, you are directing from a plan of campaign instead of waiting to recognize success when it somehow appears.

COVER IMPORTANT ASPECTS MORE THAN ONE WAY

Vital story points or important emotional transitions should be covered in more than one way so you later have a choice and can exercise maximum control over the telling moment. For instance, in a scene about a family reunion where the last of a set of wedding glasses gets broken by the mother, your major point may be to show her moment of realization and grief. The incident can, however, be given additional piquancy by shooting reactions on the part of others present. Her son may show anger at her clumsiness, her daughter may be surprised, her husband may be amused because he thinks it is just a minor accident, and her daughter-in-law may be concerned that she may have cut herself.

Covering several of these reactions allows for a variable richness in defining the moment. It also follows our often mentioned principle of abundance in which one habitually collects more than strictly necessary to allow choice and therefore control.

CONTINGENCY PLANNING

Plan your coverage minutely but still ensure against unwelcome surprises. Foresee weather changes, scheduling difficulties, and though you intend to show only one character onscreen during an intense exchange, shoot both. This allows you abundance—a fallback alternative if your plans are not fulfilled, or a reaction shot if you need to conflate the best of two takes. This caution is not artistic compromise, for no traveller of any foresight takes a two-day water supply to cross a two-day desert.

THE FLOOR PLAN AND THE STORYBOARD

Draw a floor plan to help consolidate your intentions for blocking and to use the fewest and most effective camera angles. On it show the characters' movements and the camera angles necessary for the edited version you want. Figure 10–5 is a floor plan for the scene you saw marked up in Figure 10–1. This diagram, growing out of the blocking developed during rehearsals and modified by location realities, helps further work out the editing in advance, and enables the director of photography to plan lighting and camera movements.

On a tightly planned production the art director may make storyboard sketches for each angle as in Figure 10–3B. These help ensure that the contents of each composition are as interesting and relevant as possible. The suggestions each expert contributes may be so good that the director revises the original conception. As always in a true collaboration, the whole can be greater than the sum of its parts.

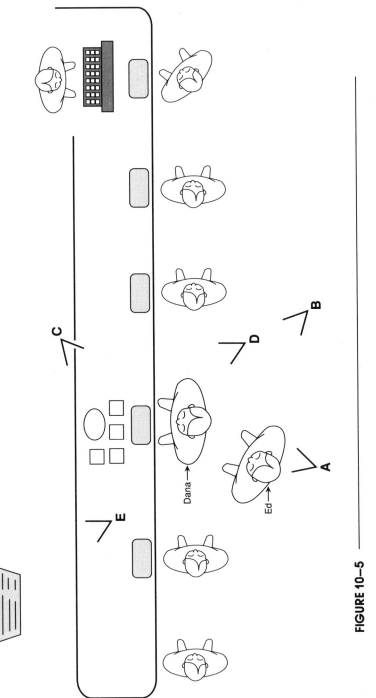

Floor plan for lunch counter scene in Figure 10–1.

Whatever the original intentions, the storyboard plan often goes out the window when you shoot. The particularities of a lens' field of view, problems with lighting, the needs of a character's movements, and even the size of the framing can all lead you to compose picture and block actors quite differently from the storyboard.

When storyboards become a fetish with a novice director, it usually foretells an overemphasis on physical design and an intolerance of the human variables during shooting. This bodes ill for the spontaneity necessary to naturalistic drama, and some of the history behind rigorous formal control is far from reassuring. The director most famous for compositional brilliance is Sergei Eistenstein, whose films were highly formalized and not at all concerned with spontaneity or even realism. As a supporter of the Marxist vision of history, he conveys powerfully the feel of inevitable historical process in a class-divided society, and the equally inevitable action and counteraction among its players. His films show individuals as part of a larger design, and elevate his historical analysis with the rhetoric of a striking but highly theatrical visual design. Ironically, his techniques are equally serviceable in the service of the opposite camp. Leni Riefenstahl's *Triumph of the Will* (1936) seductively promotes Adolf Hitler as the benevolent god of the German people. Elegant form can unfortunately substitute for intellectual content, as ten thousand TV commercials attest.

SPACE, PERCEPTION, AND BLOCKING

CAMERA EYE AND HUMAN EYE ARE DIFFERENT

The eye of the beholder during rehearsals is grossly misleading, for the human eye takes in a field of almost 180 degrees (see Figure 10–6). Although a 16mm camera lens of 10mm focal length is called a wide angle, it still only takes in fifty-four degrees horizontally and forty degrees vertically. This means that the most comprehensive wide angle lens (before fairground distortions set in) only has one quarter of the eye's angle of acceptance. This translates to a very restricted field of vision indeed and this has a resounding consequence for dramatic composition.

We compensate for such limitation by rearranging compositions to trick the spectator into the sensation of normal distances and ordinary spatial relationship. For instance, people holding a conversation may have to stand unnaturally close in order to look normal onscreen; furniture and distances between objects may need to be "cheated" apart or together to produce the desired appearance onscreen; and ordinary physical movements like walking past camera or picking up a glass of milk in closeup may require slowing by a third or more. Note, however, that comedy dialogue (though not necessarily movement) often needs to be played considerably faster than normal pacing if it is not to look slow onscreen. Screen testing helps you make all such decisions.

Packing the frame, achieving the illusion of depth, and arranging for balance and thematic significance in each setup's composition can all compensate for the screen's limited size and its tendency to flatten everything. To develop your eye in this area, do Chapter 33, Project 1: "Picture Composition Analysis". Concen-

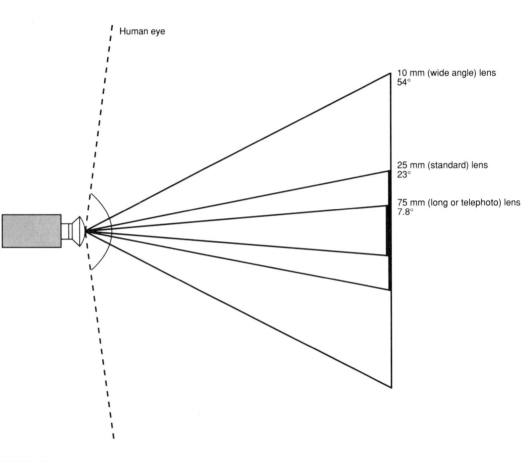

FIGURE 10–6

Human eye's field of vision compared with much more limited angle of acceptance for 16mm camera lenses. Note that vertical angles of acceptance (not shown) are twenty-five percent smaller still.

trate on realist painting and photographs, and get your own experience by taking still photos with a range of lenses. Slides are great because you can blow them up to enormous and revealing size.

CHOOSING LENS SIZE

This is an area people sometimes find forbidding, but you do not need to understand optics to use lenses intelligently. For beginners there are analogies from everyday life to help you understand and memorize the principles involved.

First, there is the normal sense of perspective as perceived by the human eye, and then there are departures on either side of normality. One such departure is represented by the telescope, which gives an almost miraculous sense of closeness but is hard to keep focussed and steady. The telescope's image is somehow luminous and isolated in space compared with that of the eye. The other extreme of departure from normal perspective is seen in the door security spyglass, which

FIGURE 10–7

Space and distance must be deliberately created on the screen. Still from Zsolt Kezdi-Kovacs' *Forbidden Relations* (courtesy Spectrafilm).

allows the viewer to see whether a visitor on the other side is friend or foe. The spyglass "sees" a lot of the hallway outside, but it produces a much reduced, distorted image. If your visitor is leaning with one hand on the door, you are likely to see a huge arm of many feet in length, diminishing to a tiny, distorted figure in the distance. These familiar optical devices allow us to pursue the range of dramatic possibilities in the camera lens.

PERSPECTIVE

NORMAL LENSES

Depending on the camera format in use, the lens that gives a normal sense of perspective will vary as follows:

Format	Focal length for normal lens
8 mm	12.5 mm
16 mm	25 mm
35 mm	50 mm

You can see there is a constant ratio between the format (width of film in use) and the lens focal length in each case. In the following examples I shall confine myself to 16mm format lenses, which are common to both 16mm film and to most video cameras.

NORMAL PERSPECTIVE

Normal perspective (Figure 10–8) means the viewer sees an "as is" size relationship between foreground and background trucks and can accurately judge the distance between them. The same shot taken with a wide-angle lens (Figure 10–9) changes the apparent distance between foreground and background,

FIGURE 10–8 ————

Normal lens.

FIGURE 10–9 ————

Wide-angle lens.

FIGURE 10–10 ————

Telephoto lens. Foreground and background distances appear quite different in Figures 10–8 and 10–9.

stretching it out. A telephoto lens (Figure 10–10) does just the opposite, squeezing foreground and background close together. If someone were to walk from the background truck up to the foreground, the dramatic implications of their walk would be very different in the three shots, all of which have the same subject but a different formal treatment through choice of lens.

PERSPECTIVE CHANGES ONLY WHEN CAMERA-TO-SUBJECT DISTANCE CHANGES

Figures 10–8, 10–9, and 10–10 produce the same size foreground truck from different lenses by repositioning the camera in each case, as in Figure 10–11. Changes of perspective result not from the lenses themselves, but from changes in the camera's physical distance from the subject and its background. Now, examine Figures 10–12, 10–13, and 10–14. Each is taken with a different lens

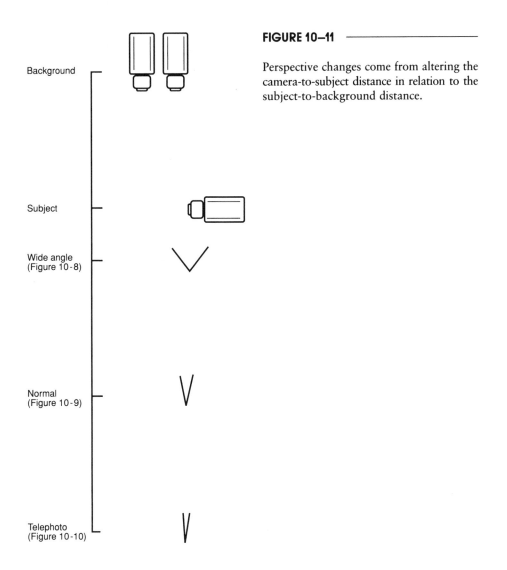

Background

Subject

Wide angle
(Figure 10-8)

Normal
(Figure 10-9)

Telephoto
(Figure 10-10)

FIGURE 10–11

Perspective changes come from altering the camera-to-subject distance in relation to the subject-to-background distance.

FIGURE 10–12

Wide-angle lens.

FIGURE 10–13

Normal lens.

FIGURE 10–14

Telephoto lens. Figures 10–12, 10–13, and 10–14 are taken from a single camera position. Notice that the stop sign remains in the same proportion to its background throughout.

but from the same camera position. The size relationship of the stop sign to the portico background is the same in all three. Here, perspective has not changed, although we apparently have three different angles. Perspective, then, is the product of camera-to-subject distance, for when this remains constant, so do the proportions between foreground and background, the means by which our eye assesses perspective.

MANIPULATING PERSPECTIVE

Using the magnifying or diminishing capacity of different lenses simply allows us to place the camera differently, so we can produce three similar shots (Figures 10–8, 10–9, and 10–10); and because camera-to-subject distance changes, perspective is different. Wide-angle lenses appear to magnify distance while telephoto lenses appear to squash different distances into the same plane.

ZOOMING VERSUS DOLLYING IN FOR CLOSEUP

A zoom is a lens capable of infinite variation between its extremes (say 10 to 100mm, which is a zoom with a ratio of 10:1). If you keep the camera static and zoom in on a subject, perspective does not alter, although apparent closeness obviously changes. With a fixed lens and a camera that dollies in close, you not only get closer, but see a perspective change with the move, just as in life.

LENS CHOICE AFFECTS IMAGE TEXTURE

Examine Figures 10–12 and 10–14. The backgrounds are very different in texture. Although in both the subject is in focus, the telephoto version has the rest of the image in soft focus, isolating and separating the subject from its foreground and background. This is because the telephoto lens has a very narrow depth of field and only the point of focus is sharp. Conversely, a wide-angle lens (Figures 10–9 and 10–12) allows a very deep focus. This can be useful, or it can produce a picture that drowns its subject in a plethora of irrelevantly sharp background and foreground detail. The telephoto has a "soft" textured background, the wide angle is "hard." Again these may be limitations, or they may have great dramatic utility.

LENS CHOICE AFFECTS LENS SPEED

Lens speed is a deceptive term that describes nothing to do with movement but instead how much light a lens needs for minimal operation. A "fast" lens is one in which the iris opens up wide so the lens is good for low-light photography. A "slow" lens is simply one that fails to admit as much light. By their inherent design, wide-angles tend to be fast (say, f1.4) while telephotos tend to be slow (perhaps f2.8). A two-stop difference like this means that the wide-angle is operative at one quarter of the light it takes to use the telephoto, which may make the difference between night shooting being practical or out of the question. Prime (that is, fixed) lenses having few elements tend to be faster than zooms, which are multielement.

SUMMARY OF LENS FEATURES

Note that lens speed refers to primes; zooms have one speed over the whole range.

	Advantages	*Disadvantages*
Wide angle lens		
Angle	Wide angle of acceptance	Can include unwanted detail
Perspective	Accentuates sense of distance	Can distort alarmingly
Speed	Fast; good for low light	
Depth of field	Large; good for deep focus	Hard overall texture
Handling	Easy; tends to absorb camera motion, so is good for handheld work, or when using an indifferent tripod head	
Effect	Dramatizes shape and movement	
Normal Lens		
Angle		Not very wide
Perspective	Normal	Dull, objective, undramatic
Speed	Modest	Too modest
Depth of field	Fairly good	Dull effect
Handling	Not easy; needs reasonably good tripod head if movements are to be acceptable	
Effect	Everything normal	"Blah"
Telephoto Lens		
Angle	Good for probing through unwanted foreground detail	Restricted acceptance angle
Perspective	Flattens and compresses	Distance hard to comprehend
Speed	Slow	
Depth of field	Narrow; good for isolating	Rack focus often necessary
Handling	Needs fluid head or camera movements are unacceptable	Hard to hold focus on moving subjects
Effect	Can be abstract and lovely	Easily overused

CAMERA HEIGHT

There is the old saying about a high camera suggesting domination and a low angle, subjugation. There are a host of other reasons to vary camera height—as many as there are relationships between compositional elements. The relationship may accommodate objects or persons in either the background or foreground, or accommodate a camera movement. This is covered below in the subsection "Relatedness: Separating or Integrating by Shot." If you carry out Chapter 33, Project 1: "Picture Composition Analysis" and take as your subject a film as cinematically inventive as Orson Welles' *Citizen Kane* (1941), you will see many occasions when the departure from an eye level camera position simply feels right. Often there is a dramatic rationale behind the choice, but these should not be turned into a filmmaking ten commandments.

In his excellent account of the craft *On Screen Directing,* the veteran Hollywood director Edward Dmytryk makes a persuasive case for avoiding shots at characters' eye level simply because they are dull. There may be another reason to avoid them. Unconsciously, perhaps the audience feels itself intruding upon the action, just as we should feel threatened by standing in the path of a duel. Being above or below eye level renders our observation safely out of the firing line. This is something to remember as your camera approaches the axis.

LIMIT CAMERA MOVEMENTS

Apart from zooming, panning, and tilting, most camera movements spell trouble unless you have an expensive dolly and tracks, and a highly experienced team to operate them. Understandably, student camera crews like to hire advanced camera support systems because it gives them practice and makes them feel professional. The price of this education may be a production repeatedly paralyzed while someone attempts to perfect a complex move that has little beyond egocentric virtuosity to offer the story.

HAVE THE COURAGE TO BE SIMPLE

The best guide to camera movement is to analyze a number of films. The best justification for camera movement may be to avoid the inherent fragmentation of cutting. Other camera movements are necessary to preserve composition and framing when characters are on the move, or to reveal something or someone formerly out of frame.

MOTIVATION FOR CAMERA POSITIONING AND CAMERA MOVEMENT

ADAPTING TO LOCATION EXIGENCIES

Making recommendations for camera positioning and movement is one of the hardest areas in which to be doctrinaire, since every situation has its own nature to be revealed and its own unique limitations. The latter are usually physical; windows or pillars in an interior that restrict shooting in one direction, or an incongruity to be avoided on an exterior. A wonderful period house you have found turns out to have a background of power lines strung across the sky, and has to be framed low when you wanted to frame high. Even when meticulously planned, filmmaking is always a serendipitous activity and often one's vision must be jettisoned and energy redirected to deal with the unforeseen.

For the rigid, linear personality this constant adaptation to the unexpected may be unacceptably frustrating, but for others it represents a challenge to their inventiveness and insight. Nonetheless, you have to make plans, and sometimes things even go according to intention.

WORK WITHIN YOUR MEANS

Any departure from the simple in cuts and camera movements should be motivated by the needs of the story if the audience is to feel it is sharing someone's consciousness. Good examples of subjectively motivated technique are Oliver's shock-cut view of the convict in the graveyard scene in *Oliver Twist* (1948) and dollying through the noise and confusion of a newsroom in *All the President's Men* (1976).

Such visual devices are dramatically justified, but for the low-budget filmmaker, dollying, craning, and other big-budget visual treatments are not strictly necessary, since few impressions cannot be achieved some other way. Whole films have been successfully made with a static camera always at eye level, or without cuts within a scene. Look at the opposite extreme: heavily scored music, rapid editing, and frenetic camera movement are mostly used as nervous stimulation to cover for a lack of true content. Just roll around the channels on your TV.

Complex camera movement is sometimes absolutely justified. In a film about dance like Emil Ardolino's *Dirty Dancing* (1987), Jeff Jur's camera cannot remain static on the sidelines. There are times when it must enter the lovers' dance and dance with them on their terms. Can this ever be done inexpensively? Using a wide-angle lens, an experienced camera operator, and a moving subject in the foreground to hold the eye, handheld camera work can often dispense with truckloads of shiny hardware and save mountains of cash.

THE CAMERA AS OBSERVING CONSCIOUSNESS

Treat the camera as a thoughtful observer and imagine how you want the audience to experience the scene. If you had a scene in a flea market, it would not make sense to limit the camera to carefully placed tripod shots. Make the camera adopt the point of view of a wandering buyer by going handheld and peering into circles of chattering people, looking closely at the merchandise, and then swinging around when someone calls out his name.

If, instead, you are to shoot a scene during a church service, with its elaborate ritualized stages, the placing and amount of coverage by the camera will be important, and it should be rock steady. Ask yourself whose point of view the audience is mostly sharing. Where does the majority of the telling action lie? With the newcomer? The priest? The choir or the congregation?

FIXED VERSUS MOBILE CAMERA

A camera on a tripod is able to zoom in and hold a steady close shot without physically crowding the actor. On the other hand, it cannot physically move to a new or better vantage point. The handheld camera gives this mobility, but at the price of a certain unsteadiness. This may be the only solution if you are shooting a semi-improvised performance. The camera on a dolly or a crane can move through a predetermined cycle of movements, but these require great precision from both crew and cast, all of whom must hit pretermined chalk marks on the floor. Here the casualty may be spontaneity in the cast.

SUBJECTIVE OR OBJECTIVE CAMERA PRESENCE

The two kinds of camera presence, the one studied, composed, and controlled, and the other mobile, spontaneous, reactive, and adaptive to change, each give a quite different sense of observing presence. Each implies a relatively subjective or objective observation of the action. Camera-handling alone may thus alter the "voice" of the film, making it either more or less personal and vulnerable. Maintaining either mode becomes unremarkable, while shifting justifiably between them can be very potent.

RELATEDNESS: SEPARATING OR INTEGRATING BY SHOT

Composition and framing alters a scene's implications drastically. Isolating two people in close shots and intercutting them has a very different feel than intercutting two over-shoulder shots where the two are always spatially related. Their relationship in space and time looks much less manipulated by the filming process in the over-shoulder shots. In the single shots, the observer is always alone with one of the contenders and inferring the unseen participant. In cinema this isolation is the exception, for normally the limitations of the frame size make us use it to the utmost to show the relationship between everything and everybody.

BACKGROUNDS

Another camera positioning issue is deciding what part background must play in relation to foreground. If a character is depressed and hungry there is a nice irony in showing that her bus stop is outside a MacDonalds and she is being watched by a huge Ronald MacDonald. The composition will unobstrusively highlight her dilemma and suggest the temptation to blow her bus money on a large french fries.

CAMERA AS INSTRUMENT OF REVELATION

Looking down upon the subject, looking up at the subject, or looking at it between the bars of a railing can all suggest different ways of seeing—and therefore of experiencing—the action that is the subject of the scene. The camera must not be a passive recorder, but should be used as an active instrument of revelation. While one can manufacture this sense of revelation through Eisensteinian editing and juxtaposition of shots, this is a blowhard technique to get your point across. More subtle and convincing is to build this multileveled consciousness into the shooting itself. Exploiting the location as a meaningful environment and being responsive to the actions and sightlines of participants in a scene can create a vivid and spontaneous sense of the scene's hidden dynamics unfolding. This is sharing the consciousness of someone intelligent and intuitive who picks up all the underlying tensions as opposed to sharing that of someone dull who merely stares passively at whatever moves.

STUDY THE MASTERS

To know how best to shoot any particular scene, study the way good directors have shot analogous situations. In Chapter 35, Project 2: Editing Analysis there is a film study project to help you define a director's specific choices and intentions.

COMPROMISES FOR THE CAMERA

When shooting action sequences, you may need to ask people to slow their movements down, since movement within a frame can look twenty percent to thirty percent faster than it does in life. Even the best camera operator cannot keep a profile in tight framing if the actor moves too fast or in focus if the actor strays from the chalk line on the floor. Such compromises on behalf of technology raise interesting questions about how much one should forgo in the way of performance spontaneity to achieve a visually and choreographically polished result. Much will depend on the expertise of your crew, but even the time of day you shoot may affect where you compromise, since tired actors are more likely to feel they are being treated like objects than fresh ones. Politics and expediency do not end here, for the crew can be disappointed and even resentful if you abandon interesting technical challenges on behalf of the cast.

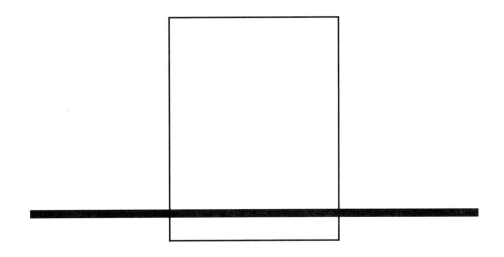

C·H·A·P·T·E·R 1·1

GETTING READY TO SHOOT

EQUIPMENT SELECTION: DRAWING UP A WANT LIST

In a book like this it is impractical to be very specific over what equipment is desirable. To prepare for shooting, sit down as a group and brainstorm over what you really need. Make lists and do not forget to include basic repair and maintenance tools. Some piece of equipment is bound to need corrective surgery on location.

How the film looks, how it is shot, and how it conveys its content to the audience are decisions that affect your equipment needs, but these decisions are about the form of the film and need to be made organically from the nature of the film's subject. Plan to shoot as simply as possible, choosing straightforward means over elaborate ones. The best solutions to most problems are elegantly simple.

Overordering and overelaboration are always a temptation, especially for the insecure technician trying to forestall problems by insisting he needs the "proper" equipment. Usually this is the most complicated and expensive. Since initially you will be trying to conquer basic conceptual and control difficulties, you will have little use for the sophistication of advanced equipment, and you cannot afford the time it takes to work out how to use it to best advantage.

Learn as much as possible about the technical decisions in the shoot so you, your DP, and your PM can decide what outlay is truly justified. Some extra items turn out to be lifesavers; others just cost money and never get used. Keep in mind it's human ingenuity and not just equipment that makes good films.

If your crew is at all inexperienced, make sure they scan all equipment manuals carefully; they contain vital and often overlooked information. At the end of this book there is a bibliography to find more detailed information on techniques and equipment.

Do not be discouraged if your equipment is not the best. The first chapters of film history, so rich in creative advances, were, after all, shot using hand cranked cameras made of wood and brass.

SCHEDULING THE SHOOT

A director needs to be familiar with details of the organization and scheduling that makes filming possible. Scheduling is normally decided by the director and the PM, and double-checked by principal crew members, in particular the DP. Much of the time you will have to make educated guesses since no film is ever quite like any other and there are few constants. Since time inevitably means money, your schedule must reflect your resources as well as your needs. Take into account any or all of the following:

- Costs involved at each stage if hiring talent, equipment, crew, or facilities (see budget form in Figure 11–1)
- Scenes involving key dramatic elements (weather or other cyclical conditions, for instance)
- Availability of actors and crew
- Availability of locations
- Relationship of locations and travel exigencies
- Availability of special or rented equipment, including props
- Complexity of each lighting setup, and power requirements
- Time of day to get available light coming from right direction

LOCATION ORDER

Normal practice is to shoot in convenient location order and to take into account cast and crew availability. During shooting, lighting setup or changes take up the most time, so a compact shoot conserves on lighting changes and avoids relighting the same set. For all these reasons and more, it is unusual to shoot in script order.

The character and location breakdown (Figure 3–4) described at the end of Chapter 3 shows which scenes must be shot at each location. It is usual for scenes from the beginning, middle, and end of the film to be shot all in the same location. This makes rehearsal all the more important if actors are to move authoritatively between the different emotional levels required. The scene breakdown also displays which characters are needed, and this, too, in association with the cost and availability of actors may influence scheduling.

SCRIPT ORDER

Few films actually need to be shot in script order, however desirable this is from the standpoint of performance continuity. A film which depends on a long, slow development (say a decline into insanity by the main character), might require this degree of progressive control by the actor playing the part. Another, depending upon a high degree of improvisation, might need to be shot in script order to maintain control over the evolving story line. Another still might be all interiors and have a small, constant cast so that shooting out of scene order is not an advantage.

Normally shooting in script order is seldom practical, so director, cast, and crew must be thoroughly prepared if patchwork filming is to assemble correctly.

SCHEDULE KEY SCENES EARLY

Some scenes are so dramatically important that there will literally be no film should they fail. Imagine that your whole film hinges upon the inevitableness of your heroine falling in love with an emotionally unstable man. It would be folly to shoot everything else trusting that your actors can make a difficult and pivotal scene work.

Such key scenes must neither be filmed too early when the cast has not yet peaked, nor too late, when failure or change might render weeks of work useless. If the scene is successful, it will give a lift to everything else you shoot; if the scene is not really working, you will want to reshoot in a day or two, and certainly before you commit yourself to shooting the bulk of the film. Problems should show up in rehearsals, but filming is only occasionally better than the best rehearsal, and often below it. While it is usual for the cast to feel more deeply during the first takes of a new scene, strong feeling is no substitute for depth of character development. When cast members realize they must sustain a performance over several angles and several takes per angle, they also begin to instinctively budget their energy level. Knowing this should make you try to mentally preedit your scene so you don't make undue and wasteful demands upon cast and crew. Drawing the line between adequacy and wastefulness is particularly hard for the new director, so it is best to err on the side of safety.

EMOTIONAL DEMAND ORDER

Scheduling should take account of the demands some scenes make upon the actors. A nude love scene, for instance, or a scene in which two characters get violently angry with each other should be delayed until the actors are comfortable with each other and the crew. Such scenes should also be the last of the day because they are so emotionally draining.

CONTINGENCY COVERAGE

Schedule exteriors early in case your intentions are defeated by unsuitable weather. By planning interiors as standby alternatives, you need lose no time. Make contingency shooting plans whenever you face major uncertainties.

BUDGETING SHOOTING TIME PER SCENE

Depending on the amount of coverage, the intensity of the scene in question, and the reliability of actors and crew, you might expect to shoot anywhere between two and five minutes of screen time per eight-hour day. Remember that

```
          S H O R T   B U D G E T   F O R M
          _____

                    Production Details

Working Title:............................................. Length: .....mins

Personnel:
     Director: ...............................Tel:..........(h)...........(w)
       Address ...............................
               ...............................
     Dir. of Photog. ..........................    ...........    ...........
     Sound:....................................    ...........    ...........
     Prod. Mgr:................................    ...........    ...........

Format (circle all that apply):
     Video: Beta/VHS/³/₄"/1"
     Film:  b&w/color  negative/reversal  8mm/16mm/35mm

Project is at stage of (circle one):  Pre-Production/Production/Post-Production

Schedule at present is:
     Pre-Production from................to...................
     Production         ..............  ...................
     Post-Production    ..............  ...................

Brief Description of subject:




Thematic focus of film is:
```

FIGURE 11-1 ────────────────────────────────

Short budget estimate form. Note high and low estimate figures. A contingency percentage is always added to budget total to cover the unforeseeable.

traveling between locations, setup, or relighting in the same location all massively slow the pace of shooting. Some directors budget setup time for mornings and rehearse the actors while the crew is busy, but this cannot work as well outside a studio setting.

```
                        Pre-Production Costs

                                                        Low      High
Travel                                                  $...     $...
Phone                                                   ...      ...
Rehearsal                                               ...      ...
Hospitality                                             ...      ...
Other (_____)     ...      ...

                                          Total         ...      ...
_____
                        Production Costs
Crew

Director    for .../....days at $...... per day         ...      ...
Camera       "  .../...   "   "   ......  "   "          ...      ...
Sound        "  .../...   "   "   ......  "   "          ...      ...
Gaffer       "  .../...   "   "   ......  "   "          ...      ...
Grip         "  .../...   "   "   ......  "   "          ...      ...
Prod. Mgr    "  .../...   "   "   ......  "   "          ...      ...

Equipment

Camera (film/Video)..... for  .../... days at $...... per day  ...  ...
Magazines (film).........   " .../...  "   "   ......  "   "    ...  ...
Changing bag (film)......   " .../...  "   "   ......  "   "    ...  ...
Clapper board (film).....   " .../...  "   "   ......  "   "    ...  ...
Nagra recorder (film)....   " .../...  "   "   ......  "   "    ...  ...
Video recorder...........   " .../...  "   "   ......  "   "    ...  ...
Lenses..................    " .../...  "   "   ......  "   "    ...  ...
Filter kit..............    " .../...  "   "   ......  "   "    ...  ...
Exposure meter..........    " .../...  "   "   ......  "   "    ...  ...
Color temperature meter..   " .../...  "   "   ......  "   "    ...  ...
Camera supports: tripod..   " .../...  "   "   ......  "   "    ...  ...
                baby legs   " .../...  "   "   ......  "   "    ...  ...
                hi-hat..    " .../...  "   "   ......  "   "    ...  ...
Tilt head...............    " .../...  "   "   ......  "   "    ...  ...
Spreader................    " .../...  "   "   ......  "   "    ...  ...
Dolly & Tracks..........    " .../...  "   "   ......  "   "    ...  ...
Video monitor...........    " .../...  "   "   ......  "   "    ...  ...
Headphones..............    " .../...  "   "   ......  "   "    ...  ...
Mike boom...............    " .../...  "   "   ......  "   "    ...  ...
Mikes:  gun.............    " .../...  "   "   ......  "   "    ...  ...
        omni............    " .../...  "   "   ......  "   "    ...  ...
        cardioid........    " .../...  "   "   ......  "   "    ...  ...
        lavalier........    " .../...  "   "   ......  "   "    ...  ...
        extension cords..   " .../...  "   "   ......  "   "    ...  ...
        mixer...........    " .../...  "   "   ......  "   "    ...  ...
Batteries...............    " .../...  "   "   ......  "   "    ...  ...
Sun gun.................    " .../...  "   "   ......  "   "    ...  ...
Open face quartz kit(s)..   " .../...  "   "   ......  "   "    ...  ...
Softlight(s)............    " .../...  "   "   ......  "   "    ...  ...
Spotlight kit(s)........    " .../...  "   "   ......  "   "    ...  ...
Extension cords.........    " .../...  "   "   ......  "   "    ...  ...
Tie-in cables...........    " .../...  "   "   ......  "   "    ...  ...
```

Figure 11–1 *(continued)*

It is best to err on the side of underscheduling, since a tired crew and cast work progressively slower, and morale (not to mention tempers) becomes frayed. You can always shorten a long schedule, but it is unpopular or even impossible to lengthen one too short. Most nonprofessional shoots (and some professional) are seriously underscheduled. When crew and cast end up working twelve- or fourteen-hour days, artistic intentions go out the window and everyone ends up

<u>Materials</u>

```
Camera raw stock .../... rolls of type.... @ $....per roll (film)   ...      ...
Nagra tape        .../...   "    "    "  .... @ $....  "      "     "  ...    ...
Develop           ...../.....ft of cam. orig @ $......per ft.    "     ...    ...
Print             ...../..... " of workprint @ $...... per ft    "     ...    ...
Sound transfer              ....hrs @ $..... per hr              "     ...    ...
Sound stock (8mm/16mm/35mm)  ......ft @ $.... per ft             "     ...    ...
Videocassettes .../...required of type........ @ $...... each          ...    ...
```

```
Total.......................................................$_____  $_____
```
<u>Talent</u>

```
_____ X _____days @ $.....per day                ...    ...
_____ X _____days @ $.....per day                ...    ...
_____ X _____days @ $.....per day                ...    ...
_____ X _____days @ $.....per day                ...    ...
_____ X _____days @ $.....per day                ...    ...
_____ X _____days @ $.....per day                ...    ...
_____ X _____days @ $.....per day                ...    ...
_____ X _____days @ $.....per day                ...    ...
Other_____            ...    ...
```

```
Total.................................................... $_____  $_____
```

<u>Other</u>

```
Transport    ..../.... days      @ $...... per day.               ...    ...
Subsistence ..../.... person days @ $..... per person per day     ...    ...
Accomodation ..../....  "    "   " $.....  "    "     "    "       ...    ...
Location or other fees                                            ...    ...
                                           Total                  ...    ...
```

<u>Post-Production</u>

```
Editor           ..../.... days @ $...... per day               ...    ...
Editing equipment ..../....  "   " $......  "  "                 ...    ...
Time coding      ..../.... hrs  " $......  at $....... per hour  ...    ...
Window dub       ..../....  "   " $......  " $.......  "   "     ...    ...
Narrator         ..../....  "   " $...... per hr                 ...    ...
Music                                                           ...    ...
Titles                                                          ...    ...
Sound mix        ..../.... hrs  @ $..... per hour               ...    ...
Transfer mag master to optical .../....ft @ $.......per ft  (film) ...  ...
Conform cam original to workprint ..../.... hrs @ $... per hr   " ...   ...
Make first answer print...../.....ft @ $....... per ft        " ...    ...
Make first release  "  ...../.....ft @ $....... per ft        " ...    ...
On-line edit, timebase correction, etc  ..../....hr @ $.... per hr ... ...
```

```
Legal                                                            ...    ...
Production Office                                                ...    ...
Miscellaneous:                                                  
   .................................                            ...    ...
   .................................                            ...    ...
   .................................                            ...    ...
                                           Total                ...    ...
```

Summary:

```
Pre-Production  total.........................................  $  ...    ...
Production      total.........................................     ...    ...
Post-Production total.........................................     ...    ...

Subtotal......................................................  $  ...    ...

Contingency addition (12% of total)..........................  $  ...    ...

GRAND TOTAL...................................................  $.....  $....
```

Figure 11–1 *(continued)*

merely aiming to survive the ordeal. The sad part is that a promising film may be sabotaged by misplaced optimism rather than any inherent need to save money.

Be prepared for the first few days of shooting to be alarmingly slow because crew are often still developing an efficient working relationship with each other. The first half of the shoot may fall seriously behind if the AD and PM do not apply the screws and keep the unit up to schedule. Not only does the inexperienced crew start slowly and get quicker over the length of the schedule, it also tends to reproduce this pattern during each day unless there is some determined progress-chasing by the DP and AD.

GOLDEN RULE NUMBER ONE: FORESEE THE WORST

Imagination expended in foreseeing the worst will forestall many potentially crippling problems before they take shape. That way you will equip yourself with particular spares, special tools, and emergency information, for example. Optimism and filmmaking do not go together. One blithe optimist left the master tapes of a feature film in his car overnight. The car happened to be stolen, and because there were no copies, the result of a vast amount of work was transformed instantly into so much silent footage.

The pessimist, constantly foreseeing the worst and never tempting fate, is tranquilly productive compared with your average optimist.

GOLDEN RULE NUMBER TWO: TEST IT FIRST

Arrive early and test every piece of equipment at its place of origin. Never assume because you are hiring from a reputable company that everything should be all right. If you do, Murphy's Law will get you. (Murphy's Law: "Everything that can go wrong will go wrong.") Be ready for Murphy lurking inside everything that should fit together, slide, turn, lock, roll, light up, make a noise, or work silently. His relatives hide out in every wire, plug, box, lens, battery, and alarm clock. Make no mistake; the whole clan means to ruin you. Make "test and test again" your true religion and leave nothing to chance.

SHOT AND SCENE IDENTIFICATION

Your crew must keep logs of important information when you shoot. These serve the same end for both videotape and film, but record-keeping and continuity observation is more stringent for film because it allows no instant replay.

CLAPPER BOARD

There are many fancy automatic **film** marking systems, but the exquisitely low-tech clapper board, with only a piece of chalk and a hinge to go wrong, is my favorite. The clapper board ritual has three main functions. Visually it identifies the shot number and the production for the film laboratory; aurally the operator's announcement identifies the track for the sound transfer personnel; and in the cutting room the closing bar provides an exact picture frame against which to sync the bang on the recorded track.

Because **video** recording normally has sound and picture on the one piece of tape, sync is not a problem. No clapper board is needed unless you are shooting high-quality double-system sound (video picture with sound recorded separately on a high-quality sync recorder like a Nagra). For either **film** or **video** double-system productions the clapper board allows sound to be synced to the picture.

You will still need a **video** shot numbering system to identify setup and take numbers even on a modest production. Using high-speed scan, one can run down to a chosen take without the need to search at sound speed for the camera stop and voice announcement. This is valuable on location when time spent reviewing tape is often stolen from much needed rest.

Film scene numbering boards carry a quantity of information used by processing labs, such as a gray scale, which includes white and black as a contrast reference, and a standard color chart for color reference. In **video** the color chart is electronically generated by the camera and is called the color bars.

To summarize, for **film** use a clapper board with announcement and for a **video** production use a number board with announcement only. For double system videotape use a clapper board and treat the operation like film, since sound will likewise have to be synced up to video action.

SETUP AND TAKE NUMBERS

The setup is the apparent position of the camera, which can be altered by a simple lens change as well as by physically moving the camera to a new position. There are two philosophies of numbering.

Scene/Setup/Take: This is the system favored in the Hollywood studio system. Numbering is based on the script scene number. For example: "Scene 104A, shot 16, take 3." Translated this means script scene 104A, setup 16, attempt number 3." Hollywood, making big highly supervised productions, needs lengthy factory part numbers. For the small, flexible production, this is unnecessary. The more elaborate a system is, the more susceptible it is to error and to breakdown if you depart from the script. Also, by taking longer to announce it wastes precious film stock.

Cumulative Setup/Take: This system is used in both documentaries and features in Europe. Shooting simply begins at one and each setup gets the next number. For example: "142 take 2." Shot numbers are often called slate numbers. This system is preferred for the overstretched small crew because it requires no liaison to coordinate numbers with the script, and needs no adaptation when the inevitable script departures come up.

SHOOTING LOGS

On a **film** shoot the camera assistant keeps a camera log (Figure 11–2) for each film magazine's contents by slate, take, and footages. Each magazine has a new camera roll number. This information comes into play during processing and

```
FILM CAMERA LOG    Production Title_____ Page_____

Operator_____ Camera #_____ Magazine #_____ Cam. Roll #____
Location_____ Film Type _____ Date ___/___/_____
-------------------------------------------------------------------------
Setup Take Comments                                                 Footage
____ ____ _____ ____ _____
____ ____ _____ ____ _____
____ ____ _____ ____ _____
____ ____ _____ ____ _____
____ ____ _____ ____ _____
____ ____ _____ ____ _____
____ ____ _____ ____ _____
____ ____ _____ ____ _____

          Process Normal Yes/ No:_____  Total Shot
-------------------------------------------------------------------------
          Notes:


                         Cam. Assistant:
          _____
```

FIGURE 11–2

Camera log for film production.

later in editing. A day-for-night scene, for example, would be shot using a blue filter to give it a moonlit look, but if the lab lacked the relevant documentation it might easily treat the filtering as an error to be color-corrected in the workprint. The film sound recordist keeps a sound log (Figure 11–3) which records

SOUND RECORDER LOG Production Title_____ Page_____
Mike Op. _____ Recorder_#_____ Tape Type_____Roll #_____
Location_____ Date ___/___/_____
Setup Take Comments   Mike(s) Sync?

Notes:

Recordist:

FIGURE 11–3

Sound recorder log for film or video double system production.

slate and take numbers, and whether each track is sync or "wild" (non sync voice or effects recording). The latter information is important to whoever does the transfer from ¼″ master tape to 16mm, since there may be no pilot tone (electronic sync reference signal).

DOUBLE-SYSTEM RECORDING

Where sound is recorded by a mechanically and electrically independent recorder, **film** camera magazines or **video** cassettes do not stay in numerical step with their sound master roll numbers because, among other reasons, the sound recordist records wild tracks and atmospheres as the production progresses. This is why separate sound and camera logs must be kept. The rushes prints actually travel to their destination in the cutting room by different routes (see production flow chart, Figure 11–4). The **film** laboratory processes the negative and strikes

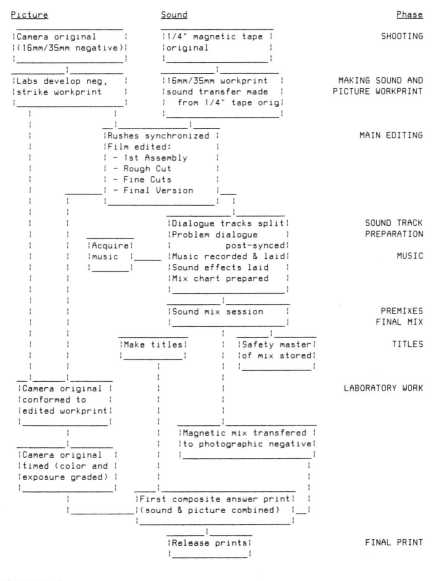

FIGURE 11–4 ————————————————————————————————————

Flowchart for a production shot on film (double system).

a workprint for the editor, while the ¼ inch magnetic master tape goes to the sound transfer suite where a copy is made onto 16mm sprocketed magnetic stock, again for the editor. **Video** master cassettes will probably go to a post-production house for time coding and/or for the editor's window dub. Thus, in double-system filmmaking, sound and picture are likely to come together for the first time when they are synchronized in the cutting room.

```
V I D E O   L O G  Production Title_____ Page_____

Cam. Operator_____ Camera_____ Date__/__/____
Location_____ Roll # _____

Counter Scene
reading # and            Description              Remarks
        take
```

Notes:

Signed:

FIGURE 11–5

Log for video production.

SINGLE SYSTEM

When shooting single system on **videotape**, records are simpler because both sound and picture are recorded on the same cassette (see flow chart, Figure 11–6). The deck operator keeps a master log by digital number and also makes a record of slate, take, and a brief description of the scene.

LOG MUST RECORD EQUIPMENT USED

In all cases, logs must identify the serial numbers of equipment used. Should a strange electronic sound be later discovered in the sound, or scratching turn up on a film negative, you are able to positively identify and examine the offending machine.

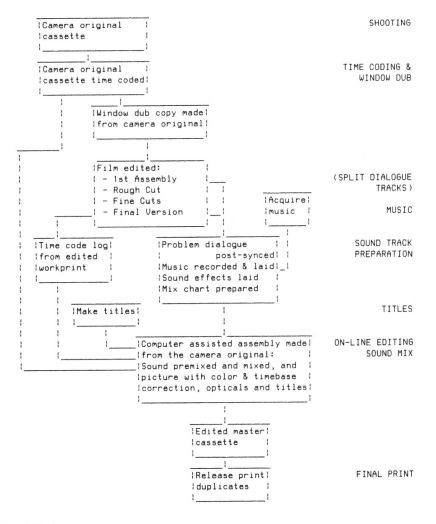

FIGURE 11–6

Flow chart for a production shot on video (single system).

SCRIPT SUPERVISOR AND CONTINUITY REPORTS

Being a director during shooting means being wholly occupied within each moment. You have planned your coverage in advance with your script supervisor and now it would be counterproductive to use some of your precious energies ensuring that the coverage is being fulfilled. That is your script supervisor's job. He or she must see that the editor is supplied with adequate coverage and see that such detail is consistent between matching shots, such as which hand a character used to open the suitcase, how long his cigarette was when he stood by the window, and which direction he turned as he left for the door.

In the event of changes or economies, the script supervisor needs to know how the revised footage could be edited together and must at all times guard against omissions.

For a feature shoot, the script supervisor produces reports that are usually masterpieces of observation. Each setup has its own sheet and each records the following:

- Production, personnel, and date
- Slate and take number
- Script scene number
- Camera lens in use
- Action and dialogue variations, successes and flaws for each take, and which are to be printed up by the lab (big-budget films are able to print selectively)
- Any special instructions from the director to the editor

Not surprisingly, a script supervisor needs fierce powers of concentration and the ability to do huge amounts of typing in spare moments. When everyone else has gone to sleep on location, you will hear the script supervisor still at work. Because one cannot replay an exposed film as one can a recorded videotape, the script supervisor's work is supremely important to feature filmmaking. Its quality later determines how readily the cutting rooms can locate material in their filing system and how well it all fits together.

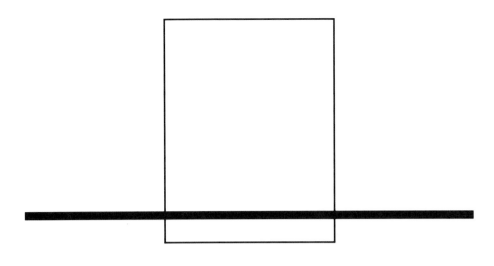

C·H·A·P·T·E·R 1·2

DIRECTING THE ACTORS

SENSORY OVERLOAD

Shooting is a time of euphoria and despair for the director, who, unlike anyone else, must scan many people's work. A supportive, enthusiastic cast and crew will endure and triumph together, but under the best of conditions this will be a time of great stress. Hardest is fulfilling the actors' needs for feedback while also trying to direct the crew.

The director's occupational hazard is sensory overload. In a typical take when you must watch the actors keenly you will hear a lamp filament humming and a plane flying nearby. Can the sound recordist hear them? Insulated inside her headphones, she only looks back at you questioningly. Next you see a doubtful camera movement, and wonder if the operator will call, "Cut!" Your heroine turned the wrong way leaving the table and your mind races to figure out if it can possibly cut with the longer shot. Now to further boggle your mind the camera assistant holds up two fingers. Only two minutes of film left. At the end of the take your cast looks at you expectantly. How was it? Of course you hardly know.

ACTORS NEED FEEDBACK

Actors learn from acting school and elsewhere to depend upon audience signals. There are few in filming, for the director is the sole audience and must try to give each actor the sense of closure normally acquired from an audience. Actors are not fooled by empty gestures. Your brain has been running out of control trying to factor all the editing possibilities that make the last performance even usable, and now you must say something intelligent to your trusting players, each of whom is (and must be) self-absorbed and self-aware. You manage something and the cast nods intently.

Now your crew needs you and the actors are already asking, "What are we doing next?" The production manager is at your elbow demanding confirmation for the shooting at the warehouse next week. The warehouse people are on the phone and they sound testy. This is what it means to direct.

PRIORITIZE

The solution lies in setting priorities and delegating as much as possible of the actual shooting to the DP, who directs the crew.

ACTORS' ANXIETIES AT THE BEGINNING

PREPRODUCTION PARTY

Try to bring cast and crew together for a picnic or pot luck party before production begins, to break the ice.

WARN ACTORS THAT SHOOTING IS SLOW

Thoroughly warn actors that all filming is slow, that even a professional feature unit may only shoot between one to four minutes of screen time per eight-hour day. Tell them to bring good books to fill the inevitable periods of waiting.

BEFORE SHOOTING

The time of maximum jitters and minimum confidence for the actors is just before first shooting. Take each aside and tell him or her something special and private. What matters is to be sincere and personally supportive. Thereafter the actor has a special understanding to maintain with you. Its substance and development will reach out by way of the film to the audience, for whom you are presently the surrogate.

TENSION AND ITS CONSEQUENCES

Whatever level of performance was reached in rehearsal now comes to the test when shooting begins. Actors will feel as if they are going over Niagara Falls in a barrel. Wise scheduling puts the least demanding material early as a warm-up. In the first day or two there will be a lot of tension, either frankly admitted or displaced into one of the many behaviors that mask it (See "Forms of Resistance by Actors" in Chapter 7). Try not to be wounded or angered; if someone is deeply afraid of failing a task, it is forgivably human to demote the work's importance. It does not mean actors are deficient as a breed (the private belief of many film technicians), but rather that actors are normal people temporarily succumbing to vulnerability and self-doubt. Having nowhere to hide, actors can easily feel exposed and humiliated. Filming is incomprehensibly slow, and the crew, enviably busy with their gadgets, seem removed and uncaring. Your appreciation, public recognition for even small achievements, and astute catering work wonders for morale in both cast and crew.

GETTING INTO STRIDE

As the process settles into a familiar routine, anxieties subside and actors fall in with the pace and demand of the shooting, arriving eventually at a craftsmanlike pride in being a member of the team. Performances improve so much that you wonder about the usability of the earlier material.

THE DIRECTOR'S AUTHORITY

While actors are visibly working their way through a labyrinth of strong feelings, the director must suffer any similar crises in silent isolation. Because cast members invest such trust in their director, he or she must play the role of all-comprehending, all-supporting parental figure. The poor novice is racked with uncertainty about whether he or she even has the authority to do the job.

How do you wield authority when you do not feel confident? In part you, too, play a role that the whole film unit wants to believe in. In practice, though, you should limit the area you oversee by delegating responsibility. Be better prepared than anyone else, and keep everyone busy. Your authority rests mainly on being able to recall and communicate what actors have just given, and to point the way forward. This is your central function, so divest yourself of anything else that impedes it.

Both cast and crew are apt to try your patience and judgment. This all too human testing procedure unfortunately falls to most leaders. Behind what seems a sparring and antagonistic attitude may lurk a growing respect and affection, but because of the parental role—supporting, questioning, challenging—you may feel thoroughly alone and unappreciated. You are an authority figure, and many experience their most ambivalent relationships with such figures. For your cast, "my director" and the other actors may be the most important people in their lives, allies with whom to play out complex and personal issues that involve love and hate, and everything in between. This is just as legitimate a path of exploration for an actor as it is for any other artist.

Finding a productive working relationship with the subtle personalities of your actors is really discovering how best to use your own temperament. There are no rules because the chemistry is always different and changing. If it comes to a choice, you should always aim to be respected rather than liked. Liking comes later if things go well.

The director stands at the crossroads to all important relationships in the making of the film, and must do whatever it takes to keep everyone focused on the good of the common enterprise. There is no set way to handle the many situations that come up, except to remain loyal to the project rather than to any individual.

DIVIDING YOUR ATTENTION BETWEEN CREW AND CAST

Often the director of a student production is using an untried crew and justifiably feels that every phase of the production must be personally monitored. But if you are to direct the human presence on the screen, directing the crew should be entrusted to the DP and the AD.

Your authority with both crew and cast lies in keeping abreast of how the material will work on the screen. One learns to do this well by taping the later rehearsals. By the time you must shoot you recognize instinctively when things work and when they do not.

Directing is easier (though hardly less stressful) for those who have arrived via one of the crafts because long years of industry apprenticeship teach people how to work in a highly disciplined team. Without this conditioning, the student director and crew are in a precarious position, but if Truffaut's *Day for Night* (1973) is as representative as I think, a lowering of ideals during shooting is a common experience.

DAILY ORGANIZATION

Be sure everyone is well prepared. This means typed call sheets for cast and crew in advance, floor plans for camera crew, and preestablished lighting design. Tricky camera setups should be rehearsed in advance and the right props and the correct costumes should be ready to go. Have your scene coverage thoroughly worked out with your DP and script supervisor. Your AD should make lists so you carry nothing in your head and nothing gets forgotten. A smoothly running organization means professionalism to the cast and creates confidence in your leadership for all working on the project.

FOR EACH SHOT

While the crew sets up the next shot, take your cast aside and rehearse intensively. The DP can borrow crew members as stand-ins for lighting and movement checks. Run through the action and remind each actor of his character's recent past and emotional state on entering the scene. This is very important and often needs to be repeated in a few words before each take. Your AD should tell you when the first shot is set up so actors can start with the minimum of waiting.

The AD should call for silence as everyone takes their working positions; important because the players are finding their focus. The director asks, "Ready to roll?" and if everyone is indeed ready, he or she next says, "Roll camera." When equipment is up to speed and stabilized, the camera operator calls back, "Speed!"

Then you say that magic word: "Action!" The word itself is actually your last direction because it can communicate something of what you expect to the actors. It can be said loudly, softly, intimately, aggressively—a hundred ways.

It is normally the director who calls, "Cut!" but the sound recordist or camera operator may do so should a technical flaw known only to them render the take unusable. Actors on the other hand should wherever possible complete a flawed scene unless the director decides to abort it.

When another take is necessary, quickly tell each actor what to aim for (whether the same or something different) and run up the camera before the collective intensity dissipates. Sometimes a further take is necessary because of a technical flaw in sound or in camera coverage, but usually you want better or different performances. This may affect each actor in a group scene differently. From one you want the same good level of performance, from another a different emotional shading or energy level. Each needs to know what you expect.

Actors themselves will often be dissatisfied with a performance and ask to do it again. The best acknowledgment is to call, "We're going for another take. Roll camera as soon as possible." While cast should always be allowed to improve, asking for just one more take can become a fetish or a manipulation of directorial decisions. Sometimes you must insist that the last take was fine and that you want to move on. Actors' insecurity has a thousand faces.

FOR THE NEW SHOT

As soon as you have an acceptable take, brief the DP what the next shot is to be, and turn to the cast to give them what they need, both positive feedback about the last shot and preparation for the next.

DEMAND MORE

In directing, the enemy is one's own passive and gullible habit of accepting what actors give as the "best they can do." Try to instill in yourself the artist's creative dissatisfaction with every first appearance. Treat it as the brilliant surface of a deep pool, a reflective facade with a teeming, complex life underneath to be found by diving deep. Treat each scene as a "seeming" beneath which hides a significance that only skill and aspiration can lay bare.

Always pushing for depth means expecting to be moved by the players, and feeding back to them how you were moved and to what degree. When the players deliver a real intensity, you are creating as you go and not just placing a rehearsal on record.

Because you are working in a highly allusive medium your audience expects metaphorical and metaphysical overtones. If you are to draw us beneath the surface of normality and make us see the poetry and conflict under the raw material of life, you will have to challenge your actors in a hundred interesting ways. This is all the more necessary because the camera itself deals with externals and surface banality.

The demands you make are what keep the cast and the crew working; to please you, but also because your demands personify their own gnawing sense of something better being possible. This dissatisfaction is as it should be.

FEEDING THE UNKNOWN INTO THE PROCESS

To revive a scene that has settled into comfortable middle age, take one or more actors aside and suggest to each some small but significant changes that will impact on other cast members. By building in little stresses and incompatibilities, you can reestablish the tension that is missing.

SIDE COACHING WHEN A SCENE IS BECALMED

When a scene goes static and sinks to a premeditated appearance, try side coaching to inject tension. This means you interpolate at a dead moment in the scene a verbal suggestion or instruction, such as, "Terry, she's beginning to make you angry—she's asking the impossible." Your voice starts a new interior process in the character addressed, but it will not work if your actors are caught by surprise. Either they are familiar with side coaching from your rehearsal methods or you should warn them to expect it and not to break character.

REACTION SHOTS

Side coaching is useful when directing simple reaction shots. The director provides a verbal image for the character to spontaneously see or react to, or an idea to consider, and gets an immediacy of reaction by feeding in something the actor does not quite expect.

Usually the best reactions are to the actual. If a character must go through a complex series of emotions while overhearing a whispered conversation, make it a rule that the other characters do a full version of their scene even though it is off camera. If, however, your character must only look through a window and react to an approaching visitor, her imagination will probably provide all that is necessary.

Reaction shots are enormously important, as they lead the audience to infer (that is, create) a character's private, inner life. They also provide vital, legitimate cutaways and allow you in editing to combine the best from all available takes. Always make sure you have thoroughly covered the reactions and cutaways for each scene.

BACKLASH AND CRITICISM

Be prepared for personality problems and other friction during shooting. It is not unknown for actors' preferences and criticisms expressed during rehearsal to surface more vehemently under duress. There will be favorite scenes and scenes the actors hate, scenes that involve portraying negative characteristics and even certain lines upon which an actor becomes irrationally fixated. One palliative in serious cases is to allow a take using the actor's alternative wording.

As knowledge of each other's limitations grows, actors become critical or even hostile to each other. Occasionally two actors who are supposed to be lovers take a visceral aversion to each other. Here, loyalty to the project and commitment to their profession can save the project from utter disaster.

However, take heart. The chances are good that you and your cast will like each other and that none of these horror stories will happen to you. But filming makes intense demands on people and a director must be ready to cope with everything human. Directors surely learn as much about the human psyche from directing as they ever do from so-called normal living.

FROM THE CAST

If the cast has become a company, creativity cannot flow only from the director. The cast may continue quite justifiably to level criticism at the script, the crew, or the director. It should be acknowledged and, if constructive, acted upon diplomatically and without guilt. A wise director stimulates and utilizes the creativity of all the major figures in the team, aware that organic development and change will always be something of a threat to everyone's security, including his own.

If, however, criticism is incompatible with the body of work already accumulated, you must say so. Remain open-minded but do not swing like a weather vane. The best way to avoid unwelcome criticism is to be so prepared and so full of interesting demands that everyone is too busy to reflect.

FROM THE CREW

Criticism by the crew should be discreet and kept out of public earshot. Actors find the spectacle of dissent among the crew deeply disturbing. Members of student crews are sometimes unwise enough to imply how much better they could direct than the director, and to publicly voice their improvements. This is an intolerable situation that must be immediately corrected. Nothing diminishes your authority faster than for actors to feel they are being directed by a committee.

Territories should have been clearly demarcated before the shooting starts, and anyone who now strays should privately but firmly be requested to tend his own area and no one else's. Where a crew has a legitimate beef, it should be routed through the DP. There will be occasions when you have to take a necessary but unpopular decision. Take it, bite your tongue, and do not apologize. Like a lot of other things, it is a test of your resolve, and the unpopular decision will also paradoxically be the one everyone knows to be right.

MORALE, FATIGUE, AND INTENSITY

Morale in both crew and cast tends to be interlocked. Giving credit and giving appropriate attention to all members of the team is the best way to create loyalty to the project and to each other. Good leadership trickles down. Even so, immature personalities will fracture as fatigue sets in, or when territory is threatened. Severe fatigue is dangerous not only because people lose their cool but because the work becomes sloppy and essentials get overlooked. Careful and conservative scheduling guards against this.

A simple insurance is to take special care of creature comforts. Your production department should make sure that people are warm, dry, have bathrooms to go to, something to sit down upon between takes, and food and drink. Avoid working longer than four hours without a break, if only for a ten-minute coffee break. Cast and crew alike infer from these attentions that the production cares about them. Most will go to the ends of the earth if they feel valued.

You are the director. Your seriousness and intensity set the tone for the whole shoot. If you are sloppy and laid back, others will outdo you and no film may get made. If you demand a lot of yourself and others but are appreciative and encourage appropriate humor, you will probably run a tight ship. Your vision and how you share it will evoke respect in the entire team. People will follow a visionary anywhere.

Try to mask all negative criticism under a request for a positive alternative. Thank people formally and individually at the end of each day's work. It is good manners and it affirms your respect for each person. By implication you demand that respect in return. Under these conditions, people should willingly accord you the authority you need to do your job.

USING SOCIAL TIMES AND BREAKS

During the shooting period, spend time outside the actual shooting with your cast. It is a mistake to retreat from the intensity of your actors to the understanding comradeship of the crew, however exhausted you may be. Try to keep cast and crew together during meals or rest periods. Frequently, while lunching or downing a beer after work, you will learn something that significantly complements or changes your conceptions. The process of filmmaking itself shakes out many new ideas and perceptions, and generates a shared intensity and sense of discovery that can bind crew and participants in a sense of intoxicating adventure. Conserved and encouraged, this sense of excitement can so awaken everyone's awareness that a profound fellowship and communication develop. Work becomes a joy.

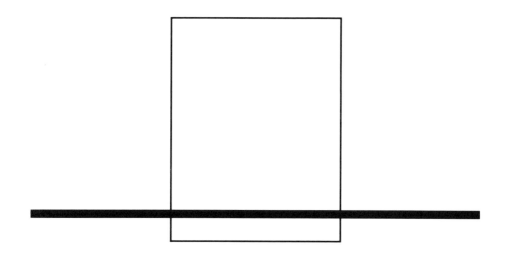

DIRECTING THE CREW

COMPARTMENTING RESPONSIBILITIES

Beginning directors in film school usually try to monitor the whole crew's work. In search of perfection you will have the urge to set the lights and operate the camera, as well as control a hundred other small details. Too often the human presence on the screen, the one aspect the audience really notices, goes neglected. A check on the camera, as we will see in a few moments, is absolutely necessary, but much else must be off-loaded. The director must be willing to give technicians and production personnel control of their areas, but delegation is a two way street. These people must be fully responsible and aware at all times, and take the appropriate initiative without waiting for explicit instructions.

INITIATIVE

Finding crew members who take initiative yet work as a team is not easy. Many people are so passive that they cannot act without instructions, and others take initiative so they can gain complete control. Status and control issues seem to absorb so much of the average person's attention that he or she is unsuited for the give and take of teamwork. Many film students get no further than fulfilling class projects because, already regimented by family and schooling, they can only produce from within a punitive monitoring structure. Most are sensitive and intelligent, but their passivity makes them unsuitable to be film crew members.

Look in a film school's credits for a particular period, and you will find the same few names over and over again in different capacities for different films. These people love the process of filmmaking and will direct one month and be a friend's gaffer or production manager the next. These are the people you hope to have as your crew.

COMMUNICATING

Before shooting begins, all crew members should read the script and contribute ideas that affect their areas of specialty. A director should understand the rudiments of each technician's craft, and be able to communicate in the craft's special terms. That is why this book contains so much about the whole production process.

From you or your delegates, the crew needs positive, concise directions with as much advance warning as possible. The crew will not rise to genuine crises if things that could have been foreseen go unattended. Avoid thinking out loud, especially when the pace heats up. Try instead to produce brief, practical instructions worded so they cannot be misinterpreted. Without being condescending, try to get people to repeat back instructions of any complexity so you are sure they understand. Everything that can be put in writing in advance should be.

Remember, wherever possible during shooting, the AD and DP should deal with all production and technical questions. This releases you to do your job properly, which is to answer the needs of the actors and to concentrate on building the film's dramatic content.

RELATIONS WITH CAST AND THE PUBLIC

Every crew member must understand some of the givens of film crew life. When actors privately seek out their opinions on the quality of the work, they must react with extreme diplomacy. However flattering, this is probably neurosis and, wrongly handled, can become dangerously divisive. To avoid such pitfalls, crew members should only be supportive, which is mainly what actors seek. When actors solicit support for negative attitudes, or communicate something the director should know about, the crew member should remain neutral and afterwards discreetly report the situation up the chain of command. Warn crew never to voice criticism that can weaken anyone else's authority, either on the set or off it. This preserves the all-important working morale.

The same caution should be exercised by the crew in conversation with bystanders on location, who may take it upon themselves to cause trouble or attract unwelcome publicity. Any purposeful questions should be referred to the AD or other crew member delegated to deal with public relations.

LOOK THROUGH THE CAMERA

When every new shot has been set up, and before the first take, it is imperative that you look through the camera (**film**) so you can confer with the camera operator and make sure the starting composition is as you expect. You should do the same at the first take's end to check the camera's finishing composition.

When there is a lot of moving camera coverage and you need to agree with your operator on compositions, angle, size of the image, etc., you should walk the actors (or stand-ins) through the take, freezing them at salient points to agree on what should appear in the frame. To stabilize these decisions, your crew will need to make chalk marks on the floor for both actors and camera dolly. Everyone will have to hit their marks. This kind of precision separates the experienced from the inexperienced. Trying to impose this degree of control on an inexperienced ensemble may be an exercise in futility that wastes time and damages cast morale.

Because framing, composition, lighting, and sound coverage are the formal structuring that translate a live world into cinema, the director needs to keep the strongest possible contact with the outcome on the screen. When shooting on **videotape,** you can watch the whole take on the monitor during recording and know immediately what you have got. With **film,** however, the results remain in agonizing doubt until the rushes return from the laboratory.

In **film,** clearly briefing the technical crew through the DP and monitoring what the camera is doing is all you can do to ensure your vision is going down on film. Not to check on these factors invariably leads to some rude shocks at the rushes viewing, when it is usually too late to make changes.

MAKING PROGRESS

Shooting is stop-start work, with many holdups for lighting or camera setups. A crew can easily slow down while everyone waits for A. N. Other. Nobody quite knows what they are waiting for, but everyone knows that someone else has not finished. Eventually someone realizes that everyone is waiting for someone else—the notorious and elusive A. N. Other. This exasperating situation easily afflicts a tired crew. A good AD is among other things a sheepdog who constantly monitors bottlenecks and who barks everyone into action the moment that shooting can continue.

WHEN YOU AND YOUR CREW ARE ALONE

When you are alone with crew members during the shoot, encourage them to discuss the dramatic elements of the shooting. Some members such as grips, electricians, and ADs do their work before shooting and stand observing during the actual take. What they notice may usefully complement your sense of what is really happening. You, after all, have goals from rehearsal to fulfill while they are seeing the action for the first time, and have an audience-like reaction.

The work of the camera operator, DP, and sound recordist demands such localized attention to quality that they cannot be open to dramatic content in the same way. You will therefore get a very mixed bag of observations, some of them way off track. Hear and encourage all views, but do not feel you must act upon or rebuff ideas that imply criticism of your work. If, however, most of the crew, including the women members, find the main female character abrasive, you should take serious notice.

WRAPPING FOR THE DAY

At the end of a working day, thank actors and crew members personally, and make sure that everything in a borrowed location has been replaced exactly as found. This attention is someone else's property signifies your concern and appreciation. It also helps ensure a welcome should you want to return. Initial reluctance to accept a film crew's presence often arises because people have heard a horror story about another crew that was inconsiderate.

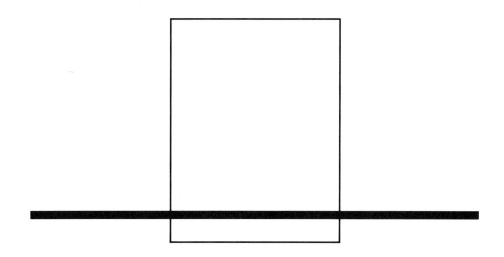

C·H·A·P·T·E·R 1·4

MONITORING PROGRESS

A director's nightmare during shooting is that an important angle or shot will be overlooked then discovered later when it is impossible to reconvene crew and cast. In low-budget filmmaking where a few people must work fast, such a catastrophe can easily occur. Working hand-to-mouth, intentions get modified and marking off a list of intended shots may incompletely reflect what was done, or may be so covered with changes that the list itself becomes a source of confusion.

Better would be a graphic representation (as always) to show the state of play at a glance. In fact one can further mark the bracketed script copy to provide a thorough and up to date version. From this anyone can see how the sequence was covered and how it might be edited. Unlike a list of scene numbers, interpretation requires no cross-referencing or special knowledge.

During the shoot, the script supervisor should carry the bracketed shooting script (see Figure 10–1) and accompanying text. As each setup is completed, he or she should ink over the pencil lines to show what was actually shot. A color system can be used for different shot sizes or angles if preferred. The start and finishing point of each setup's span and the angles and groupings it covers all become clearly visible. Where your shoot went as planned, the scrip supervisor simply overlays the pencil planning lines. Where there are changes, new markings demonstrate the difference between intentions and actuality.

At any point, director or script supervisor can glance at the marked up script to review how the sequence will cut together, or to see what alternative permutations are possible should the preferred editing strategy not work out.

DEPLETION OF RESOURCES

No matter in what order you shoot, your PM should be able to compute how much money has gone out and what should be the current camera roll number (or cassette) if the project is on track.

A production that does not keep some track of resources is like an expedition that eats steak near home and then has to boil its shoes in the wilderness to stay alive. Many beginners' shoots are liberally covered in the first stages but stretched so thin towards the end that the material can hardly be edited. If a cost projection was carried out (see Figure 4–6) it is an uncomplicated matter for the PM to track where money and stock are going, and how fast. Knowing early that a complicated sequence has consumed more resources than intended signals that you must either raise more money, economize to get back on track, or be ready to drop a "luxury" scene.

DRAMATIC QUALITY

There are various levels of thoroughness in monitoring dramatic quality. To see no rushes until the shoot is completed is to not monitor quality at all, except subjectively as the action is shot. For a low-budget **film** unit away on location, this may seem the only practical solution, although its risks are manifold. Running rushes on a silent projector is better than nothing, but you should see them synced up. Alternatively, get a cassette copy of the rushes made in home base and see them on a videocassette recorder (VCR) at the location. The rushes copy can be shot from the editing machine's screen, or from a projected image. Neither camera nor sound crews will think much of this representation of their work, but it will tell you much about essentials like acting, camera handling, composition, and so forth.

For a **video** unit a daily rushes session should be obligatory. A unit, however tired, is usually intensely interested in its own work. Do not include the actors who are likely to be thrown by seeing their own work (see "When to Show Actors Their Performances" in Chapter 7). A feature unit will see its rushes every day (hence the term *dailies* for rushes) so that any reshooting can be done before the set is struck or lighting becomes difficult to reconstruct.

The best level of quality monitoring results when the editor is employed from the first day of shooting. As the materials for a sequence come in, he or she makes a rough cut and shows it as soon as possible to the director. Here not only raw materials come under surveillance, but every aspect of the film is seen in its edited form. Any serious inconsistencies in acting, lighting, framing, sound, or continuity show up early enough to make corrections, and the director can see if stylistic intentions are working out. A rough assembly of the whole film can be seen a few days after the end of the shoot, avoiding what would otherwise be a delay of weeks or months. Because this assembly method places a premium upon speed and requires the director to trust the editor's judgment, it is seldom used by beginners.

FULFILLING ONE'S AUTHORSHIP INTENTIONS

The big questions during shooting are, am I fulfilling my authorial intentions, and do I have a film? Success is very difficult to measure except in unreassuringly subjective terms. One way to make this easier is break your intentions down into specific goals.

Earlier ("Graphics to Help Reveal Dramatic Dynamics" in Chapter 3) I talked about graphing out expectations for a scene to clarify the changes that must take place and to show where each new stage is initiated. Moment to moment, each scene by its action should impart what each character is trying to get or do. The audience needs a sense of each character's will as he or she strives under ever-changing conditions to realize one desire after another. Keeping these currents alive and flowing is your major goal. Doing so allows the audience to experience the screen's most tangibly dramatic element. Effective performances make you feel what the audience should feel while you are directing. It is something you recognize, not something you have to struggle to see.

It is extremely important to preestablish with your actors the detail in each moment of their performances; otherwise your direction may become rudderless during the shoot. Professional directors acquire so much preparatory experience along the way that their approach is internalized, like the reflexes one uses to ride a bicycle. For beginners, success lies in developing clear detail and, during the shoot, making sure the detail and clarity of performance is sustained and emotionally moving.

Even when you do all this, there remains something fundamental but less definable to assess. After every scene has been played, there is an elusive imprint left on the observer, one that interests your cast more than anything else. To capture it, ask yourself questions. To give some idea how such questions work, I have applied typical ones to two takes of a hypothetical scene set in a bus station where, late at night, two stranded passengers start a desultory conversation. Action and dialogue of each take is identical, yet each elicits different answers from the observer:

1. What life-roles did the characters adopt?

    Take 1: "Two of life's losers unenthusiastically size each other up."

    Take 2: "Two depressed, disgruntled people each decide whether they can be bothered with company at this time."

2. What truth was played out here?

    Take 1: "A person tends to instinctively despise someone else with the same shortcomings."

    Take 2: "Alienated people tend to isolate themselves further."

3. What metaphor sums up how the scene emerged?

    Take 1: "Two neutered cats circle round each other."

    Take 2: "Two exhausted convicts decide it is not worth cooperating to break rocks."

Such metaphysical questions make one transcend the tunnel vision that prevents the director from seeing beyond plot details and the intended physical movements. These answers are quite typical and reveal subtle differences between the two takes, signaling that a different subtext is spontaneously emerging from each. It arises from variables in the consciousness of the players at the time. The answers show how utterly wrong is the idea of a "finished performance." Relationship on or off the camera is alive and always in flux. All takes on all angles of all learned scenes are unpredictable of outcome and require this special sensitivity of interpretation. If as a director one has narrow expectations, such impressions, though immediately available to an audience, are hidden and evasive; hidden unless he or she deliberately digs them out.

Be aware of the dialectics in each scene and make sure they are well evidenced. By dialectics, I mean the paradoxes and opposing polarities of opinion and will that set person against person, movement against movement, idea against idea, and the parts of a person against himself or herself. These are the spars, pressures, and tensions, often insoluble and irresolvable, that stand out like majestic bridge construction in a fog of banality.

My questions, centering as they do on roles, truth, and metaphors are inconveniently metaphysical for the hurly-burly of the set. They are never easy to answer, especially for the uninitiated. But answering the larger questions is the way to break into that sealed compartment of your consciousness that already knows and recognizes the scene's underlying qualities. Having succeeded, you can be practical in remedying the shortfall between intention and execution.

MEASURING PROGRESS

Keep your intentions clear and keep them handy in list form (see "Crib Sheets" in Chapter 10) so you have access to your objectives and can check near the end that you have covered all your bases. My example of intentions for the scene looks rather rigid and locked down, but the list is only a safety net, not a sacred text. It reminds you of what to look for, what to expect, and how to get a decent range of material from the scene. It is a resource, not a straitjacket.

Keep nothing in your head that can be dumped in list form on a piece of paper. Lists are a godsend when one is too tired to think—a condition that descends rapidly during sustained shooting. At each juncture you may now assess whether you have won or lost each of the individual battles. This is hard and lonely work because one is usually underwhelmed by what takes place before the camera.

Seeing the rushes generally reveals that there is more present on film than one realized at the time. But during the shoot one often suffers a gnawing doubt just when one is supposed to be feeling creative. This, of course, is not an emotion one dares to share with anybody.

MOVING BEYOND REALISM

The point at which a film moves beyond the literalness of recorded realism, is the point at which cinema links up with its sister arts like music, dance, theatre, and literature. There is no set formula for achieving this and you cannot know if you are succeeding until the film is fully edited. Your film's inner life comes from the juxtaposition of materials, from assembling them into a provocative antiphony, from the life of the players, from the mood of the company's life together. It is also expressed through sound composition, expressionistic lighting or settings, or by other approaches germane to your piece. It's something you hope for, but not something over which you can have total and conscious control.

CEDING CONTROL

Artistic control means paradoxically that at a certain moment of conviction you actually give up your control to some intuitively felt sense of truth. Do not worry about this. If nothing like it shows itself during the shoot, it is usually manifest in the editing room, when an assembled piece will begin to make its own insistent demands, dictating to you and your editor, its creators, what it wants its final form to be. Like one's children, each of one's films turns out to have its own nature, its own imperfections and integrity, and each will start making its own autonomous decisions. What a shock and delight it is to begin assisting one's film make itself.

Similar capitulation may be required during shooting. A typical situation is an actor producing an unexpected and interesting quality that affects the character's potential or skews a certain situation you are shooting. You have to decide whether to rein it in or whether to acknowledge the new direction and live with the consequences. Whatever you do, it impacts on the other players and puts your authority on the line. You feel both your artistic control and the security of your career threatened. Yet to deny these emerging, elusive truths is to choose security over experiment. Directing is never free of moral and ethical dilemmas, nor of compromise.

The elements of authorship are analyzed in greater depth in Part IV: Aesthetics and Authorship. Here I contend that if you are engaged in authorship you are really searching for the counterparts to your own experience.

PRODUCTION SUMMARY

The points summarized here are only those most salient. Some are commonly overlooked. To find them or anything else relating to the production phase, go to the table of contents at the beginning of this part.

PLANNING ON PAPER

- With the script supervisor, turn the screenplay into a final shooting script.
- With your DP, draw a floor plan for each sequence showing characters' movements.
- Mark in the scene's axis (or axes) and camera positions.
- Mark up the script to show coverage from each camera position.
- Plan an establishing shot to clarify scene geography and character placement.
- Use movement to link angles at action-match cutting points.
- Make sure there will be plenty of overlap between angles so you will have adequate choice of cutting points.
- Use characters' eyeline shifts. Follow them with a camera movement or with a point of view shot.
- Decide where the scene will profit from changes between subjective (near axis) and objective (far from axis) camera angles.
- Cover any regrouping of characters in a comprehensive shot so that spatial changes can be made evident.
- Show relatedness through composition wherever possible so you do not have to manufacture juxtaposition through editing.
- Sketch a storyboard frame for each camera setup to make sure screen direction is maintained.
- Make up crib sheets for each scene with "must not forget" points listed.
- Cover important moments of the scene from more than one angle.

SCHEDULING AND RECONNAISSANCE

- Be pessimistic when scheduling; you will never have too much time to shoot.
- Schedule the early shooting for a slower pace.
- Arrange contingency alternatives (bad weather, etc.).
- Crews need a typewritten schedule with map details and phone contact numbers.
- PM should double-check lodging and dining arrangements for locations.
- For time economy bring food to a unit, not the unit to food.
- Check location with a compass to assess available light's direction.
- When everyone is in transit, make sure there is a central phone contact.
- Map out electrical supplies, permissible loadings, circuits, and their fuses.

GETTING READY TO SHOOT

- Remember to include tools and spares.
- For location bring first aid and basic medicine kit.
- Locate nearest medical facilities if on location.
- Research nearest point for repairs, spares, and dealers.

- PM should prepare daily cost projection.
- Make sure everyone knows his or her responsibilities. Every area of the undertaking should fall within someone's responsibility.
- Establish crew protocols for dealing with actors or the public.
- Hold a potluck party before shooting so you start out with good morale.
- Warn actors that shooting is slow, and to bring books, chess, yoga mat, whatever.

SHOOTING

- Check scene's important points on crib card.
- Delegate directing the crew to your DP.
- Make the decision for a further take quickly, so everyone stays focused.
- Make allowances for extreme tension in everyone at the beginning.
- Cater to creature comforts to keep up morale.
- Give credit publicly to anyone who deserves it.
- Use breaks for mending fences and picking up loose ends of information.
- Have personal exchange with all crew members so you are seen as a personal friend.
- Script supervisor keeps strict watch over coverage and matching.
- Sound recordist listens for any inadequate lines, and shoots a wild track.
- Sound recordist can ask for silence to pick up any atmospheres or sound effects on location.
- Keep dissent away from ears of actors.
- Ask your crew when you need advice or help.
- Do not wrap without shooting reactions, cutaways, and location presence track.
- Replace locations exactly as you found them.
- Thank everyone personally at the end of each day.
- Director and key personnel confer at day's end to lay plans for next day.

MISE-EN-SCÈNE

- Know whose point of view audience should sympathize with moment to moment.
- Use camera for storytelling, not just as a passive observer.
- Decide with DP or camera operator the size and framing of each shot.
- Look through camera often to check framing, composition, and image size.
- During shot stand close to camera so you see more or less what it is seeing.
- Make the location a character, not a mere container for action.
- Try wherever possible to create a sense of depth in the frame.
- Use characters' eyelines as guides for shooting safety cutaways.

- Use a particular lens for its dramatic revelation potential as well as to cope with limitations imposed by the shooting environment.
- Decide whether there is a simpler technical means to achieve the same effect.
- Consider varying camera height from shot to shot.
- Decide what the camera can legitimately look through.
- Slow down or simplify character movements if the camera is to follow them.

DIRECTING ACTORS

- Give actors private, personal feedback and encouragement from time to time.
- Make each character active in his or her own surroundings.
- Each situation must reveal something about the characters through behavior.
- Make sure each character has plenty to do, externally or internally, to avoid self-consciousness.
- Remind actors often where, emotionally and physically, their character is coming from.
- Be natural so you do not signal to actors that it is a scare situation.
- Support, question, and challenge. Make lots of interesting demands.
- Feed in the unexpected and side coach when a scene needs refreshing.

AUTHORSHIP AND MONITORING PROGRESS

- Hear and see the scene's actual subtext, not what you want it to say.
- Make sure each beat is clear so the dialectics of the scene become evident.
- Cover exposition and other vital points more than one way.
- Examine the imprint a take has left on you: what life roles were played out? What came from the characters this particular time? What truths emerged?
- Check your crib card to see what is being gained and what needs bolstering.
- Be sensitive to the scene's hidden meaning and energy, and allow it to exert the appropriate control.
- Make sure you have on film the necessary confrontations inherent in your movie's system of issues.
- See rushes as often as possible.

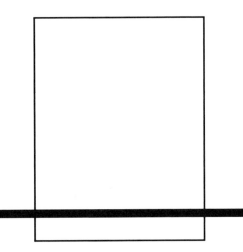

P·A·R·T I·I·I

POSTPRODUCTION

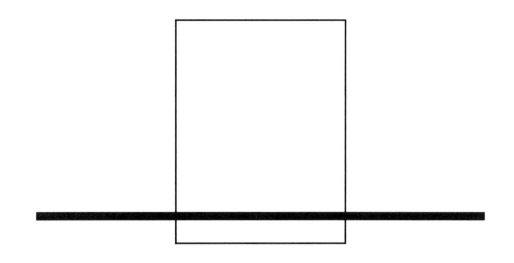

PREPARING TO EDIT

While most of the operations described in this chapter are the responsibility of the editor, a director must be familiar with the principles involved in order to get the most out of the final stages of making the film.

EDITING: FILM OR VIDEO?

For speed and inexpensive results onscreen, the beginning director is much more likely to attempt the first sophisticated work in videotape than film. Videotape equipment of all kinds is being so rapidly developed and marketed that it would be imprudent to make specific recommendations in this book. However, some generalized information about editing in either medium is likely to be useful.

Few independent filmmakers edit on their own equipment because it is too costly to purchase. Instead, one either rents editing time or talks one's way into being allowed access to free facilities. Quite sophisticated and underutilized equipment may be found at small TV stations and in audiovisual departments in hospitals, police departments, universities, and high schools. You can also rent time from a production house (more expensive) or from a film or video cooperative. Cooperatives are good because they hold prices down and provide a center of activities for like-minded people.

If you can find none of the above, do not despair. It is not unusual for the owner of a commercial operation to allow someone dedicated and impoverished to use the equipment during downtime, either at no cost or for a very modest sum. A surprising number of hard-bitten media types have a soft spot for the committed novice, and many an unlikely partnership has developed from such an initial relationship.

Film has one devastatingly simple advantage over videotape; any part of an edited workprint can be substituted, transposed, or adjusted for length, so long as you remember to make appropriate adjustments to its corresponding sound track. The situation is radically different for videotape because it is built up as a series of linear additions. To shorten the length of an early shot, for instance, means either lengthening the following shot by the deleted amount, or retransfering absolutely everything subsequent to the change.

A POSTPRODUCTION OVERVIEW

Postproduction is that phase of filmmaking where the raw materials of sound and picture rushes are transformed into the film seen by the audience. Supervised by the editor, both **film** or **video** postproduction include the following:

1. Synchronizing sound and action in preparation for first rushes screening (**film** or double system **video** recording only)
2. Screening rushes for the director's choices and comments
3. Marking up the script
4. Logging material in preparation for editing
5. Making a first assembly
6. Making the rough cut
7. Evolving the rough cut into a fine cut
8. Supervising narration or looping (postsynchronized voice recording)
9. Preparing for and supervising original music recording
10. Finding, recording, and laying component parts of multitrack sound
11. Supervising mix-down of these tracks into one smooth final track
12. Supervising shooting of titles and necessary graphics
13. Supervising the film lab or video postproduction finalization processes that in **film** involve laboratory work to produce a fine quality release print for projection, including
    - conforming (or negative cutting; the original negative is cut and reassembled to match the workprint so that fresh prints may be struck for release),
    - making a sound optical negative from the sound magnetic master, timing (or color grading) the picture negative in association with the DP in order to produce the first answer (or trial) print, and
    - producing multiple release prints

In **video** there are processes analogous to film's for producing a broadcast quality tape.

1. On-line (computerized) editing (a computerized rig is used to assemble a high-quality version of the film from camera original cassettes to match the

much degraded and almost unviewable workprint. This process is the video equivalent of the film process' conforming or negative cutting.)

2. Timebase correction (electronic processing to ensure the resulting tape conforms to broadcasting standards) and color correction

3. Copy duplication for release prints

THE EDITOR'S ROLE AND RESPONSIBILITIES

From the number and complexity of the postproduction processes you can see how important the editor is both technically and creatively. Being an editor is for this reason the most common prelude to directing.

DIPLOMACY

The editor receives the director at a time of considerable anxiety and uncertainty: the film is shot but has yet to prove itself coherent. At this time most directors, however confident they appear, are acutely aware of their material's failures, and are often suffering a sort of postnatal depression in the trough following the sustained impetus of shooting. If the editor and director do not know each other well, both will usually be formal and cautious. The editor is taking over the director's baby, and the director often carries mixed and potentially explosive emotions.

PERSONALITY

The good editor is patient, highly organized, ready to experiment endlessly, and diplomatic about trying to get his or her own way.

CREATIVE CONTRIBUTION

A good editor, whose job goes far beyond the physical task of assembly, is aware of all the material's possibilities. Directors are handicapped in this area through over-familiarity with the material's original intentions. Not being present at shooting, the editor comes to the material with an unobligated and unprejudiced eye, and is ideally placed to reveal to the director what possibilities and what problems lie dormant within the material.

On a documentary production, or an improvised fiction film, the editor is really the second director, since the materials supplied are usually capable of broad interpretation and, unlike a scripted production, require a willingness to make responsible subjective judgments. But even in a tightly scripted fiction film the editor needs the insight and confidence to know when to bend the original intentions to better serve the film's underlying goals. Editing is in any case much more than following a script, just as music is much more than playing the right notes. Indeed, composing is the closest analogy to the editor's work.

RUSHES

Feature films usually employ the editor from the start of shooting, so the unit's output can be assembled as fast as it is shot. With low-budget films, however, economics may prevent any cutting taking place until everything is shot. This is risky because errors and omissions may go undetected until it is too late to rectify them. One should therefore try to arrange to see dailies. Shooting on video permits rushes to be viewed immediately, so that any reshooting can be scheduled before quitting the location. Many 35mm feature film cameras now make a simultaneous video recording, which allows instant replay and mitigates the unit's absolute dependency upon the script supervisor's powers of observation. The low-budget filmmaker will have no such luxury, but if rushes can be synchronized at home base they can be transferred from the editing machine screen to VHS tape at minimal cost, and seen at the location on a VCR.

PARTNERSHIP

Relationships between directors and editors vary greatly according to the chemistry of temperaments, but it is usual for the director to discuss the intentions behind each scene, and to give any necessary special directions.

The editor then sets to work on making the assembly, a first raw version of the film. Wise directors leave the cutting room during this period to maintain a fresh eye for the what editor produces. The obsessive director on the other hand will sit in the cutting room night and day watching the editor's every action. Whether this is at all an amenable arrangement depends on the editor. Some like to be able to debate their way through the cutting procedure. Others prefer being left alone to work out the film's initial problems in bouts of intense concentration over their logs and machinery.

In the end, very little escapes discussion; every scene and every cut is scrutinized, questioned, weighed, and balanced. The creative relationship is intense, often drawing in all the cutting room staff and the producer. The editor must often use delicate but sustained leverage against what he senses are those prejudices and obsessions that grip every director. Ralph Rosenblum's book, *When the Shooting Stops,* shows just how varied and even crazy editor/director relationships can be.

DIRECTOR/EDITORS

In a low-budget movie the editor and director are for economic reasons sometimes the same person. This is particularly a mistake for the inexperienced. Another mind in creative tension with the director is an inestimable asset, ensuring against an early tumble into the abyss of subjectivity.

Every film is created as an experience for an audience. If the filmmakers allow their valuations to evolve into over-familiarity, cuts will get shorter and shorter and scenes will be interwoven to the point where only the film's progenitors can still understand it. Without an editor, the director never gets away from the material, and falls prey to subjective familiarity with his or her material.

Sometimes a director will personally edit because he or she was formerly an editor and cannot trust anyone else to "do it properly"; sometimes the director is imbued with the *auteur* theory, and edits in the belief that it will preserve a unified artistic identity for the film. Such impulses signal insecurities about maintaining control.

In truth, the needs imposed by collaboration, the scrutiny of the emerging work by an equal, and the editor's advocacy of alternative views all tend to help produce a tougher and better balanced film than any one person can generate alone.

PREPARING TO EDIT

Working with a professional editor can be intimidating if you do not know what the many procedures are for. All are either necessary or save time and effort, thus allowing the editor to edit instead of search for lost footage.

SYNCING RUSHES

It is beyond the scope of this book to describe the technical process of **film** rushes syncing, other than to say that the two strips of film—the picture marked at the point where the clapper board bar has just closed, and the sound track marked at the clapper bar's impact—are aligned in a synchronizer or table editor so that discrete takes can be cumulatively assembled for a sync viewing. Every respectable filmmaking manual covers this process (see Bibliography).

KEEPING A RUSHES BOOK

When assembling rushes for either a **film** or **video** viewing, make a preparatory log of slate numbers. Known as the rushes book, this should be a sturdy notebook that will not disintegrate from heavy use. Divide the pages by sequences and allow one line per take, leaving blank space for cryptic notes during the rushes viewing. Figure 15–1 shows a completed section of the rushes book.

CREW RUSHES VIEWING SESSION

At the completion of shooting, even when rushes may have been viewed piecemeal, try to let the crew see their work in its entirety. This is the only way for everyone to learn the maximum for the future, important if you expect to work

```
                         LAUNDRY SEQUENCE
         1-1   NVG
          -2   End good for David
          -3   Best, but focus change NG (slow)
         2-1   Safety cutaway only
         3-1   NG
          -2   Fair (Liz has interesting dreamy reaction to bad news)
           3   Liz angriest - try to use
           4   Best for consistency - David's reaction best in T2
```

FIGURE 15–1 ————————————————————————————

Typical rushes book notes.

with the same crew again. Screening may have to be broken up into more than one session, since four hours or so of unedited footage is the most on which even the dedicated can maintain concentration. The editor may be present at this viewing, but discussion is likely to be a crew-centered postmortem rather than one useful to the editor.

EDITOR AND DIRECTOR'S VIEWING SESSION

At the editor's rushes showing with the director, it is probably best to run one sequence at a time, and to stop and discuss its problems and possibilities. The editor will need the rushes book (see above) to record the director's choices and to note any special cutting information.

A marathon rushes viewing highlights the relativity of the material and the problems the piece as a whole may face. You might discover that certain mannerisms are used repeatedly by one actor, and must be cut around during editing if he or she is not to appear phony. Or you might see for the first time that one of your two principals is often more interesting to watch and threatens to unbalance the film.

GUT FEELINGS MATTER

Note down any unexpected mood or feeling. If, during the rushes viewing, you find yourself reacting to a particular character with, "I somehow feel she is unusually sincere here," note it down. These are seldom isolated personal reactions. Many gut feelings seem so logically unfounded that it is tempting to ignore or forget them. Yet what triggered them remains embedded in the material for any first-time audience.

The spontaneous perceptions you note down will be a useful resource when inspiration lags later from over-familiarity with the material. If you fail to commit them in some form to paper they are likely to share the fate of important dreams, which evaporate if you do not preserve them.

TAKING NOTES

It is useful to have someone present who can take these dictated notes. Try never to let your attention leave the screen, as you can easily miss important moments and nuances.

REACTIONS

There will probably be debates over the effectiveness, meaning, or importance of different parts of the filming, and different crew members may have opposing feelings about the credibility and motivation of some of the characters. Listen rather than participate, for these may be the reactions of your future audience.

THE ONLY FILM IS IN THE RUSHES

The sum of the rushes viewing is a notebook full of choices and observations (both the director's and those of the editor), and a fragmentary impression of the movie's potential and deficiencies. Absolutely nothing beyond what can be seen and felt from the rushes is any longer relevant to the film you are making. The script is a historic relic, like an old map to a rebuilt city. Put it away in the attic for your biographer. You and your editor must find a film in the rushes.

Once you confront the rushes, you change hats. You are no longer the instigator of the material but a surrogate for the audience. You must have no knowledge of prior intentions and your understanding and emotions must come wholly from the screen.

SYNC CODING

This **film** process is also known as edge numbering or Dupont numbering. After the rushes have been viewed (to ensure that they are indeed in sync), a film laboratory prints yellow ink numbers every foot or six inches. Sync code numbers, printed in parallel on both sound and picture, function as unique, unambiguous sync marks, allowing original sync to be restored at any time. Recorded in a log, they also allow almost any length of anonymous-looking film to be reunited with its parent trims or off-cuts.

POOR MAN'S SYNC CODING

Because edge coding is expensive and not strictly necessary, subsistence-level filmmakers handwrite numbers every three feet or so, using a three-foot loop in the synchronizer as a length guide.

TIME CODING AND WINDOW DUB

When shooting on **video** a time code is necessary if you are to later use on-line (computerized) postproduction editing. Time code is either generated at the time of recording and electronically interwoven with the video signal, or, more usual in small-format recorders, the camera original is sent after shooting to a post-production house for time coding and window dubbing. First a digital time code is laid down in whichever sound track was unused. Be sure you have clearly marked on each cassette which track is free or you will lose original sound. Next a copy cassette is made from each original tape with the time code displayed visually at the bottom of the frame in a window as cassette number, hours, minutes, seconds, and frames (see Figure 15–2). Every frame in your production now has an individual identifying set of numbers, necessary for on-line editing.

LOGGING THE RUSHES

In any log, since scenes will be shot (and therefore logged) out of order, it is a good idea to start each new sequence on a fresh page so it can eventually be filed in script order.

In **film,** every new camera start receives a new clapper board number (see Chapter 11, "Shot and Scene Identification" for a fuller explanation of different marking systems). As we have said, the clapper is there to allow the editor to easily synchronize the separately recorded picture and sound. With **video,** since picture and sound are usually recorded alongside each other on the same tape, no syncing up is necessary and a simpler marking system can be employed. Scene

FIGURE 15–2

Time-coded video frame.

numbers (and clapper boards) are not even strictly necessary because videotape editing methods do not permit working materials to be physically dismantled.

The **film** editing log on the other hand may have to facilitate easy access to thousands of small rolls of film. The filing system and the log format will depend upon the editing equipment in use. If an upright Moviola—still the fearsome workhorse of many cutting rooms—is to be used, the workprint will be broken down into individual takes, and filed numerically in cans or drawers. If a table editor, such as Steenbeck or Kem is used, the editor is more likely to withdraw selected sections from large rolls, each containing materials for a single scene. Even then, practice will depend on the work preferences of the editor. If large rolls are used, film logs may be organized like videocassette logs to reflect what is to be found cumulatively in that particular rushes roll.

Film, using separate sound and picture in the cutting room, requires that you log photographic edge numbers and the inked-on sync code numbers (or hand-applied sync code numbers) for the beginning and end of each take. Figure 15–3 is a typical film log entry for script scene 29. A log like this is a mine of useful information. We can see how many takes were attempted, how long each

Scene	Edge #	Sync Code #	Cam Roll	Sound Roll	Date
29-1-1	29J6 434114- 158	000 - 018	14	6	13 Aug 87
2	434159- 207	019 - 038	"	"	"
3	434208- 222	039 - 050	"	"	"
29-2-1	34Z7 945781- 879	051 - 099	15	"	"
2	945880- 904	100 - 151	"	"	"
29-3-1	945905- 965	153 - 186	"	7	"
2	945966- 971	187 - 193	"	"	"
3	945972-6034	194 - 224	"	"	"
29-4-1	21X3 100676- 771	225 - 277	9	MOS	14 Aug 87

FIGURE 15–3

Typical film log book entries.

scene and each take were, where to find particular takes in camera original rolls if we need to make reprints, even at what points the camera magazine was changed and which magazines started a new day.

The **video** editing log is a set of cumulative numbers that allows the editor to quickly locate the right piece of action in a cassette that may hold from 20 to 120 minutes of action. It gives the starting point for each new scene and take. Descriptions should be brief and serve only to remind someone knowing the material what to expect. Note that the log (see Figure 15–4) records function, not quality; there is no attempt to add the qualitative notes from the rushes book. To do so would overload the page and make it hard to use.

The figures at the left are minutes and seconds, but might be cumulative numbers from the digital counter on your player deck, or if your materials are time-coded, would be the code displayed in the electronic window.

In the log examples there are a number of standard abbreviations for shot terminology which are listed in the glossary. Rule a dividing line between sequences and give the sequence a heading in bold writing. Since the log exists to help quickly locate material, any divisions, indexes, or color codes you can devise will assist the eye in making selections and ultimately save time. This is especially so for a production with many hours of rushes. When logging is complete, the editor is ready to prepare the script.

MARKING UP THE SCRIPT

Each page of the script should end up looking like Figure 15–5. Although the editor's markings appear to duplicate the script supervisor's marked up pages (Figure 10–1) they are made in the peace of the cutting room and show only the footage that finally and definitively exists in the cutting room. At a glance the editor can see from the bracketing and notations what angles exist for every moment of the scene, and which takes were considered best. This greatly speeds

```
            Cassette 12 SCENE 15: HOTEL LOBBY (NIGHT)

  00:00   43-1   WS Henry entering hotel lobby.
  00:31     2
  00:59     3
  01:41   44-1   MS Henry seen through palm tree.
  01:51     2
  02:24     3
  03:02     4
  03:35     5        (uses whip pan)
  03:54   45-1   CS clerk's hands writing.
  04:17   46-1   MCS clerk's face as he works. Stops, smelling smoke.
  04:46     2
  05:11   47-1   Phone grabbed (4 rounds)
```

FIGURE 15–4 ————————————————————————————

Typical videocassette log entries.

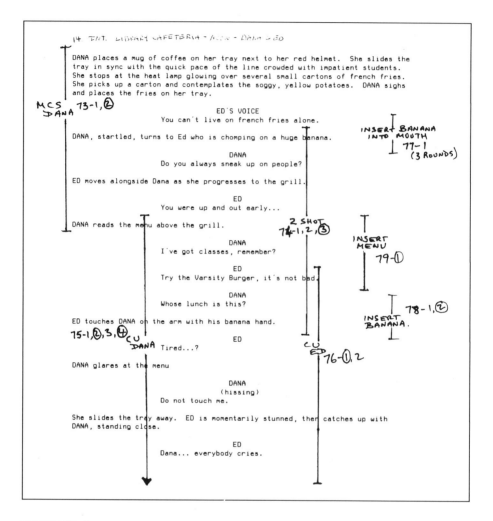

FIGURE 15—5

Editor's script marked up with rushes coverage.

up assessing alternative cover during the lengthy period of refining the cut. This is a time of problem-solving when graphic representation instead of thickets of description can save untold time and energy.

To mark up the script, run the rushes on a viewing or editing machine, concentrating on one scene and running one camera setup at a time. Note that a change of lens is treated as a new setup, for although the camera may not be physically moved, the framing and composition will have changed. Each setup is represented as a line bracketing what the angle covers. Shots that continue over the page end in a arrow. Leave a space in the line and neatly write in the scene number, all its takes (circling those chosen), and the briefest possible shot description. More detailed information can now be quickly found in the continuity reports or rushes book.

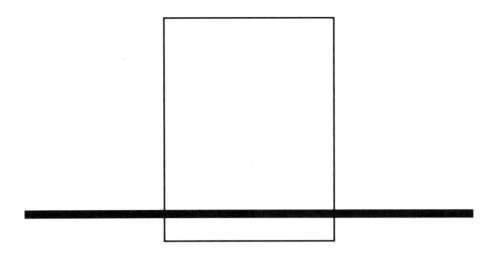

C·H·A·P·T·E·R 1·6

EDITING THE FIRST ASSEMBLY

THE PHYSICAL PROCESS FOR FILM

MACHINERY

For those unused to handling **film,** the best piece of equipment is undoubtedly one of the excellent flatbed table editors such as the Steenbeck (Figure 16–1). It keeps sound and picture in constant sync but allows either to be moved in relation to the other. Sound and picture are simply spliced into the left hand side of the film's passage through the machine.

SOUND TRACK EVOLUTION

Until the fine-cut stage, the sound track is dialogue only, assembled into a single track. This is a temporary compromise, for within a single sequence several mike positions may be cut together and the sound may vary in level and quality. Since the priority at this stage is to achieve a correct dramatic balance, the simplest assembly method is used to allow rapid changes during the lengthy and experimental business of achieving a fine cut.

Once a fine cut is achieved, dialogue tracks are split into separate tracks to allow the appropriate control over each, and effects (FX), music, and atmosphere tracks will be laid as appropriate. Some sequences may need postsynchronizing (also known as looping) because the original dialogue tracks, perhaps recorded by an expressway, are insufficiently intelligible.

A chart is made of all tracks laid, especially because the sound editor will probably have laid extra tracks to allow for experimental alternatives. Editor,

FIGURE 16–1

Steenbeck flatbed table editing machine.

chart, and tracks then go to a sound studio where specialists mix the tracks under the director's and editor's guidance into a final mix, a process determining much of the film's artistic effectiveness with an audience.

PICTURE EVOLUTION

The final-cut workprint picture will eventually go to a conformer, who very carefully cuts the camera original (nowadays a negative, but formerly quite often a reversal original) to exactly match what is by now a very tired and beaten up workprint. The conforming process uses cement splices, which require an overlap and therefore lost frames of camera original to each side of the splice. While editing workprint, therefore, never use adjacent shots without dropping out three frames between them. These frames you keep in case you later decide to reconstitute the two shots back into one. This precaution, and this alone, allows a conformer to edit the camera original to the butt-spliced workprint.

In the lab a photographic sound track is made from the magnetic master, ready to combine with the picture. The A and B rolls of negative are first timed (color- and exposure-graded) then contact-printed. The print stock passes three times through the contact printer to print (1) picture A roll, (2) picture B roll (alternate scenes printed in A roll spaces), and (3) sound negative (sound photographically printed on the edge of the film).

Occasionally there will be additional picture rolls, should titling or subtitling require it. The A/B roll printing process allows a print with no splicing marks showing, with low-cost dissolves and fades.

COMPOSITE PRINTS

The resulting composite print (sound and action) is one that has had adjustments made for inequities of color or exposure in the original. An answer print demonstrates the viability of these changes. If perfectly acceptable, it becomes the first release print. If further changes are required, they are incorporated into the next print, and the first acceptable print becomes the first release print.

THE PHYSICAL PROCESS FOR VIDEO

MACHINERY

The most common format for off-line video editing machines has been the ¾″ U-Matic, but ½″ VHS editing seems likely to become the standard. If you shoot in one format and want to edit in another, you simply dub (electronically transfer) from one to the other before editing. Though there is some quality loss from one generation to the next, especially in picture, this is a minor consideration since most off-line editing leads to final "conforming" by way of an on-line postproduction edit. Later, when you are competent to shoot material for broadcasting, you will need to research the current minimum requirements for each link of the chain; that is, for camera, recorder, editing, time base correction, and so on.

FIGURE 16–2

Video editing console.

EDITING MECHANICS

Cassette-to-cassette editing is quite simple in principle and the mechanics do not take long to master. Essentially it is the progressive transfer of sections from one machine to another. You pick an out-point to material already cut, and then in- and out-points for the new section to be added on. On pressing the review button, your rig will line up the already recorded and the new material at their cutting points, and in a review pass will let you see how your choice of cut looks and sounds. If you are satisfied and want to record it, you hit the record button and magically, the machine will once again back up, stop, roll forwards for five to ten seconds of preroll, and go into record mode at the prearranged cutting point. You see it all on the monitor: the last seconds of previously compiled material, and then the new segment cut onto the old.

SOUND CONSIDERATIONS

Figure 16–3 shows in diagramatic form how sound is transferred from the feed deck to the recorder. I have assumed that the original tape was a two-microphone setup, with each mike's output appearing on a separate track. The two tracks are adjusted for level (or volume) at the mixing board, and the mixed result is routed to the recorder. At the mixing board, you send the mixed track alternately to track 1 and track 2, scene by scene, in checkerboard fashion. At a later stage (Figure 16–4) these individual scenes' tracks can be further mixed down and equalized (made consistent through adjustment of individual tone controls) and adjusted for level, resulting in a smooth, seamless sound mix. Figure 16–4 includes a cassette player supplying a nonsync atmosphere (might be wind, traffic, or TV sound coming from an adjacent motel room).

Figure 16–4 shows how at each recording stage two tracks are combined into one. This always leaves an unused track on the newly recorded tape, upon which you can, as the next step, record additional materials for a further mix. Each stage prior to the final mix is called a premix.

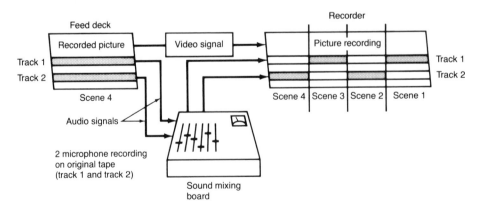

FIGURE 16–3

Two-track dialogue recording mixed and transferred in checkerboard fashion to allow sound mix-down later.

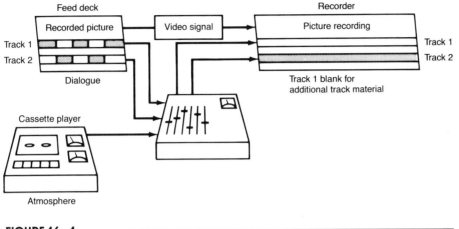

FIGURE 16–4

Checkerboarded tracks mixed with atmosphere track and recorded as a premix.

MINIMIZING GENERATIONAL LOSSES

Repeated audio premixes as in Figure 16–5 lead to a generational deterioration audible as an increased hiss level, but there are more sophisticated ways of using time code and a multitrack recorder to keep degeneration to a minimum. Generational losses through retransfering the picture are disturbingly evident, and are seen as increasing picture noise (picture break-up), particularly in shadow areas, and a deterioration in color fidelity and overall sharpness. You can, however, shunt a sixth (or any other) generation sound track back onto an earlier generation picture. The last stage is risky because it involves wiping a track from the second generation combined picture and sound cassette, and replacing it with the sixth generation mix, starting from a common sync start mark. Practice with unimportant copy tapes before you take risks with vital materials.

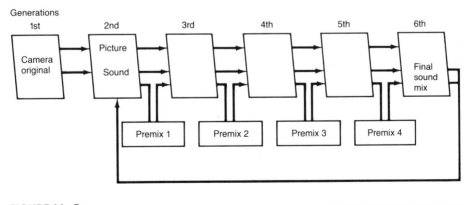

FIGURE 16–5

A succession of video premixes leading to a final sound mix. This is dubbed back onto second-generation picture (caution—see text).

OPTICALS

Rather sophisticated equipment is needed to do picture dissolves and wipes, and fairly advanced electronics are needed to do title and other superimpositions. However, it is perfectly possible to make a professional film without these optical effects. Having access only to a basic editing machine need not hold you back in any significant way.

TIME CODE: ON-LINE AND OFF-LINE EDITING

As mentioned in the previous chapter, time-coding provides every frame of picture (or sound only if shot on videocassette recorder) with its own unique time code number. The window displays cassette number, hours, minutes, seconds, and frames. The window dub, a copy of the camera original where the time code is displayed in a window (see Figure 15–2), is used as the editing master. The window with its time code copies through to subsequent editing generations. Most importantly, it lets you dub from one generation to another, knowing that when cutting is complete a computerized (on-line) editing setup will use a log of code in and code out points, recover the sound or action from in the camera-original tapes, and reconstruct a pristine copy. On-line editing is expensive compared with off-line, and the whole process is only economically viable if you have good reason to aim for broadcast quality.

EDITING CONCEPTS

Basic editing can be self-taught using common sense, but both basics and the further reaches of sophistication can be better learned from a detailed analysis of finished films (see Chapter 33, Project 2: "Editing Analysis"). You should also carry out the hands-on shooting and editing projects designed to develop particular skills (Chapter 34, Projects 5 through 10). What follows here is an overview of the conceptual process.

THE FIRST ASSEMBLY

Putting the material together for the first time is the most exciting part of editing. You should not worry at this stage about length or balance. Keep in mind how little you can premeditate a film from knowledge of rushes, just as there is a limit to how much planning you can do before using a surfboard. Experimental adaptation to what you find is everything.

To make a first assembly, work on one scene at a time and put the film together in whatever order is convenient, as follows:

1. Run all the material for the scene to refresh your memory.
2. Referring to the marked-up script (example in Figure 15–5) figure out how the coverage might best be assembled. At this stage, use a lot of the master shot, and do not bother yet with closeups or with double-cutting (repeatedly cutting between, say, two speakers when single cuts would adequately relay

the action). Nor should you use any overlap cutting (where a speaker's dialogue, for instance, overlaps the listener before the listener replies).

3. Assemble the simplest version that is faithful to the script, avoiding any questionable changes in the actors' pacing.

SEE A ROUGH DRAFT FIRST

I believe that it is vital to see the whole film as soon as possible in a long, loose form before doing any detailed work on any sections. Of course, you will be longing to go to work on a favorite sequence, but fixing details would be avoiding the need to assess the film's overall identity and purpose. Once you have seen the whole ungainly epic, you can make far-reaching resolutions about its future development. These may have to do with performances, pacing, parallel storytelling, structure, or overall meaning. Again, I must emphasize that what you intended is now completely irrelevant. This viewing is where you come to terms with what is and consign to oblivion what was meant to be.

FIRST ASSEMBLY VIEWING

NO INTERRUPTIONS

Run the first assembly without stopping and without interruption of any kind. Make no notes because this will take your attention from the screen. You want to look at the film as an audience would. Someone should "ride gain," that is, adjust sound levels, for the smoothest effect.

WHAT DO YOU HAVE?

The assembly viewing will yield some important realizations about the character, dramatic shape and best length of the film. Fundamental issues now come out of the closet. You will sense an overall slowness, that scenes include unnecessary exposition, or hang on beyond a good ending point. You may find you have a film with two endings, one false and one intended, or that one character is stronger than another. A sequence you shot in miserably cold conditions by a river at night turns out to stall the story's advance, and ought to be dropped.

The first assembly is the departure point for the denser and more complex film to come. As a show it is long and crude, yet it can be affecting and exciting because of its artlessness.

RUN THE FILM A SECOND TIME

Now run the film again to confirm original impressions. After further discussion with your editor, collaborate in making a list of aims for each sequence, arranging them by priority.

DIAGNOSTIC QUESTIONING

To sense a likely audience response, one must view the film as if seeing it for the first time to question the imprint the film has made. At this point one is dealing with the film in its crudest form, so the aim is to methodically elicit one's own dominant reactions.

A useful strategy after seeing an assembly is to rapidly list the memorable material and then refer to the script and make a second list of whatever you forgot. The human memory discards quite purposefully what it does not find meaningful. All that good stuff you could not recall was forgotten because it simply did not work. This does not mean it can never work, only that it is not doing so at present.

Why does material not deliver? Here are some possible reasons, each suggesting a different solution.

- Writing is poor in comparison with other sequences. (Cut the whole scene? Shorten? Rewrite and reshoot?)

- Acting is at fault. (Dramatic rhythms are too predictable, actors are not in character or in focus. Help but not cure is available in further editing.)

- Scene outcome is predictable. (Scene structure at fault? Too long or too slow?)

- Two or more sequences make a similar point. (Repetition does not advance a film's argument unless there is escalation, so make some choices and ditch the redundant.)

- Dramatic intensity plummets. (A useful analogy is the idea of a rising or falling emotional temperature. Now you are seeing the material in its context, correct relative temperatures become clearer. If your film is raising the temperature then inadvertently lowering it before the intended peak, the viewer's response is seriously impaired. The transposition of one or two sequences will sometimes work wonders. Naturally, this can only be done if the scenes are not locked into a fixed time development.)

- The viewer is somehow set up by the preceding material to expect something different. (We read film by its context, and if the context gives misleading signals or fails to focus awareness in the right area, the material itself will seem flat.)

These areas of examination all belong in the mainstream of dramatic analysis that a playwright or theatre producer would employ during rehearsals of a new work. These considerations are particularly important after the first audience reactions have been monitored. Just as a playwright routinely rewrites and adjusts a work based on audience feedback, the filmmaker makes a vast number of adjustments, large and small, before admitting a work is finished. Because a filmmaker has no true audience until the work is finished, assessments are hard to make, and they certainly are not objective. First you dig for your own instincts through feeling the dramatic outcome of your material. Later when you have a fine cut and the material becomes showable, you will call in a few people whose reactions and tastes you respect. You will probably find quite a bit of unanimity in what they tell you.

While still in this assembly stage you and your editor begin by examining your own audience reactions and asking basic questions.

1. Does the film feel dramatically balanced? (If you have a very moving and exciting sequence in the middle of the film, the rest of the film may seem anticlimactic. Or, you may have a film that seems to circle around for a long while until, suddenly, it starts really moving.)

2. When is there a definite feeling of a story unfolding, and when not? (This will help locate impediments in the film's development, so you can analyze why the film stumbles.)

3. Which parts of the film seem to work?

4. Which parts drag, and why? (Some of the acting may be better than others. Sometimes the problem is that a scene is wrongly placed or repeats the dramatic contours of a previous one.)

5. Which of the characters held your attention most, and which the least?

6. Was there a satisfying alternation of types of material, or was similar material indigestibly clumped together?

7. Which were the effective contrasts and juxtapositions? Are there more to be found? (Sometimes a sequence does not work because the ground has not been properly prepared, or because there is insufficient contrast in mood with the previous sequence. Variety is as important in storytelling as it is in dining.)

8. What metaphorical allusions did you notice your material making? Could it make them more strongly? (That your tale carries a metaphorical charge is as important to your audience as a water table is to pasture.)

PRIORITIZE

When you tackle problems that show up in any cut, you should arrange the problems by hierarchy and, just like building a scene in rehearsal, plan to deal only with those of the largest dimension. If the film's structure is at fault, reorder the scenes and run it again without making any refinement to individual scenes. If there is a serious problem of imbalance between two characters who are both major parts, go to work on bringing forward the character presently deficient.

LENGTH

Look to the content of your film itself for guidance over length and pacing. Films have a natural span according to the richness and significance of their content, but the hardest achievement in any art form is the confidence and ability to say a lot through a little. Most beginners' films are agonizingly long and slow, so if you can recognize early that your film should be, say, twenty minutes long at the very most, you can get tough with that forty-minute assembly and make some basic decisions.

STRUCTURE

Most of all you need a good dramatic structure to make the movie into a well told tale. Bear in mind that a good plan does not guarantee a satisfying experience for an audience. Other criteria will come into play as a result of the emotional changes and development an audience will actually experience. These now become apparent for the first time.

LEAVE THE EDITOR TO EDIT

Having decided what the next round of changes should be, leave the cutting room until summoned back. Not all editors or directors can work this way but it is important to try. The reason is simple: the editor loses objectivity while correcting the many problems and so will the director who remains present. But a director returning with a fresh eye to see a new cut can tell which changes are a positive development. The director acts throughout as a surrogate audience whose keenest tastes must be satisfied.

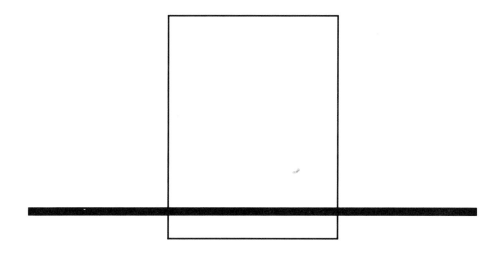

C·H·A·P·T·E·R 1·7

EDITING FROM ROUGH CUT TO FINE CUT

THE ROUGH CUT VIEWING

The cut following the first assembly is called the rough cut. Here the full range of material is deployed toward goals decided from seeing the assembly. No sequence is yet fine-tuned, but the editor tries to make each sequence occupy its right place and be dramatically successful.

The scrutiny you give this new cut is similar to those previous, and it remains important to deal with the large-scale dimensions first.

1. Is there adequate, too little, or too much expository detail?
2. Is exposition integrated with the action or does the film pause to inform the audience?
3. What exposition, if excised, could still be inferred by the audience?
4. Does the film have a sense of momentum from the beginning?
5. Where does the momentum falter and why?
6. Does the film breathe so that, like music, each movement feels balanced and inevitable, or is there a misshapen, unbalanced feel to some parts?
7. What material is redundant?
8. How logical and satisfying is the development of each major character?
9. Is anything misleading or alienating about the characters that needs fixing?
10. Is there a satisfying balance between interiors and exteriors? (This often means dealing with a claustrophobia the film generates. Well constructed

films alternate between intensity and release much as a person must alternate intimacy with solitude, indoors with outdoors, family with work, day with night, and so on)

11. What is the film's present thematic impact?

After seeing the rough cut again you might ask more localized questions.

1. Which sequences could have later in-points and/or earlier out-points?
2. What needs to be done for each character to exert maximum impact, and in which sequences?
3. Which sequences cry out for special attention to rhythm and pacing?
4. How effective is the ending?

Again, ask the editor to attend only to what you agree are the glaring faults before having another showing.

SEE THE WHOLE FILM

Even if work has been done to two sequences alone, make a practice of running the whole film. A film is like a tent: change one pole or guy-rope and you alter stresses throughout the tent's structure. Examine changes to your film in the context of the whole work, and examine the whole work for its potential for further change.

THE PROBLEM OF ACHIEVING A FLOW

After you have run your evolving cut a few times, it will begin to strike you more and more as a series of clunky blocks of material, with a distressing lack of flow. Dialogue scenes in particular seem to bog down, being centered as they probably are upon showing each speaker. First there is a block of this speaker, then a block of that speaker, then a block of both, and so on. Even sequences themselves go past in a blocky way, like boxcars in a goods train watched from a level crossing, each quite different and having a link device joining it to its fellow. I think of this kind of editing as "boxcar cutting."

How does one achieve the effortless flow seen in the cinema? To discuss that, we must first investigate the way human perception functions.

HOW EDITING MIMICS AN OBSERVING CONSCIOUSNESS

This section expands upon principles you may already have explored elsewhere (in the Chapter 8 editing analogy exercise under "Blocking," in Chapter 33, Project 2: Editing Analysis, or in Chapter 34, Project 8: Edited Two-Character Dialogue Scene). How and why we cut between speakers in a dialogue scene is based on how our attention shifts. This is best seen by examining eye contact and eyeline shifts, which the practiced editor uses extensively as an editing foundation.

THE MYTH AND THE REALITY OF EYE CONTACT

Take the commonly dramatized situation of two diners having an intimate conversation. Inexperienced actors play this kind of scene by gazing into each other's eyes as they speak. This is an idea of how people converse, but it is not true to life and gives phony results, either for acting or as a guiding principle for editing. Go to a restaurant and do some sleuthing. You will see what really happens between different pairs of people talking. As always, reality is far more subtle and interesting. It is unusual for either to make eye contact more than fleetingly. The situation varies with the individual and with the situation, but generally we reserve the intensity of eye contact for special moments. Usually it is to (1) search out information from the other person's expression, (2) check what effect we are having, and (3) put pressure on the other person.

In each case we glance into the other person's face to rapidly gather information. In subtle ways, each speaker is either pressing, or being pressed. Only at crucial moments does one search the other for facial or behavioral enlightenment. Much of the time the listener's gaze rests upon isolated or neutral objects while mentally searching out what the other person means.

APPLYING THE ANALOGY TO FILM

We have said all along that film, unlike literature, has difficulty in portraying interior life. But where a person looks and what he sees indicates what he feels, so we can show these shifts through editing and imply a special significance to each moment of change. We can in fact imply inner lives and imply character revelation through editing choices.

Now play the role of interested observer again, but this time be aware of how your own eyeline shifts between the speakers. Notice how often you follow up the shifts in their eyelines, involuntarily switching your gaze from subject to object. As you watch, you will be conscious not only of a rhythm and motivation to their eyeline changes (controlled by the shifting contours of the conversation itself) but also how your eyes made their own judgment over where to look. Independently, your center of attention switches back and forth, often following the pair's action and reaction, their changes of eyeline, and their physical action, but also making independent choices. Notice that you often leave a speaker in mid-delivery to examine his effect on the listener.

Unconsciously, the observer edits according to his own developing insight in order to extract the most telling information.

To film what you have been observing, you would need to cover each speaker's viewpoint of the other, and a third viewpoint encompassing both, which represents the perspective of you the observer. This last is outside the enclosed consciousness of the two speakers and tends to show them in a more detached, storytelling way. Two over-shoulder shots and a wide two-shot would be a basic coverage.

According to choices made in editing, the audience can identify with either of the characters inside the story, or with the more detached perspective of the invisible storyteller/observer. While character A talks, the film might allow the audience to look detachedly at either A or B, to share the perspective of either one upon the other, or to look at both of them in long shot.

This flexibility of viewpoint allows the director to structure not only what the spectator sees, but whose point of view and whose state of mind he shares at any particular moment. This probing, cinematic way of seeing is modelled upon the way we unconsciously delve into any event that interests us. The film narrative process is thus never objective but mimics the selective consciousness of a particular observer.

ALTERING PERFORMANCE RHYTHMS

A very significant dramatic control now rests in the cutting room for any scene that has been adequately covered. This concerns not only who or what is shown at any particular moment, but how much time each character takes to process what he sees or hears. This timing is initially controlled by the actors and contributes very much to the power and consistency of a scene's subtext.

THE POWER OF SUBTEXT

Let us take the example of a two-person, interior scene where a man asks a simple question of a woman visitor: "Do you think it's cold out?" This could be interpreted several ways. It could mean

- "Tell me I don't have to change into heavier clothes."
- "Tell me if you think I will be uncomfortable."
- "What clothes do you think I should wear?"
- "Let's not go to the party after all."
- "Do you want to stay the night with me?"

Depending on context and what has previously happened, any of these implications may be present. How do we the audience judge, or even conceive of these possibilities? How the speaker says the line may tell you a lot, but as much may be inferred from the listener's reactions. An easy and unreflecting "No" is very different from one that is delivered with more difficulty, or one that is long delayed, indicating an internal struggle or perhaps concern over what may come next.

CONTROL IN EDITING

From repetition, actors tend to drop into a standardized rhythm of delivery and reaction time that levels the characters' inner lives to a shared average. This is, of course, deadly, and often needs to be varied to recover the changeableness and unpredictability of spontaneous action. Even when performances are uniformly excellent, there is another reason to want to exert fine control over playing rhythms. An edited scene, like a jazz performance, acquires its own intensity and context and becomes an entity that nobody could quite foresee. This, too, requires control over the original rhythms of reply, eyeline changes, action, and reaction.

No editor can change the rate of speech or, in an unbroken take, the timing of reactions. But the situation changes radically if the director shot more than one angle. Look at Figure 17–1. Diagram A is a representation of the master take, a timing that the actors reproduced in all subsequent takes. The diagram shows picture and sound as separate strands, much as one sees them while cutting film.

```
 !2S: Him                                        Her
 _____
 /   "Do you think it's cold out?"               "No"
 _____
                           <----t------>

           Example A: Master Two-Shot (actors' timing "t" as played)


 \    Him                        2S  ! CS: Her                             !
 _____!_____/
 /   "Do you think it's cold out?" !       "No"                           !
 !_____!_____\
                           <------t---->

     Example B: Cut from Two-Shot to CS (still actor's timing as played)


 !    Him              2S  ! CS    Her                                     /
 _____!_____/
 /  "Do you think it's cold out?" ! "No"                               /
 !_____!_____\
                           <-->

       Example C: Reply Now Comes Quickly Using Picture Overlap Reaction


 \    Him                        2S  ! CS        Her              /
 _____!_____\
 \ "Do you think it's cold out?"     !             "No"               /
 /_____!_____/
                           <-------- t x 2 ---->

     Example D: Reply Delayed by Summing Reaction Time from Both Shots


 \  Him                      2S  !Her reaction!His reaction!Her reaction    /
 /_____!_____!_____!_____\
 "Do you think it's cold out?"   !           !           !            "No" /
 _____!_____!_____!_____\
                           <------------------ t x ? ---------------->

        Example E: Double Cutting Reaction Shots Creates Maximum Delay
```

FIGURE 17–1 ——————————————————————————————————————

How original pause timing (t) between lines can be removed or augmented to alter the rhythm of dialogue responses.

In Example B the cut to close up simply preserves the actors' original timing, though by isolating her it suggests a greater degree of significance to her reply. Example C uses overlap cutting (see below for extended explanation) to make her reply come as quickly as possible. Example D, however, by adding together the pauses from both takes doubles her reaction time. Example E goes still further by double-cutting her thinking and his waiting reaction before cutting back to her thinking and replying. To create this length of delay you will need a complementary closeup reaction shot on him, and a second take on her from which to steal the extra close shot (CS) reaction.

By using the coverage resourcefully we have considerable choice over the pace of the playing (though not of speech itself until digital techniques makes all kinds of manipulation possible). Intelligent rebalancing of performances can add massively to the credibility of the characters' inner lives and to the believability of choice and reaction that compel them to action or speech.

In fact, intelligent editing has much to do with the credibility of all subtexts. It coaxes our imaginations and lends enormously to the overall impact of the film, aiding and abetting performances and creating the grounds for us to infer thought, feeling, and reaction.

VISUAL AND AURAL EDITING RHYTHMS: AN ANALOGY IN MUSIC

The interplay of of rhythmic elements through editing needs further explanation if the possibilities are to be fully appreciated. Though editing is carried out by the mechanical means of viewing, splicing, or transfer, decisions can no more be made by measuring the script or by calculations with a stopwatch than music can be composed with a metronome.

RHYTHMIC INTERPLAY

Music offers a useful analogy here if we examine an edited version of a conversation between two people. We have two different but interlocked rhythms going. First there is the rhythmic pattern of their voices in a series of sentences that ebb and flow, speed up, slow down, halt, restart, and continue. Set against this, and often taking a rhythmic cue from the sound rhythms, is the visual tempo set up by the complex shifts of visual choice, outlined above and evoked in the interplay of cutting, camera composition, and movement. The two streams, visual and aural, proceed independently yet are rhythmically related, like the relation of music and the physical movements of a dancer.

HARMONY

When you hear a speaker and you see his face as he talks, sound and vision are allied. We could, however, break the literalness of always hearing and seeing the same thing (harmony) by making the transition from scene to scene into a temporary puzzle.

COUNTERPOINT

We are going to cut from a woman talking about her vanished husband to a shot panning across a view of tawdry seashore hotels in Florida. We start with the speaker in picture and sound, and then cut to the panning shot while she is still speaking, letting her remaining words play out over the hotels. The effect is this: while our subject is talking about her now fatherless children and the bitterness she feels toward him, we glance away and in our mind's eye imagine where he might now be. The film version of this scene can suggest the mental (or even physical) imagery of someone present and listening. The speaker's words are powerfully counterpointed by the image, and the image lets loose our imagination so we ponder what he is doing, what is going on behind the crumbling concrete facades of the hotels.

This counterpoint of one kind of sound against another kind of image has its variations. One usage is simply to illustrate. We see taking place what the woman's words begin to describe: ". . . and the last I heard, he was in Florida. . . ."

Many an elegant contrapuntal sequence in a feature film is the work of an editor trained in documentary trying to raise the movie above a 1940s scriptwriting technique, as Ralph Rosenblum relates in *When the Shooting Stops . . . the Cutting Begins*. Directing and editing documentaries has contributed importantly to the screen fluency of Robert Altman, Lindsay Anderson, Carroll Ballard, Werner Herzog, Louis Malle, Alain Resnais, Alain Tanner, and Haskell Wexler, to name but a few of the better known modern fiction directors.

DISSONANCE

Another usage exploits discrepancies. For instance, while we hear a salesman telling his new assistant his theory of dynamic customer persuasion, we see the same man listing the virtues of a hideaway bed in a monotone so dreary that his customer is bored into a trance. This discrepancy, if we pursue the musical allusion, is a dissonance, spurring the viewer to crave a resolution. Comparing the man's beliefs (heard) with his practice (seen), the viewer is driven to conclude, "here is a man who does not know himself." It is interesting to note that this technique of ambiguous revelation is equally viable in documentary film, where it seems to have originated.

COUNTERPOINT IN PRACTICE: UNIFYING MATERIAL INTO A FLOW

Once you have improved on the script's order for the material, you will want to combine sound and action in a form that takes advantage of counterpoint techniques.

In practice this means bringing together the sound from one shot with the image from another, as we have said. To return on my example where a salesman with a great self-image proved to have a poor performance, one could show this on the screen by merging two sets of materials, one of him talking to his assistant over a coffee break (sequence A), the other of him in the salesroom making a pitch to clients (sequence B).

In editing we can bring these materials into juxtaposition. The conservative, first-assembly method would alternate segments as in Figure 17–2A, a block of explanation then a block of sales talk, then another block of explanation and another of sales, and so on until the point had been made. This is a common though clumsy way to accomplish the objective, and after a few cuts both the technique and the message become predictable. It is boxcar cutting because each chunk goes by like freight cars as you stand at a level crossing.

Better would be to integrate two sets of materials as in Figure 17–2B instead of crudely alternating them. Let us start Harold explaining his sales philosophy (sequence A) during the salesmen's coffee break. While he's showing off to the younger men, we begin fading up the sound from the salesroom (sequence B) in which we hear Harold's aggressive greetings. As he reaches full volume we cut to the salesroom picture (sequence B) to see he has trapped a reluctant customer and is launching into his sales pitch. After this is established we fade up the coffee break conversation again (sequence A). We hear the salesman say how he first fascinates the customer. We cut to sequence A's picture and see Harold has moved uncomfortably close to his juniors. He tells them one must now make the customers admit they like the merchandise. While the voices continue we cut back to the salesroom (sequence B) picture only and see the customer backing away angrily. We bring up sequence B's sound as the customer says she only came to buy a pillow.

Notice that in the overlap areas (x, y, and z), picture from one sequence is being countpointed against sound from another. Instead of having description and practice separate as discrete blocks of material, description is laid against practice, ideas against reality, in a much harder-hitting counterpoint.

The benefits are multiple. The total sequence is shorter and more sprightly. Conversation is kept to an interesting minimum while the behavioral material—the salesroom evidence against which we measure his ideas—is now in the majority. The counterpointing of essentials allows the combination of materials to be pared down to essentials, giving what is presented a muscular, spare quality usually lacking from theatrically conceived film writing. There is a much closer and more telling juxtaposition between vocalized theory and actual performance,

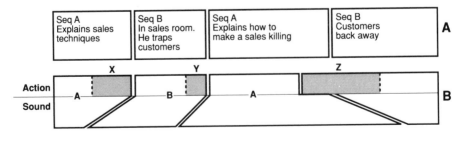

FIGURE 17–2

Counterpointing the content of one sequence against another.

and the audience is challenged to reconcile the man's ideas with what he is actually doing.

Counterpoint editing cannot really be worked out in scripting, because entry and exit points depend on the nuances of playing or even camerawork. But if both scenes are shot in their entirety, one becomes a parallel action to the other. The resulting sequence can be worked out from the materials themselves, and will reliably and effectively compress the two.

There is a shooting/editing project to practice these skills in Chapter 34, Project 6c, "Vocal Counterpoint and Point of View." This adds a vocal counterpoint to action, but you might want to try improvising the salesman scene used as an example above, using one scene as parallel action to the other and fusing the two in counterpoint.

DRAMA SHOULD TAKE PLACE IN THE AUDIENCE'S IMAGINATION

By creating a texture of sound and picture that requires an interpretation, a film can juxtapose the antithetical with great economy and kindle the audience's involvement in its dialectical tensions. The audience is no longer passively identifying and submitting to the controlling will of the movie, but rather stimulated to live an imaginative, critical inner life in parallel with the film. This is what Brecht, striving to break down the audience's capacity for identification, set out to accomplish in the theatre.

THE AUDIENCE AS ACTIVE RATHER THAN PASSIVE PARTICIPANTS

This more demanding texture of word and image puts the spectator in a new relationship to the evidence presented, encouraging active rather than passive participation. The contract the storyteller has developed with the audience is no longer just to imbibe and be entertained. Instead, the challenge is to interpret, to weigh what is seen against what is heard, an idea against its contrary. The film will now sometimes confirm and other times contradict what had seemed true. As in life, the viewer's critical judgment is invoked when a man's ideas turn out to be an unreliable self-image.

But there are yet more interesting ways to use juxtaposition and counterpoint when the basic coupling of sound and picture is altered. For instance, one might show an interior with a bored teenage girl looking out of a store window at people in the street. A radio somewhere offscreen is broadcasting the report of a boxing match as she watches a boy and his mother having a violent argument outside. The girl is too abstracted to notice the counterpoint. Though we see the mother and child, we hear the excited commentator detailing the punishment being inflicted. There is an ironic contrast between two different planes in view; an argument is raised to the level of a public spectacle, yet our main character's consciousness is too naive or too inward-looking to notice. Very succinctly and with not a little humor, both her unconsciousness and a satirical view of mother-child relationships have been compressed into a thirty-second shot. That is economy.

FILLING IN THE GAPS

Counterpointing visual and aural impressions is only an extension of what was called montage early in film's history. Because film was silent, film grammar developed the juxtaposition of two shots to imply either relatedness or continuity. But the audience's imagination is what supplies the relational link between shots and, in a larger plane, between scenes. It is important to remember that the audience's enjoyment comes not from what it sees and hears, but from what it imagines in pursuit of subtexts. Few filmmakers seem consciously aware of this, and for this reason, grasping the principle and finding effective ways to put it into effect will immediately mark your work as different.

The use of contrapuntal sound came relatively late and was, I believe, developed by documentary editors in search of narrative compression for lengthy actuality materials. In fiction filmmaking, Robert Altman's films from $M*A*S*H$ (1970) onwards show great inventiveness in producing a dense, layered counterpoint in their sound tracks. Altman's sound recordist even built a special sixteen-track location sound recorder capable of making individual recordings from up to fifteen radio microphones, so the whole problem of miking shots was eliminated.

THE OVERLAP CUT: DIALOGUE SEQUENCES

Another contrapuntal editing device useful to blur the unnatural seams between shots is called the overlap cut. It works like counterpoint between sequences, bringing a speaker's voice in before his picture, or vice versa, and dismantling the procession of level cuts resulting from the assemblage of dialogue material in blocks.

Figure 17–3 is a straight-cut version of a conversation between A and B. Whoever speaks is shown on the screen and before long this becomes predictable and boring. You could alleviate this by slugging in some reaction shots (not shown).

Now look at the same conversation using overlap cutting. Person A starts speaking, but then we hear B's voice (during overlap x). We wait a sentence before cutting to him. B is interrupted by A (during overlap y), and this time we hold on B's frustrated expression before cutting to A driving his point home. Before A has finished, because we are now interested in B's rising anger, we cut back to him shaking his head (during overlap z). When A has finished, B, whom we have seen waiting, caps the discussion and this ends the sequence.

How do you decide when to make overlap cuts? Usually it is done at a later stage of cutting, but we shall need a guiding theory. Let us return for a moment to the example of human consciousness, our trusty guide to editing. Imagine you are witnessing a conversation between two people; you have to turn your head from one to the other. You will seldom turn at the right moment to catch the

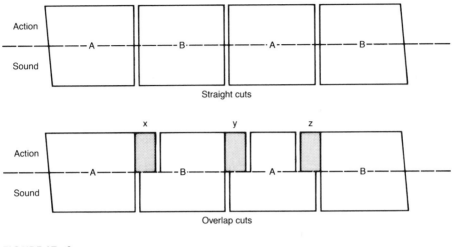

FIGURE 17-3

Straight-cut dialogue sequence and its overlap-cut version.

next speaker beginning; only a suspiciously omniscient being could be so accurate. Such omniscience in a movie destroys the illusion of watching something spontaneous. Inexperienced or downright bad editors often make neat, level cuts between speakers, and the results have a prepackaged, premeditated effect.

In real life one can seldom predict who will speak next and usually it is the new voice that tells you where to look. If a film or video editor is to convince us that a dialogue sequence comes from real life, he or she must replicate the disjunctive shifts we unconsciously make as our eyes follow our hearing, or when our hearing (that is, concentration) catches up late with something we have just seen.

The guideline to effective cutting is always to be found in the consciousness of the story's point of view, which it is useful to think of as the involved observer.

The spectator is engaged not just in hearing and seeing each speaker as he speaks (which would be boring), but also in interpreting what is going on inside each protagonist through clues embedded in moments of action, reaction, or subjective vision. Through what the "involved observer" notices, through the evidence shown on the screen, the storytelling consciousness of the film itself is subtly established in addition to that of point-of-view characters.

For filmmaking the message is clear. If the editor is to be true to life, to implant in the audience the developing subjectivity of the critical observer, he or she must make sound and picture changeover points as staggered cuts more often than level ones.

THE OVERLAP CUT: SEQUENCE TRANSITIONS

In the most uncinematic scene transition, a character exits the frame leaving an empty set, and the film cuts to another empty set in anticipation of his arrival. This is really proscenium arch theatre, and its scene shifting puts an artificial hiatus in a film's momentum. Inexperienced directors often engineer scenes to start and stop this way, but a good editor quickly looks for ways to axe the dead footage.

Just as there are dialogue overlap cuts, there are live transitions from one sequence to another by using the staggered cut. Imagine a scene with a boy and girl talking about going out together. The boy says he thinks her mother will try and stop them. The girl says, "Oh don't worry about her, I can talk her round." Cut to the next scene where the girl asks the question of her mother who closes the refrigerator with a bang and says firmly, "Absolutely not!" to the aggrieved daughter.

First of all, it is not necessary to restate the girl's situation. A level cut would take us instantly from the boy/girl sequence to the mother/girl scene where the mother answers, "Absolutely not!" A more interesting way of leaving the boy/girl scene would be to cut to the mother at the refrigerator while the girl is still saying " . . . I can talk her round." As she finishes, the mother slams the fridge door and says her line, "Absolutely not!" and the camera pans to show the girl already in the scene.

Another way to create an elision instead of a definite scene change would be to hold on the boy and girl and have the mother's angry voice say "Absolutely not!" over the tail end of their shot. You would use the surprise of the new voice to motivate cutting to the mother in picture as the new scene continues.

Either of these devices serves to make less noticeable the seams between one sequence and the next. Though one sometimes wants to bring a scene to a slow closure, perhaps with a fade-out, more usually one wants to keep up the momentum. People choose dissolves because a level cut jerks the viewer too rudely into a new place and time, but dissolves insert a rest period between scenes and dissipate storytelling momentum.

The answer is the overlap cut; it keeps the track alive, draws the viewer after it, and makes a natural transition while keeping up the pace.

SOUND EFFECTS AS SCENE ELISION

You have seen this overlap technique done with sound effects. It might look like this: The schoolteacher rolls reluctantly out of her bed, then as she ties up her hair in a scarf we hear the increasingly loud sound of a playground until we cut to her on duty at the school door. Here anticipatory sound drags our attention forward to the next sequence. Because our curiosity demands an answer to the riddle of children's voices in a woman's bedroom, we do not find the location switch arbitrary or theatrical.

Another type of overlap cut makes sound work the other way; we cut from the teacher leading kids chanting their multiplication tables to her getting food out of her refrigerator at home. The dreary class sound subsides slowly while she exhaustedly eats some leftovers.

In the first example, anticipatory sound draws her forward out of her bedroom. In the second, holdover sound persists even after she gets home. In both cases, the storyteller suggests that the din persists in her mind, implying that she finds her workplace unpleasant. This is not just a way of softening transitions between scenes, but a way of suggesting what dominates our character's inner consciousness. We could suggest something different by playing it the other way, and let the silence of her home trail out into the workplace, so that she is seen at work with her bedroom radio playing softly before being swamped by the rising uproar of feet echoing in a corridor. At the end of the day, her TV sitcom could displace her voice giving out the dictation, and make us cut to her relaxing at home.

By using sound and picture transitions creatively, we can transport the viewer forward without cumbersome (and expensive) optical effects like dissolves, fades, and wipes. We are also able to scatter important clues about the characters' subjective lives and inner imaginings, something film cannot otherwise easily do.

SUMMARY

In the examples above, we have established that our consciousness can probe our surroundings either (1) monodirectionally (eyes and ears on the same information source) or (2) bidirectionally (eyes and ears on different sources). Our attention also moves forward or backward in time, and film recreates all these aspects of consciousness by making the audience share the sensations of a character's shifting planes of consciousness and association. A welcome and money-saving result from creative overlap cutting is that one can completely dispense with the fade or dissolve.

HELP, I CAN'T UNDERSTAND!

These cutting techniques are hard to grasp from a book even though, as I have said, they mimic the way human awareness shifts. If this is getting beyond you, do not worry. The best way to understand editing is to take a complex and interesting sequence in a feature film and, by running a shot or two at a time on a VCR, make a precise log of the relationship between the track elements and the visuals. Chapter 33, Project 2: "Editing Analysis" is an editing self-education program with a list of editing techniques for you to find and analyze. Try shooting and editing your own sequences from directions in Chapter 34, Projects 5 through 10. After some hands-on experience return to this section and it should be much clearer.

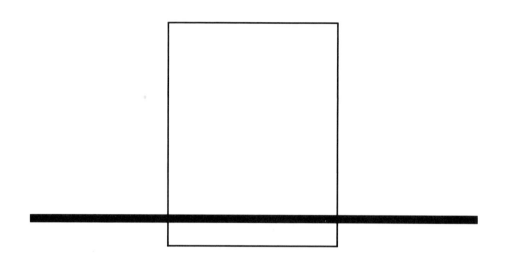

VIEWINGS AND TRYING TO STAY OBJECTIVE

After perhaps months of sustained editing work on a film, a debilitating familiarity sets in. As you lose objectivity, your ability to make judgments on behalf of an audience departs. Every alternative version begins to look the same. All seem too long, and you may become so obsessed with particular faults in your footage that they seem overwhelming.

This disabling condition is particularly likely to overwhelm the hyphenate, the director-editor, who has lived with both the intentions and the resulting footage ever since their inception. But it afflicts whole crews during postproduction and is the main reason why one begins calling on other people's reactions to the piece at this stage.

Before showing the working cut to outsiders, you should first make an abstract of your film in the form of a block diagram to help you spot anomalies.

DIAGNOSIS: USING A BLOCK DIAGRAM

Whenever one needs to better understand something, it helps to translate it into another form. Statisticians, for instance, know that the full implications of their figures are not evident until expressed as a graph, pie chart, or other proportional image.

In our case, we are dealing with the mesmerizing actuality of the film, which, as we view it, concentrates our attention within its unfolding present to the detriment of any sense of overview. It is tempting to regard all of one's earlier production work as something that renders unnecessary any further dramatic analysis, but this is far from being true, especially after you may have altered, abbreviated or transposed much of the original. Through using a block diagram you can in fact regain a fresh and a more objective perspective of your work.

Figure 3–1 is a useful dual-purpose form that speeds the job of analysis. To use it, run your film a sequence at a time and, stopping after each, make a brief note of the sequence's content in the box (name of characters and what is the main action). Next to the box, write what main point the sequence contributes to the development of the film as a whole. This might be factual information, it might introduce a setting, a character, or a relationship to be developed later in the film, or it might be there because it sets a special mood or feeling.

Soon you have a flowchart for your film. This representation has its limitations since film sequences are not like a succession of soloists, each singing a self-contained song, but more like the delayed entry of several parts in a choral work. Each entering voice joins and cross-modulates with those coming before. Draw and annotate lines indicating any special relationship existing between each new sequence and those preceding. This may indicate in parallel storytelling, for instance, that one sequence is too far away from another that it affects.

The benefit of this kind of analysis is that one is forced to conceptualize what actually comes from the screen, to translate conveniently inchoate sensations into hard-edged statements. It is vital, therefore, to do this work from the life on the screen and not from memory or the script. Another useful trick is to give each sequence an impact rating so you can assess the development of the film's dramatic pressures.

Through articulating what each sequence contributes you will begin to see dispassionately and functionally what is truly there for an audience. What does the progression of contributions add up to? As with the first assembly, you will again find it reveals some of the following:

1. The film lacks early impact, or has an unnecessarily pedestrian opening that makes it a late developer (fine for nineteenth-century Russian novels but fatal for a film that may depend on TV showings).

2. The main issues are unclear or unclear for a long time (writing problem, but in editing it is sometimes possible to reposition a scene earlier, even ahead of titles, to commit the film to an interesting line of development).

3. The type and frequency of impact is poorly distributed over the film's length (feast or famine in dramatic development and progression).

4. There is a nonlinear development of basic, necessary information about characters, backstory, and environment, including

   - omissions,
   - duplication,
   - backdoubles,
   - redundancy,
   - information too far ahead of place where audience needs it.

5. The same kind of dramatic contribution is made in several ways (three scenes reveal that the hero has a low flashpoint; choose the best and reposition or dump the rest).

6. A sequence or group of sequences do not contribute to the thrust of the film (be brave and dump them).

7. The film's resolution emerges early, leaving the remainder of the film tediously inevitable (rebalance indicators in the film to keep resolution in doubt, this way audience keeps working and remains interested).

8. The film appears to end before it actually does (false or multiple endings are a common problem).

Naming each ailment leads to finding the cure. When you have put these remedies into effect, you will sense the improvement rather than see it. It is like resetting a sail; the boat looks the same, but the vessel surges under new power.

After several rounds of alterations, make a new block diagram to ensure that housecleaning has not introduced new problems. I cannot overstress the seductions film practices upon its makers. You will find more anomalies by repeating the process, even though it seems utterly unnecessary.

With some years of practice, a lot of this formal process will become second nature to you and will occur in the earlier stages of the cut. Even so, filmmakers of long standing invariably profit from subjecting their work to such formal scrutiny and much of the discussion during the cutting of a feature film centers on the film's dramatic shape and effectiveness.

A TRIAL SHOWING

Preparing a block diagram has an additional benefit. Having defined what every brick in your movie's edifice is supposed to accomplish, you are excellently prepared to test your intentions during a trial show for a small audience.

AUDIENCE

Your audience should be half a dozen or so people whose tastes and interests you respect. The less they know of your aims the better.

PREPARATION

You should warn your audience that it is a work in progress, still technically raw. Tell them that music, sound effects, and titles have yet to be added. Incidentally, it helps the film if you cut in a working title or, in its absence, if you tell the audience what it is, since a title legitimately signals a film's purpose and identity to its audience. While the film is running, you may also want to describe in three words any vital sound component that is missing.

SOUND CONTROL IS CRITICAL

When you show the film, carefully control the sound levels or you will get misleadingly negative responses. Even film professionals can drastically misjudge a film whose sound elements are inaudible or overbearing. A simple but effective way is to feed the two tracks of the VCR into a hi-fi and use balance and volume controls to adjust the levels, and bass and treble tone controls to provide maximum listener comfort and involvement.

SURVIVING YOUR CRITICS AND MAKING USE OF WHAT THEY SAY

LISTEN, DO NOT EXPLAIN

After the viewing, you should ask for impressions of the film as a whole. You will probably need to focus and direct your viewers' attention or you may find the discussion quite peripheral to your needs. Asking for critical feedback must be handled carefully or it can be a pointless exercise. You need to say little and listen very carefully, and you must also retain your fundamental bearings towards the piece as a whole. Avoid the temptation to explain the film or to explain what you intended. Explanations at this stage are irrelevant and only confuse and compromise the audience's own perceptions. Your film must soon stand or fall on its own merits among strangers, so you must concentrate on listening to your audience.

Taking in reactions and criticism is an emotionally draining experience. It is quite usual to feel threatened, slighted, misunderstood, and unappreciated, and to come away with a raging headache. You need all the self-discipline you can muster to sit immobile, say little, and listen. Make an audio recording of the proceedings so you can listen again in peace.

LINES OF INQUIRY

Because you will often need to direct the inquiry into useful channels, here are some questions that move from the large issues toward the component parts.

1. What is the film really about?
2. What are the major issues in the film?
3. Did the film feel the right length or was it too long?
4. Were there any parts that were unclear or puzzling? (You can itemize those you suspect fit the description, since audiences often forget anything that passed over their heads.)
5. Which parts felt slow?
6. Which parts were moving or otherwise successful?
7. What did you feel about _____(name of character)?
8. What did you end up knowing about _____(situation or issue)?

You are beginning to test the effectiveness of the function you assigned each sequence. Depending on your trial audience's patience, you may be able to survey only dubious areas, or you may get feedback on most of your film's parts and intentions.

BALANCING CRITICS' VIEWPOINTS

Dealing with criticism really means absorbing multiple views and, after the dust settles, reviewing the film to see how such varying impressions are possible. When you return to the cutting room, you and your editor see the film with the eyes of those who never understood that the messenger was the workmate seen in an earlier scene. You find a way to put in an extra line where the woman asks if Don is still at work, and without compromising the film in any way the problem is solved. You must, of course, take into account the number of people reporting a difficulty and its nature before rushing to fix anything. Where comments from different audience members cancel each other out, there may be no action called for. Make some allowance for the biases and subjectivity of your individual critics.

THE EGOCENTRIC CRITIC

An irritation one must often suffer, especially among those with a little knowledge to demonstrate, is the person who insists on talking about the film he would have made rather than the film you have just shown. Diplomatically redirect the discussion.

MAKE CHANGES CAUTIOUSLY

On the whole, make no changes without careful reflection. Remember that when people are asked to give criticism, they want to leave a contributory mark on your work. You will never under any circumstances be able to please everyone. Nor should you be tempted to try.

HOLD ON TO YOUR CENTRAL INTENTIONS

Never let your central intentions get lost and never revise them unless there are overwhelmingly positive reasons to do so. Act only upon suggestions that support and further your central intentions. This is a dangerous phase for the filmmaker, indeed for any artist. Let go of your work's underlying identity and you lose your direction. More important is to keep listening and to think deeply about what you hear. Do not be tempted by strong emotions to carve into your film precipitously.

MEA CULPA

It is quite normal by now to feel that you have failed, that you have a piece of junk on your hands, that all is vanity. If this happens, take heart. You might have felt this during shooting, which would have been a lot worse. Actually, things are never so awful as they seem after showing a workprint. Keep in mind that the conditions of viewing invite mainly negative feedback and audiences are disproportionately alienated by a wrong sound balance here, a missed sound dissolve there, a shot or two that needs clipping, and a sequence that belongs earlier. These imbalances and rhythmic ineptitudes massively downgrade a film's impact. The glossy finish you have yet to apply will greatly upgrade the film's reception.

THE USES OF PROCRASTINATION

Whether you are pleased or depressed about your film, it is always good if at all possible to stop working on it for a few weeks and do something else. If this kind of anxiety and depression is new to you, take comfort; you are deep in the throes of the artistic experience. It is the long and painful labor before birth. When you pick up the film again after a lapse, its problems and their solutions will no longer seem overwhelming.

TRY, TRY AGAIN

With a film of some substance that requires a long evolution in the editing room, you should expect to try it out on several new audiences. You may want to show the last cut to the original trial audience to see changes in what they report. While this is not reliable, you can sometimes get a real sense of the progress you have made during the editing process.

As a director with a lot of editing background, I feel that a film truly emerges in the editing process. Magic and miracles appear from the footage, yet even film crew members seldom have much idea about what really happens. It is a process unknown and unguessed at by those who have not lived through it, and for the beginner it will be extremely slow. A year of part-time work to make a thirty-minute film live up to its potential is not unusual.

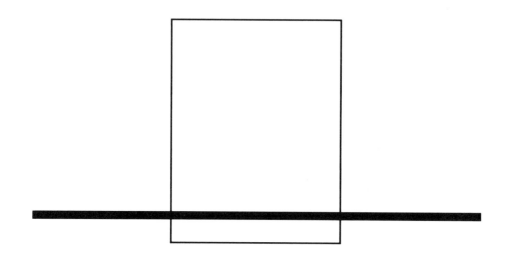

C·H·A·P·T·E·R 1·9

EDITING FROM FINE CUT TO SOUND MIX

THE FINE CUT

With typical caution, filmmakers call the result of the evolutionary editing process the *fine cut,* not final cut, for there may still be minor changes and accommodations. Some of these arise out of laying sound tracks in preparation to produce a master mixed track.

SOUND AND MUSIC TREATMENT DISCUSSIONS

Sound is an imcomparable stimulant to the audience's imagination, and I have given it a very full treatment so you are alert to sound composition possibilities during postproduction. Poor control of sound can also disrupt the dreamlike quality that good film attains. Depending on the experience and imagination of your editor and sound mixer, you may get only what you insist you want. It is important to develop your own ideas and not to think that all magicians can pull a rabbit out of the hat. If the director has not monitored and directed the sound treatment throughout, it may be too late to do anything at the sound mix.

The editor, before going to work on splitting tracks and laying sound effects, should hold a detailed discussion with the director to determine how each sequence should be handled from the sound point of view. Music in particular needs careful thought, as well as participation by the composer before the music is written. Commissioning original music obviates the difficulty of getting (or paying for) copyright clearance on music already recorded. Music is most commonly used as a transitional filler device, or as a mood enhancer, so you will need to agree on the start and finish points. Getting a music segment started is relatively easy, but ending one so the audience does not feel deprived takes careful planning. A good rule of thumb is to conclude or fade out music when something more commanding begins. You might take music out during the first seconds of a noisy street scene, or under the beginning of dialogue. The best guide is to study films that successfully integrate music with the kind of action in your film.

POSTSYNCHRONIZING DIALOGUE

Postsynchronizing dialogue means creating new speech tracks in lip sync with existing picture, and is variously called dubbing, looping, or automatic dialogue replacement (ADR). It is a procedure to be avoided because newly recorded tracks invariably sound flat and dead in contrast with live location recordings. This is not just a question of background sounds (they can be added). It is more a question of sound perspective and location acoustics (impossible to recreate in a studio), and of the artificial situation in which the actor finds himself working to reconstitute a few seconds of dialogue.

SYNC SOUND EFFECTS

Most **film** sound effects can be created wild and fitted afterwards. Sounds that must fit an action (knocking on door, shoveling snow, or footsteps) can often be recreated by recording a little under speed and then cutting out the requisite frames before each impact's "attack." This is not practicable with **video**, where in common with more complex sync effects (two people walking through a quadrangle) the tracks will have to be postsynced just like dialogue, paying attention to the different surfaces that the feet pass over (grass, gravel, concrete, etc.). Doing a postsync session makes one understand how critical it is that the location recordist procure good original recordings in the first place.

Sound effects are professionally created, or recreated, in a special effects theatre called a Foley stage. On a complex production with a big budget, the cost is economically justified. For the low-budget filmmaker, some improvisation can cut costs enormously. What matters is that sound effects are appropriate (always difficult to arrange) and that they are in sync with the action onscreen. Where and how you record them need not matter if they work. Sometimes you can find appropriate sound effects in sound libraries. Never assume that a sound effect listed in a library will work with your particular sequence before you have tried it.

MUSIC

Music sections are logged in minutes, and to the nearest half second. Figure 19–1 shows what a composer's cue sheet looks like.

```
                    "THE WATER-PEOPLE" MUSIC SECTION 4

00:00.0  Music segment begins as Robert jumps in car
00:03.5  Engine starts
00:05.0  Car lurches forward
00:10.5  Cut to Robert checking fuel gauge
00:14.5  Looks in rearview mirror
00:19.0  Frowns, realizing that a motorcycle is behind
00:27.5  Cut to Carl gunning his Harley-Davidson
00:38.0  Cut to Robert staring in mirror, car going off track
00:46.0  Shriek of tyres for 3 seconds as Robert drags car back on to road
00:58.5  Cut to Carl lying forward on motorcycle tank
01:06.5  Cut to BCU Robert's face realizing it's Carl behind
01:08.5  Begin Robert's line: "So you want trouble.  I can give you trouble"
01:12.0  End of line.
01:14.5  Cut to BCU hand opens glove pocket, takes out revolver
01:16.0  Revolver visible
01:17.5  Cut to flashing ambulance light, zoom back and siren drowns out
         music fades to silence and...
01:29.0  music ends here.
```

FIGURE 19–1 ——————————————————————————————————————

Typical scene measurements for a music segment.

COMPOSING AND RECORDING TO SYNC POINTS

An experienced musician will compose to these very precise lengths, paying attention to track features such as the tire screech and the dialogue line so there will be nothing too "busy" in the music to compete with them. The score will be marked at strategic points with the cumulative timing so that as the music is recorded (normally to picture as a safeguard) there is a running check that the sync points line up. The composer might put a melodramatic "sting" on the first appearance of the pursuing motorcycle at 27.5 seconds and on the appearance of the revolver at 01:16, for instance.

THE SESSION

The editor makes the preparations to record music and attends the recording session because only the editor can say whether a particular shot can be lengthened or shortened to accommodate the slight mistimings that always appear during recording. Adjusting the film is easier and more economical than paying musicians to pursue perfect musical synchronicity.

FITTING MUSIC

After the recording session, the editor fits each music section and makes necessary adjustments. If the music is appropriate, the film takes a quantum leap forward in effectiveness.

WHAT THE SOUND MIX CAN DO

The culmination of the editing process, after the film has reached a fine cut, is to prepare and mix the component sound tracks. A whole book could be written on this preeminent subject alone. What follows is a list of essentials along with some tips.

When you have finalized your film's content, fitted music, recorded and laid narration, and laid sound effects and atmospheres, you are ready to make a mix-down of the tracks into one master track.

The mix procedure determines the following:

1. Comparative sound levels (say, between a dialogue foreground track of a voice played over a noisy factory scene)

2. Consistent quality (for example, two tracks from two angles on the same speaker, need equalization [tone control adjustments] and level [volume] adjustments to make them sound similar)

3. Level changes (fade up, fade down, sound dissolves, and level adjustments to accommodate new track elements such as narration, music, or dialogue)

4. Equalization (the filtering and profiling of individual tracks either to match others, or to create maximum intelligibility, listener appeal, or ear comfort; a voice track with a rumbly traffic background can, for instance, be much improved by "rolling off" the lower frequencies, leaving the voice range intact)

5. Sound processing (adding echo, reverberation, telephone effect, etc.)

6. Dynamic range (a compressor squeezes the broad dynamic range of a movie into the narrow range favored in TV transmission; a limiter leaves the main range alone but limits peaks to a preset level)

7. Perspective (to some degree, equalization and level manipulation can mimic perspective changes, thus helping create a sense of space and dimensionality through sound)

8. Stereo channel distribution (if a stereo track is being compiled, different elements go to left and right channels to create a sense of horizontal spread)

9. Noise reduction (Dolby and other noise-reduction systems help minimize the system hiss that would intrude upon quiet passages)

It is vital to note that with a manually operated mixing board changes cannot be done instantaneously at a cut from one sequence to the next. Tracks are checkerboarded so that a channel's equalization and level adjustments can be set up in a silent section prior to the track's arrival. This is most critical when balancing dialogue tracks, as explained below.

SOUND MIX PREPARATION

Track elements are presented here in the conventional hierarchy of importance, although the order may vary; music, for instance, might be faded up to the foreground and dialogue played almost inaudibly low. When cutting and laying sound tracks, be careful not to cut off the barely audible tail of a decaying sound, or to clip the attack. Sound editing should be done at deafening volume, so you hear everything that is there.

Laying **film** tracks is easier than in video because it follows a logic visible to the eye. Each track section is of brown magnetic stock interspersed with different-colored spacing. Fine control is quick and easy since one can cut to the frame (one twenty-fourth of a second) and conceptualizing what one is doing is aided by physically handling the individual tracks.

Because **videotape** editing is accomplished by a transfer process it is more of a remote-control process, but the working principles remain identical.

NARRATION OR VOICE-OVER

If narration is laid to a quiet sequence, you will need to build up the gaps between narration sections with "presence" so the track remains live. Getting actors to make a written narration sound spontaneous is next to impossible, so you should consider using the improv method. Here actors, given a list of particular points to be made, improvise dialogue in character. By making a number of passes, and judicious side-coaching or even interviewing, the actor produces a quantity of entirely spontaneous material that can be edited down. Though laborious, the result will be more spontaneous and natural than anything read from a script.

DIALOGUE TRACKS AND THE PROBLEM OF INCONSISTENCIES

Dialogue tracks for **video** should have been checkerboarded during the editing stage (see Chapter 16), and if not, tracks must be split in preparation for the mix. **Film** dialogue tracks will only now be split up into separate tracks according to the needs imposed by the original mike positioning. In a scene shot from two angles and two mike positions, all the close shot sound goes on one track, and all the medium shot sound goes on the other. Equalization (EQ) settings can now be determined to make the two mike positions sound compatible and the same will apply to multiple sections as they come and go.

Film mixing can handle many tracks, but **video** can often only handle two at a time. Each succeeding section is alternated between the recorder's two available tracks (see Figure 16–3) to allow prior mixing board adjustments during the sections of silent or blank track. Through rehearsal, the mix engineer can set up the controls for each track section to balance the following.

Inconsistent Backgrounds: The ragged, truncated background is the badge of the poorly edited film, its inadequacies of technique stealing attention from the film's content. Frequently when you cut between two speakers in the same location, the background to each is different either in level or quality because the mike was angled differently. Because one angle was recorded subsequent to the other, there may be a different amount of background activity. Be sure to shoot presence tracks on location so one can add to and augment the lighter track to match its heavier counterpart.

Inconsistent Voice Qualities: A variety of location acoustical environments, different mikes, and different mike working distances all play havoc with the consistency of location voice recordings. Intelligent adjusting with sound filtering (EQ) at the mix stage can massively decrease the sense of strain and irritation arising from one's ear having to make constant adjustment to unmotivated and therefore irrational changes.

MUSIC

It is relatively easy to lay in music, but remember to cut in just before the sound attack so you do not hear telltale studio atmosphere or record surface hiss prior to the first chords (see Figure 19–2). Arrow A represents the ideal cut-in point; to its left is unwanted presence or hiss. Following A are three attacks in succession leading to a decay down to silence at arrow B. A similar attack-sustain-decay profile is found for most sound effect—footsteps, for instance—so you use the same editing strategy. By removing sound between x and y we could reduce three footfalls here to two.

SPOT SOUND EFFECTS

These sync to something onscreen, like a door closing, a coin placed on a table, or a phone being picked up. They need to be appropriate and carefully synchronized. Sound effects, especially tape library or disk effects, often bring problematical backgrounds of their own. You can reduce this by cutting into the effect immediately before a sound's 'attack' (Figure 19–2, arrow A) and immediately after its decay (arrow B), thus minimizing the unwanted background's intrusiveness. Mask unwanted sound changes by placing them behind another sound: an unavoidable atmosphere change could be masked by a doorbell ringing, for example. Sometimes you can bring an alien background unobtrusively in and out by fading it up and down rather than letting it thump in and out as cuts.

Bear in mind that the ear registers a sound cut-in or a cut-out much more acutely than a graduated change.

ATMOSPHERES AND BACKGROUND SOUND

One lays in an atmosphere either to create a mood (birdsong over a morning shot of a wood or woodsaw effects over the exterior of a carpenter's shop) or to

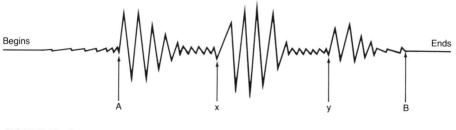

FIGURE 19–2

Sound modulations: attack, three bursts, and decay. Arrows indicate best cutting points.

mask inconsistencies by using something relevant but distracting. Always obey screen logic by laying atmospheres to cover the entire sequence, not just a part of it. Remember that if a door opens, the exterior atmosphere (children's playground, for instance) will rise for the duration that the door is open. If you want to create a sound dissolve, remember to lay the requisite amounts to allow for the necessary overlap.

MIX CHART

Once tracks have been laid to picture, you will need to fill in a mix chart blank (Figure 19–3). In the sample (Figure 19–4) each column represents an individual track. By reading down the chart one sees how individual tracks play against each other, like instruments in a vertically organized music score. The sync pip or "BEEP" at 00.30 is a single frame of tone that serves as an aural sync check when the tracks begin running. Track segment starts and finishes are marked with timings (or footages for a film mix). A straight line at the start or finish represents a sound cut (as at 04:09 and 04:27), while a chevron represents either a fade-in (track 4 at 04:10) or a fade-out (tracks 2 at 02:09). Timings at fades refer to the beginning of a fade-in, or the end of a fade-out. At 02:04 to 02:09 there is a fade-out on track 4 overlapping a fade-in for the cassette machine. This is a cassette machine. This is called a cross-fade or sound dissolve. You can see that ours is a five-second cross-fade. It is prudent to lay in more on both tracks in case you later decide you would like a longer dissolve.

Vertical space on the chart is seldom a linear representation of time. You might have seven minutes of talk with a very simple chart, then half a minute of railroad station montage with a profusion of individual tracks for each shot. To avoid either unwieldy or crowded mix charts, use no more vertical space than is necessary for clarity to the eye. To help the sound mix engineer, who works under great pressure in the half-dark, shade in the track boxes with a highlight marker.

SOUND MIX STRATEGY

PREMIXING

One reel of a feature film may mix down from forty or more tracks. Since only one to four sound engineers man a mix board, it requires a sequence of premixes. The same principle holds true for a much humbler production, with only a four- to eight-track mix, especially if the medium is videotape, where only two tracks at a time can be played off tape. It is vital to premix in an order that reserves control over the most important elements to the last. If you were to premix dialogue and effects right away, then a subsequent addition of more effects or music would uncontrollably augment and thicken the competition to the dialogue. Since the intelligibility of most films depends on audible dialogue, you must retain control over dialogue-to-background level until the very last stage of mixing.

```
SOUND  MIX  LOG  Production_____

Date__/__/____ Reel #____  Page # ____  Premix #____  Editor_____
```

Action cues	Track 1	Track 2	Track 3	Track 4	Cassette/Disc

FIGURE 19–3 ————————————————————————————————————

Sound mix log form.

Note that for **video** in particular, each generation of analogue sound transfer introduces additional noise (system hiss) that is most audible in quiet tracks such as a slow speaking voice in a silent room, or a very spare music track. The order of premixes may thus be influenced by which tracks should most be protected from repeated retransfer.

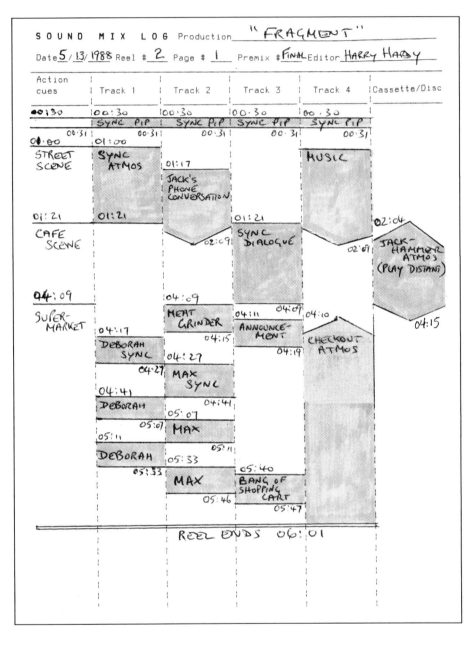

FIGURE 19–4

Specimen sound mix log.

USING A WILD (NON SYNC) SOURCE

To decrease premixing, one can feed in nonsync atmospheres from a cassette player or other high-quality sound source (see Figure 16–4). Sound must usually be faded in and out since frame-accurate cut-ins or cut-outs may be impossible.

TAILORING

Many tracks if played as laid will enter and exit abruptly, giving an unpleasantly jagged impression to the listener's ear. This negatively affects how people respond to your subject matter, so it is important to achieve a seamless effect whenever you are not deliberately disrupting attention. The trouble comes when you cut from a quiet to a noisy track, or vice versa, and this can be greatly minimized by tailoring; that is, making a very quick fade-up or fade-down of the noisy track to meet the quiet track on its own terms. The effect onscreen is still of a cut, but one that no longer assaults the ear (see Figure 19–5).

COMPARATIVE LEVELS: ERR ON THE SIDE OF CAUTION

It is common for mixing facilities to use expensive hi-fi speakers. For **video** work the results are dangerously misleading. Low-budget filmmakers must expect their work to be seen mostly on domestic TV sets, which have miserably small, cheap speakers. Not only does the unsuspecting consumer lose frequency and dynamic ranges, he loses the dynamic separation between loud and soft, so that foregrounds previously separated become swamped by backgrounds. If you are mixing a dialogue scene with a traffic background atmosphere, err on the conservative side and make a deliberately high separation, keeping traffic low and voices high. Many mix suites keep a TV on hand to give the customer a salutory reminder of what the home viewer will actually hear.

REHEARSE, THEN RECORD

Mixing is best accomplished by familiarizing oneself with the problems of one short section at a time, and building sequence by sequence from convenient

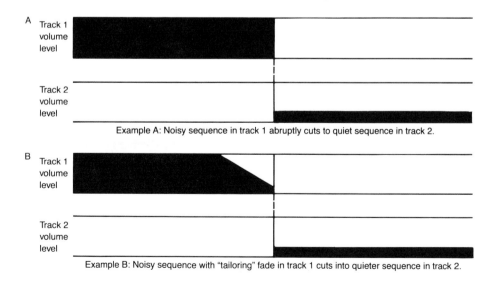

Example A: Noisy sequence in track 1 abruptly cuts to quiet sequence in track 2.

Example B: Noisy sequence with "tailoring" fade in track 1 cuts into quieter sequence in track 2.

FIGURE 19–5

Abrupt sound cut tailored by quick fade of outgoing track so it matches level of the incoming track.

stopping points. Check your work as you go, and at the end, check the whole mix without stopping.

FILM MIXES

The **film** medium is sprocketed so tracks or a premix are easily synced up to a start mark in the picture reel leader. The final mix will be transferred by a film laboratory to an optical (that is, photographic) track and photographically combined with the picture to produce a composite projection print. Sometimes television will transmit from double system; that is, picture and the magnetic mix will be loaded on a telecine machine with separate but interlocked sound. The track is taken from the high-quality magnetic original instead of from the much lower quality photographic track. As hi-fi TV catches on, this will happen more often.

VIDEO MIXES

Providing there are unbroken **video** control tracks, it is possible to transfer in absolute sync using a sync start mark from one tape to another (see Figure 16–5 and accompanying text). In practice this means that video mixing is done from a number of generations away from the master edit, with resulting picture degradation. Subsequently, the master mix is dubbed back onto the master cut, which is only a second generation picture. A word of caution: Since eventually this means erasing original tracks to make way for the mix, always first experiment with copies to verify the procedure.

KEEP A SAFETY COPY OF THE MASTER MIX

Because a mix requires a long, painstaking process, it is professional practice to immediately make a safety or backup copy. The safety copy is stored safely in another building and copies are made from the master mix.

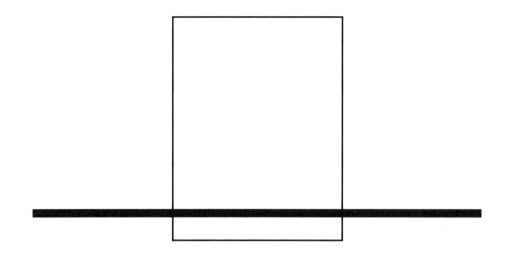

C·H·A·P·T·E·R 2·0

TITLES AND ACKNOWLEDGMENTS

Although every film has a working title, the final title is often decided late because it must epitomize the film's concerns and intentions. Bear in mind that your film's title may be the only advertising copy your audience ever sees. TV listings and festival programs rarely have space to describe their offerings, so the title you choose may be your sole means of drawing attention to your film.

A sure sign of amateurism is a film accompanied by an egocentric welter of credit titles. The same name should not crop up in four key capacities, and acknowledgments should be brief. An actor should not be described as "Starring Sherry Mudge" unless Sherry's fame makes the claim realistic. With union actors there will often be contractual obligations over the size and wording of title credits, and these must be scrupulously observed.

Titles should be few in words and short in duration. There are plenty of examples available on TV. Locate models of a length and budget commensurate with your own. Many of the most artistically ambitious European films have brief and classically simple white on black titles.

Appropriate onscreen timings can be assessed by reading the contents of each card (which represents one screen of titling) one and a half times out loud. When you shoot the titles, be sure to shoot at least three times as much as you need. This allows for a title to be extended if needed and for the all-important **video** editing preroll.

White titles on a moving background are nice, but unless you have access to video superimposition technology they are out of your reach, as will be dissolves and wipes. Plain titles on a colored artwork, or a still photo background can be tasteful and effective.

Many favors are granted filmmakers merely for an acknowledgment in the titles, and of course promises made must be carried out. Funding often comes with a contractual obligation to acknowledge the fund in a prescribed wording, so this and all such obligations should be carefully checked before titles are specified. Spelling should be carefully gone over by at least two highly literate checkers. The spelling of people's names should receive special care.

Titling work has to be done carefully and meticulously, since even small inequities of proportion and straightness show up badly and make titles look amateurish. In general, a wide-contrast ratio between lettering brightness and background brightness is best avoided in **video**, as the circuits that adjust for exposure tend to go haywire and give you out-of-focus lettering. Even with **film**, white titles are easy to overexpose, and this leads to a similar loss of definition.

Never assume that titles will be "all right on the night." They are often tricky to get right, especially if you are at all ambitious and want fancy effects. Titles, like troubles, are sent to try us, so give yourself plenty of time in case you must reshoot.

Do not forget to include the © symbol before your name and the year as a claim to the copyright of the material. To file for copyright in the United States, write to the Registrar of Copyrights, Library of Congress, Washington, DC 20450, and ask for current information on copyrighting.

LOW-COST TITLING

If you are meticulous, quite professional-looking titles can be made using press-stick lettering available from art shops and stationers. There is a bewildering choice of typeface, and you should choose one that reflects the nature of your film. Keep in mind that spindly or ornate lettering may be illegible on the TV screen. Lettering size can be adjusted by using either loose or tight framing, always assuming your layout permits the latter within the camera's frame, and assuming that your lens will focus close enough.

You can create black letters over a still frame by projecting a 35mm slide into a rear projection screen and placing the lettering on a clear plastic sheet (called acetate sheet) over the screen. Rear projection (with the slide reversed so it reads the right way around from the front) allows you to keep both slide projector and videotape camera on the same axis, so the lettering does not suffer from keystone distortion (see Figure 20–1). You will, however, see the grain of the screen with any rear-projection work.

White lettering on a graphic background (a still photo or dark-toned painting, for example) can be achieved by using white lettering mounted on an acetate sheet, which can be laid over a choice of still background. The whole sandwich can be lit and shot from the front. You can change white titles on a black ground to any color you want, simply by putting the appropriate filter gel in front of the camera lens, or altering the camera's color balance. If your camera has inverse video, you can change black letters on white to white letters on black at the flick of a switch.

A character generator is a computerized device that electronically produces lettering and symbols on the screen. It is useful for producing rapid, nicely spaced,

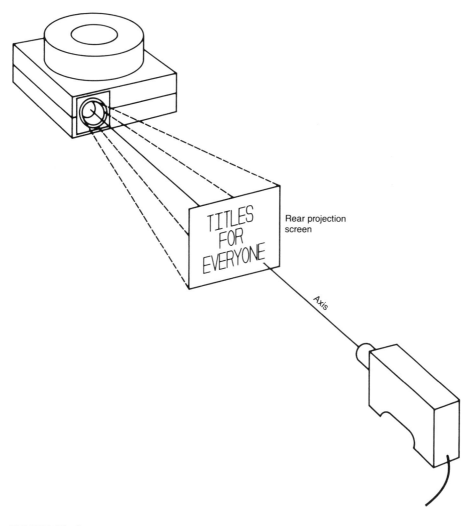

FIGURE 20–1

Rear projection only works if camera and slide projector are on the same axis.

centered, and legible titling, but the low-priced ones are likely to have an electronic typeface inappropriate for most films.

GETTING TITLES MADE COMMERCIALLY

Larger cities have companies that specialize in making up and shooting titles, and it may be a wise investment to give a good film professional-looking titles. Since the bulk of optical house work is for wealthy commercials producers, you should check prices carefully in advance, as titling can be vastly expensive. Be sure to meet and discuss with the person who will be making them up. Ask what further charges you face for reshooting should you be dissatisfied.

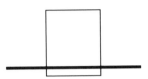

POSTPRODUCTION SUMMARY

The points summarized here are only those most salient. Some are commonly overlooked. To find them or anything else relating to postproduction, go to the table of contents at the beginning of this part.

EDITING IN GENERAL

- Interesting discrepancies of information drive the audience into an active, problem-solving relationship to the film, instead of the usual passive one.
- Every call to imagination or judgment is an acknowledgment of equality with the audience, and an invitation to participate in discovery.
- Are there dramatic advantages to be gained from disrupting the subject's natural advance in time?
- Cross-cutting between two stories allows time to be telescoped or stretched, and aids comparison and irony.
- The operative word falling on each new shot helps us interpret the image's meaning.
- Changing the juxtaposition of words and shots can imply different meanings.
- It is easier to shorten a film than to pump substance back into one prematurely tightened.
- If an edited version is different from what you expected, see it again before commenting.
- Stay away from the cutting room and preserve your objectivity.

VIEWING RUSHES

- Avoid taking your attention away from the screen.
- In the rushes book note down chosen takes, special comments, and any ideas and transient impressions; they will be an important resource later.
- Note down moods and feelings evoked by scenes or individuals.
- Nothing outside the rushes is relevant to the film you can make.
- The director discusses intentions for each sequence with the editor and encourages early, loose assembly of whole film.

PREPARING TO START EDITING

- Time spent making a consistent, intelligent log is time liberated for creativity later.
- From rushes mark up script to show actual coverage and number of takes for each angle.

EDITING PROCEDURE

- In **film** do not forget to put aside three frames minimum between adjacent lengths of film to allow for cement splices in conforming.
- Assemble **film** workprint sound as one track containing main dramatic elements (dialogue, atmosphere, or music). Later you will split these tracks apart.
- Assemble **video** tracks, especially dialogue, in checkerboard fashion to allow early premix with equalization.
- Leave spaces in dialogue for featured sound effects.

FIRST ASSEMBLY

- Make first assembly long, loose, and simple using master shots and a minimum of intercutting so you get an early view of the whole film.
- See first assembly without interruption and make quick list of what was memorable.
- See first assembly a second time and see if your impressions are confirmed.

ROUGH CUT

- Work on each sequence to make use of all material, but still keep pace slow and cutting simple.
- View whole film, and pay attention to material that is not working.
- Tackle only top level of problems in each pass and see new version before addressing a further level of problems.

DIAGNOSTIC METHODS

- Make block diagram of movie to spot invisible anomalies (blank form is in Figure 3–1).
- After recutting and viewing, check results by making revised block diagram.

FINE CUT

- Where necessary, alter performance rhythms in action and reaction according to time needed by characters to process particular information.
- Use eyeline changes and reactions to alter those moments of special awareness that give us access to a character's inner life.
- Where you have multiple angle coverage, experimentally rebalance subjective and objective angles so the sequence feels right.
- Try counterpointing visual against speech to suggest subjective vision.
- In dialogue sequences, examine cuts for balance between showing the speaker and the listener. Frequently the character acted upon adds more dimension to the exchange.
- Introduce overlap cutting to set up a visual cutting rhythm that is separate and meaningful in contrast with speech and sound effect rhythms.

- Tighten transition cuts where action flows from one composition to another.
- Examine sequence transitions for sound overlap or sound dissolve possibilities.
- Put the film aside for a week or two, and see it again before deciding the fine cut is final.

EVOKING A TRIAL AUDIENCE RESPONSE

- You can't please everyone.
- Tell your audience the film's title and warn them of what is missing (music, sound effects, atmospheres, etc.).
- In a trial showing, exert maximum control over sound.
- Direct audience attention to issues over which you need information, but ask nondirective questions and listen carefully for what is really being said.
- Do not abandon any central intention without long, hard thought.
- Do not rush into changes of any kind.
- Expect to feel depressed about the film, that it's failing, etc.

MUSIC

- Choice of music should give access to interior of character or subject.
- Music can signal emotional level at which audience should approach the scene.
- You can not know that music works until you try it against the picture.
- Better no music than indifferent or bad music.

FINALIZING SOUND

- Decide what, if anything, needs postsynchronizing.
- Start looking for sound effects early; they are part of your orchestra.
- Plan featured sound effects to go in dialogue gaps (or vice versa).

SOUND MIX

- Premix, retaining control over balance of important elements until last.
- Soften ragged sound cuts by tailoring the louder to the quieter.
- When mixing foreground speech with background (music, FX, atmosphere, etc.) err on the side of caution and separate foreground well from background.
- Check completed mix against picture at end without stopping.

TITLES

- Keep credits short and few.
- Each title card should be on the screen long enough to be read aloud one and a half times.
- Choose a legible, clean typeface that goes with the period and style of your film.

- Double-check all spelling, especially of people's names.
- Include acknowledgments, funding sources, dedications, etc. exactly according to contractual obligations.
- Copyright your film with the Library of Congress.

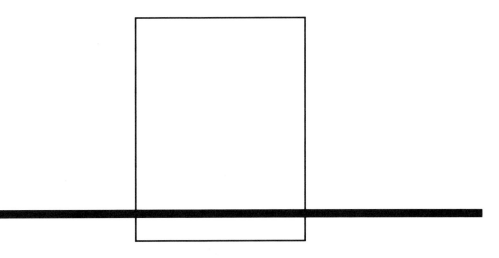

P·A·R·T I·V

AESTHETICS AND AUTHORSHIP

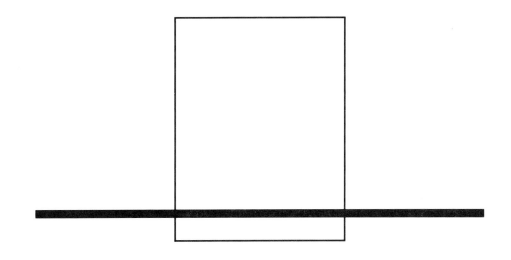

C·H·A·P·T·E·R 2·1

MAKING THE VISIBLE SIGNIFICANT

Parts I through III of this book deal primarily with the requirements of the director interpreting a given script. Here in Part IV are ideas for the most advanced filmmaker and guidelines for the *auteur;* that is, the writer/director wanting to exercise an integrated control across the spectrum of the writing and realization processes. Necessarily, such control is linked to advanced concepts about how work of depth and resonance is created, how screen works achieve a strongly individual identity, and how the narrative form itself might be expanded and developed.

Curiously, the *auteur* exists both at the beginner level and at the pinnacles of the world film industry, but much less apparently in the middle ground. A typical evolution begins in film school where the filmmaker starts as a Renaissance figure doing anything and everything. Wanting to produce more sophisticated work, he or she soon specializes in one of the crafts. Competently handled, that craft becomes the bridge into the film industry where initially he or she makes a slender living as a free-lancer. Now a specialist technician, our filmmaker becomes known and established and living becomes less precarious. If during the following years the drive to direct results in a break, early directing work is likely to be cautious and commercial, for death at the box office means dropping down the ladder again. With two or three modest successes a director can expand into more personally meaningful work. Even when limited by survival instincts and money interests to popular work, the astute director can flex artistic muscle and learn to control the medium. This is even true to a more limited degree in commercials.

When a director gains a mature control both over the medium and over what he or she needs to say through it, audiences begin to detect and be excited by an authorial identity at work. The filmmaker who once upon a time had total control over a very small film now regains similar ubiquity over an immensely expensive and popularly significant medium. The *auteur* reemerges, now driving a better car.

Part IV examines advanced authorship concepts as they apply to subjects and sources of ideas, screenwriting and adaptation, screen archetypes and genre, and stylization in environment and characterization. It analyzes alternatives in structure, form, style, and point of view, and offers ways of refreshing invention through improvisation.

Throughout this book I have suggested that memorable cinema communicates an integrated point of view, not just as the occasional subjective camera angle or interior monologue, but as a sense of access to a fellow spirit's inward and outward vision. I do not mean the heroic and idealized characters enshrined by the star system, but rather the cinema through which one recognizes unfinished business in one's culture or even in one's personal life. Charles Foster Kane, for example, is a man blinded by his own rhetoric and corrupted by the power he has gathered, but *Citizen Kane* (1941) shows how much his actions are directed by the hurt child within. The lovers in David Lean's *Brief Encounter* (1945), at first stuffy and ludicrous, gain stature and poignancy as we comprehend the degree to which each belongs within a code of honor that places loyalty to commitments above passion and experiment. Somewhere in our lives, each of us has done the same, been the same as these.

How should one go about reflecting such things on the screen? Robert Richardson goes to the heart of the problem filmmakers face in comparison with writers: "Literature often has the problem of making the significant somehow visible, while film often finds itself trying to make the visible significant" (*Literature and Film,* chapt. 5 [Bloomington, IN: Indiana University Press, 1969]). Unfortunately, film's surfeit of realistic detail invites the audience to look no deeper than the surfaces rendered so minutely and attractively by the camera. This leads us to make simplistic valuations. In Claude Jutra's *Dreamspeaker* (1978) the delinquent boy running away from a remedial institution seems to be doing the inevitable, and the fact that he is sheltered by two North American Indians is a simple act of human goodness. By looking deeper, however, one sees that the story is really a parable comparing modern, clinical concepts of human care with ancient, animistic ones.

As so often happens with film, Jutra had to solve the problem of making what is apparent—the film's actions and its events—also function as a more probing, metaphysical inquiry. There are many subtle ways, of course, that film authorship can draw our attention to a film's subtext, but without a very astute use of film language and structure, an underlying discourse can go completely unnoticed. If it does get through, it may seem too intellectually rarefied to raise its head amid the exuberant physicality of the material world. Film has the uniquely modern mission of finding and validating the spiritual underlying the material world.

One must admit that literature, portable and consumed contemplatively at one's own pace, is still a superior forum for intellectual discourse. The cinema, moving at a predetermined pace and compelled to approach the spirit by way of the physical, is handicapped. Film, like living, cannot be contemplated at the time, although the popularity of the VCR is allowing people to interrupt the movie and reexamine a passage. By its nature, film is not ideas but sensory impressions that take root in the memory and imagination, inhabiting and haunting us for days or even years. Some screen works beckon one to return for the rest of one's life, like profound and uncompleted relationships.

The fiction film, the documentary, and the short story have something in common. All are consumed at a sitting and so perhaps carry on the oral tradition. Like it, they seem best suited to representing personally felt and experienced history rather than issues and ideas in abstraction. Perhaps that restriction lies more with the way we use film than with film's inherent limitations, but surely any short, immediate form must entertain if it is to connect with the emotional and imaginative life of a mass audience. Like all entertainers, the filmmaker has a precarious economic existence, and either understands his audience or goes hungry. Richardson (ibid., chapt. 1) argues convincingly that the vitality and optimism of the cinema in contrast to other twentieth-century art forms results from its collaborative authorship and its dependency upon public response. While it would be foolish to claim that only the appreciation of the common people matters, surely the enduring presence of traditional forms should remind us of how much we still share with the unacademic and intuitive tastes of our forebears.

Actually, the ordinary person's tastes and instincts—yours and mine—are not simple at all, but highly cultivated and accultured. But because we seldom discuss them or use them to make statements through art, we lack confidence when it is time to consciously live by them.

Making a film is exciting precisely because it demands that one expose one's perceptions and judgments, for an audience and for oneself. The cinema's strength and popularity lies with its power to make an audience see from someone else's point of view. In works for the screen we see communally through different eyes and experience visions other than our own. For significant sections of the world, recently divested of thousands of years of spiritual beliefs, this is a reminder of community and something beyond self, whose value cannot be underestimated. Just as importantly, the best cinema is relativistic, that is, it allows us to experience related but opposing points of view in juxtaposition. Used responsibly this is an immensely civilizing force to offset the conformity imposed by merchandizers striving to normalize us in every imaginable sphere.

As a filmmaker, then, you will need to concern yourself not only with self-expression (which untethered can be a narcissistic display of conscience or feelings), but with serving your society through entertainment that has an underlying seriousness of purpose. Even then, the most perceptive in your audience may still miss what your film says unless you find special ways to drive the audience's awareness beyond the obvious.

To use the screen or any other medium well is surely to give access to another person's subjectivity, to communicate the poignancy and transience of his separate existence, and to outline the tragedy implicit in his limitations. Intelligently used, the screen can recreate the intensity of existence with breathtaking economy and precision. For the filmmaker striving to create this dramatic resonance, filmmaking must always be experimental, always pushing toward metaphysical meanings, or external realism will engulf with its tedious familiarity our sense of sharing the characters' (and filmmakers') inner existences.

Ideas about how to reveal subjectivity, and about the way an audience inhabits and explores the main characters' reality, must therefore permeate any useful theory uniting the elements of filmmaking, whether in scriptwriting, directing actors, planning coverage, or editing. This is the subject of the next chapters.

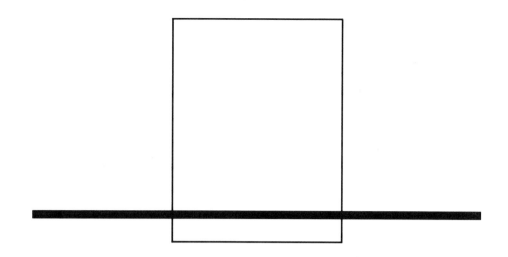

C·H·A·P·T·E·R 2·2

ON THE PROCESS OF WRITING

This chapter supplements *Chapter 2: On the Screenplay* by examining the work of the director who wishes to work from original ideas. Screenwriting was once a discrete craft, but today screen authorship is increasingly seen as a hybrid skill that starts with the typewriter and develops through *mise-en-scène* and editing. No book on contemporary directing techniques would be complete without some comments on original writing.

By the inexperienced, scriptwriting is handled as a literary undertaking. But a screenplay is a blueprint, not a complete form of expression, so this is the beginning of a false trail. Screenwriting must be tempered by knowledge of the film medium and the process by which films reach the screen. Films are much less a transcription of language and ideas from paper than they are a self-referential stream—sights and sounds attuned to an audience's sensibility.

In any case, turning a script into a polished, professional film is not accomplished alone, as writing is. It requires the input of other specialized, idiosyncratic minds. For example, dialogue that one assumes to have a set meaning has in the mouth of an accomplished actor an unforeseen range of shading and subtlety—nuances impossible to prescribe in the script even if you happen to think of them.

As a scriptwriter one tries to put on paper the movie one runs in one's head; but only what can be written down survives from that mental composition. Even then one cannot be sure that what is on paper can effectively be translated to the screen. What would you put on the screen for, "By the light of a melancholy sunset she broods upon the children she will never have"? Plainly, making films goes beyond what goes down on paper, but what does go down matters very much indeed.

The mechanics of screenwriting are well described in a number of script-writing manuals (see Bibliography). They represent a large reservoir of professional experience to help you write a good traditional screenplay.

WRITING YOUR OWN SCREENPLAY

The act of writing is really the mind contemplating its own workings and thus being able to go further. How one approaches writing very much affects the quality and quantity of one's output.

Needless to say, one must learn to type. Touch typing takes ten or fifteen lessons but it is the most useful skill you will ever acquire. If at all possible, write on a computer. The worst word processor is better than the best typewriter because you can alter and restructure at will, and never have to retype anything. I am writing this on an old Kaypro that I love dearly and that one can find used for a few hundred dollars.

WRITE NO MATTER WHAT!

Set aside regular periods of time and make yourself write whether the results are good, bad, or indifferent. The first draft is the hardest so do not wait to feel inspired, just keep hacking away. Write scenes that interest you, rather than writing scenes in order. Once a few things are down on paper, you can develop and connect what you have written. Try always to write for the silent screen. Writing for the camera means dealing with human exteriors. To make your characters' inner lives accessible, keep in mind that a person has no inner experience without an outward sign in their behavior.

If this or any other advice stops you writing, then write early drafts any way you can. Write any way, anywhere, anyhow—just write.

IDEA CLUSTERING, NOT LINEAR DEVELOPMENT

Most people who want to write and cannot are suffering the effects of doctrinaire teaching earlier in life. The most common block results from the writer trying to write in a linear fashion—beginning, middle, and end in that order. At some point the writer ends up in a desert with nowhere to go. But at any stage one can always resort to one's associative potential. Where the pedestrian intellect fails, the exuberant subconscious will obligingly run rings around it. Here is one way to turn it loose.

Take a large sheet of paper and put down a central idea in the middle, such as "happiness" or "rebuilding the relationship." As fast as you can write, surround it with associated words, no matter how far removed or wacky. The circle of words should look like satellites around a planet. Now around each of these individual ideas put a ring of words you associate with it. Soon your paper will be crammed with a little solar system.

Now look at what you have and start making lists classifying the ideas into families, groups, hierarchies, systems, anything that speaks of relationship. While doing this you will find all kinds of solutions to your original problem taking shape.

WRITING IS CIRCULAR, NOT LINEAR

Finished writing is of course linear, but the process is anything but. Scripts are not written in the order of concept, step outline, and screenplay, nor even as beginning, middle, and end. Although the odd screenwriter may work this way, he or she is just as likely to write the most clearly visualized scenes first, making an outline to gain an overview, and later filling in the gaps and distilling the concept from the results.

Like any art process, scriptwriting—indeed filmmaking itself—looks untidy and wastefully circular to the uninitiated, and totally alien to the tidy manufacturing processes dear to the commercial mind. This produces much friction and misery in the film industry, where artists handling people and concepts must work within financial structures imposed by managers wanting to make filmmaking efficient, that is, profitable.

FILTER OUT RULING ESSENCES

Writing a step outline and a dramatic premise is a vital part of gaining control over what the script is truly about. It sounds paradoxical that a writer should ever need to discover the themes and meanings in his or her own work, but the creative imagination functions at several different levels, some of the most important activity taking shape well beyond the reach of the conscious mind. The summarizing, winnowing process of making outline and concept statements helps raise the submerged into view.

The amended step outline and concept following each new draft will point the way to further revision and rewriting. It is thus an important way station between drafts that makes analysis unavoidable and development inevitable.

WORK TO CREATE A MOOD

Settings that are bland or unbelievable compel the audience to struggle against disbelief with every scene change, something the theatre makes us do each time the curtain rises. Using locations and sound composition intelligently will provide a powerfully emotional setting, and thrust the audience into the heart of a situation.

WRITE FOR THE CINEMA'S STRENGTHS

To avoid a theatrical film, turn conversations into behavioral exchanges comprehensible to a foreigner. Where you are forced to use dialogue there is probably a real need, and in any case a screenplay with sparse dialogue raises words to a higher significance. We are impressed most by a person's acts because the verbal is abstract and uncommitted until endorsed by acts. Perhaps for that reason the German director Werner Herzog did not telephone or write to his beloved mentor Lotte Eisner lying sick in Paris, but trudged all the way from Munich on foot. Decide for yourself what you like about the cinema and consciously compose to take advantage of these strengths.

WRITE WITH THE AUDIENCE IN MIND

If drama is to reach beyond the egocentricity of therapy, the writer must be aware of the broader implications of the material for an audience. To write for an audience means not exploitation but trying to conceive works that participate in modern thought and modern dilemmas, and that prompt questions and ideas cutting across conventional thinking.

TEST YOUR ASSUMPTIONS

The author writes from experience, imagination, and intuition as well as from assumptions stored in the unconscious. The author knows her character Harry would never perjure himself in court, but her audience knows nothing of the sort unless his honesty is first established. To do this, we might make Harry go back into a store to pay for a newspaper he unthinkingly carried out with the groceries. Now his honesty is demonstrated.

It is important to stress that any form of writing—for print, song, or screen—creates significant spaces that the audience must constantly fill in from its own values, imagination, and life experience. The reader of a novel, for example, supplies an image of the setting and the characters' appearances. A film audience does not have to visualize the physical world of the story, but it does constantly decide on characters' motives and morals. Just as a painting implies life going on beyond the edges of its frame, so does a narrative work have characters and ideas that extend beyond what we see and hear. Not only do they have additional, unseen life but they acquire a resonance that is universal.

For the writer, anything that is to be implied must first be named, if there are not to be counterproductive ambiguities and contradictions. Then the writer must figure out how to make each intention reach the audience, and to make each event or implication fit into the character's logic.

In a film about a man adopted in childhood who searches for his biological mother, it would be illogical for him never to examine his birth certificate or to question his foster parents. These are the first steps in any serious inquiry, and a screenplay must carefully take account of such imperatives. At a later point it would be equally baffling if he was immediately happy and fulfilled when he found her. This would be simplistic, either on his part or on the writer's. If it is the character who is naive, we should expect his gullibility to land him in situations of stress that would ultimately lead to greater understanding. If the naiveté is actually the writer's, the audience will realize with disappointment that it is smarter than the movie.

A piece of fiction, though it is a self-contained world with its own set of rules governing the characters' lives, cannot capriciously violate what the audience knows from life. It must be interesting, representative, and consistent if it is to suggest the depth of real life. This requires that the authors (writer, director, actors, editor) share a body of knowledge that is a great deal more complete than what appears in the film itself. It also means withholding just enough of that information to keep the audience guessing and involved, but not baffled or confused.

TEST YOUR SCRIPT EXHAUSTIVELY ON OTHERS

To go ahead with an imperfectly tested script is to leave unexamined a Pandora's box. All kinds of demons will eventually emerge. To avoid this, you will need to acquire a complete and accurate sense of what the audience knows and feels at each stage of the proposed film. You get this from exhaustive discussion with critical readers, who should be replaced over time when they, like the writers themselves, become overfamiliar with the material. In seeking responses, try to find mature listeners or readers whose values you share and respect. As with responses to a fine cut, you are not interested in a film the respondent would make. You want to know what, as an audience member, he or she understands from the script, what the characters are like, what seems to be driving them, which scenes are effective, and so on.

It is also good practice to explain one's ideas to anyone smart who will listen. If "the unexamined life is not worth living," the unexamined story idea is not worth filming. Hearing yourself telling your own story is the very best way to see your ideas from another's point of view. Repeatedly exposing your ideas to skeptical listeners also makes one confront the clichés in one's own thinking. After all, one's first thoughts are the same junk as everyone else's. Originality is not innate talent but something that appears only when you repeatedly reject the conventional.

ACT ON CRITICISM ONLY AFTER REFLECTION

In an audience medium the director must want to speak to a general audience, and seeking individual responses to a script is an early and, it must be said, potentially misleading exposure. Doing this is also a test of self-knowledge, for if you resist all suggestions and argue with the validity of the responses, you are probably insecure. If instead you agree with almost everything, set about a complete rewrite, or scrap the project, you are very insecure. If, however, you continue to believe in what you are doing but recognize some truth in what your critics say, you are progressing nicely.

Never make changes hastily or impulsively. Let the criticism lie for a few days, and see what your mind has filtered out as valid. If in doubt, do not make changes or abandon your intentions. Work on something else until your mind quietly tells you what must be done.

Do not show your work to family or intimates until it is finished because, knowing you so well, they will want to save you by hiding your many faults and naiveté from public view.

Be ready to keep changing the script all the way up to the day of shooting. A script is not itself an artwork that finds a final form; it is like the plan for an invasion that must be altered in the light of each day's fresh intelligence.

TESTING WITH A SCRATCH CAST

Before you cast a script, assemble a scratch cast to read the whole thing through. Each actor, however inexperienced, will identify with one character and bring your script under a new kind of scrutiny. It is important when you cast and rehearse that you do not get taken unnecessarily by surprise. You should be able to wholeheartedly justify every word of dialogue and every stage direction in the script.

REWRITE, REWRITE, REWRITE

In the theatre, it is not unusual for the author of a new play to be on hand for weeks of rehearsal, and for many of the early audience performances. Every night, director, writer, and cast will review how the audience reacted to each part of the show. Editing, compressing, or expanding your material where needed, simplifying and even wholesale rewriting of it will further shape the material to take advantage of the way "reading audiences" receive the piece.

In filmmaking, finished versions cannot be tested on audiences the way they can be in the theatre, so reshaping must be accomplished during the script development and cast rehearsal period. Rewriting is frequently omitted or resisted by student production groups out of inexperience or because it threatens the writer's ego.

No matter if the screenplay is your own or the work of another hand, the director must be ready to independently follow up lines of development by rewriting as the need arises. By this I do not mean just the fine-tuning of dialogue, but the addition, deletion, and substitution of whole scenes, should the need emerge. Feature films I worked on were regularly undergoing rewrites the day before shooting. Writers hate this compulsive rewriting, but their standards for completion arise from habits of solo creation, while filmmaking is an organic, physical process that must adapt to the unfolding reality of cast and shooting— both in negative and positive implication.

ON DIRECTING FROM YOUR OWN SCREENPLAY

If you are preparing to direct from your own script, work hard to distance yourself by treating it like someone else's work. Unless one has learned over a period of years to be professionally rigorous with one's own writing, there are many unexamined assumptions waiting to surface later as full-blown problems that can easily sap the writer/director's confidence and authority. By carrying out all available analytical steps you can with difficulty gain an objective understanding of your own work.

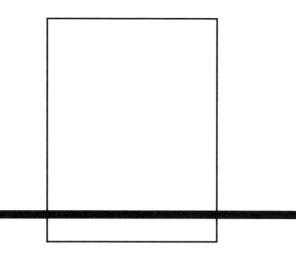

C·H·A·P·T·E·R 2·3

SELF-EXPRESSION, SUBJECTS, AND ADAPTATION

GENERATING IDEAS

Most people by the age of twenty have experienced the full range of human emotion, and have already glimpsed most of what human life can offer. In your home, family, school, games, friendships, and solitude you have analogously experienced war, politics, dictatorship, fear, hate, rage, despair, vindictiveness, theft, rejection, and rebellion as well as tenderness, generosity, growth, affection, harmony, companionship, collaboration, acceptance, and being in love. The work of the storyteller is to interpret what is personal, to project it to more embracing conclusions, and to place it in the mainstream of human experience.

You could now withdraw like Proust into his cork-lined room and write for the rest of your life in pursuit of the meanings inside your wellspring of experience. All the sources you will ever need are already there. It is now a matter of confronting the mysteries, discovering what is significant, and connecting causes and effects to find the order and inevitability that underlies your life. You will never find them all, and what you do find will constantly grow and change.

Let me demonstrate from personal experience what this means. I grew up as an isolated middle-class child in an English agricultural village. Sometimes the other kids jeered at my accent and I was derided, envied my possessions, and ambushed. I absorbed several things from this: that fear was a constant in life that one must endure alone, that the individual was different and unacceptable to the majority, that one could expect little help from the adults who had power, and that one must adopt a different persona to be acceptable outside one's own home.

In essence I needed and developed a ghetto survival mentality. My experience has equipped me to empathize with what the black person in a white neighborhood feels, or the Jew among Gentiles. I represented a class deeply resented by the village and was made to pay for it. Much later I began to see how my victimization was not my fault for being cowardly, nor was it even a personal matter on the part of my tormentors. The village children and I were blindly carrying out roles in an historical opposition of which we knew nothing. Years later, coming to understand how the rural poor were suppressed and exploited in the previous century, I also came to understand and even sympathize with the bitterness in their actions. Losing my fear, becoming aware of how a class's history molds its children, my relationship in the Royal Air Force with fellow conscripts from similar backgrounds was quite different and very gratifying.

In earlier life, then, I lived on both sides of an invisible but very old historical barricade. Now I can participate in the reality of others in analogous situations. I understand why I am drawn to foreigners and the displaced, to outsiders with unorthodox vision. Their issues are mine. As a child I wore a scarlet letter and as a result I feel for others. Whites stereotype blacks, blacks stereotype whites, men stereotype women, the rich stereotype the poor, and on and on.

I am less interested in this as an abstract political notion than I am moved by the plight of the unaware individual caught in a web, struggling to survive and adapt. Any story containing these trace elements quickens my interest. I see the counterparts everywhere: in news stories, fiction, the lives of friends and acquaintances, myths and legends, folk stories, and historical or cultural figures.

Others respond to quite different issues. Many male film directors, working in an industry that preeminently respects power, make films about achieving manhood and power. Donna Deitch in her *Desert Hearts* (1985) deals with the different kinds of love that women can give. Alain Tanner has repeatedly made films about people trying to live out impractically romantic ideals in a drearily unimaginative setting. Oliver Stone in *Platoon* (1987) concentrates on a young Everyman patriotically catapulted into a war so indecipherable that he must concentrate on physical and spiritual survival. A biography by Paul Michaud about the late Francois Truffaut links such films as *The 400 Blows* (1959), *Jules and Jim* (1961), *The Wild Child* (1969), and *The Story of Adèle H.* (1975) with trauma Truffaut suffered as a child on being estranged from his mother. His characters' rootless lives, their naive impracticality, and his study of Adèle Hugo's neurotic, self-destructive hunger for love all reflect aspects of Truffaut as his friends knew him. If this seems reductive, I do not mean to "explain" Truffaut so much as point to the energizing self-recognition that lay at the source of his prolific output, and to suggest how diverse are the means by which self-recognition can be expressed and made universal.

DEFINING AND DEVELOPING ONE'S INTERESTS

All filmmakers worry whether their chosen subject will be "good enough." Suppose it proves neither exciting nor original over the long haul? Films take time and effort to get started and even longer to finish, so an unwise choice can leave one dying in the desert. If younger people are more prone to lose confidence in projects than older, the difficulty of making a confident commitment afflicts everyone. Comedy or sci-fi may initially seem a less "serious" and threatening choice than drama or tragedy, but in the end they make equally high demands on the director. Having a comedy on your hands that you no longer think funny is the loneliest feeling in the world.

FEW SUBJECTS EXCLUDE OTHERS

Those people with dramatic life experience (say, of warfare, life in labor camps, or being orphaned) seldom doubt what subjects they should tackle, but for the rest of us living more ordinary lives, finding a sense of mission can be baffling.

We are each, however, invisibly marked by life in unique ways and there are always a handful of issues that arouse us to strongly partisan feelings. Few and personal though they may be, this narrow range of interests sincerely explored can deeply touch your audience and keep you busy for life.

MAKE FILMS FOR PEOPLE LIKE YOURSELF

If you try to anticipate "audience issues" through a project in which you have no investment of strong feeling, you will sever yourself from your own best sources of energy. While it is inadvisable to make straight autobiography, your own true subjects lie within the imprint your life has left on you. Nobody is without drama in his life to draw upon. This is easiest to see among artists; for example, in the films the French director Jean Vigo made before his early death. There is a striking connection between his antiestablishment vision and the ambivalent impact his father made upon him. A revolutionary who deserted the boy and his mother, Vigo's father was later strangled in prison while awaiting trial.

Invariably, there is a unity between a person's key experiences and his acts throughout life. The artist invests his life with meaning by finding and imposing an order on it, by identifying what would otherwise seem chaotic. The resulting work is usually displaced from the original experiences.

Few are so obviously stigmatized in their growing up as Jean Vigo, but everyone's journey to adulthood leads through a war zone; each is different and special, and each participates in a larger fabric of truths.

One can only make good films (write good novels, paint good pictures, sing good songs) by making each attempt for people like oneself. One cannot do more than make hack commercial work by talking down or by cynically trying to fulfill a market, for it requires isolating oneself from self-inquiry. To tell stories as a means of inquiry, to have one's purpose grasped by an audience, are steps that renew energy and bring focus for the next project.

FIND YOUR LIFE ISSUES

There are right and wrong ways to come into possession of your own particular life issues. A wrong way is to regard someone else's tastes and expertise as more authoritative than your own. Change authority and you change identity—but do you?

Avoid following the herd by rejecting all fashionable subjects or approaches unless you can subvert them. Most student films about Vietnam or about the exploitation of women were indistinguishable because they reflected the clichés of received opinion and offered nothing of their makers' feelings and discoveries. To find your own life issues means to confront yourself impartially and honestly and to reject everything that is alien to what you see. This is made extremely difficult by the shimmering, ambiguous nature of actuality itself. What is true? What is real? What is cause and what is effect? To sustain our focus and answer such questions we end up making art.

TAKE INVENTORY OF YOURSELF

To find your issues and what you can give to others, make a nonjudgmental inventory of your most moving experiences. This is not as difficult as it sounds, for the human mind retains only what it finds significant. Write rapid, short notations of each major experience as it comes to mind until you have at least ten or a dozen. Some will be positive, most will be negative and painful. Make no distinction, include everything that is true.

Now stand back and organize them into groups and give names to the groupings you find and the relationships between them. Ask yourself, what kind of person has had this experience? Do you already see yourself in a new light? Do you see trends, even a certain vision of the world clustering around these experiences?

Even if you think you already have a good handle on your own underlying issues, make the inventory anyway. You can survey all your life, or a recent period only. Honestly undertaken, it will confirm which life events formed you and urge that you work on the underlying issues they represent. You will probably see how you have resonated to these issues all along in your choice of music, literature, and films, not to mention in your friendships, love affairs, and dreams, where incidentally the mind expresses itself unguardedly and in surreal images.

The British novelist John Fowles started both *The French Lieutenant's Woman* and *A Maggot* from single images, one of a woman gazing out to sea, the other of a mysterious group of horsemen crossing a hillside. Whole complex novels came from investigating the characters "seen" in these tantalizing glimpses.

Character, they say, is destiny. Because we unconsciously participate in designing our own destiny, there are always hidden patterns and propitious images waiting in the wings to be recognized and developed.

FINDING YOUR WORK'S PATH

This search for one's own paths, for the truths underlying one's own formation and patterns, starts feeding itself once you make a commitment to expressing something about it. This is the artist's journey: at the beginning you get clues, clues lead to discoveries, discoveries lead to movement, and movement leads to new clues. A piece of work—whether a piece of writing, a painting, a short story, or a filmscript—is therefore both the evidence of movement and a prime mover in further progress.

FOLLOW YOUR FASCINATIONS

In getting ready to produce, search for that special element that fascinates you. It might be expressed through mountaineering, the rescue of animals, something involving water and boats, or love between schoolfriends. You explore that fascination by producing something external to your own thoughts: the piece of work. What begins as a circumscribed personal quest soon leads outward. You might take two opposing parts of your own character during a trying period of your life and make them into two separate characters, perhaps well known political or historical characters. Profiling historical personalities, social assumptions, political events, or the temperaments of the people most influential in your life will all contribute to further shaping your consciousness. Doing such things well entertains and excites your audience, who are also, whether they know it or not, on a private quest and starving for a sense of direction.

FIGHT THE CENSOR AND FINISH

Very important is to finish projects. Work left incomplete is a step taken sideways, not forward. It is tempting halfway through a project to say, "Well, I've learned all I can learn here so I think I'll start something new." This is the internal censor at work, your hidden enemy who whispers, "You can't show this to other people, it isn't good enough; the real you is better." One's work seldom feels good for long, but do not let that make you halt or change horses. Only intermittently will you feel elation, but finishing will always yield satisfaction and knowledge.

YOUR WORK IS NOT YOU

Remember that your work is only an interim representation, like a core sample from a subterranean drilling. The next piece of work will show advances, will strengthen you and sharpen your journey's purpose. Truffaut, admitting late in his life that it was just as difficult to make a bad film as a good one, became a kinder critic of other directors' work after he, too, had experienced the failures that prepare us to succeed. The integrity and perseverance of the explorer is what matters. Keep going, no matter what.

DISPLACE AND TRANSFORM

After a period of careful inquiry and reflection, take the best of what you have discovered and, even though they are temporary and subject to change, assume they are your own real issues. If you are working directly from events and personalities in your own life, transform the screen version away from the originals. This has numerous benefits. It frees you from self-consciousness and allows you to tell all the underlying truths instead of only those palatable to friends and family. Most importantly, it allows you to concentrate on dramatic and thematic truths instead of getting tangled up in biographical accuracy.

To obscure your sources you can give characters alternative attributes and work, make them composites by amalgamating the attributes of two life models, place the story in a different place or epoch, or even switch the sex of the protagonists.

One student director whose script told his own story—about the painful choice he had made to abandon a suburban marriage and a well paying job to become a film student—inverted the sex of the main characters and made the rebel into a woman. In rethinking the situation to give her credible motivations, he made himself inhabit both the husband's and wife's positions and came to more deeply investigate what people trapped in such roles expect out of life. Displacement forced him into a more objective relationship with his characters and raised the level of his film's thematic discourse.

SOURCES FOR STORIES

Stories are never really "original." Anyone sitting down to write something "new" and purely from imagination soon finds himself in trouble. The truth is that we borrow incessantly—from sources in life and from other creators. Have no compunction about this borrowing process, because you are going to put the original materials through such a long and complex transformation process that just about everything of the original gets subsumed in the process of making them your own.

Returning to the transformation of life events, a real-life story also contains characters, events, settings, situations, and conflicts just like a piece of drama— that is what makes it a story. It expresses particular themes and tends to relay a particular vision of life, whether comic, satirical, realistic, surreal, melodramatic, or tragic. In a good story, the parts fuse together into a whole, but if you take the framework and change one or two of the elements, the meaning and impact of the entire work will be affected, probably beyond recognition.

At first, searching for relatively whole stories, you will feel there is nothing dramatic in your life to draw upon. Perhaps the tensions you have witnessed or experienced never matured into any action. But maybe the writer's gratification, even the main purpose of authorship can be to make happen what did not happen, to project situations and conflicts into the confrontation and change you need.

Let us say that you want to make a film about the incompatible natures of your parents. Since nothing more than irritation has ever been expressed, you do not know how to do it. In the newspaper, however, you see a true story about a peaceable civil servant, married for thirty-eight years, who at Thanksgiving dinner suddenly rose from the table because his wife put the salt cellar down in the wrong place on the table. Irrevocably crossing some invisible inner threshold, he left home to begin tracing his childhood sweetheart. You are attracted to what makes people (like your parents, perhaps) follow the "wrong" path, do work and live lives that do not feel right, what aspiration it is that keeps them in the paths of conformity, and what kind of incident makes them shear off at a tangent at one particular moment in their lives.

You can digress imaginatively away from biographical fact or you can stick closely to it. John Boorman's *Hope and Glory* (1987) is modeled upon the lives and emotional evolution of his own family during World War II when he was a boy, and explores with imagination and sympathy his mother's unfulfilled love for his father's best friend.

JOURNAL

Keep a journal and note down everything that strikes you, no matter what its nature. You can also keep clippings or transcribe anything that catches your interest. Rereading your journal becomes a journey through your own most intense ideas and associations and can prime the creative pump or suggest a mass of alternatives when you run dry of inspiration.

NEWSPAPERS

There is nothing like real life for a profundity of outlandish and true tales, so going back through the files of newspapers of perhaps fifty years ago will supply you with a profusion of rich sources. You find a story about two business partners, one of whom absconds with the company bank balance to blow it all in Las Vegas. It reminds you of your best friend's father, and the ruin a similar incident caused her family. That sets you thinking about your role in trying to help her through the period of disaster, and what you both learned. Here, you realize, are characters and a plot; all you need do is put it in the present, find a point of view, and help the story to develop itself.

The agony columns, or the personals, even the ads for lost animals can all suggest subjects. Newspapers are a cornucopia of the human condition at every level, from the trivial to the global. Local newspapers are particularly fertile because the landscape and the characters are circumscribed and accessible, reflecting local economy, local conditions, and local idiosyncrasies.

HISTORY

Look at why history is written and you will find not objective truth but the distillation and interpretation of what someone somewhere considers significant. There are figures in history who have already in some way enacted the dramas that particularly interest you. No matter what happens to fascinate you—be it charismatic leadership, practical jokers, crooked doctors, polygamous family groups, neglected inventors, or old ladies who fill their houses with stray cats—there is a wealth of fully realized characters waiting to be employed. Intelligent research finds them in the great casting agency of the past.

MYTHS AND LEGENDS

Each culture has its own myths and legends, most of which are translatable into a modern setting. They are useful because they enshrine conflicts that man has found enduringly important. The human truths in Greek mythology (for instance) do not lead to easy or happy resolution, but instead leave a bittersweet aftertaste that is perversely uplifting. Each generation regenerates myths for its own purposes, using them as frameworks for contemporary characters and action that is usually unresolvable. This quality of paradox and the unanswerable is peculiarly modern. We have entered an age that admits once again that humans have more questions than answers.

FAMILY STORIES

All families have favorite stories that define particular people. My grandmother, for instance, was someone who "found things before people had lost them." In all respects a morally conventional woman, she nevertheless had mild klepto-mania, especially for flowers and fruit, and at an advanced age during breaks in long car journeys would hop over garden walls to borrow a few strawberries or liberate a fistful of chrysanthemums. How a family explains and adjusts to these characteristics might be the subject of an endearing short film. Family tales can be heroic or very dark, but they are always vivid and trenchant, as oral history invariably is.

CHILDHOOD STORIES

If you write down two or three of the most intense things that happened to you as a child, you will have several ready-made short film subjects that are intensely meaningful, have a strong and inbuilt visualization, and contain great thematic significance for your subsequent life.

DREAMS

A sure indicator of one's underlying concerns lies in one's dreams. Keep a note-book by your bed and write down each dream while you still remember it. Look back over an accumulation of entries and you will see a pattern of recurring motifs and archetypal characters. Here are your deepest concerns expressed in surreal action and imagery. What more could a filmmaker ask?

SOCIAL SCIENCE AND SOCIAL HISTORY

If you are interested, for example, in the exploitation of farm workers, you can find books on the subject, many containing bibliographies. The list of works will tell you what other books exist on the subject, perhaps in both fiction and nonfiction, and the more modern your source, the bigger the bibliography. Many books now contain filmographies too.

Case histories can be a good source of trenchant detail. If one of your characters is a shoplifter, reading about actual shoplifters will supply you with what is typical (you need to know that) and also with detail that is quirky and interesting, so your shoplifter is not a stereotype.

Case histories are generally interpreted, so they supply the dramatist with good material and ideas about its significance. Social scientists are chroniclers and interpreters; their work can confirm your instincts and provide the kind of background information that allows you to root your fiction in what we know about the real world.

SUBJECTS TO AVOID

Many subjects come easily because they are in one's immediate surroundings or are being pumped up by the media. You are also well advised to stay away from

- Worlds you haven't experienced and cannot closely observe,
- Any ongoing, inhibiting problem in your own life (if you have not found a perspective on it you will not do so directing a film unit; see a good therapist),
- Anything or anyone that is "typical" (nothing real is typical, so nothing typical will be interesting or credible),
- Preaching or moral instruction of any kind, and
- Films about problems to which you already have the whole answer (so does your audience).

Your films will be your portfolio, your precious reel that alone tells others who you are and what you can do. Try to make films for the outside world and not just for your film school peers. If you show short films that look into a larger world and that do not have a central character suspiciously like yourself, you will avoid the narcissistic tunnel vision afflicting many student films. Try taking what you know from your own life and applying it elsewhere to say something about the human condition.

ADAPTATION FROM LITERATURE

There is an inexhaustible fund of stories in the constantly growing supply of plays, novels, and short stories. Libraries keep copies of an amazing range of indexes to help you find what interests you. Someone has already analyzed or indexed the very thing you are interested in by characters, subject, or theme. All you need do is to find the index. Short stories, for example, are indexed by theme.

If you make any adaptation that bears any identifiable likeness to its original make sure you have the legal right to use it. Copyright law is changed periodically. In the United States you can obtain current information from the Copyright Office, Library of Congress, Washington, DC 20559. Many works first published fifty-six years ago or more are old enough to be in the public domain, but do not assume this without careful inquiry, preferably through a copyright lawyer. The law is extremely complicated, especially as it applies to a literary property's clearance in other countries.

The short story is a favorite source of material for both short and full-length films. Like all literature it can be treacherous, for the magic of language can seduce the filmmaker into assuming it will make an equally fine film. This may not even be possible if the author's writing style and literary form have no cinematic equivalency. A story relying upon a subtly ironic storytelling voice, for instance, might be a bad choice because there is no such thing as ironic photography or ironic sound recording.

Effective literature never automatically contains the basis for a good film. Most of the criteria for judging material for an adaptation remain the same as those used to assess any script.

1. Does it tell its tale through visual, behavioral means?
2. Does it have interesting, well developed characters?

3. Is it contained and specific in settings?

4. Are the situations interesting and realizable?

5. Is there an interesting major conflict and is it dramatized?

6. Does it imply interesting metaphors?

7. Does it have a strong thematic purpose?

8. Is the thematic purpose one you can relate to strongly?

9. Can you invent a cinematic equivalency for the story's literary values?

10. Can you afford to do it?

11. Is the copyright available?

FAITHFUL ADAPTATION

Any well known work comes with strings attached. Even if J.D. Salinger person-ally handed you the rights to *The Catcher in the Rye,* you would not have a free hand at adaptation. The book has touched so many people that meeting their expectations would be well nigh impossible. For this reason alone, effective lit-erature adapted to the screen almost always disappoints its fans. Other works, long or short, may pose narrative or stylistic problems that can only be satisfac-torily solved by boldly seizing a cinematic form that radically departs from the original. For instance, John Korty's version of John Updike's five-and-a-half–page story "The Music School" (The American Short Story series) takes a story that happens contemplatively inside a man's mind, develops it into interwoven events, and propels them upon a musical theme of increasing texture and con-fidence. The result is a short film gem no less profound than Updike's over-compressed original and a good deal more accessible, yet true to the original's spirit.

Karel Reisz's 1981 screen version of John Fowles' *The French Lieutenant's Woman,* however, suffers badly. Fowles' novels tend to overflow with ideas, and this one more than any. The movie version, although scripted by the supremely intelligent Harold Pinter, is forced by time limitations to strip away most of the sociological exposition and philosophical speculation by which the novel assesses the nineteenth century against its twentieth century offspring. Like most adap-tations, the movie concentrates on the plot and action at the expense of dis-course, and emerges with a bad case of malnutrition.

FREE ADAPTATION

A more fertile union of literature and screen can happen when the filmmaker abandons the reverential processing of literary or theatrical icons and instead employs aspects of a written work to seed a fully autonomous film. Many of Godard's ground-breaking movies of the 1960s were free adaptations of theatre or sociology, works by Alberto Moravia and Guy de Maupassant, and, interest-ingly, transformations of pulp fiction.

The implication is that inventive, original cinema takes what it needs from anything and everything, while "great" novels or plays processed for the screen are diminished, as paintings are when reproduced as tapestry.

DEVELOPING AN AUTONOMOUS SCREENPLAY FROM FICTION OR A LIFE EVENT

ALTERING THE GIVENS

By taking over a story framework (from a literary work or from a life situation) and substituting some of one's own choice of main elements, an entirely new work can emerge, since everything else, including the main issues, will be affected. In the search to integrate all the parts, the work will inevitably evolve and begin to impose its own demands that the writer must satisfy. Elements you might alter could be

Characters: Placing a new character in any situation creates pressure for new outcomes (and therefore a changed destiny). Strong characters can steer a story to new conclusions that express a different resolution and meaning.

Situations and conflicts: Changed characters almost certainly generate changes in the events, and changes in some or all of the main conflicts.

Period: One can tell an old story in a modern setting, as Leonard Bernstein did by adapting Shakespeare's *Romeo and Juliet* to New York City in the musical show *West Side Story*.

Settings: New characters demand their own settings to express what is particular to them. Changes of class, changes of region, or changes of occupation all have far-reaching consequences. A change of setting will produce changed pressures on the characters.

Point of view: In her novel *The Wide Sargasso Sea*, Jean Rhys reinterprets the situation in Charlotte Bronte's *Jane Eyre,* taking the point of view of the mad, imprisoned Mrs. Rochester. It is a radically different story arising from Rhys' outrage at the injustices suffered by neglected wives, something she experienced during her early years in Paris. Any story that draws one emotionally into its web is capable of reinterpretation, especially when one violently disagrees with the conclusions reached by the original author.

Thematic purpose: You might keep similar characters but adjust the situations to produce a different thematic outcome. Here you may be attracted to interpreting the same events differently.

As soon as one admits that one is surrounded by rich resources for storytelling, and that one may legitimately borrow and adapt from any source, provided the new entity gains its own identity and purpose, the emphasis is no longer "I don't have any stories to tell" but becomes "What is the basis for my choices and adaptations?" and "Why do I like this particular story so much?"

Whatever causes a deep response in you throws light on your underlying storyteller's identity. Self-knowledge should enable you to further build into the story whatever else fascinates you, and permit you to design a vehicle so freighted with personal significance that you become possessed by it, drawing out characters, events, and situations that impell themselves forward to their own conclusion. Indeed, the sign of an effectively rigorous writing process is that your characters detach themselves from their originals and become empowered and autonomous within their own world. Such independence comes from knowing that your story instills belief in its audience, that you can let go of the security blanket represented by a fictional original or by remembered fact.

ACTOR CENTERED FILMS AND THEIR SCRIPTS

Your vision can only reach an audience through what you put on the screen, much of which will be the human presence. Quite simply, the credibility and quality of that human presence will make or break your film. Every film makes its passage from page to screen almost wholly through its actors, yet seldom are scripts much influenced by the individuality of those who most give them life.

Actors whose effortless-looking performances we take for granted arrive on the screen through a rigorous apprenticeship and selection process. Beginning filmmakers, on the contrary, must try to match the commercial cinema's professionalism using actors with little or no experience. Unfortunately most still do this by following the cinema industry's assembly line operation which processes the script first, then adds cast and begins shooting. This creates handicaps. You can hardly bring together people unknown to each other and unfamiliar with the process of filming and expect them to be relaxed and focused in their roles. There must be an induction process to bring the anxiety levels down and build an ensemble that works well together.

Even with a professional cast it is a mistake to assume they can easily enter the script. Jessica Lange, an actress as professional as they come, deplores the fact that she has never worked on a film allowing rehearsal time to develop the emotional life of the characters (*American Film,* June 1987). The need to explore and interact is even more urgent for the inexperienced cast, and the prudent director plans time and activities in which cast and script can evolve. Careful and lengthy rehearsal is a must, but intelligent improv work exploring the ideas and emotional transitions in the script can bring that magic quality of spontaneity to the screen.

Though this is a nontraditional approach to screen authorship, it is one used increasingly and with significant results. This is a scripting method that uses human beings as well as the typewriter.

INTEGRATING THE CAST INTO THE SCRIPT

Some directors already write in an unconventional, actor-centered way, foremost among them Ingmar Bergman, who does not favor the screenplay:

> If . . . I were to reproduce in words what happens in the film I have conceived, I would be forced to write a bulky book of little readable value and great nuisance. I have neither the talent nor the patience for heroic exercise of that kind. Besides, such a procedure would kill all creative joy for both me and the artists. (*Four Stories by Ingmar Bergman* [New York: Doubleday, 1977])

Bergman develops his films from an annotated short story. For *Cries and Whispers* (1972) he supplied notes on artistic approach, the intended characters and their situations, the settings and time period, fragments from Agnes' diary, details of a dream, and the dialogue and narrative of the events. These Bergman hands to all participating, and the developmental work begins from a thorough assimilation of all the inherent possibilities. Much of the creation of characters and action then lies with actors whose careers and talents Bergman has been instrumental in developing.

In the United States, actor/director John Cassavetes has also long given primacy to his actors, either improvising completely as in *Shadows* (1959) or basing his written script upon structured improvisations as in *A Woman Under the Influence* (1974). "The emotion was improvised," he said, "but the lines were written."

Alain Tanner, a Swiss director who came to feature films through television documentaries, has gradually evolved his fiction works toward the spontaneity of his documentary beginnings. In *Jonah Who Will Be 25 in the Year 2000* (1976) he showed photos of his chosen cast to his collaborator John Berger. The associations Berger made with each face became the basis for a script. In his more recent film *In the White City* (1985) Tanner used no script at all, relying

FIGURE 23–1

Tanner's *Jonah Who Will Be 25 in the Year 2000*, a film developed from its actors (courtesy New Yorker Films).

instead upon the ability of his fine actors to improvise upon a framework of specified ideas. This takes expertise all around.

Before the reader lines up behind any particular creed, it may be important to glance at the fundamentals of modern realistic cinema. If the object is to create believable life on the screen and to expose credible contemporary issues, there must not only be viable ideas and situations present, but most of all credible characters. Today's audience has spent upwards of eighteen thousand hours watching the screen and is an expert judge of acting. People are quite unmoved by the representational styles that audiences accepted years ago. Unless an actor finds an adequate emotional identification with his character, we reject his performance and with it, much or all of the film.

Unsophisticated or untrained actors tend to model their performances not on life but upon other, admired actors. They will signify a character's feelings and perform at a mass audience they imagine to exist just beyond the camera lens. The director must have a set of strategies to break through to something true. As a matter of survival you should give first priority to developing your actors' potentials. Good acting can survive indifferent film technique, but nothing can rescue lousy acting; not good color, not good music, not good photography or good editing, none of these separately or combined.

Actors' qualities and limitations should influence the way you realize your authorial intentions. Even the very intentions themselves may need alteration to bring them in line with the intrinsic personal qualities found along the way in your cast.

A SCRIPT DEVELOPED FROM ACTORS IMPROVISING

Let us imagine you are going to make a film about the conflicts and paradoxes in a young man leaving home, and want to show it as an ordeal by fire. It is possible and even desirable to begin without a full-fledged script. The experience is so universal that any cast member will have strong feelings on the subject. You decide to find an interesting cast, knowing that each actor's ideas are going to be engaged in developing your thematic concerns. John Cassavetes' *A Woman Under the Influence* (1974) began this way. Cassavetes and his actress wife Gena Rowlands, playing the wife in the film, were interested in what happens in an Italian-American blue collar family when women's liberation ideas penetrate the home. The wife becomes aware that her role as wife and mother is preventing her from growing into an autonomous adult. The script, developed from improvisations, was founded upon the experiences and personalities of the players. Uneven as the movie is, Gena Rowlands' performance is disturbingly memorable.

In Giles Walker's National Film Board of Canada comedy *90 Days* (1986) the subject grew out of a favorite actor's idea for making a film about an ordinary guy who orders an Oriental mail-order bride. After casting, the film was improvised in three stages, each section then scripted and shot as a prelude to conceiving the next. What makes this comedy so touching is that the main characters are all fully realized, and although the film is very funny, it also displays a wealth of sympathetic insight into everyday Canadian life and the difficulty the ordinary man has in articulating unfamiliar emotions.

By finding an interested cast and by posing the right questions, it is possible to draw upon their interests and residual experience of life. When interesting and credible situations have been identified, they can be experimentally played out. As this happens, consistent characters begin to emerge from each player, and in emerging, demand greater clarity and background. The director and cast find their attention turning from ideas to character development, and from character development inevitably to situations, and from situations and characters to the specific past events—personal, cultural, political—that seeded each character's present. Gradually a world is formed of tensions and conflicts that belong to everyone taking part, because each has had a hand in the development.

Naturally a ship with several uncoordinated oarsmen needs a firm hand on the tiller. Leading a project of this nature takes subtlety, patience, and the authority to make binding decisions. Dramatically the results may be a mixed bag, but at the very least such a process is a tremendous way of building rapport among cast and director. I have found that the cast tends to retain what is successful by concensus, so that gradually what began as improvisation becomes, as attention turns increasingly toward details, much more like collaborative scripting.

Another more open-ended method is to start not from a social theme or idea, but from a mood or from the personality and potential of individual cast members. If "character is fate," let your characters develop their fates. By getting each to generate an absorbing character and by letting situations grow out of the clashes and alliances of these characters, themes and issues inevitably suggest themselves. A project like this is good for a theatre company used to working together, or as a follow-up film project when the cast and director have come to trust each other and want to go on working together, which is not always the case.

As everyone knows, there are only so many plots. But there is no limit to the interaction possible between characters. Alternatively, both characters and issues might be developed from the influence of a particular location, say a deserted gravel pit, the waiting room in an underground car park, or a street market. More potent, perhaps, is the site of an historical event, such as a field where strikers were martyred, or the house where a woman who had apocalyptic visions grew up.

Experiments of this kind are excellent for building the cast's confidence to play scripted or unscripted parts with unselfconscious abandonment, and the daring to act upon intuition—all priceless commodities. Playful work like this generates energy and ideas, and when the dramatic output is rounded up and analyzed, a longer work can be structured. A firm hand guiding the piece is imperative or the results will lack integration and fail to make any recognizable statement. This is true for all improv-generated ideas.

Techniques useful for this kind of work appear as a structured sequence in Part VI: Director and Cast Development Projects.

THE VIDEO NOVEL: IMPROVISATORY APPROACH

Just as the theatre in England was revitalized in the 1960s when local theatre turned its back on cocktail plays in favor of local history and local issues, it now seems possible, with increased local television programming and as more port-able, inexpensive video equipment is manufactured, that local fiction video groups will emerge to begin producing the modern equivalent of the regional novel. That nothing like it has yet happened is not because of the system, but because regional film production remains imitative and third rate. A few first rate con-temporary voices would send distributors rushing to make money from a new source of product.

The most likely point of origin is in city theatres producing works of con-temporary social and political criticism, and having a fairly stable ensemble. It has been done before. Both the German director Rainer Werner Fassbinder and the fine actress Hanna Schygulla, who played in his *Marriage of Maria Braun* (1978), emerged from such an institution, the Munich action-theatre, which later became the *anti-teater*. The company made no less than six of Fassbinder's early films together, and his astonishingly prolific and creative film career is plainly rooted in this early experience of creating instant theatre out of contemporary personal or political issues.

Why not elsewhere? Of course, there are many arguments against a grass-roots screen drama movement. Funding, distribution, the continuity of the en-semble and the homogeneity of their vision are all difficult to sustain at the present time. However, rather than debate these points, I will just point out a possible niche for an enterprising group.

Let us take an example. During the last fifteen years in Chicago the steel industry has gone silent and the hardworking ethnic communities that clustered around it have become unemployed. They have participated in the American Dream for two or three generations, and suddenly it has all died. What happens to such people? What happens to their sons and daughters? What happens to people who have lived their lives with a sense of virtue tied to hard, dirty work and who now have no more "man's work" in the offing? How do they explain their losses? This is really a story being repeated all over the industrialized west-ern world. Such people and their fate are of wide significance and of wide inter-est. It is not hard to find out about them, for they have ample time for the researcher.

At first sight it seems more of a documentary subject, but when you begin to read articles and interviews, to visit with union leaders, local historians, doc-tors, and clergymen, as well as with the unemployed steelworkers and their families, you find that the story is diffuse and complicated. Perhaps some of the men live on false hope. Some drink too much. Some take meaningless jobs that pay only a fraction of what they earned before. The wives now begin to go out to work, and this changes the family dynamic. Most of the men are traditional husbands and feel a sense of failure. There is a dull anger, a depressed, moody resignation. There is also an ugly side to this resentment; the community becomes inturned and racist. There is a neo-Nazi group that meets in its own well guarded headquarters. There are some demonstrations, some harrassment of blacks in a neighboring district, a burning garage or two.

Then there are the young people. They either stay because for one reason or another they cannot leave, or they get out and go to college, leaving their parents' decaying neighborhood ever farther away, yet feeling guilty for their betrayal and sorrowful at the ruin of their embittered, once-proud parents.

What we have here is a situation with so many possibilities, so many things happening, that the only way to handle it is to decide which are specially interesting and make a dramatic construct out of those chosen. What we begin to see is perhaps a representative family whose members are composites inspired by people we met and who left an indelible impression. We know what the key events are in the life of the family: father loses job, scenes of mounting pressure in the family, the mother finds a job as a checkout clerk at a supermarket, the daughter begins going to a college downtown and becomes increasingly critical of her family and its assumptions. Her brother drops out of school and hangs out on street corners, identifying more and more with the neo-fascist messages of revenge and hatred.

We have built up a series of pressures. Now we urgently need ideas about how these pressures will resolve, what kind of contortions this family and this bereaved community are going to suffer, and what "coming out the other side" may mean. A fictionalized treatment of these very real circumstances must, therefore, have an element of prediction to propose to its audience, a prediction about the way human beings handle this kind of slow-motion catastrophe.

To be such a social analyst or prophet is an exciting job to give yourself. It is a job that can arouse much interest, one requiring some of the abilities of journalist, sociologist, documentarian, and novelist to make work. But look what is already available: a host of characters to play minor roles; a landscape of windswept, rusting factories, and rows of peeling houses; a circuit of bars, dance halls, and ethnic churches with their weddings, christenings and funerals. Sound too depressing? Then go to the amateur comedian contests and make Dad into an aspiring stand-up comic. The community where you are going to film has all sorts of regular activities to use as a backdrop, and within reason you can make the characters do and be anything you want.

What is happening in your area that needs to be understood? A rash of teenage suicides? A cult? A new and dangerous form of racing? A cosmetician who has found a way to get rich quick? A UFO society? An archeological hoax by a hitherto reputable academic? A purity movement among teenagers? Industrial espionage? An aging beauty queen who has run away with her priest? A computer nerd reorganizing the town's bank accounts for no personal profit?

Committed regionalists need to reach out and inhabit interesting, broadly significant local situations that can be filled out from imagination and experience. Newspapers, magazines, and bookshops are full of models, and the filmmaker needs only to choose well from the local storehouse.

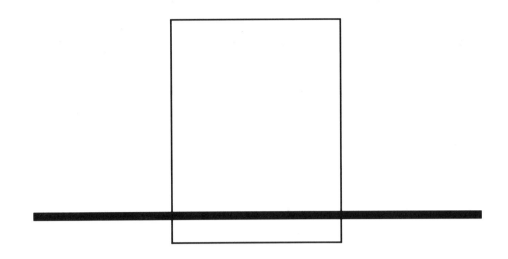

C·H·A·P·T·E·R 2·4

POINT OF VIEW

SUBJECTIVITY AND POINT OF VIEW

Most people prefer to learn by active inquiry rather than by passively receiving instruction, and this holds true for what we want of the screen. From a film version of *Anna Karenina* we expect to experience what Tolstoy's adulterous heroine suffers, not simply be told that she is immoral. We wonder what it is like to be a young woman married to a stuffy older man, to feel isolated and loveless, to be approached by a romantic admirer. What is it to be tempted and yet viewed by society as a temptress? If the movie is good, we pass vicariously through these conditions and come away expanded in mind and heart from all we have felt.

To make us participate in other realities, the cinema must be able to project us into a main character's emotional condition, for our main and perhaps only desire is to be transported into another's world.

In a love triangle like *Anna Karenina* there is more than one such world, available because there are the separate perceptions of each character—Anna's, her husband's, and her lover Vronsky's. With the husband Karenin we might view the situation as a betrayal; with Vronsky, see it as a romantic adventure that turns sour; with Anna, feel night turn into brightest day, and then change to a long, bloody sunset.

From Tolstoy's novel the story might seem the tragedy of double standards that make women into property and deny them the same freedom of choice as men. Under a shaping hand in the theatre or cinema the story could emerge differently as a parable about the unfulfillability of romantic love. By favoring Karenin's point of view over that of his wife's in some scenes, the storyteller could imply without changing the events that Karenin is also a misunderstood or even pitiable figure. Another director might conceivably make the whole story into a metaphor for Mother Russia caught between servitude to the Czars and manipulation by the revolutionaries, making Tolstoy a prophet of the Russian Revolution.

Evidently there are dimensions beyond those of the story's inhabitants: there is that of Tolstoy the storyteller, and also that of anyone reinterpreting Tolstoy's story. This altered perspective need not change the interaction Tolstoy specifies between the characters. It simply represents the differing slant of an adaptation, one drawing upon the contemporary mood and the personal perspective of the screenwriter. Additionally, there is the point of view that the audience itself brings to the piece.

THE CONTROLLING POINT OF VIEW

The point of view of a film controlling the story is usually that of a central character—in *Anna Karenina,* Anna herself—but point of view is switched in film as in literature whenever it usefully augments the audience's perception. This might be done through parallel action, through a choice of angle, or by subjective coverage placing us with the alternate character. The switch can be made more subtly by an interaction that invokes our sympathy but needs no attention-guiding technique like a special angle or shot.

The controlling point of view is generally rooted in the consciousness of the person or persons at the center of the work. After Lewis Carroll's Alice passes through the looking glass, she enters a world of inverted logic. To the child in us, *Alice in Wonderland*'s looming, swollen personages are alarming magnifications of those encountered in our own youth. We see not only Alice's new and bizarre world, but through her efforts at coping we also see her in action, and come to appreciate her resourcefulness and courage. Dorothy in *The Wizard of Oz* (1939) makes a similar journey through a bewitched landscape, but she is joined by the Lion, the Tin Man, and the Scarecrow, alter egos whom she inspires to continue.

Alice and Dorothy each acts as the focus of attention in her particular world but also as a means through which we see it. As surrogates for ourselves, each heroine acts as a lens of temperament through which the audience experiences the land of Oz and the Victorian eccentrics beyond the looking glass.

Werner Herzog also makes a character cross a major threshold in *Kasper Hauser: Every Man for Himself and God Against All* (1974). In a setting of early nineteenth-century Germany, the viewer accompanies a young man into daylight for the first time. Like the feral boy in Truffaut's *Wild Child* (1969), Kasper has practically never seen, spoken to, eaten with, or walked amongst other human beings. Modeled on an actual wild child of the period, Kasper is a completely innocent human being confronting all the beauty, complexity, and hypocrisy of civilization. In accelerated succession he suffers the amazements of childhood and the child's sense of bereavement at discovering the world's moral bankruptcy.

It is an astonishing, sustained parable that makes us reexperience the familiar through Kasper's naiveté of spirit. But we also share the perspectives on Kasper by the professor of logic, the pastor, the travelling showman, the dandy, and the kindly family who teach him basic table manners—all those who try to help, classify, civilize or exploit the strange young man. Their view of him heightens

Kasper's point of view by juxtaposing his innocence against the puzzled, derisive, or antithetical reactions of those who want to change him.

Many other films have established powerful worlds through the eyes of young people, notably de Sica's *Bicycle Thief* (1949), Ray's *Pather Panchali* (1954), Truffaut's *400 Blows* (1959), Saura's *Cria* (1977), Schlondorff's *The Tin Drum* (1979), Babenco's *Pixote* (1981), and Bergman's *Fanny and Alexander* (1983), which, in spite of its title, is really Alexander's point of view.

One should also mention some recent films among the thousands that create powerful worlds through an adult's point of view: Truffaut's *The Story of Adèle H.* (1975), Resnais' *Providence* (1977), Scorsese's *King of Comedy* (1982), Wenders' *Paris, Texas* (1984), Forman's *Amadeus* (1984), Luis Puenzo's *The Official Story* (1985), and Paul Leduc's *Frida* (1987).

VARIATIONS IN POINT OF VIEW

BIOGRAPHICAL

Kasper Hauser being in the form of a biography focuses on a single character, keeping him center stage almost all the time. It develops its philosophical abstractions by showing Kasper's collisions with different small-town factions, and

FIGURE 24–1

Survival through the eyes of a street urchin in Babenco's *Pixote* (courtesy New Yorker Films).

FIGURE 24–2

A novelist transforms his family into the characters of dark fiction in Resnais' *Providence* (courtesy Almi Distributors).

by amassing a catalogue of specific reactions. Boldly and poetically, the film imparts the violence of Kasper's sensations and of his chaotic inner life, beginning with a lyrical shot of a field of blowing corn. Over pastoral music a quotation is superimposed: "But can you not hear the dreadful screaming all around that people usually call silence?" At a stroke, Herzog establishes the juxtaposition of summer beauty and inner despair that will tear Kasper apart.

In our basic biographical form, we saw Kasper objectively in his interactions with others, then through using music and through seeing things as Kasper might see them, Herzog makes us see through Kasper's subjectivity. Framing these viewpoints we now discern Herzog showing us his own point of view, that Kasper is an undefended Everyman. Through the storytelling itself, we find Herzog making an impassioned and poetical comparison between the nobility of a human's potential, and the muddle and corruption called civilization. Herzog's is a romantic vision, movingly appropriate from a child of World War II Germany.

CHARACTER WITHIN THE FILM WHO ARTICULATES A POINT OF VIEW

A film's apparent vantage point may come directly from a character within the film itself who directs us through the main events by narrating them. Again these are frequently children. In Malick's *Days of Heaven* (1978) there is a voice-over narration by the fugitive's young sister. The country lawyer's daughter is the narrator in Mulligan's *To Kill a Mockingbird* (1963), and the boy houseguest

FIGURE 24–3

Leduc's highly visual *Frida:* love and art through the transcendent vision of the Mexican painter Frida Kahlo (courtesy New Yorker Films).

writing in his diary effectively narrates Losey's *The Go-Between* (1971). In Truffaut's *Jules and Jim* (1961) the narrator is a novelist and participant in the love triangle.

The perceptions of a narrator make us aware of his or her subjectivity and limitations. In extremity a character may subjectively see either magic or monsters and a film that portrays these is really depicting the narrator's state of mind. Limitations and distortions of vision make us painfully aware of the narrator's vulnerability and create a sense of rising dramatic pressure.

MAIN CHARACTER'S IMPLIED POINT OF VIEW

In mainstream cinema, characters and their issues are often established through a series of realistic events. Their world is objectively normal and the world is not distorted by how they perceive. The coolness and distance of this mode allow the audience to think as much as feel. Here a character's point of view must be implied rather than verbalized since there is no commentator. The audience long retains its status as nonidentifying observers and merges with the main characters only through empathy and by choice. Jiri Menzel's *Closely Watched Trains* (1966) is about a youth adapting to his first job in a railroad station. Obsessed by the shameful fact of his virginity, he finds himself surrounded by the sex lives of others. This seems more the humor of the gods than a situation he has influenced. Tony Richardson's *A Taste of Honey* (1961), on the other hand, focuses upon a provincial teenager who at a time of great loneliness gets pregnant and is befriended for a while by a homosexual boy. Showing how she is led by raw emotion from one situation to another, the film demonstrates how a person's destiny is the outcome of a subtle balance of environment, chance, and character. Her world, like that of the young Czech railwayman, is still an alien environment with which she must struggle, but she bears more responsibility for her destiny.

Two of Hitchcock's most famous films each hinges upon the validity of its main character's subjective judgment. In *Rear Window* (1954) an injured photographer confined to his room and compelled to look at the building opposite becomes convinced that a murder has taken place, and takes on some of the guilt of the murderer. In *Psycho* (1960) Marion Crane battles to deny her instincts that something malign is afoot in the Bates Motel. In each case, the audience must constantly decide what reality is, until at the end Hitchcock provides the key that unlocks the suspense.

Very different in intention is Fassbinder's *The Marriage of Maria Braun* (1978), which shows a German war bride working her way from rags to riches while awaiting the return of her husband. Maria seems to personify Germany's return from destruction and at the same time implies that its passage to wealth really has led to moral bankruptcy.

Two films about women center upon very different concerns. Teshigahara's *Woman of the Dunes* (1964) tells of a woman trapped in her house in a sand dune, who must dig constantly to prevent her home from being obliterated by the drifting sand. Villagers lure a male tourist into sharing her life and her fate. The film is notable for its abstract and erotically charged photography, so the viewer is constantly striving to relate the close up shapes he sees to their parent whole—arm, knee, breast, sand dune, eddy, kitchen vessel—each threatening to engulf the viewer just as the woman's sandy environment threatens to engulf her. The film leaves an almost palpable sense that sexuality and the struggle for survival are inextricable.

In another world altogether is the heroine of Polanski's *Tess* (1980), a film treatment of Thomas Hardy's ballad-like novel about a country girl seduced by one man and later abandoned by her new husband when he learns of it. While the novel constantly but subtly thrusts the reader into understanding Tess's awareness, Polanski's version fails to find the cinematic equivalency to Hardy's poetic language, and the viewer remains distanced. Further threatening the viability of this adaptation, the seducer emerges as the most complex and interesting character of the three.

DUAL CHARACTERS

In Malick's *Badlands* (1974), Penn's *Bonnie and Clyde* (1967), and Godard's *Pierrot le Fou* (1965), the subjects are partnerships and there are two point-of-view characters. All three films involve journeys by road that end in self-destruction. In the two American films, the partnerships seem to exist primarily to define male and female roles within a dissident or criminal subculture, while Godard's work uses the same self-immolating subculture as a vehicle to explore the incompatibilities between the male and female psyches. Each film studies the tensions generated between their characters, and uses the way each step is (or is not) resolved to energize the next move. *Pierrot le Fou* in particular makes a rewarding study of dramatic form, because character and dramatic tension are developed in action between the characters rather than from external pressures applied by the chase.

Wim Wenders' *Alice in the Cities* (1974) is another journey but the dialogue is between unequals: a journalist reluctantly helps a nine-year-old girl find her grandmother. The film manages to avoid the pitfalls of kitsch sentiment as it explores the gulf between adults and children.

Gregory Nava's *El Norte* (1983) alternates between the vantage points of brother and sister accomplices as they escape Guatemala toward the promised land of El Norte (North America), where exploitation and disillusion await them. Other films that alternate between two points of view often represent a more direct struggle between dialectical opposites. In Woody Allen's comedy of manners *Annie Hall* (1977) the duel is between Allen and Diane Keaton as neurotically self-protective New Yorkers; in Bergman's *Scenes from a Marriage* (1974) the tension is between the sundered halves of a marriage gone bad. Bergman's *Autumn Sonata* (1978) instead explores what is "mysterious, complicated and charged with emotion" in a mother/daughter relationship. A most imaginative and heightened duel comes in Babenco's *Kiss of the Spider Woman* (1985) in which a heterosexual political prisoner and his despised transvestite cellmate spar their way toward understanding and trust.

FIGURE 24–4

A child's and an adult's world compared in Wenders' *Alice in the Cities* (courtesy Museum of Modern Art/Film Stills Archive).

MULTIPLE CHARACTERS

In Altman's two films *M*A*S*H* (1970) and *Nashville* (1975), as well as in Tanner's *Jonah Who Will be 25 in the Year 2000* (1976), individual point of view is not an issue since each character is a mosaic fragment in a large pattern. All three films have a cast of characters reaching into double figures, and all focus on the patterns that emerge during a collective endeavor rather than upon the consciousness and destiny of the individual. This concern with the texture of collective destiny reaches back to Lewis Milestone's *All Quiet on the Western Front* (1930), which follows a group of young German recruits during World War I from their schoolroom to their ignoble and futile deaths on the battlefield. Like Oliver Stone's *Platoon* (1987), it shows the disintegration of self-worth that comes with disillusion, but while Stone's Chris Taylor remains an individual with individual choices, Milestone's boy soldiers are stripped of life one by one like cogs in a self-destroying machine.

One of Bergman's most remarkable films, *Cries and Whispers* (1972), sets in motion the dark web of emotions—guilt, blame, fear, and remorse—that well up in a family attempting to close around one of its members dying of cancer. Within the lavish interplay of emotions expressed by the three sisters there glides the silent, caring servant Anna who late in the film cradles her dying mistress, regressed to childlike terror, against her bare bosom. A gesture stunning in its elemental tenderness, it stands in total contrast to the narcissistic emotion issuing from the sisters destined to survive.

AUTHORIAL POINT OF VIEW

This is a difficult category to separate from films that contain individual points of view, but here for the sake of argument are three films all different but all dealing with ideas about humanity more than individuality.

Michael Cacoyannis' version of Euripides' *Iphigenia* (1978) is the least stagey of his trilogy that includes *Elektra* (1961) and *The Trojan Women* (1971). By exposing a family to pitiless pressures, the film shows how Agammemnon rationalizes sacrificing his beloved daughter in return for favorable conditions in his war against the Trojans. Iphigenia, the daughter, grievously betrayed by her father, must accept that the choice he has made was agonizing and for the good of their people. Anyone with experience of institutional politics will here recognize the forces at play and appreciate the inner torment of characters forced to make such choices. With changes of time and place, you have the dissolution of a Tennessee Williams family. Here, too, the characters are more archetypal than individual. The same thread runs through the genre of the western, which produced many stars but few deeply realized screen characters.

Volker Schlondorff's adaptation of Heinrich Boll's novel *The Lost Honor of Katharina Blum* (1975) centers on a blameless young woman who harbored a fugitive radical. She is so hounded by a yellow press reporter that she finally acts contrary to her gentle, conforming nature and shoots him. So concerned is the film with the policeman's and journalist's distorting perspectives of Katharina's character that she remains strangely unindividualized even though on the screen most of the 102 minutes. Perhaps because it fails to arouse identification with its central character the film is polemically successful and raises disturbing issues about the rights of the state, of the public to news at any cost, and of the individual to privacy.

Orson Welles' *Citizen Kane* (1941) is also about perceptions and distortions in a person's character, but treats the late Charles Foster Kane as an enigma to be unraveled. While Katharina was a small person caught in the momentary spotlight of state security phobia, Kane is the great man whose driving motives remain tantalizingly obscure to the little people around him. The key to Kane's underlying mood of unassuagable deprivation is revealed only to the audience— a sled that epitomized the loss of home to Kane as a boy. It is also the mechanism that allows Welles' argument about pain fueling human creativity to finally unfurl and reveal itself.

These storyteller-point-of-view films are concerned with patterns of cause and effect and employ characters to animate patterns of behavior rather than as subjects worthy of empathy. The same might be said of Hitchcock's films, which dwell upon the subtle, misleading interplay of human constants rather than seeking to confer recognition upon human individuality. These dramatists are polemicists whose passions are more passionate in the head than the heart.

Where a director's intelligence and character are stamped on a body of work, one may trace out the recurring signs of vision and philosophy, and this we think of as the directorial point of view. Like that of a character, this may be interestingly polarized and in conflict. A storyteller like the novelist F. Scott Fitzgerald, who also wrote for Hollywood, may create a world of which he disapproves. Fitzgerald participated enthusiastically in the hedonism of the 1920s flapper generation, but a part of him loathed its privilege and egocentricity, and he wrote about it extensively. Serious artists often create beleaguered characters and unpromising situations as an act of self-exorcism. One must be on the lookout for the storyteller's implied ambiguities and paradoxes, just as one does with an interesting and complicated friend. Authorship involves characterizing the world one sees, a world containing people like oneself and about which one is deeply ambivalent.

AUDIENCE POINT OF VIEW

If the director invites us to look over his shoulder at the world he and his unit have created, and if he occasionally signifies a personal bias against his characters and their world, there is still another point of view to be considered: that of the audience. It measures him, his film, and the assumptions the film expresses. For us to look at a patriotic World War II film is to experience an eerie gap between our own values and those guiding the film's creation. Individually and collectively we have our own perspective into which we fit the entirety of an artwork, including the authorial frame of reference within which it was fashioned.

ROUNDUP AND RECAP

Point of view can be likened to a set of Russian dolls: the audience's point of view encloses the film's point of view, the film's contains the point of view character's, which embraces that of the subsidiary characters, each of whom is holding up a mirror to the others. It is the most difficult aspect of narrative art to conceive and control, and in films often emerges by default, resulting from the subject in hand and the idiosyncrasies of the team that made the film. If it seems chimerical, it is worth bringing under control, and perhaps the most practical means is by thinking in terms of applied subjectivity. To expose this we might ask the following questions at any point during the telling of a tale:

1. Whose mind is doing the seeing?
2. What are the idiosyncrasies in the way they see?
3. What disparity is revealed between their world and that of others?
4. What is the function of a particular moment of subjective revelation?

We amassed four different point of view dimensions. Starting within the film frame, and backing away from the screen toward the audience, we find

1. Main character(s) or controlling point of view, whose subjectivity affects the mood of both what is shown and how it is shown. This controlling point of view influences both content and form of the film and shows up in a number of ways:
   A. It may be explicit in the form of a character who speaks as a narrator to the audience, but more often it is
   B. implicit as we empathize with a particular character or characters. Usually artful *mise-en-scène* contributes heavily (see Chapter 10: Mise-en-Scène Basics).
   C. The characters' attention is usually directed within the action toward each other, perhaps in a dialogue, but may be
   D. a retrospective point of view (the body of the film is perhaps a diary or memoir) or
   E. a character may directly address the audience, as Woody Allen does.
2. Subsidiary characters' points of view, whose subjectivity is called upon to heighten or counterpoint where useful. Sometimes a movie lacks a central character or characters, and concentrates on a texture of equal points of view.
3. Authorial point of view. Authorship of a film is a collective effort, like that of an orchestra under a conductor, so the origin of authorial viewpoints remains uncertain; one cannot know that an actor rather than the director thought of a particular and effective feature. Authorial point of view has two main polarities which often overlap:
   A. A personal or *auteur* point of view in which the film expresses a central personality and attitude toward the characters and their story.
   B. In genre, authorial point of view is vested more diffusely in the handling of archetypes and archetypal forms, such as the film noir or the western.
4. Audience point of view is the critical distance the audience senses between itself and the film. Escapist films, which seek to engulf the audience in sensation, lead the viewer to identify with a heroic figure and annihilate the audience's critical identity. Other directors such as Godard and Tanner, following the lead of Brecht in the theatre, have stressed the cinema as an arbitrary show, not an escapist's substitute for reality. They intend the audience not to identify but to gain a heightened critical perspective.

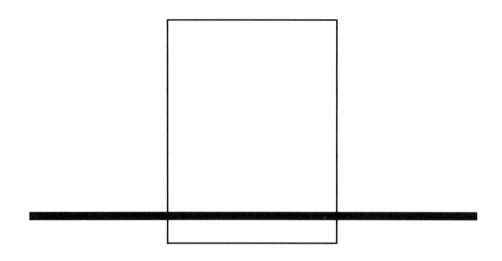

C·H·A·P·T·E·R 2·5

AUTEURISM AND GENRE

The cinema exploits our consciousness so successfully that a recently seen movie can afterwards feel more like personal experience. Through the screen we enter an unfamiliar world or see the familiar in a new way. We share the intimate being of people who are braver, funnier, stronger, angrier, more beautiful, more vulnerable, or more beset with danger and tragedy than we are. Two hours of concentrating upon a good movie is two hours during which we set aside the unchangeability of our own lives, assume other identities and live through the trials of a different reality. This reality can be dark and depressing, or it might be that of a Godard film that circles around the unanswered questions of the age with wit and intelligence, yet either way we emerge energized and refreshed in spirit, having looked "what is" in the eye.

This cathartic contact with the trials of the human spirit is a human need as fundamental as eating, breathing, or making love. It is the essence of living life fully. In our daily lives either excess or poverty of emotional movement will send us to the arts in search of reflected light. Quite simply, the arts, of which the cinema is the newest, nourish us in spirit by allowing surrogate emotional experience and by implying patterns lying behind that experience. They help us prepare for the future, make sense of the present and the past, and turn what seems isolatingly personal into a part of shared human experience.

Films must necessarily choose an area in which to work, and a common language through which to speak to an audience. Let us look at some types of film to see what they are and therefore how they might be handled by the filmmaker.

FIGURE 25–1 ————————————————————————————————————

The human condition according to Jean-Luc Godard in *A Woman Is a Woman* (courtesy Museum of Modern Art/Film Stills Archive).

ON GENRE AND DRAMATIC ARCHETYPES

In French, *genre* simply means kind, type, or sort, and is a convenient way of referring to films that can be grouped together. Under *genre* James Monaco's *How to Read a Film* lists black film, buddy film, chase, comedy (screwball), detective story, film noir, gangster film, horror film, melodrama, musicals, samurai, science fiction, thriller, war film, westerns, youth. For television it lists action shows, cop shows, docudrama, families, professions shows, soap opera, comedy (sitcom).

These classifications are evidently archetypal. Each contains characters, roles, or situations somewhat familiar to the audience and each category promises to explore a known world running under agreed rules and limitations. The buddy film will always be about male friendships, though it may contain works as diverse as Kramer's *The Defiant Ones* (1958), Hill's *Butch Cassidy and the Sundance Kid* (1969), and Hughes' *Planes, Trains and Automobiles* (1988). The gangster film, the sci-fi film, and the screwball comedy like any genre will embody a subject and an approach that similarly function within known limits.

Understandably, much is prescribed and even traditional, and this kind of film does not normally strive for individual vision. In fact, the antithesis to genre is said to be the *auteur* film; that is, one bearing a recognizable personal signature in its style and content. In reality no film belongs entirely at either extreme.

Screen archetypes have their roots in a cultural history infinitely longer than that of the cinema. As we said in Chapter 1 "On the History of Dramatic Presentation," audiences have always craved something beyond realism, so it is no surprise that horror and fantasy have been staples throughout cinema's short history. They are folktale and folk drama modernized, forms in which man can again indulge his taste for demons, ogres, wizards, and phantom carriages. Under the guise of futurism, Schaffner's *Planet of the Apes* (1968) and Lucas's *Star Wars* (1977) are really old fashioned morality plays whose settings obscure but do not efface their ancient origins.

Like any drama, the morality play profits from finding a metaphorically charged setting, and in the fantasy film the unreal setting has the advantage of being remote from the banal world of the audience. Twentieth-century space travel has refreshed the genre by providing a boundless new world for imaginative storytelling. It is a nice paradox that scientific and industrial progress provides an excuse for Odysseus, Penelope, Hercules, Bluebeard, and Merlin to return in new outfits.

The horror film is a genre whose very profitability makes one wonder why people will pay money to be frightened. Presumably the horror tale dates from when our cave-dweller ancestors, bored in the long hours of winter darkness, told scary stories and dared one another to walk away from the campfire and tempt the evil spirits and wild beasts lurking in the shadows. Today we watch Clouzot's *Les Diaboliques* (1954) or Carpenter's *Hallowe'en* (1978) and explore the same exquisite flirtation with dread. Horror films, inviting us to test the strength in our emotional reserves and belief systems, also have their roots in the morality play, the difference being only that disproportionate power is given to evil.

Though fiction cinema allows us to court most imaginable fates, there is nevertheless a conspicuous silence on nuclear attack and holocaust. True horror seems to be nothing we really care to contemplate. With the possible exception of Resnais' *Hiroshima Mon Amour* (1959), Kramer's *On the Beach* (1959), and Kubrick's *Dr. Strangelove* (1963), global disaster is mainly displaced into the safer realm of high fantasy. Surely it is no coincidence that Japan, the only nation to yet experience nuclear attack, specializes in films and comic books featuring world-destroying monsters. It is interesting to note that in time of war when tensions and personal drama run at their highest, nations are most likely to produce realistic cinema, and the monsters and ghouls of folklore shrink to the relatively human form of the prevailing enemy.

The different forms of genre comedy also fit the notion of a world with constants to which the audience can turn with pleasurable anticipation. Chaplin, Keaton, Mae West, W.C. Fields, Red Skelton, Laurel and Hardy, as well as Tati, Lucille Ball, Woody Allen and John Cleese, each plays a type of character recognizable from film to film. Each new situation and dilemma functions as a pressure cooker in which to place a familiar and unchanging personality under a different comic stress.

Comedy's underlying purpose is perhaps to create catharsis by making audiences laugh at their own deepest anxieties and trauma. Harold Lloyd hanging from Manhattan skyscrapers and Chaplin working frantically to keep up with a production line or playing the dictator are obvious examples, but more recent sex comedies or sitcoms involving men carrying out women's roles and women taking over male preserves all illustrate the way comedy relieves the pressure that, like geological stress, lies as a threatening substratum to social change.

That audiences should want to vicariously investigate anxiety, fear, or deprivation is a good deal easier to understand than other kinds of experiment. The sex exploitation film with its portrayal of women as willing objects of mysogenistic violence, and the "slasher" film, striving to portray the ultimate in sadistic brutality, each prompt disturbing questions about manipulation and responsibility for the darker side of the (mostly male) human imagination. Perhaps secular middle class living has so effectively banished fear and uncertainty that we recreate the primitive and supernatural to allay that worst of all bourgeois ills: terminal boredom.

In every age, art supplies a surrogate experience to exercise hearts and minds. Sometimes (as, for instance, in wartime) actuality is dramatic and mysterious enough on its own, and at other times we gravitate toward works presenting elaborate metaphors for our own condition, particularly as we approach our own taboos.

But how does the poor filmmaker, surrounded by the paraphernalia of scripts, budgets, and technical support, know when to shear away from the kitchen sink realism so basic to photography? What we need here are guidelines to put individual perception into a manageable frame. I wish there were a magic formula, but instead we must talk about dialectical worlds, those animated by the creative tensions of opposition.

DUALITY AND CONFLICT

Have you ever received one of those tedious photocopied family newsletters around Christmas time:

The Russell News for the Year

David received his promotion to area manager but has a longer drive to work. Betty has completely redecorated the dining room (with an avocado theme!) after successfully completing her interior decorator course at Mallory School of the Arts. Terry spent the summer camping and canoeing and thoroughly enjoyed being a camp counselor. In the fall he learned that he had a place at Hillshire University to study molecular biology. In spite of what the doctor said, Joanne has successfully adapted to contact lenses . . . .

What makes this so insufferably boring? For me, it is because the writer sees life as a series of happy, logical steps. In the Russell photo album everyone faces the camera wearing a glazed smile. There will be nothing candid, spontaneous, or disturbing. I do not doubt that, strictly speaking, the newsletter events are all true, but the selection applied has rendered them lifeless. By avoiding all hint of conflict, the account is dehydrated. It totally suppresses the dissent, doubt, and eccentricity that makes every home turbulent behind its neat front door.

Family life is like a pond; calm on the surface but containing all the forces of warring nature below the surface. So, too, is an individual. For that reason a person's life does not move forward in a series of linear steps like an adding machine. Instead it moves like a flying insect, a zigzag pattern in response to a series of conflicting needs and random conditions. Joanne Russell needs her mother's emotional support, but cannot bear the way she criticizes her. Terry Russell wants to go to college, but dreads leaving friends and home behind him. Each has conflicting feelings over these issues, and feels contradictory impulses in dealing with them.

The individual can be pictured therefore as a raft on the ocean moving irregularly under the impetus of a number of oarsmen (representing the passions) rowing from all four sides. Most row peaceably together in one direction, but the raft's capricious progress is because of the dissident oarsmen, each struggling to send the raft in a different direction. Imagine now several such rafts in a territorial conflict and we have an analogy for the battle of individual wills in a piece of drama.

Let us enlarge our illustration and make the rafts into an Elizabethan sea battle between two warring nations. With our all-seeing eye, we soon make out strategies, signaling, misunderstandings, failures, strokes of luck, changes of wind and direction, the onset of fog and storm. Then comes the arrival of allies, boardings, sinkings, the death of an admiral, and a rebellion of men below decks. By dawn the triumphant victors and their wounded go limping onward. This is an analogy for a piece of large-scale drama.

MICROCOSM AND MACROCOSM

A Eugene O'Neill play or an Ingmar Bergman film fits in well with this analogy for the forces in drama. What is fascinating is that because there is a similar pattern of conflicts in an individual, the dramatist can take what is internal to a human subject and make of him something like an exploded diagram, dramatizing each aspect of personality as a separate character and setting him in conflict with the others. This makes visible a struggle that would otherwise be largely internal and mental. In Wajda's *Ashes and Diamonds* (1958) the drama is an externalization of what is really Maciek's inner struggle on the eve of peace, what Wajda calls "the soldier's eternal dilemma, to obey orders or to think for himself." For dramatic legibility the interior has been made large scale and exterior, the microcosm into a macrocosm.

Conversely, when a diffuse, complex situation needs to be presented coherently, it can be miniaturized and personalized by making the macrocosm into a microcosm. Oliver Stone's *Wall Street* (1988) concentrates and simplifies the trends in the stockbroking industry into a representation. His story revolves around a young stockbroker seduced into illegal practices by the charisma of a powerful and amoral patron. His counterbalancing influence is the pragmatism of his working class union leader father. Interestingly a similar configuration of influences vie for the soul of the hero in Stone's *Platoon* (1987). In each case, a complex and otherwise confusing situation is played out accessibly by having individuals represent typical forces. By compelling the Everyman character to make choices we see him tempered in the flame of experience.

THE SUBJECT AND HOW ONE'S OUTLOOK AFFECTS THE VISION

How the storyteller decides to interpret an event or a world depends on a number of factors, not the least being the idiosyncrasies of the subject at hand and what needs to be said about it.

There is also an important temperamental element that guides the filmmaker's choice both in subject and its presentation. The political historian or social scientist, for instance, may see a naval victory or defeat as the interplay of inevitable forces, probably the result of the technology used and the different leaders' strengths and weaknesses. This deterministic view of human behavior might produce a genre film. It is a relatively detached and objective kind of vision that expresses itself similarly whether it works through the medium of comedy, mystery, or psychological thriller.

The *auteur* dramatist, probably more concerned with the individuality of human experience, would treat a battle differently—going below decks, looking into faces and hearts, and seeking out the conflicts within each ship and within each sailor, the great and the humble. His film might place us in the heat of battle to show not so much the constants in human history or the eternal repetition of human error, but the human potential inherent in moral choice. This kind of film is likely to show a more individual vision and a less predictable world, as it is concerned with raising questions rather than in fulfilling certain audience expectations.

Whether you show a deterministic world or one where individuals influence their final destinies will be a matter of what story you want to tell, since most of us happily subscribe to contradictory philosophies, depending on our environment, mood, and the situation under scrutiny.

DRAMA, PROPAGANDA, AND DIALECTICS

Drama and propaganda handle duality differently: drama sees the live organism of the sea battle while the propagandist knows before he starts where the truth lies and drives his audience singlemindedly through a token opposition to arrive at a prescribed truth. His drama is not a process of exploration but of jostling the spectator into accepting a predetermined outcome, as a salesman's stories might be directed not toward celebrating understanding but to selling encyclopedias. Much "message" television or cinema arouses our hostility because under the guise of entertainment we are being sold a bill of goods, and instinctively we resent it.

The dramatist, valuing the complexity, integrity, and organic quality of struggle and decision, treats the protagonists more evenhandedly. Truly dramatic

writing evolves from exploring unknowns and represents to some degree a journey to an unknown destination by the author. I believe this is why so much well
intentioned educational and corporate product is stultifyingly boring. The makers have either forgotten or are incapable of recreating the sense of discovery.
The viewer is treated as a jug to be filled with information, a passive receptacle
and not an active partner in discovery. The educator with a closed mind wants
to condition us, not to invoke free-ranging intelligence. That is why art under
totalitarianism comes from the dissidents, never the establishment.

What we face is a range of dialectical oppositions between which any film
will be suspended. Here are those we have mentioned as well as a few extra.

Either	*Or*
Auteur (personal, authorial stamp)	Genre (film archetype)
Subjective (character's) point of view	Objective (storyteller's) point of view
Realistic	Nonrealistic
Duality requires audience judgment	Conflicts are generic and not analyzed
Conflicts are interpersonal	Conflicts are large scale

How do you decide which of these (and other) oppositions to invoke in your
particular piece of storytelling? A guiding principle is to return to the idea of the
concerned observer. What would the concerned observer notice in a given situation? What would he or she feel? How would the sequence and structure of his
impressions and emotions be?

BUILDING A WORLD AROUND THE CONCERNED
OBSERVER

The concerned observer is really the audience, but an audience relieved of cor-
poreal substance so that it becomes invisible and weightless like a spirit. The
concerned observer sees and feels for the characters, yet accompanies the storyteller, sometimes standing on the periphery, sometimes flying into the center of
things, but always mobile and involved, always alert to significance and larger
meaning.

The concerned observer develops empathy and knowledge of the characters,
but the storyteller also creates an environment and an identify for the concerned
observer, sending him through a series of experiences that invoke his identification with the characters, strain his powers of understanding, and stress his
emotions. Following are some made-up examples for discussion.

SURVIVAL FILM

You have set your film in the rubble after World War III. Your choice is to use
realism to allow the audience no escape, and to make the audience identify with
a family that has survived by a freak. There are some interpersonal conflicts
(over what is the best direction to follow in search of water, for instance), but

most of the conflict is objectively between the family and the hostile environment. The trials that the individuals face are trials of survivorship that involve bravery and ingenuity rather than self-knowledge and human judgment. You want your audience to be affected by the bleakness of the environment, the tragedy of humankind wiping itself out, and the futility of your lone family's efforts. Their hope is to meet others. Their fear is of never finding enough food or shelter to survive an endless winter. You want to show the resourcefulness and compassion of a family unit under extreme duress.

LOTTERY WINNER FILM

An elderly widower goes from genteel poverty to stupendous wealth by winning the lottery. He decides to indulge his two best friends with everything they have ever wanted. Each according to his minor flaws becomes distorted by the bounty in a different way, and each finds that getting what you want brings more troubles than it is worth. In the end the three are forced to separate and begin new lives where they are unknown.

Here there is the possibility of showing three different characters in three different phases of reality, all very subjective, and of occasionally dropping back to a more objective storyteller's mode. The conflicts each character suffers are mostly an internal conflict over suddenly having to opt for what makes one happy. There is much doubt and self-examination here, and perhaps conflict between the three friends as they find themselves in deep waters. The lottery winner feels responsible, and often we will see things through his eyes. The world, first a desert, becomes a cornucopia of delights; then it becomes complicated and troublesome. The lottery winner finds he likes his friends less and less until they all agree to give up the life they have taken on. They only regain peace of mind by separating and living with financial security in obscurity.

Your intention is to show how security and a sense of self-worth comes from facing problems, and that people get into deep trouble when they suddenly have nothing left to push against. This is a subtle subject, for it shows how fragile people are when accommodating good fortune.

Neither of the above are unusual subjects, yet the world you show and the roles in which you successfully place the audience enable you to create a sequence of experiences that allows a great deal to emerge about the human condition. The same would be true for any form of film you choose, provided you decide not only upon the characters' careers, but also the role of the subjective, watching audience, a role that normally emerges by default rather than by conscious design.

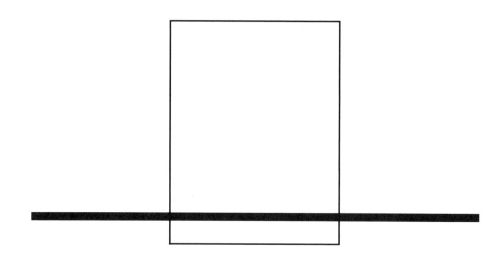

C·H·A·P·T·E·R 2·6

STYLIZED ENVIRONMENTS AND PERFORMANCES

In a film like Lang's *Metropolis* (1926) the stylized environment is so pervasively visionary that it becomes a leading component in the film's formal argument. Such a degree of expressionism in any film, especially one set in the present, creates the feeling of a reality molded by an extreme subjectivity.

If mainstream cinema generally uses a realistic mode it is mainly for economic reasons. The stylized environment makes a passing appearance either to reflect a character's temporary unbalance (euphoria, fear, insecurity, etc.), or to represent a storytelling inflection and share confidential information with the audience much as an author does in a literary aside. Withheld from characters, this privileged information (symbolic objects, foreshadowing devices, special in-frame juxtapositions, etc.) places us ahead of the characters in some way and gives us a broader perspective.

It must be said that making rules and even drawing demarcation lines between realistic and nonrealistic or stylized environment and subjectively observed environment is at best ambiguous unless tied to a specific example. Even then, a noticeable degree of stylization may be traced to nothing more remarkable than a choice of lens, a mildly unrealistic lighting setup, or an interestingly unbalanced composition. Stylization may even be present in the sound treatment, as, for example, in Frank Tashlin's *The Girl Can't Help It* (1956) when a man walking up with a hangover hears the smallest sound as an abrasive uproar.

Because film is such a relativistic medium, practical definitions of a visual or aural device can only take place in their context, something beyond the scope of this book. What follows are some loose guidelines designed to focus attention on issues that arise constantly in film authorship. They show, I think, that point of view and environment are extricably interwined. A character's environment, the way he perceives it and interacts with it, serves to explain him to us and illuminate his temperament or mood. We must also recognize, in a chicken-and-egg reversal of logic, that the movie's world is in some degree a projection of his vision. Polanski's *Repulsion* (1965) makes the apartment occupied by its paranoid heroine seem like the embodiment of threatening evil. Though logically we know this is the creation of her deluded mind, we are engulfed nonetheless, and the outcome is an unpleasantly memorable sense of the psychotic's terrible vulnerability.

OCCASIONALLY STYLIZED

By occasionally sharing the intensity of a character's subjective vision we can enter his or her reality without giving up our observer's immunity, that comparative objectivity against which we measure the character. In the famous shower scene in *Psycho* (1960) we temporarily merge with the killer's eyeline after he begins stabbing. The point of view switches to show the last agonized images seen by Janet Leigh's character. Finally the killer runs out, and as Janet Leigh's character is now dead, we are left with the storyteller's point of view, alone with the body in the motel room.

This brief foray into immediate, limited perceptions—first of the killer, then of his victim—is reserved for the starkest moment in the film, when Hitchcock disposes of its apparent heroine. Elsewhere we are allowed more distance from the characters. Were we to remain confined throughout within the characters' point of view we should often be denied an adequate exposure to the signs and portents of the terror to come. A storyteller's purpose is occasionally to raise the audience's sense of an enveloping destiny above and beyond that of the characters themselves.

The deranged or psychotic subjectivity of *Psycho* and *Repulsion* is of course a favorite model for films designed to create suspense. In Carpenter's *Hallowe'en* (1978) we occasionally circle and stalk the small town inhabitants along with the revengeful but unseen murderer, occupying his reality even to the point of sharing the sensation of his breathing.

Many of the films listed in the preceding chapter under single-character point of view expose us only sparingly to the point-of-view character's circumscribed vision, much of the drama being shown from a relatively detached standpoint. While the switch to a subjective point of view catapults us into vulnerable perspectives at times of peak emotion, it is important to reiterate that an audience's empathy builds through identifying with the character's general situation, and not just through eyeline-dominated impressions. The island scene in Carroll Ballard's *The Black Stallion* (1979) creates the boy's interior state of rapture over the horse through a lyrically edited vision of the horse prancing, galloping, and dancing in the waves of the island foreshore, yet the camera is usually distant from both boy and horse.

After the intensity of early childhood we are seldom as alert to our environment, registering only what holds special significance at special moments. Using this principle in a film needing an ominous setting means that no radical transformation of an environment is necessary; all you need do is select from it. By

showing only what a character thinks is ominous one assembles physical externals to sketch psychologically or emotionally skewed vision. The psychopath
Travis Bickle in Scorsese's *Taxi Driver* (1975) is shown in an entirely recognizable but heightened New York City. The traffic is denser, the street sounds more
jarring, the night sidewalks more overflowing with pimps, pushers, and trans-
vestites. The vision is actually intensified by selection. It crystallizes both what
registers in Travis's consciousness and what acts upon his warped psyche. The
film subjects us to the pressures acting on Travis's susceptibilities but stops short
of showing anything from a recognizably "mad" and therefore impossible perspective. Slowly and relentlessly we are driven to identify with Travis, to go out
along the limb of his emotional logic. When the worst happens, Scorsese seems
to be saying, it happens because nobody intercedes to challenge the isolate's
unbalanced reading of reality. The film's power comes from switching us back
and forth across the threshold between Travis's normality and our own, a breathing motion between alternates.

Film art constantly makes us compare by creating heightened awarenesses
and moving us between sensations unavailable in normal experience. It does this
by editing between different-sized shots, cross-cutting, parallel storytelling, and
through juxtaposing events, periods, places, objects, and people.

So far we have dealt with movement from a safe base of normality into a
character's subjectivity and back again, just as the closeup takes us temporarily
closer than would be permitted in life in order to explore some development of
high significance in a character, or (in the case of an object like a clock or a time
bomb) some high significance to the mood or advancement of the story.

FULLY STYLIZED

Some films—to the purist, perhaps all—set aside realism for a stylized environment throughout. Usually the film is deliberately distanced in time or place.
Period films fall readily into this category, from Griffith's *Birth of a Nation*
(1915) and Victor Fleming's *Gone with the Wind* (1939), and including such
recent nostalgia items as Barry Levinson's *Diner* (1982) and Coppola's *Peggy
Sue Got Married* (1986).

Any film profits from being removed in time and place from the present, for
the audience applies less stringent standards for credibility and more readily
grants artistic license to anything filtered through memory. Legend is, after all,
only unauthentic history and the cinema enthusiastically extends the oral tradition.

From a practical standpoint, it is straightforward (if expensive) to ask an art
director to create a heightened or even caricatured past environment. In Law-
rence Olivier's *Henry V* (1944) art director Carmen Dillon wonderfully evoked
the atmosphere of medieval illustration by having large figures lean out of small
towers.

EXOTIC ENVIRONMENT

Another way to achieve a tension between figures and environment is, instead
of transporting them in time, to place them in a specialized or alien setting, such
as the nuclear plant in Nichols' *Silkwood* (1983), or to Africa with Bogart and
Hepburn in Huston's *African Queen* (1951). Herzog transplants his naive Ber-

liners to heartland America in *Stroszek* (1977), and Antonioni leaves his urbanites on a deserted island in *L'Avventura* (1960). Wherever you have a confrontation between different values, it allows the film to be impressionistic and to create powerfully subjective moods.

FUTURISTIC ENVIRONMENT

The flight from the here and now also jumps forward in time. Fritz Lang's *Metropolis* (1926) is the classic example, but there is no shortage of good examples. Chaplin's *Modern Times* (1936), Godard's *Alphaville* (1965), Truffaut's *Fahrenheit 451* (1966), and Gilliam's *Brazil* (1986) all paint futuristic worlds. Each shows Kafkaesque distortions in the social, sexual, or political realms that place the characters under duress. Plucked from the familiar and invited to respond as immigrants to a world operating under different assumptions, we are shown the totalitarianism of governments dehumanized and made powerful through technology.

EXPRESSIONIST ENVIRONMENT

Some films construct a completely stylized world. Kubrick's strange, violent *A Clockwork Orange* (1971) is a picaresque tale played out by painted grotesques in a series of surreal settings. Even if one quickly forgets what the film may be about, the visualization is unforgettable, and owes its origins to the expressionism of the German cinema earlier in the century. Robert Wiene's *The Cabinet of Dr. Caligari* (1919) borrowed from contemporary developments in the graphic arts that sought to reproduce the wholly altered reality. In it characters may have unnatural skin texture, move without shadows, or occupy a world full of oversized, distorted architecture and machinery. Fritz Lang's *Dr. Mabuse* (1922) and Murnau's *Nosferatu* (1921) sought to create the same unhinged psychology by a more subtle use of the camera. We no longer touch base with the familiar, but find ourselves enclosed in a fully integrated, nightmarish world expressing an alien state of mind, one that makes its political and satirical comment much as Kokoschka, Grosz, and Munch were doing in the graphic arts of the 1920s and 1930s.

In *Taxi Driver,* Travis Bickle insanely misinterpreted a world we recognize as familiar but intensified. In the expressionist film, the audience is thrust into a subjectively distorted cosmos, and must hold on to its own sanity. In each work the central characters tend to be people like ourselves challenging the normality of a world gone mad. We are invited to identify with them and to protest against a system peopled by characters who neither reflect nor doubt. Secondary characters are often no longer psychologically individualized, and tend to be the flat archetypes of genre, as in Truffaut's *Fahrenheit 451* (1966) or Terry Gilliam's *Brazil* (1986), both of which owe a heavy debt to George Orwell's novel *1984*.

ENVIRONMENTS AND MUSIC

As we see, the past can be selectively distorted and the future can be projected as an ominous caricature. But there are ways to remain in the present and to display realistic events in a nonrealistic way. Musicals are one way. Jacques

Demy's *The Umbrellas of Cherbourg* (1964), though visually formal and lyrical in composition and camera movement, tells a conventional small-town love story using natural dialogue. The difference is that it is sung, giving the effect of a realistic operetta (if that is not a contradiction in terms). The Gene Kelly films do much the same thing with dance, but use unashamedly abstract, theatrical sets. Busby Berkeley's dance films on the other hand veer toward fantasy by merging human beings with the hypnotic fascination of kaleidoscope geometry.

Music itself, when its use goes beyond conventional mood intensification, can impose a formal patterning upon the life onscreen. In Losey's *The Go-Between* (1971), Michel Legrand's exceptionally fine score starts with a simple theme from Mozart and develops and modulates it hauntingly, carrying us deep through a boyhood trauma and onward to the ultimate tragedy—the emotionally withered, unused life of the old man who survives.

THE STYLIZED PERFORMANCE

Perhaps the only truly unstyled performance is the one caught, documentary fashion, by a hidden camera, as Joseph Strick often did in *The Savage Eye* (1959). Here we face a paradox: if the actor is unaware he is acting, he is in reality not acting but simply being. Performers know they are performing, and make choices over what they present, consciously and unconsciously adapting to the situation. All performance is therefore stylized to a greater or lesser extent.

Here it seems prudent to draw a working distinction between the performance that strives for realism—the art that hides art—and that which is deliberately heightened for dramatic effect. The adaptations of Dickens's novels, such as George Cukor's *David Copperfield* (1934) or David Lean's *Oliver Twist* (1948), have a young person as their point-of-view character and through him present a subjective perspective upon the adult world. Fagan, Bill Sykes, and the other thieves verge on the grotesque, while Oliver remains a touchingly vulnerable innocent caught in their web. Here we have a good example of what E.M. Forster called flat and round characters, the round character being psychologically complete and the flat characters being filtered through Oliver's partial and subjective perspective.

How much a character should be played as subjective and distorted can be decided fairly easily by examining the controlling point of view. In Welles's version of Kafka's *Trial* (1962), it is the character of Joseph K. whom we identify with and against whose perceptions all the characters are directed. Likewise, in *The Wizard of Oz* Glenda and the Wicked Witch of the West are each designed to act in opposite ways upon Dorothy, mirroring her conception of benevolence and evil.

In such films a polarization is implied between the point-of-view character and those in his or her surrounding world, who bear in on the character like the spokes of a wheel in relation to the hub. Often these peripheral characters have an allegorical function and correspond to roles in a morality play. Some characters remain uniform in purpose (threatening, demanding, manipulative, life-saving, generous, teasing, good, evil, etc.), while some might appear hostile but turn out to be benevolent saviors (the convict in *Oliver Twist)*. Others become

FIGURE 26–1

Lovers amid encroaching darkness in Cox's *Cactus* (courtesy Spectrafilm).

the object of compassion or pity (the Cowardly Lion in *The Wizard of Oz*). Misperceived at first, and perhaps misunderstood by the world, the Cowardly Lion moves us because ultimately he contributes to Dorothy's education, and grows as a result of their partnership. Thus, the film celebrates collaboration and implies that fellowship alone overcomes life's more overwhelming obstacles.

It is the director's job to set the levels of heightened characterization and to determine the nature of the pressure each spoke must transmit to the hub, or point-of-view character. It is important, too, that the level of writing and playing be consistent, and that there be change and development as the film is played out so that no part, whether spokes or hub, becomes predictable and static.

The personification of human qualities implied by the stylized performance points back to the early theatre's masks and its stock characters mentioned in Chapter 1, "On the History of Dramatic Presentation." Nonrealistic or flat characters are especially likely to function as metaphors for the conflicting aspects in the round character's predicament, and so draw our attention to a metaphysical subtext that might otherwise be elusive to the point of invisibility.

NAMING THE METAPHORICAL

If characters play metaphorical roles in an allegory (and it is always revealing to scrutinize a drama as if this were true), then finding potent metaphors to describe each, as discussed in Chapter 2: On the Screenplay is an important tool of clarification. This is equally true for the worlds they inhabit. Paul Cox's *Cactus* (1985) is about the developing relationship between an angry and desperate woman losing her sight after a car accident and a withdrawn young man already blind. His chosen refuge is a cactus house where she visits him to explore her fate. Having settings and analogies either dramatized, as here, or on hand as an explanation to actors will greatly help you explain how you want each to play the role, and why.

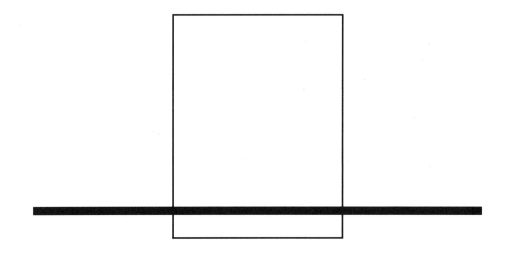

PLOT AND STRUCTURAL ALTERNATIVES

The structure of a film is a design whose details can originate in any number of unforeseen ways and can be influenced by any number of considerations. Composition, visual and aural rhythms, amount and complexity of movement within the frame, and length and placement of shots all play a role in determining a film's final design. On the whole, most of these elements are not more than generally present in the filmmaker's mind at the outset, and their specific influence usually makes itself known organically in the cutting room more than at the typewriter.

My purpose here is to deal only with the largest concerns in determining a movie's structure—the handling of plot and time.

PLOT

The plot of a drama is the design that arranges or patterns the incidents befalling the characters. Since we do not and cannot show everything in the world that happens to them, a film selectively puts on the screen only certain incidents and actions. By concentrating our attention, a film's plot therefore acts as a useful frame within which to focus authorial intentions.

The emphasis on plot may be light or heavy, and heavy plotting tends to place a stress upon the logical and the deterministic side of life. In modern drama, plot may be deemphasized in favor of a looser and more episodic structure where chance and randomness can legitimately play a larger part. Type and degree of plotting may therefore be a clue to a film's underlying philosophy of life.

Though a film may ardently promote a theory of randomness in life, cause and effect in the language it must use is fixed and inescapable. The relationship between shots, angles, characters, and environments in film language is fashioned precisely the way that most of the audience will best understand. No more randomness here than with any other language. We all have to agree on rules if we are to understand one another so that film language is the result of a collusion between filmmakers and audiences. Plot plays its part in the pact not just by reconciling the characters' motivations—why character A manipulates a confrontation with character B, for example—but by steering our attention to the issues at hand. It also maintains the tension that makes us keep actively watching.

Since a character's temperament largely determines his actions, plot must be consonant with character. Conversely, characters cannot be arbitrarily plugged into a plot, since again plot and character must work hand in hand so that as the story advances, each episode stands in logical and meaningful relationship to what went before. Failures in the plot will be those weaknesses or breaks in the chain of logic that cause a breakdown in credibility. The audience will in consequence feel confused or even cheated.

We must also make a distinction between how things happen in reality and what is permissible in drama. If in real life an oppressed, docile factory worker suddenly leaps to the center of a dangerous strike situation and averts tragedy by inspired oratory, one is led to ponder what signs of latent genius went overlooked by coworkers, but one cannot doubt that it actually happened. If, however, we model a fiction film upon such material, our audience would simply dismiss the events as unlikely. We have to carefully arrange selected incidents to show that our heroic character does not acquire courage for dramatic convenience during the salient events, but is freed by them to realize his or her true potential.

Common weaknesses found in plotting are an excessive reliance on coincidence, or on the *deus ex machina*, the improbable action or incident inserted to make things turn out right. Audiences know when drama forces a development that is untrue to life, so you must ask a great many searching questions when writing to ensure that your plot is as tight and functional as good cabinetry. The well crafted plot has a sense of inevitable flow, because it is unimpeded by anything gratuitous or facile. It generates a sense of energizing excitement, each step arousing the audience to actively speculate on what can happen next.

THEMATIC DESIGN

When directing a play or a film, one needs to be well aware of its thematic design. Because most films use realism there is often little incentive for their makers to employ the kind of metaphoric thinking that, in any case, seldom comes easily to anyone reared in today's literal-minded society. Yet audiences crave the resonance that deeper meanings bring. Former generations, reared on the allusions and poetry of religious texts, were more attuned to thinking on dual levels. The artist of today must recapture this skill, and a helpful tactic is for the filmmaker to invent a graphic image or diagram that represents the movement of elements and characters in the story. This brings the film's underlying statement to the surface through posing a problem that can only be solved by deep and sustaining thinking.

In discussing *The Wizard of Oz* (1939) earlier, I noted how each of the characters exerts—for good or ill—different pressures upon Dorothy, who is like a hub at the center of a wheel with many spokes. Movement in the film is like a journey in which the wheel revolves a number of times, each spoke bearing upon her more than once. The image usefully organizes one's ideas about how *The Wizard of Oz*'s thematic design applies a rotation of pressured experiences, each testing Dorothy's stamina and resourcefulness.

Altman's *Nashville* (1975) is very different. We have the trajectories of many characters converging at a single concert where there will be a gunshot. This one sound to which everyone reacts is the point of ultimate convergence—the one shared moment in all of their lives and the target (no pun intended) for all the film's lines of development. *Nashville*'s country music scene and its gunshot focal point are quintessentially American. The film points to all those moments of terrible unity in American consciousness when leaders fell to the assassin's bullet. The film's design and metaphors are anything but random.

In choosing a thematic design, one may be trying to describe a journey that is emotional and metaphysical rather than one purely physical and actual. Bo Widerberg's *Elvira Madigan* (1967) tells the true story of a nineteenth century Swedish count who deserted both the army and his family to run away with a beautiful circus acrobat. Perfectly in love, the two are unequipped for practical life and do not take the material steps to survive. Thematically their romantic flight is like the inverted elliptical flight of a doomed airplane, beginning as an ascent but flattening out before turning downwards with increasing inevitability. This, or the pyramid shape, is actually the classical developmental shape (Figure 27–1) for tragedy.

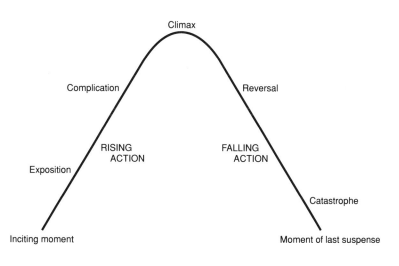

FIGURE 27–1 ———————————————————————————————

Development curve for the traditional tragedy.

This shape might be applied to a whole film or to a single episode among many. Another shape could be called the crossover, in which, for example, the strong is revealed as vulnerable, and the weak turns out to be strong. This happens in Chris Bernard's *Letter to Brezhnev* (1985) made on a low budget for Channel 4 TV in England. In this tale of two impoverished but feisty Liverpool friends it is the more conforming girl who eventually turns away from her home city to follow her Russian lover, not the more aggressive and demonstrative one. One might represent the stages of this movement as in Figure 27–2.

In Louis Malle's *My Dinner With André* (1982) one might think of the pattern of waves washing ashore as the tide goes out—a constant rhythm and repetition with a slow descent. Here we have two interlocking cycles; the undulation of the waves in ceaseless motion, and the enclosing cycle of the tides. The tides represent the cyclical repetition of conversations through a person's life, and the waves represent the texture of the individual exchange. Implicit is the idea, too, of different seasons (the different ages and growth stages of a protagonist) and different weathers (moods) as well as the changelessness of the sea itself (human nature).

For Milos Forman's *Amadeus* (1984) one might graph Mozart's rise and fall in a repeating sawtooth fashion, as each of Mozart's successes are followed either by sabotage or self-inflicted setback.

The hero of Scorsese's dark comedy *After Hours* (1986) is like a rat trying to escape from a labyrinth. Indeed there is a caged rat in one scene where Paul finds himself trapped in a talkative woman's apartment. The film could be plotted out as a labyrinthine journey, each compartment holding out the promise of a particular experience, almost all illusory and misleading.

Sometimes the image for a film's thematic development is completely encapsulated in the film itself, as in Gregory Nava's *El Norte* (1983). The illegal Guatemalan immigrants cross the American border through a rat-infested land drain, which aptly summarizes their long, perilous journey fraught with dangerous, individual obstacles.

Each of my examples is no more than a rough beginning. Films under the microscope yield many additional thematic elements that cross-modulate within the larger pattern, as in the *My Dinner With André* example above. Each work's full design really only emerges at the end of postproduction. A problem in editing turns out to be a misjudged scene that subtly disrupts and negates the overall pattern, and must either be changed, moved, or eliminated. Often it is the dis-

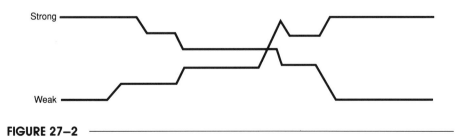

FIGURE 27–2

Graph representing the development of a character initially weak in relation to one stronger.

covery of a disruptor that establishes the harmony elsewhere, like one false note in an experimental chord progression.

Before you direct, make a close, written analysis of more than one film that moves you. This is true critical interaction and will help enormously when you come to abstract the thematic development from a script you intend to film. In developmental work following the initial script, produce a graphic representation of the whole film along the lines above, and then write about it. As always, the act of writing will further develop an analysis that had initially seemed complete.

Finding and illustrating the thematic progression in a script is of course a large step toward identifying the right structure for your film; the two are so closely related.

HANDLING TIME

For every potential film there is an optimal structure, one that best presents the content and fulfills the film's underlying purpose. Arriving at it will always involve deciding how to handle time. As with all design, the simplest solution is usually the strongest.

TIME PRESENTED CHRONOLOGICALLY

The most straightforward structure is a film whose sequences jump forward through time in a linear fashion. Chronological sequencing is likely to produce a relatively cool, objective film because the narrative flow is least interrupted or redirected. Effect follows cause in predictable but potentially unchallenging rhythm.

To depart from chronological time is always to risk confusing the audience, but something can also be lost when the conservative, linear approach is used. In Volker Schlondorff's film version of *The Lost Honor of Katharina Blum* (1975) the adaptors abandoned as too complex the flash forward technique of Heinrich Boll's novel, substituting instead a conventionally linear structure that muted the novel's contemplative, inquiring voice and produced a polemical film in the Costa-Gavras tradition.

NONLINEAR TIME: SCENES FROM THE PAST

Chronology may be broken up and the blocks of time rearranged in response to the subjective priorities of a character's attention or recall, or because the storyteller has a narrative purpose for reordering time.

Resnais, perennially fascinated by the way the human memory edits and distorts time, intercut *Muriel* (1963) with 8mm movie material from the Algerian war to create a series of flashback memory evocations. In his earlier *Hiroshima Mon Amour* (1959), the French woman and her Japanese lover increasingly recall (or are invaded by) memories of their respective traumas—his, the dropping of the bomb on Hiroshima; hers, a love affair with a German soldier in occupied France—events central to the anguish suffered by each. The placing and frequency of these recollections indicate the movement of their inner lives, and provoke us to search for what in their developing love affair brings these withheld memories to the surface. Both films pose questions about the effect of repressed personal history upon present behavior.

NONLINEAR TIME: SCENES OF THE FUTURE

A scene from the future can be a useful foreshadowing device. A familiar comedy routine can show this. We see a man start walking and cut ahead to a banana skin lying on the sidewalk. Cutting back and forth between the man and the banana skin creates expectation so that when he falls on it, we are in a state of receptive tension and laugh when chance takes its toll. A variation that subverts expectation instead of fulfilling it makes him step unaware over the banana skin at the point where the pratfall should occur.

Since the victim is unaware of the banana skin, any revelation of what is to come necessarily arises from a storyteller's point of view, not that of the character. If instead the banana skin has been laid as a trap by a hidden boy, then flashing back and forth between victim and banana skin becomes the waiting boy's point of view, and is now a piece of continuous present. Point of view here determines the tense of the footage.

In an example of dramatic foreshadowing, Jan Troell's *Journey of the Eagle* (1985) starts with unexplained shots of human bones in a deserted arctic encampment. The film is about an actual balloon voyage to the arctic at the turn of the century, a hastily prepared expedition that concluded with the death of the aviators. We see the actual aviators' fate first, and the rest of the film leads toward this tragic destiny.

Alain Tanner uses different foreshadowing in his *The Middle of the World* (1974). The authorial narration mentions at different stages how many days remain in the affair we witness between the engineer and the waitress. Because the ending is known in each film, our attention focuses on human aspiration and fallibility rather than on the outcome.

Another very different flash-forward technique is used in Nicholas Roeg's *Don't Look Now* (1974). The lovemaking scene is repeatedly intercut with shots of the couple getting dressed later in a state of abstraction. The effect is complex and poignant, suggesting variously the idea of routine and that the mind of each is preoccupied with what must be done after they have made love. The sequence also implies that each act of love has not only a beginning, middle, and end, but a banal aftermath waiting to engulf it.

NONLINEAR TIME: CONDITIONAL TENSE

A favorite device in comedy is to cut to an imagined or projected outcome, as in John Schlesinger's *Billy Liar* (1963), whose hero takes refuge in fantasy from his dreary job in an undertaker's. It is used altogether more seriously in Resnais' *Last Year in Marienbad* (1961), in which a man staying in a vast hotel tries to renew an affair with a woman who does not know him. The film is sometimes maddeningly experimental, moving between past, present, and future, and extending to multiple versions of scenes that function as repeated attempts by the central character to remember or imagine. Here Resnais is using film as a research medium and providing us with an expanded, slowed-down model of human consciousness.

COMPRESSED TIME

All narrative art must select and compress in the interest of intensification, juxtaposition, and brevity. Film does this supremely well. Newsreels at the beginning of film history showed that a number of fragments could be jumped together and that a world was inferred from them by the audience, both the one beyond the edges of the frame, and one imagined from the dialectical tension between images, compositions, and subjects. Over the years film narrative shorthand has become more concise as audiences and filmmakers have colluded in evolving a common language. Ironically, this process has been much accelerated by that thorn in our flesh, the TV commercial. In the cinema, Jean-Luc Godard has probably done more than anyone to demonstrate that cumbersome transitional devices are superfluous. The jump cut is an economical substitute, but a much tighter overall editing style is yet another. Such narrative agility is hardly possible if the film starts from a ponderous scripting style that over-explains and relies on hefty dialogue exchanges.

For a sustained narrative style that is elegant, compressed, and highly allusive, one can hardly do better than study Nicholas Roeg's *Don't Look Now*. Unfortunately the movie does not transcend the superficially explored goals of Daphne du Maurier's short story. Owing to its modest intellectual reach the film is fully accessible and richly rewards analysis.

I should mention that American experimental cinema of the 1960s and 1970s rebelled against the conservatism of Hollywood and tried drastically altering assumptions about audience attention and the length both of films and of their shots onscreen. Eight hours of the Empire State Building made a statement at the long end of the spectrum, while Stan VanDerBeek's two-frame cuts and manic compression of scenes stand at the other. Overall, as the cinema has had to define itself away from television, the most conservative approaches have been left for the little screen. Cinema films have matured into becoming longer, more reliant on mood and emotional nuance, and less tied to the laborious plotting associated with formulaic attitudes to screen narrative.

The danger with too much narrative compression is the risk of distancing the audience from a developing involvement with personalities, situations, and ideas, and of generating a generalized, even ritualized drama, like the western serials that at one time dominated television. Compressing or even eliminating prosaic details should not simply allow the markers to shoehorn more plot into a given time slot; it should make way for the expansion of what is significant. Here the Godard films of the early 1960s reign supreme.

EXPANDED TIME

The expansion of time onscreen allows a precious commodity often missing in real life—the opportunity to reflect in depth upon the significance of something as it takes place. Slow-motion cinematography is an easy way to do this, but nowadays we are all heartily tired of seeing lovers endlessly flying towards each other's arms. The same hackneyed device distended the race sequences of Hugh Hudson's *Chariots of Fire* (1981).

Two films that expand time are Robert Enrico's masterly short, *Occurrence at Owl Creek Bridge* (1962) and Paul Leduc's *Frida* (1987). The first, while it

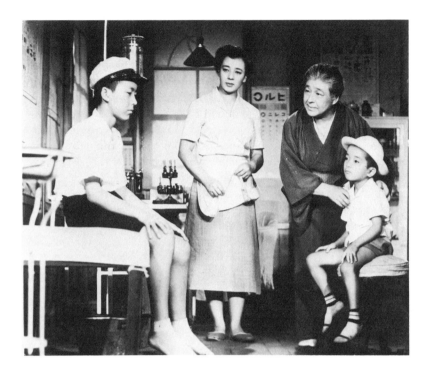

FIGURE 27–3

Minimal technique and a slow pace concentrate attention on the tragedy of old age in Ozu's *Tokyo Story* (courtesy New Yorker Films).

contains the seminal slow-motion lovers, is a brilliant expansion of a Civil War victim's momentary fantasy of escape as he is about to be hanged, while the second is a retrospect of her key memories by the Mexican painter and political activist Frida Kahlo during the night on which she is dying. Both films dwell extensively and without regard for objective time upon the act of introspection.

Yasujiro Ozu's *Tokyo Story* (1953) and Antonioni's *L'Avventura* (1960) subvert the popular action form by slowing both the story and its presentation to expose the more subtle action within the characters. *Tokyo Story* is about an elderly couple journeying to the capital only to find that neither of their children has time for them. The two hours and fifteen minutes of film is engrossing, yet the film is almost entirely in medium shot, and has one camera movement, a gentle pan.

Both films center on the tenuousness of human relationships, something that would be impossible in a torrent of action. Needless to say, an unattuned audience will find such films boring. *L'Avventura* was ridiculed at the Cannes Film Festival, but later found success in Paris and became a cornerstone in Antonioni's career.

OTHER WAYS TO HANDLE TIME

There is literal time. Agnes Varda's *Cleo from 5 to 7* (1961) lasts two hours and shows exactly two hours in the life of a woman who has just learned she may be dying. Conceivably there could be retrograde time, or time played backwards to a source point, which might be a format for handling a story about regression in psychiatry to a buried moment of truth. And there is parallel time, or parallel story telling, as in Altman's *Nashville* (1975).

Since the screen treatment of subjective experience is inseparable from time and memory, there must be other designs for screen time yet to be explored.

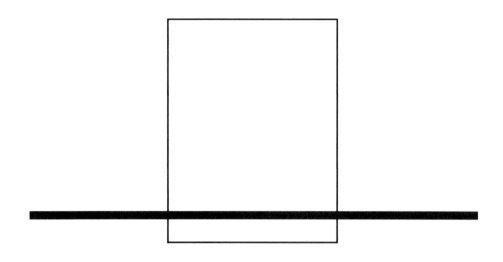

C·H·A·P·T·E·R 2·8

FORM AND STYLE

FORM

Form is really the manner in which content is presented. For a film to have a coherent and provocative outlook on the life that it shows, the story must be shown in a particular and purposeful way; that is, the makers must find the story's own unique form. The possible variations, although theoretically unlimited, are in fact confined by allied concerns, which we will look at in a moment. Designing form involves more than figuring out where to put the camera and what lens to use before shooting. It means articulating a clear and provocative purpose for telling the tale.

If, for instance, we want to show a holdup in a grocery store, we would need to first decide whose was the controlling point of view. It could variously be that of the store owner, the frightened clerk, a short-sighted old man, the off-duty policeman buying a loaf of bread, or the robber himself. Because each would see the events with a different significance, each would tend to notice different things, and this way of noticing lets the audience infer the dilemma of that character. There is also, as we have mentioned before, the storyteller's point of view; this might shift narrative focus between three of the characters, treating the point of view of each as equally important.

So, in considering form, the chosen point of view can usefully limit and shape your decisions. Subsequent choice of lenses, camera positions and angles, and lighting all contribute to the cumulative impression you want to build up in the audience. This adds up to a progression of distinct moods and to a particular way of seeing.

We must also consider the structuring of time. The crime need not necessarily be shown in chronological order—one might also show it in portions, as remembered by a survivor, perhaps, or from the stage-by-stage retrospect of the court case following the arrest of the robber. Different witnesses might have conflicting memories of the different actions, and so on. Chronology, as these examples show, is really another facet of point of view.

The controlling point of view and the limitations inherent in the story's structure largely determine the form of any film, but good formal choices are seldom obvious nor can they be made without analysis and insight.

FORM, CONFLICT, AND VISION

Events do not achieve significance just because someone frames them. A quite average audience is already subconsciously aware that good fiction is not a reproduction of life but an enactment of ideas about it. If your topic is robbery, your audience expects you to reveal something fresh about what robbery means—socially, culturally, and emotionally. Who carries it out, where, in what way, and why are questions of basic story philosophy, all of which run back dependently to the film's vision of life. The only way such questions can be answered is by putting each major character under duress so his or her basic makeup is revealed.

Every human being has a character and that character is a mix of innate temperament, environmental influence, and what his or her peculiar history has instilled. Almost all of what is visible about people's characters—what moves them to act the way they do and what causes them to forge their own destinies—arises from their personal baggage of unresolved conflicts, both the internal ones they carry everywhere and the external ones they confront, or cause.

Such conflicts already exist in yourself, the reader reading these words. They are your unfinished business in life. However old or young you may be, however much you feel yourself to be lacking in "interesting" experience, you are stigmatized in certain ways, and within yourself there are buried memories of events that still smolder, whose cause and effect you feel very deeply, and whose significance, once grasped, you can work out through telling analogous tales. By this token, the storyteller tells a tale not just to entertain, but to grow in spirit.

Form, therefore, derives first from knowing what you want to show, and then from finding the best framework and visual/aural language to impart it. The examples below are to highlight the elements of form you should take into consideration.

VISUAL DESIGN

This is the aspect of a film that people most readily notice, and it can be affected by lighting, choice of lenses, camera height and movements, costuming, set dressing, and by the locations and terrain themselves. A film gains power when it finds visual equivalencies to its thematic concerns. Wim Wender's *Paris, Texas* (1984) finds in the flat, depopulated, and arid terrain of Texas the perfect counterpart to the dehydrated emotions of the numbed, inarticulate man stumbling through life in search of his lost wife and child. *Elvira Madigan* (1967) used long takes and telephoto lenses to merge the runaway count and his mistress into a lyrical, floating oneness with the Swedish landscape during its brief period of summer. Bergman's *The Seventh Seal* (1956) goes to the opposite extreme; set in the Middle Ages, when superstition and fear of the plague ruled men's hearts, the film's heavy forests, dark figures, and low-key black-and-white photography make us aware of the mixture of magic and terror at a time when life was "nasty, brutish, and short."

Jacques Rivette's *Celine and Julie Go Boating* (1974) has an ingenious and effective development in its visual style. Two young women discover a locked house in which a stagey domestic drama is slowly unfolding. Obsessed with the characters and the play's outcome, they are compelled to keep returning, eventually discovering that they can even participate in the action, quite unnoticed by the play's characters. As the piece develops, and as the missing parts drop into place, the characters and their setting gradually become more and more unnatural in color. What starts as realism gradually becomes more surreal, distanced, and artificial until it has become a dynamic genre painting.

SOUNDTRACK DESIGN

Too often film sound is diagetic, that is, something that merely provides the logical and realistic accompaniment to what we see on the screen. However, as

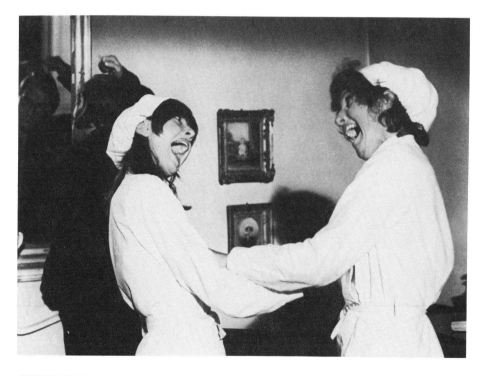

FIGURE 28–1

Two friends discover each is playing the same part in the drama they have infiltrated. Rivette's *Celine and Julie Go Boating* (courtesy New Yorker Films).

Bresson so perceptively said, "the eye sees, but the ear imagines." The cooing of doves floating in through a sunny bedroom window, the echo of footfalls in a church, the calling of children distantly playing hide-and-seek, or muffled weeping in a darkened room can work miracles upon our imagination and receptivity. Dialogue can be used in poetic counterpoint, as in Chris Marker's extraordinary short film made of still photos, *La Jetée* (1963). Songs and sayings, snatches of story, old recordings, street sounds, the sounds of the natural and the manmade world, as well as the shock and tension of silence can all be composed into a *musique concrète* that is poles away from the literal what-you-see-is-what-you-hear world.

RHYTHMIC DESIGN

On the face of it this suggests music or sound (such as footsteps) to supply a rhythmic identity to a scene, but there is quite a list of elements in a film that can supply rhythms:

- music
- sound effects
- speech patterns (and breathing)
- frequency of sound changes
- frequency of picture cuts
- inherent rhythm of shot (affected by content and its movement, movement of camera, and less definably by composition)
- inherent rhythm of action itself.

Here you can see that cinematic rhythms are being simultaneously generated from several sources at any given time. A good editor and an experienced director are acutely sensitive to their combined effect, and know as instinctively as any musician when the combined effect is not working.

An audience's involvement, as any showman will tell you, is best sustained by variety. Shakespeare, who had a large company to support through satisfying the tastes of the common people, switches scenes from action to monologue to comedy, long scenes to short scenes, group scenes to duologues, duologues to soliloquoys. While there is a continuous thematic development through these varying orchestrations, there are very different textures and rhythms juxtaposed. Without consummate form, Shakespeare could never have delivered such profound themes to his unlettered audiences.

Good film technique aims to refresh the ear and eye with variations and comparisons that cause us to keep experiencing differently, to pass through a succession of perspectives and moods.

Linked to variations in rhythm is the idea of changes of dramatic pressure. One can increase or relax the audience's sense of pressure by ringing the appropriate rhythmic changes. It is for this reason that Bergman insists film is a musical rather than a literary medium: "Film is mainly rhythm; it is inhalation and exhalation in continuous sequence." (Introduction, *Four Screenplays of Ingmar Bergman* [New York: Simon & Schuster, 1960]).

MOTIFS

These devices placed by the storyteller alert the audience to recurring thematic aspects. Any repeated formal element, aural or visual, can be a motif.

Aural: In Carpenter's *Hallowe'en* (1978) there is a strange synthesizer sound accompanying the presence of the vengeful escapee. It is a nondiagetic sound (that is, heard by the audience and not by the characters) and serves to heighten our sense of their danger. Most films using specially composed music also use the *leitmotiv* principle, that is, a special instrumentation and/or special musical theme running through the film assigned to a character, situation, or sentiment. Many will know this from Prokofiev's delightful *Peter and the Wolf,* composed to introduce the different instruments of the orchestra and their tonal range to children through the medium of a fable.

Visual: Certain repeated camera movements, like the crabbing shots through the trees in Enrico's *Occurrence at Owl Creek Bridge* (1962), can be a motif. In Abraham Polonsky's *Tell Them Willy Boy is Here* (1969) it is an action. The fugitive Indian is so often seen running that running itself becomes emblematic of his existence (as it once was for Polonsky, badly victimized during the Mc-Carthy witch-hunt years). Shots of trickling sand in Teshigahara's *Woman in the Dunes* (1964) repeatedly characterize the woman's constantly threatened situation. In Roman Polanski's *Tess* the use of color becomes a motif, as Hardy specifies in the novel. The young peasant heroine, moving unconsciously between what society sees as innocence and sin, is repeatedly associated with either white or red (the white dresses in the opening May walk, the red of the strawberry Alec puts between her unwilling lips, for example). The color red is also a motif connoting danger throughout Roeg's *Don't Look Now* (1973).

COUNTERING AUDIENCE IDENTIFICATION

The suspense film and the action thriller both aim to make the spectator identify with a particular character, and to "lose himself," as the success of the string of James Bond films testify.

BRECHTIAN DEVICES

Because of its innate limitations, the cinema has so glorified action at the expense of contemplation that by now we are inclined to assume that all films should promote such audience identification. This assumption was also applied to the theatre until Berthold Brecht's pioneering work in a Germany turning toward the Nazis. Realizing that the contemporary audience habits were incompatible with his purpose, Brecht redefined how theatre might work upon an audience's sensibility. Wanting to stimulate his audience into thinking about the dialectics of political and social life, rather than in getting them to dream their way through the fate and fortunes of a unique individual, Brecht devised a theatre of mixed and constantly changing forms, to keep the audience aware it was watching a dialectical show, not an imitation of life.

The same constantly changing mode of address can be found in Jean-Luc

Godard's films of the 1960s, or in some of Alain Tanner's work of the 1970s. Films with this purpose may employ an authorial narration, titles, songs, musical interludes, or surreal events peopled with bizarre, allegorical, or historical characters. Often using elliptical forms, such films disrupt the audience's ever present desire to lapse into that waking dream of identification which Brecht, surrounded by incipient fascism, saw as suicidal escapism. Though mass audiences have yet to be drawn by Brecht's rather demanding alternative to traditional narrative form, his work and that of filmmakers influenced by him can be immensely moving and intellectually invigorating.

To keep an audience consciously thinking and entertained—not just feeling—is a rare skill in the cinema that awaits development on a wider scale. Wim Wenders' *Wings of Desire* (1988) points most excitingly in the right direction.

LONG TAKES VERSUS SHORT TAKES

Without abandoning his wish to keep the audience at a distance, alive to the meaning of the characters' lives rather than participating in their emotions, Alain Tanner in *Jonah Who Will be 25 in the Year 2000* (1976) adopted a quieter and less confrontational technique by playing whole scenes as single takes, with only the simplest of camera movements. The result is a cool and welcome distancing that invites one to follow the film's underlying intention: to ponder how the characters should still live out their ideals when their 1968 revolution has failed.

To eliminate the need for editing, the long take needs astute blocking and rehearsal. In conventional technique, editing and mobile camerawork inject nervous excitement into the events shown and enable the point of view to constantly migrate around a central character, both classic ways of seducing the spectators into identifying. Tanner uses some minimal camera movement to avoid making locations appear flat like a backcloth. Otherwise he uses one take per scene; yet one feels no loss of the conventional apparatus of cinema. In shooting, the level of playing and its consistency are of prime importance, so this apparently simple approach may save nothing in time or filmstock, since actors or technicians can at any time spoil not just a take, but the whole scene.

In the long take, the audience sees the whole picture, so far as practicable, and closeups are produced by blocking actors to move close to the camera. In the conventionally shot and edited scene, the audience will more often be shown only enough important fragments (of a room, for instance) to infer the whole. The act of imagining the result of the environment seems to make us enter the reality of the person whose experience the scene represents. In so doing, says the theory, we yield intellect to sensation.

Somewhere between the extremes of utter Eisensteinian fragmentation at one end of the spectrum and monolithic presentation at the other lie the choices that reflect not just convenience, but, as always, your special attitude to the audience as you tell your tale. Surely there is a place for both the emotions and the intellect in any intelligent film, if not in every single scene it contains.

SHORT SUBJECTS

The short subject is often considered beneath the director with serious intentions. This is a pity. It is like would-be novelists rejecting poetry and the short story form as a practice ground. The short film is actually closest to the poetic form, for it requires deft characterization, a compressed narrative style, and something original to say. In some ways, it is actually more difficult to make a good five- to ten-minute film than a passable thirty-minute one.

The short form is essential for beginners because it is economic in outlay and forces the filmmaker to come to terms with the essentials of one's craft. Good short films will get an easy showing in film festivals, while for obvious reasons even good longer films (thirty to sixty minutes) are much less likely to be shown and therefore to get awards. To earn recognition, you need to win prizes, so be kind to yourself and compete in the easier arena, save money, and get invaluable experience. You can make five eight-minute films for the price of one sixty-minute film. By the time you have finished five short films, you will handle a long film five times as well because of the many times you will have tackled demanding conceptual problems like characterization, blocking, dra- matic shape and flow, and editing. You will also have directed a host of actors and given life to a gallery of characters.

What makes a good short subject? It requires much the same qualities as a good short story: a limited but evocative setting, characters engaged in a signif- icant form of struggle, and a resolution that opens the audience's eyes in some way to a hidden aspect of the human condition. Such a film can be a comedy, a farce, a *film noir,* a lyrical piece, a Chaplinesque allegory (like Polanski's early shorts), a sitcom—anything. However, it must declare its issues and its person- alities as quickly and economically as animators do in their works. It should be as well acted, as interestingly shot, and as tautly edited as the best five minutes in a first-rate feature film. Once made, a good short film stands as a superb advertisement for what you could do with a bigger canvas.

The key to the short film lies in defining what situations most test and reveal a given character. This is almost always at some turning point, where pressures have built up and the character is forced to take action. When he or she acts, there follow the inevitable consequences to which he or she must adapt. Since the turning point marks the onset of change, it is the true starting point of the story, to which the buildup is a necessary prelude, to be kept as brief as practic- able. In Polanski's nondialogue *The Fat and the Lean* (1961) the thin man serves the fat man in all manner of humiliating ways, all the while visibly yearning to escape toward the Paris skyline. Eventually, to our joy, he runs away, only to be recaptured by the fat man, roused to action by the loss of his slave. On one level a vaudeville comedy, on another a grisly political allegory, the film shows how neither slave nor master are free. Who can wonder that Polanski was soon entrusted with bigger things?

STYLE

The word 'style' is often and confusingly interchanged with 'form.' Godard, apparently speaking of form, said, "To me, style is just the outside of content, and content the inside of style, like the outside and inside of the human body— both go together, they can't be separated" (Richard Roud, *Jean-Luc Godard* [London: Secker & Warburg, 1967]). Roud himself seems unsure of what God- ard means, and of course the ambiguity may reside in translating from the French.

Style is really the visible influence on a work that is characteristic of its maker's identity. This is complicated in film by the fact that it is a collective, not individual, art form. But a Godard film, even when you hate it, is immediately recognizable. Partly this is content, partly the forms he chooses, and partly it is because they have the mark of his personality, politics, and tastes all over them. It is this last subtle and virtually uncontrollable element that is properly style.

Because personal identity at any meaningful level is neither chosen nor manipulated, you should let style take care of itself. You can of course locate your film within a genre, and to the best of your ability design its content and form to be an organic whole. If over a period of time you serve each controllable aspect well, people will come to recognize a continuity in your films—something hard to pin down—that will be called your style. From your audience and your critics you may even learn what it is, rather as one sifts out the image of one's character from the reactions of friends, enemies, family, flatterers, and detractors.

My feeling is that setting out to develop a style or an artistic identity only leads to superficialities and attention-demanding gimmickry. More important is to work at finding one's deepest interests and at making the best possible cinema from the imprint left by formative experience. Working sincerely and intelligently at that level of integrity is what really makes a director available to an audience.

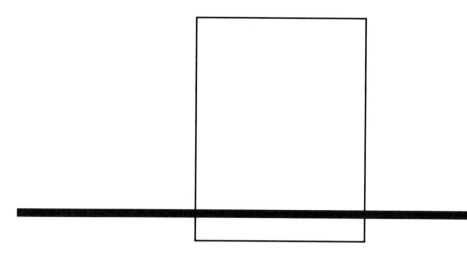

P·A·R·T V

CAREER TRACK

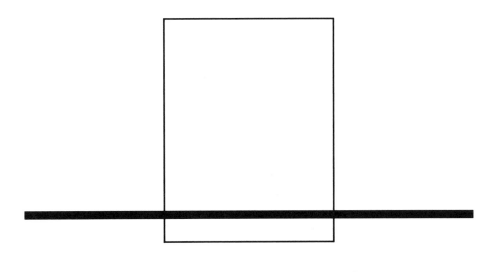

C·H·A·P·T·E·R 2·9

PLANNING A CAREER

Filmmaking, unlike engineering or real estate management, does not have a career ladder with predictable promotion steps. It is a branch of show business, and how far you get and how long it takes depends on your ability, tenacity, and to a smaller degree, your luck. If your primary loyalties are to family, a community, and material well-being, then sustaining a commitment to filmmaking may be impractical because the industry is informally structured, unpredictable, and assumes initiative and complete commitment in the individual.

There are three kinds of candidate for filmmaking: the craftsman, the craftsman who is also a visionary, and the craftsman with a visionary inside struggling to get out. Only the second is ready to direct, and this is discussed in Chapter 30: Breaking into the Industry.

Anyone lacking in allegiance to film craft attitudes is unsuited to the work; that is, the undisciplined, the unreliable, or those whose egos prevent them from working with other people as equals. Filmmaking is long and slow, so it also has no place for those who cannot work without immediate gratification.

After years of film industry work and of teaching in a film school, I still have found no way to predict who "has it." One only knows after someone has proved himself or herself over the long haul. Getting established in the industry is equally slow, but few drop out. After all, where else can the ordinary person so profoundly affect so many lives? If the profession is insecure, at least you never have to ask yourself why you go to work every day. All these things seem more or less true for every country's film industry.

So, if you love the cinema and are willing to invest a long, uphill, and penurious struggle to gain recognition, then you might like working in film very much. How do you get started? Old-timers used to scorn any form of schooling, but that is changing as film school alumni like George Lucas, Frances Ford

Coppola, Terence Malick, John Milius, Susan Seidelman, and Roman Polansky show how a career can follow schooling.

Should film school be out of the question, this book allows you to undertake much self-preparation outside the available educational structures. The best education will always be that that one gives oneself. Formal schooling is, and must be, geared to the common denominator; it can be frustrating for those who learn more rapidly or who are more than averagely motivated. In short, there are no sure routes, only intelligent traveling.

APPRENTICESHIP AS A BEGINNING

Prior to the rise of the film school, most entered, like myself, as an apprentice. This initiation may seem like a dream come true, but I want to warn how slow and dangerous to one's self-esteem this method can be. My time as filmmaker and teacher has brought me to believe ardently in the value of a good formal education for filmmakers.

Older people in the film and TV industries often say that only on-the-job experience counts. Because such people tend to value procedural knowledge and professionalism (often deficiencies in recent graduates), they assume schooling fails. But school cannot teach the consistency, tact, and reliability that make up the hallmark of professional responsibility, nor should it drill students on the niceties of industrial procedures at the expense of a conceptual education.

Many holding down media jobs who received no college-level education still contend that their training was enough. They will tell you that college education fills your people's heads with idealistic dreams unrelated to the business. This view is eagerly bought by some students, who drop their schooling when an industry opening comes their way. This is almost always a terrible mistake.

As a scarred survivor of industry apprenticeship I want to stress the benefits of a purposeful education. One example should suffice: I see students in a fifteen-week editing class mastering techniques and gaining insights that took me ten years on the job to invent for myself. My experience of learning so slowly and in isolation is quite representative. The explanation is simple and stark: in the free-lance world, know-how and experience are earning power, so workers systemically avoid enlightening their juniors. Most are not secure enough to share their knowledge, live pressurized lives, and consider it no part of their job to prepare you for more responsibility. Either you are prepared through prior schooling to assume more complex duties, or you must devise an education for yourself while serving as the company peon.

WHAT FILM SCHOOL CAN DO

A good education imparts a broad cultural and intellectual perspective on your chosen medium, a knowledge of the history your role grows out of, some marketable skills, and aspirations to use your professional life for the widest good. By encouraging collaboration and unbridled individual vision, the process helps you determine early where your talents, skills, and energies truly lie. Most important, by exposing you to a holistic experience of filmmaking, it allows you to form long-range ambitions and to recognize the appropriate opportunities as they arise, something the underprepared worker is usually mortally afraid to do.

Almost every entering film student wants to be a director. The true visionaries (they are few and far between) direct all through film school and go straight into directing when they leave. Others of promise graduate with a useful technical skill and, most importantly, with a personal artistic identity firmly established. Most on leaving school will not be ready to direct and will not even want to direct for a number of years.

How does one know what kind of person one is? Only by going through all the stages of making a film—no matter how badly—can the aspiring director begin to truly see the strengths and weaknesses in his or her own (and other people's) work. Film is such a dense and allusive language that a director must develop two separate kinds of ability. One is the slew of human and technical skills to put a well conceived, well composed series of shots on the screen and make them tell a story. The other is hardest to acquire; that of knowing oneself, what one has of value to offer the world, and the capacity to remain true to oneself even when one's work comes under attack.

The beginning filmmaker not only relives and reinvents the history of film during early growth, but discovers with a shock how much personal identity and perception he or she has taken for granted, and how precarious one feels putting ideas and assumptions before an audience.

A good film school is the place to have this experience, for learning is structured, there are technical facilities and enthusiastic expertise available, and contemporaries with whom to collaborate. Most importantly, one can experiment and afford failures. Unwise experimentation in the industry spells professional suicide, so the low-level worker quickly learns to play it safe, further slowing his own development.

Film school is the place to find peers, become familiar with every aspect of one's medium, and fly high on exhilarating philosophies of filmmaking and of living life. An established school also lets students develop a network of contacts; each as he or she becomes established tends to aid the others.

FINDING THE RIGHT SCHOOL

Many schools, colleges, and universities now have film courses. While no serious study of film is ever wasted, be careful and critical before committing yourself to an extended course of study. Many film departments are underequipped and underbudgeted. Often film studies is an offshoot of the English department, perhaps originally created to bolster sagging enrollments. Avoid departments whose course structure shows they are lukewarm about field production. Film studies are good in a liberal education for sharpening the perceptions, but divorced from film production they become criticism, not creation. The measure of a film school is what the students and faculty produce. Quite simply, you must study with filmmakers.

However, there are a number of film teachers whose own films are so far from the mainstream that they lack appeal for almost any audience. During the

1970s some of the more colorful experimentalists got tenured positions in universities and art schools. School administrations welcomed them because they
symbolized buccaneering independence to students of the day, and because they
were used to working with little equipment and small budgets. Some experimental cinema is undoubtedly significant but, while there must always be room for
the inventive iconoclast, what passes under the label experimental film normally
departs from or even despises mainstream forms. Experimentalists are thus
equipped neither technically nor philosophically to teach what goes into creating
the modern, mass-audience film.

One must also be cautious about film departments in fine arts schools. Usually
they undervalue content and craftsmanlike control of the medium and overvalue
exotic form presented as personal vision. Instead of working collaboratively,
students tend to be reclusive soloists like the painters and sculptors around them.
This encourages gimmicky, egocentric production with poor basic control over
the medium. Leaving school with no work that film or TV companies can take
seriously, the student finds developing a career next to impossible.

At the opposite extreme is the trade school, much more technically disciplined and infinitely less therapeutic. The atmosphere is commercial and industry
oriented, concerned with drilling students to carry out narrowly defined technical
duties for a standardized industrial product. Union and Academy apprenticeship
schemes tend to follow these lines; technically superb but often intellectually
arid. They do lead to jobs, unlike the hastily assembled school of communications, which offers the illusion of a quick route to a TV station job. For every
occupation there is somewhere a diploma mill. In the TV version expect to find
a private, unaffiliated facility with a primitive studio where students are run
through the rudiments of equipment operation. Needless to say, it is doubtful
whether more than a token few ever find the career they hope for.

A good school balances sound technical education with a strong counterpart
of conceptual, aesthetic, and historical coursework. Foundation courses should
lead to specialization tracks, such as screenwriting, camera, sound, editing, directing, and production management. Animation is an advantage, but utterly
separate from live action filming and closer to the graphic arts in its training.
There should be a respectable contingent of professional-level equipment as well
as enough basic cameras and editing equipment to support the beginning levels.

Most important of all, a good school should be the center of an enthusiastic
film-producing community, where students routinely support and crew for each
other. The school's working attitude towards students and how they fit into the
film industry is the key. A school that rewards individualist stars or one divorced
from working professionals can not prepare its students for reality. And a school
too much in awe of Hollywood is likely to promote ideas about success that
destroy real talent. Oliver Stone's *Wall Street* (1988) stands as a warning not
only to young stockbrokers but also to young filmmakers who fly too near the
big money.

If the film school of your choice has been in existence for a while, successful
former students not only give visiting lectures, but come back as teachers. In
turn they either employ or give vital references to the most promising students.
In this networking the lines separating many schools from real life are being
crossed in both directions. The school filmmaking community tapers off into the

young (and not so young) professional community to mutual advantage. In the reverse flow, mentors not only give advice and steer projects but exemplify the way of life the student is trying to make his own. Even in the largest cities the film and video community operates like a village where personal recommendation is everything.

Much practical information can be gleaned from the *American Film Institute Guide to College Courses in Film and Television* (Princeton, NJ: Peterson's Guides [Peterson's Guides, Dept 7591, PO Box 978, Edison, NJ 08817]). Being so comprehensive, it allows one to make comparisons and to guess at a department's emphasis. Even a promising statement of philosophy from a department of communications may be undercut when you scan equipment holdings and course structure. Sometimes a department has evolved under the chairmanship of a journalist or radio specialist, so film and television production may be public relations orphans within an all-purpose communications department.

Here are some questions to ask as you decide if a film school fulfills your expectations:

1. How big is the department and what does its structure reveal? (Number of courses, number of students, subjects taught by the senior and most influential faculty.

2. How long is the program? (See model syllabus.)

3. How much specialization is possible? How far do upper level courses go?

4. How much equipment is there, and what kind? (This is a real giveaway.)

5. How is the school coping with the massive increase in video use?

6. What kind of backgrounds do the faculty members have, and what have they produced?

7. How much equipment and materials are supplied out of tuition and class fees, and how much is the student expected to supply along the way?

8. What does the department say about its attitudes and philosophy?

9. What does the place feel like? (Try to visit the facilities.)

10. What do the students think of the place? (Ask to speak to senior students.)

11. How much of a specialty are your special interests?

12. What kind of graduate program do they offer? (An MFA is a good qualification for production and teaching, while a Ph.D. signifies a scholarly emphasis that generally precludes production).

One way to locate good teaching is to attend student film festivals and note where the films you like are being made. A sure sign of energetic and productive teaching, even in a small facility, is when student work is receiving recognition in competitions.

Some of the larger and well recognized film/video schools are listed below.

Australian Film and Television School
Box 126, North Ryde
N.S.W. 2113
Australia

Brooks Institute
801 Alston Road
Santa Barbara, CA 93108
Tel: (805) 969-2291

Canadian Centre for Advanced Film Studies
2849 Bayview Avenue
North York
Ontario, Canada M4W 3E2
Tel: (416) 445-1446

Columbia College Chicago
Film/Video Department, Columbia College
600 S. Michigan Avenue,
Chicago, Illinois 60605
Tel: (312) 663-1600

Columbia University
Graduate Film Division
513 Dodge Hall
116th Street and Broadway
New York, NY 10027
Tel: (212) 280-2815

Deutsche Film- und Fernsehakademie Berlin GmbH
Pommernalle 1
1 Berlin 19
West Germany

Dramatiska Intitutet (The Swedish Media School)
Filmhuset
Borgvägen,
Box 27090, S-102
51 Stockholm
Sweden

Film and Television School of India
Law College Road
Poona 411 004
India

Film and Television Institute of Tamil Nadu
Department of Information and Public Relations
Government of Tamil Nadu, Madras
Adyar, Madras-600 020
India

Hochschule fur Fernsehen und Film
Ohmstrasse 11
8000 Munchen 40
West Germany

L'Institut des Hautes Etudes Cinematographiques (I.D.H.E.C.)
4 Avenue de L'Europe
94360 Bry-sur-Marne
France

London International Film School
24 Shelton Street
London WC2H 9HP
England
Tel: 01-240-0168

National Film and Television School
Beaconsfield Film Studios
Station Road,
Beaconsfield, Bucks HP9 1LG
England
Tel: 04946 71234

New York University
Tisch School of the Arts
Department of Film and Television
Undergraduate Division
721 Broadway, 9th Floor
New York, NY 10003
Tel: (212) 998-1700

Tisch School of the Arts
Department of Film and Television
Graduate Division
721 Broadway, 10th Floor
New York, NY 10003
Tel: (212) 998-1780

Pańswowa Wyzsza Szkola Filmowa, Telwizyjna i Teatraina
im Leona Schillera, U1
Targowa 61/63
90 323 Lódz
Poland

San Francisco Art Institute
Filmmaking Department
800 Chestnut Street
San Francisco, CA 94133
Tel: (415) 771-7020

Sundance Institute
19 Exchange Place
Salt Lake City, UT 84111
Tel: (801) 521-9330

University of California
Department of Theater, Film and Television
Los Angeles, CA 90024
Tel: (213) 825-7891

University of Southern California
Division of Cinema/Television
School of Performing Arts
University Park
Los Angeles, CA 90007
Tel: (213) 743-2235

University of Texas at Austin
Department of Radio, Television and Film
School of Communications
CMA6.118
Austin, TX 78712
Tel: (512) 471-4071

Vsesoyuzni Gosudarstvenni Institut
Kinematografi Ulitsa Vilgelma Pika 3
Moscow 129226
USSR

Some of these schools only take advanced or specially qualified students, in particular New York and Columbia Universities' graduate schools, the Sundance Institute, the Canadian Centre for Advanced Film Studies, and the National Film and Television School in Britain. The AFI Guide and Jan Bone's *Opportunities in Film* (Lincolnwood, IL: Ballantyne, 1977) list other schools in Canada, Australia, New Zealand, and European countries. Many Americans assume that work and study abroad is easily arranged and will be an extension of conditions in the United States. Be warned that most film schools have very competitive entry requirements, and that self-support through part-time work in foreign countries is usually impossible to arrange. As in the United States, immigration policies exclude foreign workers when natives are underemployed. That situation changes only when you have special, unusual, and proven skills to offer. Check local conditions with the school's admissions officer and with the country's consulate before committing yourself. Also check the length of the visa granted and the average time it takes students to graduate—sometimes these durations are incompatible.

SELF-HELP AS A REALISTIC ALTERNATIVE

Since many can afford neither time nor money to go to school, they must find other means to acquire the necessary knowledge and experience. Werner Herzog has said that anyone wanting to make films should waste no more than a week learning film techniques. Given his flair for overstatement, this period would appear a little short, but fundamentally I share his attitude. Film and video is a practical subject, and can be tackled by a group of motivated do-it-yourselfers. This book is intended to encourage the reader to learn filmmaking by making films, to learn through doing, and, if absolutely necessary, through doing so alone.

Self-education in the arts, however, is different from self-education in a technology, because the arts are not finite and calculable. They are based upon shared tastes and perceptions that at an early stage call for the criticism and participation of others. Even the painter, novelist, poet, photographer, or animator—artists who normally create alone—is incomplete until he engages with society and experiences its reaction. Nowhere is public acceptance more important than with film, the preeminent audience medium.

PROS AND CONS OF COLLABORATION

If you use this book to begin active film/video-making, you will recognize that filmmaking is a social art, one stillborn if there is no spirit of collaboration. You will need other people as technicians to do any sophisticated shooting, and you will need to earn the interest of other people in your end product. If you are unused to working collaboratively—and sadly students learn to compete for honors instead of gaining them cooperatively—then you have an inspirational experience ahead. Filmmaking is an intense, shared experience and no relationship is left untouched. Lifelong friendships and partnerships develop out of it, but on the negative side, flaws emerge in one's own and other people's characters when the pressure mounts.

Somewhere along the way you will need a mentor, someone to give knowledgeable and objective criticism of your work and to help solve the problems that arise. Do not worry if none is in the offing right now, for the beginner has far to go. It is a law of nature in any case that you find the right people when you truly need them.

PLANNING A CAREER TRACK DURING YOUR EDUCATION

Whether you are self-educated or whether you pursue a formal education at school, the way your work is received will indicate whether you are a visionary and it is realistic to try entering the industry as a director, or whether you belong with the vast majority for whom directing is a distant dream. In the latter case you must develop a craft specialty in order to make yourself marketable and gain a foothold in the industry. These decisions are considered in detail during the next chapter.

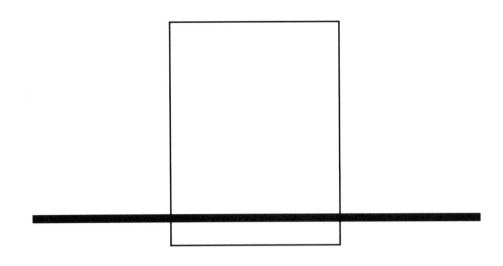

C·H·A·P·T·E·R 3·0

BREAKING INTO THE
INDUSTRY

THE PATH TO THE DIRECTOR'S CHAIR

In the last chapter I spoke of there being three good kinds of candidates for filmmaking—the craftsman, the craftsman also a visionary, and the craftsman with visionary potential. Everyone enters film school wanting to direct, but it soon becomes evident who is equipped with ideas and leadership and who is happiest in an interpretive or technical role. Only the visionary with a fully formed artistic identity is at all likely to go straight from film school into commercial directing. Others will wisely choose a more gradual ascent through one of the crafts. Most craft practitioners never go on to direct, sometimes because they lack the self-confidence to take chances, but mostly because they like what they do and find it wholly rewarding.

To make the best use of your present potential, be realistic about what kind of person you are. In the final analysis, you are what you do. Look at what you have actually done near the end of your time in film school, and solicit the opinions of the faculty you respect.

THE VISIONARY: DIRECTING STRAIGHT OUT OF SCHOOL

It is very rare to move into directing work after schooling and it happens to people whose early work gains them immediate recognition as "having something special." If you look at Roman Polansky's earliest films, *Two Men and a Wardrobe* (1958) and *The Fat and the Lean* (1960), it is already apparent what an unusual talent was at work, already expressing a view of the human condition in surreal allegories.

To be a director is really to be an author, to have something to say. For most people this comes later in life—if at all. For those already deeply marked and deeply ambitious, the time is now. For these few, clarity and urgency will open up the Red Sea. For the rest it will be a slow maturing process while working in less exposed positions. The resistance to your advancement may seem to be in other people, but really it lies within yourself. It is extremely challenging to forge a clear artistic identity. Most people's lives are centered on more mundane things. When you begin to have it, this identity will be sensed and implicitly recognized by others as they see your work.

Film school is the place to find out whether you have the vision and sheer leadership drive to put together outstanding films. Such films win festival prizes and these in turn give you momentum. To succeed in the capitalist system you also have to become an entrepreneur and assemble "packages," about which there is much written to help the novice (see Bibliography). You will also, if you expect to be paid for your work, have to have tastes that are shared by a chunk of the paying public. You can no more decide to become a popular director than you can decide to become Shakespeare or Elvis Presley. The best you can do is to know yourself, since that is what you have to work with.

CRAFTSMAN WORKER

Most people do not have a clear and novel vision of life, and know they will not be ready to direct features until extensive life experience has given them time and the maturity to figure out what they have to say.

Let us suppose that through schooling you have acquired a reasonable knowledge and initial experience in the field of film- or videomaking and are ready to make the transition from student to paid worker in the medium. If you have won prizes and have an excellent body of work, you might conceivably direct either commercials, educational, or industrial work straight away on commission, and get experience with actors. But is is more likely you will enter the field in a lowly position, so during the latter half of your education you need to develop a craft specialty and the appropriate industry contacts. Plenty of people get work as grip, assistant editor, or camera assistant straight out of school, but it happens only if you have proven skills, professional discipline, and great references to prove it.

PERSONAL QUALITIES REQUIRED

How fast you advance and what responsibilities people care to give you will hinge upon your maturity. Everything said in this book about reliability and realism for every film crew member must become your undeviating norm if you are to build a positive reputation. The sign of the committed professional is that he or she puts the film before everything, particularly himself or herself.

Such stern necessities run contrary to undisciplined and immature personalities who assume others will adapt to their needs. The true creativity behind any film is organized and tenacious, and you will need the same combativeness to get established. If as a director or crew member you consistently do good work, on time, and within the agreed parameters, then your reputation will slowly spread through the grapevine, and you will naturally rise. Make a costly mistake, and you will fall back. There are no reliable shortcuts to recognition and reward, for filmmaking is a long, slow, pragmatic business. As a way of life it will only gratify those who value the process as much as the product, just like any other art.

WHAT YOU CAN DO TO MAKE GOOD PROGRESS

If you are a craft worker with a director inside struggling to get out, contrive to keep producing your own work after you graduate. Keep contact with those peers whose values you share. Film and video production has always been an area for the self-starter, so unless you are accepted by a going concern as a full-time employee, you and your friends must make cooperative efforts to get established. You can form an entrepreneurial film unit around a likely script and shoot on speculation, knowing that everyone's skills will be furthered even if the piece never finds a distributor. With a wise choice of script, and professionalism from everyone concerned, there is a fair chance of getting costs back, even of making a modest profit over the long haul.

To get a cautionary sense of the market forces at work, grit your teeth and read *Variety* regularly. Study recent low-budget production and its tortuous relationship to distribution. Work your way through recent copies of *International Film Guide* for a sense of international trends. Try to see examples of every kind of likely work so you know in what area and at what level you are competing.

FREE-LANCING TO GAIN EXPERIENCE

The aspiring director will for a long time have to use his or her craft skills (camera, editing, sound, or production management) to fulfill quite ordinary commercial needs. You may find yourself expending lots of imagination and effort crewing for industrial, training, or medical films, and occasionally even shooting conferences and weddings. Learning to do this reliably and to your own high standards will teach you a great deal. A training in industrials and documentaries served Robert Altman and many another director well. Commercials, too, are a good training ground since incredible expense and effort are focused on very limited ends. The superb technical and production knowledge you gain can be transferred to the features setting—if you can wean yourself away from the living.

In general, American TV produces very little drama itself, unlike its European counterparts (British, German, Swedish, and Italian especially) which have nurtured many fine directors and actors. There is a crying need for first rate regional production to break down the stale formulaic vision of the present production centers.

Most crew work is free-lance, which means feast or famine living conditions until demand for your services becomes regular. As an aspiring director, you aim to be in the right place at the right time, taking other craft work until something turns up. While making a modest or even good living as a free-lance technician, you try to continue making your own films with contemporaries also struggling to gain experience and recognition. By investing in your own talent and developing it to a point where you have concrete, proven abilities, you then have something to offer an employer or a sponsor. Once you get a little paid directing work, you start building up a track record and a reputation. It is this and festival prizes alone that recommend you for more interesting and demanding work.

WHICH CRAFTS LEAD TO DIRECTING

It is important to be clear that some craft areas lead to directing much more readily than others. Editing is a common route since the editor orchestrates acting, directing, camerawork, sound, and everything else. Writers and directors of photography make the transition, and occasionally actor/writers. ADs, handling logistics and organizational details, rarely ever become directors.

If you really want to become a feature film director you should perhaps make a choice between editing or camera, with a strong emphasis on screenwriting. If you can contrive to have both spare time and spare cash (often mutually exclusive for free-lancers) you should try to work with a theatre group to gain experience with actors, and make several short dramatic films.

DIRECTING DOCUMENTARY FILMS STRAIGHT OUT OF SCHOOL

If you have also studied documentary form and production, you may prefer to think about starting on a low rung of the film industry in nonfiction filmmaking (travelogue, industrials, corporate, promotional, or educational films). Here you will work with a small crew and can gain a high degree of personal control in a relatively short time. Being a big fish in a small pool is good for many who are highly motivated but do not have the confidence to break into the larger game. While it will not be possible to compete immediately and on equal terms with nonfiction professionals, there is marginal film and video work to be picked up and jobs you can make for yourself. These pay a slender living but you will be working for yourself and also getting a great further education. Many people with long-term goals who start in these areas migrate to documentary work, or to commercials (if their technical control is good enough), and then perhaps go on later to do feature film work. Many more get stuck for life in one of the good livings encountered along the way, and elect to have children and a mortgage instead of produce works of art. And who is to say that is wrong?

If you want to consider documentary work and you liked this book, see its sister volume that I wrote earlier, *Directing the Documentary* (Boston: Focal Press, 1987). Look first at the career section.

IMPORTANCE OF THE PORTFOLIO

It can not be overstated that you are what you have done. A film degree is nice (indicating you are educable and committed) but more than anything you need a portfolio of your work that demonstrates your true capabilities to prospective employers or money backers. If you have some original directing work, this will help you get interviews for feature crew work and perhaps even some modest commissioned work, especially if you have festival awards.

COMPROMISING YOURSELF

The emphasis on becoming known and fitting into a commercial system may seem like the slipway to compromise. It does not have to be. After all, the films on which we were raised were produced for profit, and some were good art by any standards. Almost the entire history of the cinema has its roots in commerce, with each new work predicated upon ticket sales. If cinema and capitalism go hand in hand, one must also recognize a certain cantankerous democracy about the business of selling tickets; they are votes from the wallet preventing the cinema from being irrelevant or from straying too far from the sensibilities of the common man. Shakespeare and his company flourished under the same system.

FINDING FICTION SUBJECTS

Read Chapter 23 for a full treatment of sources for stories. What follows now places this work in a more commercial perspective.

It is sad but true that people who invest in films do so to make money, not films. Any feature film you want to make must have audience appeal, and you must be very persuasive in showing that. There are a few cheerfully amoral personalities who steer instinctively towards pornography and exploitation, but they still find they need stories, characters, situations, dramatic development, and thematic resolution in order to sustain the fantasies of their clients. We are not concerned here with pornography and exploitation, but with the majority who are serious and socially responsible and for whom planning the rest of their working lives poses some difficult and worrying questions.

The search for subjects is really a search for counterparts to oneself, the issues that stir one at a deep level. Most of the population will never unlock the shadowy rooms in which those parts are stored, having opted instead to live in pursuit of comfort and happiness. Maybe because of the deprivation such selectivity brings, they live vicariously through the cinema.

You who search for subjects to move a wide audience are in reality searching at a deep level for the ways in which you connect with, and represent, a slice of contemporary humanity. The seeker must plunge into the mainstream of modern awareness, must have a keen curiosity about the ebb and flow of currents in contemporary society, not just those egocentric concerns circulating within.

This means to read omnivorously, to feel that political and international affairs are your responsibility, and to assume that poets, novelists, and songwriters are your equals and share a common mighty endeavor. It means that you must strive to discover the humanity you share with painters and philosophers of the present and past, and that you look for your own history in tales, myths and legends. It means that you are willing to feel the suffering and dreams of other people, and other peoples.

Living out this quest you will find your fellow spirits. Some will be dead, their voices speaking to you urgently and personally through their works. Some will be very much alive, modestly struggling to make sense and give utterance. Some will become your friends and collaborators, allies with whom you face the world and tell the story of what it is like to be alive at this moment in this century.

You have probably noticed a strange omission from my list of recommended sources—other films. Of course you will be seeing films and will be influenced by them, but film subjects and approaches should be developed from life, not from watching films; that road leads to derivative and imitative work lacking identity. Good art extends a tradition, of course, but its source and its destination is in life, not in other art.

If there is a writer whose tastes and interests you share and with whom you can collaborate, you should jointly explore subjects and make a commitment to meet regularly even if he or she is not currently writing. Truly creative partnerships are tougher, more resilient, and more likely to lead to a strong, marketable story idea than writing solo. The director also retains some objectivity over the evolving script if he or she does not physically write it.

FORM AND MARKETABILITY

A film is not content alone but also a way of seeing. The implication is important: how a film sees is more important than what it sees. As everyone knows, there are only a limited number of plots, but there are infinite ways of seeing, as many as there are original characters. The special subjectivity of characters and of the storyteller means that creativity in form is just as important as ingenuity at finding content.

To build an artistic identity for yourself, you not only need a subject of interest to an audience, but also a stimulating way of seeing it. Part IV deals with the many issues that affect form.

CONTINUING TO LEARN FROM OTHER PEOPLE'S WORK

It is possible to see other people's films and learn very little of use from them. The problem is that good films fascinate us to the exclusion of our critical and analytical abilities. Partly you will overcome this by the change of perspective that comes from making films yourself, but the best plan is to actively analyze with a VCR the films that speak to you strongly, so you observe more purposefully and methodically and absorb whatever can be useful for future use.

A basic study method is suggested in Project 3: A Scripted Scene Compared to Its Filmed Outcome, which you might modify as follows:

1. See the whole film through as an audience does, without allowing your expertise to make you reflect upon technique.

2. Write down dominant impressions, especially what the film conveys thematically. Most importantly, what does it leave you feeling?

3. Run the film one sequence at a time. Make a block diagram of the movie as a whole.

4. Analyze each sequence for its contribution to the whole.

5. Analyze any special technique each sequence uses to achieve its ends, and assess the language or form chosen. Was it appropriate? Could you see a better way of reaching the same communicative ends?

6. Keep a journal of thoughts, ideas, techniques, and approaches and add to it regularly.

From doing something along these lines you will learn an immense amount about the way a movie affects people, and about the art used to create certain kinds of impression. Another valuable outcome is the ability to intelligently question the makers of the film if they happen to appear in your area. Nobody who labors to create something as complex as a film, no matter how famous, is so secure and aloof that he is indifferent to truly informed questions and comments. Out of such conversations links are formed. Informal though they are, contacts of this nature frequently lead to work of some sort. If you genuinely admire someone's work, it is not unlikely that he or she will take very seriously your desire to work and learn. Film work is irregular and unpredictable; film crews may suddenly need a gopher or find room for an observer. Once you show by your dedication how much you value that position, you become someone special, someone everyone will remember. Film people do not forget how hard it is to get started and work will most often go to someone who has earned a warm spot in everyone's heart.

FUNDS, JOBS, AND TRAINING SCHEMES

GETTING A FICTION FILM FUNDED

For anyone who has made a short fiction piece attracting acclaim there is the possibility of packaging a feature film proposal and going out to raise money. No absolute and set way to do this exists since the laws and regulations that affect investment and fund disbursement are subject to change, but those who follow this route often publish or give interviews about their process. To locate methods recently successful, do a thorough bibliographical search giving particular attention to film periodicals.

In the United States there is a complex and shifting system of federal, state, and private funding agencies, each of which has guidelines and a track record in funding some special area. Usually only local organizations will fund first films. Fund money is good money because you usually are not required to pay it back.

As a general rule, private grant funds prefer to only give completion money to "issue" films that are shot and viewable. In general, arts funding of all kinds has shrunk in recent years.

If your track record is slender (perhaps a short film that has won a festival award) and are seeking either preproduction, production, or completion money, you should investigate your state or city arts council, which is probably affiliated with the National Endowment for the Arts. If it does not fund film or video-making, its officers usually know about the other local sources of funding. As with all research, use one expert's knowledge to get to the others. The national organization's guidelines can be obtained by writing to Grants Office, National Endowment for the Arts, 2401 E Street N.W., Washington, DC 20506.

Each state has a state humanities committee that works in association with the National Endowment for the Humanities. This agency works to fund groups of accredited individuals (usually academics) producing work in the humanities. Conceivably your film furthers the humanities (literature, for example). National guidelines can be obtained from The National Endowment for the Humanities, 806 15th Street N.W., MS 256, Washington, DC 20506.

Many states and big cities have a film commission or bureau that exists to encourage and facilitate filmmaking. A full list can be obtained through the American Film Institute (AFI) or through *Opportunities in Film* (both listed below). These offices develop formal and informal relationships with the whole local filmmaking community, and can also be an excellent source of information on all aspects of local production.

AFI either administers funds or serves as an intermediary, and for anyone looking for internships, funding, or special information, membership of the AFI is imperative. AFI has published a range of fact files, those of special interest being

\# 1   Film and Television Periodicals in English

\# 2   Careers in Film and Television

\# 3   Film/Video Festivals and Awards

\# 6   Independent Film and Video

\#11   Film/Television: A Research Guide

\#12   Film/Television: Grants, Scholarships, Special Programs

AFI administers the Academy of Motion Picture Arts and Sciences annual Internship Program, in which successful applicants spend time observing on shoots by well known directors (AFI, 2021 North Western Avenue, Los Angeles, CA 90027). It has held drama directing workshops specifically for women and, like the Sundance Institute and the Canadian Centre for Advanced Film Studies, functions mainly to educate advanced students. Entry is very competitive.

A good move is to take out a subscription to the monthly *American Cinematographer,* a west coast publication that will keep you abreast of the latest technical innovations, and that also includes news, interviews, and a great deal of useful "who is doing what" information (*American Cinematographer,* American Society of Cinematographers, Inc., PO Box 2230, Hollywood, CA 90028).

Three books that contain a vast amount of interlocking information on the structure of the film/video industry, job descriptions, pay scales, funding agencies, proposals, grants, budgeting, contracts and distribution are Mollie Gregory's *Making Films Your Business* (New York: Schocken, 1979), Jan Bone's *Opportunities in Film* (Lincolnwood, IL: VGM Career Horizons, 1983), and Michael Wiese's *The Independent Film and Videomaker's Guide* (New York: Focal Press, 1984). All of these works give case histories and examples; collectively they represent a mine of information.

There are survey organizations to help you find the appropriate private fund or charity to approach. Chicago, for instance, has the Donors Forum (208 N. LaSalle Street, Chicago, IL 60601) as a clearing house that publishes local information periodically, and in New York there is the Foundation Center (888 7th Avenue, New York, NY 10106), a center for nationwide reference collections for study by those wishing to approach donors and donor organizations.

PRESENTING YOURSELF

Naturally a good resume is important when you seek work, but quite the best references, apart from letters of recommendation from established filmmakers, are awards won at festivals. AFI lists upcoming festivals, and you should enter your work in as many as you can afford. Most film and video competition entries are abysmal, so if you do good work it is realistic to hope to win. Prizes are inordinately persuasive in swinging votes during a funding application, or in securing an interview.

Nothing, they say, succeeds like success, and people with judgmental responsibilities often seem most impressed by prizes and honors of which they may know nothing. Make sure you get some.

Whoever you approach for work or money, make full inquiries first. Take the trouble to learn all you can about the business of the individual or organization you are approaching. People accustomed to dealing with a volume of job seekers learn to distinguish rapidly between the realists and those naive souls adrift in alien seas. This judgment is made not on who you are but on how you present yourself—on paper and in person. You can only do this well if you first do your homework, through resourceful reading and networking on the phone. Remember that anyone can get to anyone else in the world in five or less phone calls.

When you send your resume to an individual or company enclose a brief, carefully composed, individual cover letter that shows your goals and how you might best contribute. You should send this letter to the appropriate individual by name in the company or group. After a few days, follow this up with a phone call and ask when you might stop by for a ten-minute chat in case a position opens up in the future.

If you are granted an interview, dress conservatively, be punctual, and have all relevant information at hand. Know what you want and show you are willing to do any kind of work to get there. Let the interviewer ask the questions and be brief and to the point when you reply. Tell the interviewer concisely what skills and qualities you think you have to offer. This is where you can demonstrate your knowledge of (and therefore commitment to) his or her business. Interviewers often ask if you have any questions; here you can demonstrate your involvement by having two or three good questions ready.

If you know that shyness is going to hold you back, do something about it now. If you need assertiveness training, get it. If none is available, join a theatre group and force yourself to act, preferably in improvisational material. You alone can make the moves to start believing in yourself.

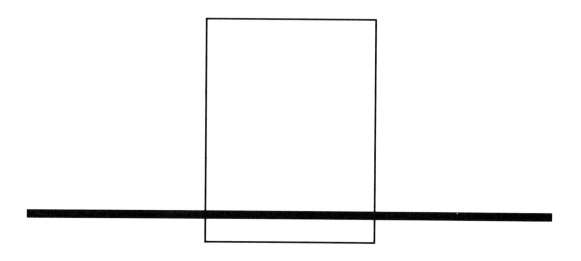

P·A·R·T V·I

DIRECTOR AND CAST
DEVELOPMENT PROJECTS

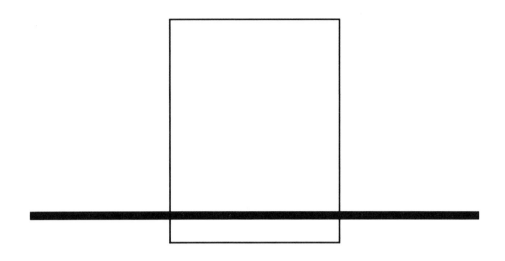

I·N·T·R·O·D·U·C·T·I·O·N

AN ALTERNATIVE WAY TO USE THIS BOOK

Many people find conceptual theory either uncongenial, or too abstract to absorb without some ongoing practical application. Those who wish may cheerfully and without guilt jump in here where the things to do begin. Here are group improvisation exercises, exercises for interpreting a text, film study projects, and film (or video, of course) production exercises that vary from ground level film techniques all the way up to very sophisticated directing goals.

Once actively involved you will run into fascinating problems of method, approach, and philosophy. Further discussion can be found as you need it under the part dealing with your particular stage of production (preproduction, production, or postproduction). Use the very full table of contents at the beginning of each part. If what you find is insufficient, the index should yield still more references.

Also in Part IV: Aesthetics and Authorship is an extended discussion of the invisible elements that underpin any accomplished film. Dip into it before, after, or during your earliest production.

USING THE EXERCISES AND PROJECTS

I have supplied both exercises and projects with basic information and some provocative ideas. These should help you make good progress before you need to refer to the body of the book. Do not be put off when a project seems to demand excessive depth. Each is designed to go a long way for those willing. Do a little more than is rewarding and move on.

THE COURAGE TO BE FOOLISH

A directing class working together in the dual roles of director and actor learns how to relinquish those instincts of self-preservation that prevent the exploration of emotions in public (alias, acting). This happens through building trust. It means taking chances on looking a fool and finding that one survives. It also means supporting and appreciating others as they push their own limits. For this reason, Exercises 1 through 20 are all improvisational. Many will be familiar to anyone with an actor's training.

You will discover that just about anyone can act when the fears subside and the armor is laid aside. Once this is established, directing becomes a matter of searching for the right keys to unlock the potential in each individual.

FINDING THE BEATS

Throughout improvs and scripted scenes one works constantly to find the beats. A beat is a moment of fulcrum in a scene when the pressures that have been building produce a changed balance. This may be a subtle change, or it may be a massive one; either way it represents a step up the developmental stairway that drama always aims to be (for more on this see chapters 5 through 8).

The buildup of forces—of establishing the situation, building pressure, increasing that pressure, then of change to a new set of circumstances that produce new pressures—can only be accomplished if the characters have mismatched volitions, and therefore the potential for conflict. Conflict may be between characters, internal to a single character, between characters and a system, or between characters and a natural force.

THE JOURNAL

Each director should keep a journal. In it describe honestly your thoughts, observations, and feelings about assignments and peers. Periodically the instructor can collect them and report trends or significant observations back to the class. No names are disclosed without writers' prior permission and if something is to be shared with the instructor alone the writer stipulates confidentiality.

The journal functions as a safety valve, a channel for feedback allowing the instructor to be fully aware of common insecurities and personal triumphs. Through it the instructor gets to know everyone on his or her own terms.

NOT ALL ACTING IS A DUET

The acting exercises sometimes read as if acting always takes place between two people. Of course, an actor will often be alone or in a large group with many interactions to sustain. To allow for all eventualities in a commentary would produce unreadable English, so I have treated the duet as the standard.

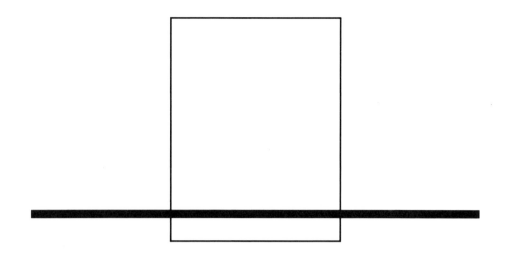

C·H·A·P·T·E·R 3·1

IMPROVISATION EXERCISES

The director is the link between the text, the cast, and the crew. More than anyone else, the director must empathize with the cast, must truly know what it feels like to expose one's emotions to a nonreacting camera and crew, and must understand the mental and emotional process of a player dependent on an audience of one. Acting exercises are included here for directing students because I am convinced that one learns to direct best from firsthand experience of the actor's reality.

WHAT IT IS

Improv is a series of skill-building games. The initial atmosphere should be light-hearted enough to be fun, but serious-minded enough to pump the collective adrenaline. The object is to develop the ability to act upon impulse and intuition. I use these exercises extensively with nonactors wanting to become directors. They arouse interest in the craft of acting and deep respect for the committed actor, and give people a vocabulary of experience that serves them well. Sometimes the exercises I have given incorporate a degree of premeditated structure, sometimes the actor has virtually no guidelines beforehand.

ACTORS, MAKE YOUR AUDIENCE SEE

Using no props, see your surroundings and the things you handle with such conviction that the audience is able to see them too. When the actor believes, the audience also believes and is captivated.

MIX IT UP

Be sure to change partners from exercise to exercise so you work with people you do not know. Wear loose, comfortable clothing that you will not mind getting dirty. Try to play people whose characters and circumstances are removed from your own.

STAYING FOCUSED

The biggest challenge is to achieve and maintain focus; to think one's character's thoughts, to see one's character's mental images, and as a result, experience one's character's feelings. Because improvisation constantly springs surprises, the actor is repeatedly flushed out of his hiding places. Through improv he can learn to trust his instincts, discover the supportiveness of other cast members, and gain confidence that dealing with the unexpected will not cause him to fall out of character.

THE DIRECTOR'S ROLE

On the face of it, to direct an improv is a contradiction in terms. Most of these exercises need nothing beyond the actors understanding the ground rules for the particular exercise. The more advanced exercises, however, will benefit from having a director select and coordinate cast ideas and take spot decisions so the piece can start without delay. Remember that the director is really the surrogate for an audience. All exercises will benefit from directorial feedback so that the cast can tackle specific problems in subsequent versions.

DURATION OF SKETCHES

Either the instructor can call, "Cut!" or, as confidence develops, audience members give a show of hands when a piece runs out of steam. This way actors get used to satisfying audience demands and directors learn to make independent judgments rather than relying on their instructor.

ASSESSMENT AND DISCUSSION

During an exercise look particularly for the combination of spontaneity and intensity that comes when actors are fully accepting the demands of a role. Reward courage with a round of applause at the end of the piece. After each exercise, brief and concentrated discussion is valuable, but the audience should speak mainly about what was communicated and avoid discriminating between good and bad. Very important also is to avoid all theorizing; concentrate on what you felt and what you saw at each stage. When discussion becomes academic it drains away the momentum and the director should not hesitate to suspend it. Actors and director should not justify what they did but instead listen to the comments attentively. In all your work, your audience is the most important arbiter.

EXERCISE 1: SEE OR BE SEEN

Purpose: Exploring the idea of focus.

Activity: Half the class is in the audience and remains seated. The other half, the performers, stand in a row facing the audience looking above them into space. Audience members should carefully study the faces and body language of the performers. The instructor

1. tells the performers to empty their minds and to concentrate on simply being themselves;

2. after a minute or two, tells the performers to mentally visualize a room they know well and everything in it; and

3. after a minute or two, tells audience and performers to switch roles and repeats steps 1 and 2 with the other half of the class.

Discussion:

1. Performers: How did it feel to focus on being oneself?

2. Audience: How did the performers' feelings show in their behavior and appearance?

3. Both: What did you see when the performers switched to visualizing?

4. Performers: What kinds of work can an actor legitimately undertake to avoid feeling self-consciousness?

EXERCISE 2: DOMESTIC APPLIANCE

Purpose: To become in spirit something you are not.

Activity: First study a domestic appliance or activity in action. Announce in class what you are, then do a full impersonation using only your body and vocalized sound effects. Try to convey its spirit as well as its shape, actions, and sounds. The class should choose one for the instructor, who breaks the ice by going first. It is quite normal to feel foolish and painfully self-conscious. Use what you learned from Exercise 1 to maintain focus.
   Examples:

Coffee percolator	Overfilled garbage bag removed
Toilet flushing	Cold car engine that will not start
Electric can opener	Tomato sauce pouring
Rubber plunger opening drain	Dripping faucet
Washing machine changing cycles	Upright vacuum cleaner
Autochange phonograph	Toothbrush at work
Blender with lumps	Electric toaster
Nutcracker	Rusty door lock
Honey pouring	Steam iron

Coffee grinder
Corkscrew
Garbage disposal unit

Photocopier
Ice cream cone melting
Clock radio coming on

Discussion:
1. When were you self-conscious?
2. Where in your body could you feel tension from self-consciousness?
3. Did you get into focus, and if so, how?
4. As an audience member, which impersonations made you see the real thing?

EXERCISE 3: FLYING BLIND

Purpose: Exploring trust and dependency.

Activity: The rehearsal space is made into a disordered jumble of obstacles. Divide into pairs. One person closes his eyes, and is turned several times to disorient him. He now walks as fast as he dares with his partner whispering instructions on which way to move. A variation is for the seeing partner to guide through touch. After a few minutes switch roles on the instructor's command.

Discussion: What were your feelings and sensations, being so utterly dependent on another person? (Instructor: what did the body language differences tell you about the different reactions to dependency?

EXERCISE 4: "TIMBER!"

Purpose: Exploring trust, equal partnership, and tactile defensiveness.

Activity: Using pairs (same sex or different), one person is a piece of timber, and the other must try to balance the timber upright. You can use any part of your body to catch and steady the timber except your hands. After a few minutes, swap roles on command.

Discussion:
1. What are one's thoughts and feelings, being in bodily contact with someone you do not know well?
2. How free and true to gravity was the timber? (Did he or she protect the two of you by making it easier?
3. How willing was the timber to trust you to catch him or her? To fall backwards and stay rigid?
4. Was one partner tending to control the situation?

Actors must be able to make physical contact and even play love scenes with people they may neither know nor find attractive. In any acting situation, each must share control equally, being ready to "catch" a partner, or be caught, yet neither taking more than momentary control. Neither should fall into a habitually dominant or a submissive acting relationship. When things are working right both actors are sensitive to each other, actively creating, conscious of the unique nuance of the moment, and able to work from it. This confidence comes from the relaxation that goes with having trust in one's partners and in the audience's approving reaction.

EXERCISE 5: MIRROR IMAGES

Purpose: Close observation and moment-to-moment adaptation without anticipating.

Activity: You arrive in front of the bathroom mirror, coming close to its surface, and go through your morning routine. Your partner is your image in the mirror, doing everything you do as you do it, inverted as a mirror image actually is. Swap roles after a few minutes.

Discussion:
1. How successful was the "mirror" at replicating the actions?
2. How difficult did the mirror find it to neither anticipate nor lag?
3. Did the person stay in character?
4. How frank and complete was the "person's" routine? Who took risks and was therefore self-revealing?
5. What analogous situations is an actor likely to face?

EXERCISE 6: WHO, WHERE, WHEN, WHAT

Purpose: Immediate character and situation development without props.

Activity: Instructor designates an actor, then asks successive people for one each of who/where/when/what. The actor then carries out some appropriate action, in character, for a minute or two. The instructor calls "Cut!" when the action is long enough or if development levels off. The class reports what it saw happening and what was communicated. The actor then says briefly what he or she intended.
  Example:

Who [is present]?	"Mary Jo Sorensen, thirty-five"
Where [is she]?	"In an airport lounge"
When [is this]?	"Christmas Eve, late at night"
What [is happening]?	"Waiting for her parents to arrive. Must tell them she has lost her job."

Our designated actress thinks a moment, then slips into character. She sits moodily tearing up a styrofoam coffee cup, looking sidelong with fatigue and distaste at some people nearby. From another direction she notices evidence of some change, and stands apprehensively, straightening her skirt.

Discussion: The class should say what it felt was going on inside the character. This may divide up into what was convincing, and what were false notes, intentions that did not come across as natural. In our example the actress focused on being anxious, tired, and depressed, but did not forget to interact with her environment. Built into the action was a significant change, a heightening of awareness as her long wait suddenly promises to end. On balance the class believed that Mary Jo had not told her parents about the change in her employment, and liked the action with the styrofoam cup, which most "saw" in her hands. They also liked the irritability, but were unclear what was its source. One person thinks it was because of cigar smoke, another thought it was carousers the worse for drink. However, most felt that the change of awareness was imposed and that the actor lost focus at that moment.

The actress said she had believed in her character while she had the cup in her hands, but then had imagined a man with a loud voice but had been unable to see his image. In confusion she had decided to make her parents appear at the arrival gate, but this image too refused to materialize because she had forced it.

EXERCISE 7: SOLO, NO WORDS

(From this Exercise onward, a piece can be ended when the majority of the audience, through raising hands, signifies to the director/instructor that dramatic development is past its peak.)

Purpose: Use unremarkable, everyday action to communicate something of the inner thoughts and feelings of a character whose life is quite unlike that of the actor.

Activity: From an action (the what) and using no props, invent a who, where and when to sustain your character sketch. Avoid storytelling or high drama of any kind. Try out any or all of these:

1. Alone in someone's house (whose?) where you explore: (a) the refrigerator, (b) the bathroom, (c) the bedroom you have been given
2. Finding a box of your childhood toys you haven't seen for many years
3. Unwrapping a long-awaited parcel
4. Waiting in the dentist's office
5. Making a grocery list
6. Trying on a new coat
7. Taking medicine

8. Caring for a pet

9. Taking a bike out after the winter

10. Cleaning out the attic

11. Wrapping a gift

12. Cleaning shoes

13. Looking out of the window

14. Waiting for a phone call

15. Dividing up the laundry

16. Watching a sport

17. Overhearing an interesting conversation in a store

Discussion: Audience: In a particular performance, what was interesting and what did it make you see? When did the player break focus? Why?

EXERCISE 8: DUO, NO WORDS

Purpose: Through interaction, to communicate something of the inner thoughts and feelings of two characters using an everyday action that involves some element of conflict.

Activity: From an action (the what) and using no props, invent a who, where, and when to sustain your character sketch. Avoid storytelling or high drama of any kind. Try these:

1. Mending a car

2. Making a double bed

3. Buying a magazine

4. Pulling a sliver out of a finger

5. Carrying a heavy garbage can

6. Washing dishes after a special meal

7. Washing a child's hair

8. Photographing a model

9. Putting up a tent

10. Playing pinball

11. Maneuvering heavy furniture through doorway

12. Waiting in a doorway for a heavy rainstorm to ease

13. Writing out a speeding ticket after the talking is done

14. Watching a TV program; one likes it, the other does not

15. A stranger in a plane who is falling asleep against you

Discussion: Did the actors create

1. two distinct character identities (who)?
2. a believable and recognizable environment—country, area, city, place, or room—and use it (where)?
3. a distinctive period and time of day (when)?
4. a believable tension?
5. a situation in which speech was not called for?
6. an interaction in which neither was controlling the movement of the sketch? Was there communion and adaptation?

EXERCISE 9: GIBBERISH

Purpose: To use the voice as an expressive instrument and to compel the actors to use their bodies and voice quality as tools of communication. Too often actors cease to act with the whole body once they have lines to speak. This exercise stimulates speech but deemphasizes verbal meaning in favor of underlying intention.

Activity: Using the examples in Exercise 8 carry out an activity, with a conflict, using gibberish as the characters' language.

Discussion: As in Exercise 8, but omitting (5). How did the actors handle the gibberish conversations? Did they become natural?

EXERCISE 10: SOLO, WITH WORDS

Purpose: To create a character, using the usual who/where/when/what, using both actions and speech.

Activity: In creating your character, remember to develop him or her through actions. Do not sit still and rely on a monologue. Here are some suggestions:

1. A difficult phone conversation (phone has a long cord)
2. Reconstructing a painful conversation
3. Writing the opening remarks of an important speech
4. Rehearsing in front of the bathroom mirror for a traffic court appearance
5. Planning a dinner party
6. Getting ready to tell someone about a betrayal or infidelity
7. Working up to approaching your boss for a raise
8. Rehearsing the way you will evict a rich, peppery relative who came to visit and has long overstayed

9. Explaining to your new employer why you must do your first day's work in full clown costume

10. Imagining different approaches to someone who attracts you deeply but whom you hold in awe

11. Your head is stuck between the railings enclosing a war memorial. Someone has gone to call the fire department and you are trying to figure out an explanation.

12. It is Judgment Day and you are rehearsing an explanation of your sins to a recording angel

13. You are preparing to audition for the role of "Talk Show Host With a Difference"

14. A practical joke has gone wrong and you must explain to the victim

Discussion: Did the actor

1. create a believable character?

2. keep up a developing action?

3. make the situation develop?

4. make you see all the physical objects and surroundings?

EXERCISE 11: DUO, WITH WORDS

Purpose: To maintain conversation and developing action at the same time.

Activity: Each of these sketches requires both a conversation and accompanying physical action, which should be purposeful. Do not take it too fast, and do not feel you have to be talking all the time. Examples to try:

1. Eating a meal and discussing a prearranged topic

2. Demonstrating a kitchen appliance to a family member

3. Cleaning the car, discussing something

4. Getting a large piece of furniture through an awkward doorway

5. Discussing your son's or daughter's rotten grades

6. Asking for some money that you are owed

7. Buying something embarrassing from a pharmacist

8. Rearranging a room

9. Showing someone they have not done a good job of work

10. Teaching a friend to drive

11. Discussing a change in hairdo

12. Teaching someone a dance step

13. Meeting someone you had hoped to avoid

14. A confession you would rather not hear

Discussion: Did they

1. keep both the topic and the actions going?
2. keep the physical world they created consistent?
3. work off each other?
4. share the initiative equally?
5. allow the piece to develop spontaneously?
6. develop interesting characters?

EXERCISE 12: MAKE YOUR OWN CHARACTER

Purpose: To place the actor, as a character, in the hands of the audience.

Activity: Go before the class, in costume, as a character based on someone you know or have met who made a powerful impression on you. The class asks you probing questions about yourself. You answer in character.

Each character should be onstage for about ten minutes, and two or three performances per session is the maximum, as the interaction can be very intense.

Discussion: This, honestly undertaken, can be magical, a powerful exercise in portrayal that tells much about the actor's values and influences. There may be little need for discussion if the exercise goes well. Play it by ear.

EXERCISE 13: ENSEMBLE SITUATIONS

Purpose: To engage the whole group in a collective creation.

Activity: These are situations in which individual characters contribute to a whole. The where and when will need to be agreed on beforehand. The aim is to keep up your character while contributing to the development of the piece. You might want to reuse a character developed earlier, perhaps the one from Exercise 12. Specimen situations include the following:

1. A tug of war
2. Dealing with an obstreperous drunk
3. Someone is hurt in the street
4. Surprise party
5. A person faints in a crowded train
6. Bus driver stops bus because passenger will not pay
7. Unpopular coach berates a team
8. Party interrupted by protesting neighbor
9. Busy hotel kitchen with waiters and waitresses coming and going

10. Airline with badly delayed flight dealing with irate passengers

11. Exercise class in an institution for severely disturbed people

12. Policeman tries to arrest person at demonstration; crowd argues

13. Subway train stops in tunnel due to power cut

14. Someone arrives with news that may have serious consequences.

Discussion: How many subordinate actions were there going on during the main action? Did everyone stay in character? (The temptation is to lose focus unless you are important.) How did the piece develop, and what compromises did people make to sustain the whole?

EXERCISE 14: DEVELOPING AN EMOTION

Purpose: Here the actors are supplied with an emotion to reach for.

Activity: This exercise should not be attempted until the class has developed considerable rapport and experience. The players must invent characters and a situation, then develop it to the point where the specified emotion is reached. The class can stop the sketch when the emotion is reached, or if the piece is not going anywhere. Emotions one character might feel include

1. anger	6. suspicion	11. sympathy
2. relief	7. jealousy	12. condescension
3. rejection	8. love	13. stupidity
4. disbelief	9. friendliness	14. release
5. superiority	10. empathy	

Discussion: This is a tricky demand because it asks that actors build to a known conclusion, and this tempts them to manipulate the situation. All the prior criteria apply, but important considerations here are

1. Was the interaction credible?

2. Did it arrive at the specified emotion?

3. If not, why not?

4. Was the development even or uneven?

5. Was the initiative shared equally?

This exercise can dramatically reveal the cardinal weakness of improvisation: unevenness of inspiration producing an inconsistent pace of development. The symptoms are lengthy periods when the actors are circling a problem, unable to break through or, alternatively, breaking through by decision instead of by the characters' process. This happens from frustration or panic at making the audience wait. A sign of confidence in both players and company (audience) is that the players do not short-circuit the process in pursuing the goal, and the audience remains supportive.

EXERCISE 15: BRIDGING EMOTIONS

Purpose: To make a credible change from one emotion to another.

Activity: Same as Exercise 14 except the players start in the middle of one emotion and find their way to the next. Start with two emotions, and then, if you want to make it truly challenging, specify three.

Discussion: Same as Exercise 14.

EXERCISE 16: GENERIC SITUATIONS ON TV

Purpose: To involve a group in immediate and unpremeditated invention.

Activity: Divide the class into players and audience. The audience is watching a TV program that leads up to one of the generic situations below. The players are TV actors who must instantly become a program showing the chosen situation. When the situation is running out of steam, an audience member may come up to the TV and change the channel and announce what the new program is. The players must now develop the same situation in the new program format, until someone changes the channel again. After a while, students swap roles. Suggested situations:

1. Persuasion
2. Trapped
3. Returning
4. Interview
5. Making a difficult request
6. Successfully stopping an argument
7. Cheating
8. Being authoritative
9. Avoiding something
10. Complaining
11. Disaster
12. Surprise
13. Laughing out of relief
14. Jeering

Discussion: How inventive were the players able to be? How authentic were the situations to actual TV programs? How quickly were they able to make the change? Here the accent is upon experiencing the same situation and probably the same emotions through very different characters, and feeding into different but set expectations in the audience.

EXERCISE 17: VIDEO CONVENTION

Purpose: Same as Exercise 16.

Activity: Same ideas as Exercise 16 except the situation is a huge video dealer's convention offering unsold video programs at big discounts. The audience is comprised of potential buyers at a stand where everything imaginable is on sale:

do-it-yourself tapes on kitchen rehab or carburetor tuning, nature films, social documentaries, comedies, tragedies, slasher films, soft porn films, biology lessons, music videos, teen romances, farces, beauty procedures for the over-forties, etc. When the audience decides to see a new sample, an audience member calls out the title of the new video.

Discussion: Similar to Exercise 16. Accent is upon spontaneity and speed of adaptation. Since these are videos that have not sold, they probably are obscure or third rate, and full of genre cliches. Did all the cast contribute equally?

EXERCISE 18: BLIND DATE

Purpose: To work with interior monologue.

Activity: A man and a woman have been set up by friends with a blind date. They meet in a bar and discuss how to spend the evening together. Character A has several conflicting personality traits, each represented by a class member. As the conversation between the two slowly proceeds, each of the voices chimes in, speaking its biased reaction or tendentious thought. Character A must listen to his or her interior voices, react realistically to his or her own "thoughts," and act upon the most appropriate in his or her next words or action. Character B must disregard everything except what Character A says or does. There may be a chorus of inner voices, or there may initially be none. The voices will overlap, and argue with each other. Take your time and react to them, remaining credibly in character. Personality traits could include

1. the need to be liked
2. fear of rejection
3. the need to be different
4. the need to be normal
5. the need to make conquest
6. fear of being manipulated
7. worry about expense
8. guilt
9. worry that he or she will find out your secret

Discussion: This one is a lot of fun, and demands tremendous concentration from all concerned. How did Character A handle all the input? What were his or her noticeable influences? This is a key exercise to help understand a prime source of focus: if an actor keeps his character's interior voices going, he or she will never lose focus, and will consistently bring a richness of ambiguity to each moment of the part. Remember, the real action of any part takes place inside, behind the character's outward words and physical actions.

EXERCISE 19: INNER CONFLICT

Purpose: To portray a character's contradictory tensions but never directly reveal them.

Activity: An actor is designated to play an intelligent person who wishes to be correctly understood. The character can be modeled upon someone prominent in the news. This character has gone through life denying certain aspects of his or her character, so sometimes "puts a good face on things" and rationalizes what he or she cannot change. The character begins with the sentence, "Because I think you may have the wrong idea about me, I'm going to tell you what most people don't know." After he or she has spoken for a while, the audience can help by asking questions.

Discussion: When was the actor sincere, when was he or she suppressing the truth? How did you know? When was it believable and when did it look contrived? What was interesting, what was less so? The actor must portray his or her character's conflicts by denial, which must flow from the character's rationale about what can or cannot be admitted in public.

EXERCISE 20: THROWN TOGETHER

Purpose: To bring together in a common activity two characters each of whom is using it to gain emotional satisfaction from the other. The exercise seeks to explore the idea that in real life we almost never express what weighs on our minds; instead we recreate our own unsolved issues through the situation at hand and use them to seek satisfaction, occasionally with success.

Activity: Take two of the least compatible characters developed in Exercise 12 or 19 and put them together in a credible work situation. Within the bounds of ordinary, decent, civilized behavior, each follows his or her usual agenda in relating to other people. The actors should take the time to keep up an interior (and silent) monologue. No issues are ever named; their needs and reactions must be expressed through the work they are doing together. Whether they get along or whether they find mutual accommodation should not be predetermined.

Discussion: Did each character

1. develop?
2. find a way to play out his/her issues through their work?
3. choose a credible path?
4. stay in focus and in character?
5. find a believable way of cooperating?

Did you believe the outcome? Did one "win?" Did both find satisfaction? Neither? What was the obligatory moment in the scene? What made it the obligatory moment?

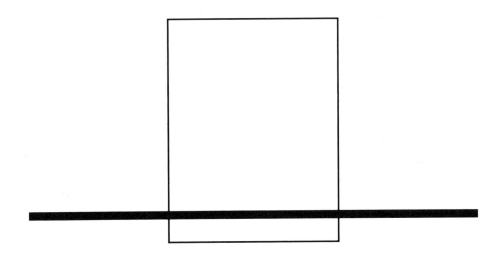

C·H·A·P·T·E·R 3·2

EXERCISES WITH A TEXT

Interpreting a text is explained in Chapter 3: The Director Prepares, and re-hearsing actors is covered in chapters 5 through 8. The exercises here are intended to develop particular skills, but each can also serve as a resource later to correct some common problems that emerge during rehearsals or even shooting.

TEXTS

Because you should learn the rehearsal process without ever having to doubt the quality of the writing, I advise using a good one-act drama rather than your own writing at this stage. Use something short so discussion can be narrowly (and therefore deeply) focused. Avoid the theatrical comedy because more than anything it requires a live audience. I have found several of Harold Pinter's short works to be ideal, in particular *The Dumb-Waiter*. In Pinter there is always a fascinating tension between what characters say and what is going on in their minds.

BEFORE THE EXERCISES

After casting, everyone should carefully read the whole play, make brief definitions of the characters, and do an ensemble read-through of the whole piece. Actors must not learn lines until instructed!

DEVELOPMENTAL PROCESS

Do not anticipate problems. Particularly when you direct actors of some experience, it is dangerous to impose any developmental technique arbitrarily, as they may feel it is unnecessary or beneath them. Let your actors get as far as they can with minimal directing, and when problems appear use an appropriate technique to break the logjam. After one or two successes, your credibility will rise.

USEFUL WHEN

Each exercise is also a resource to help solve common problems during rehearsal or production of any work in progress. Its medicine chest utility is given under "Useful When."

EXERCISE 21: WHAT THE ACTORS BRING

Useful When: Adjusting one's thematic intentions for the piece around the cast and to make use of what each individual brings.

Purpose: To make decisions about the special qualities and characteristics of the actors for use in your thematic interpretation.

Activity: After the read-through

1. make notes that capture the intrinsic quality of each actor. For example:

    <u>Dale</u> has a slow, quiet, repressed quality that masks a certain pain and bitterness. He is watchful, highly intelligent, intense, and his first reaction is often a protective cynicism, but really it matters very much to him that he be liked. He reminds me of a stray cat, cornered and defiant, but hungry and cold, too.

2. make a projection of how the actors' qualities can legitimately be used to polarize the performances, and how this will affect your thematic interpretation of the piece. For example:

    <u>Dale</u> has the quality of honorable victimhood and this stacks the cards interestingly against the father, whom we assume has practiced subtle violence against his son in the distant past, without the mother being aware of it.

EXERCISE 22: MARKING BEATS IN A TEXT

Useful When: Actors cannot be relied upon to make an instinctive and complete dramatic analysis of a text.

Purpose: To find the beats, that is, the fulcrum points of emotional change.

Activity: Director and actors should separately study the scene looking for the beats. These may be triggered by dialogue, by an action, or by outside information coming in, such as a phone call. Emotional change does not happen continuously and smoothly like the hands of a clock. It is more like the move-

ment of a heavy object being pushed across a rough surface. Pressure to move
it mounts and mounts until suddenly it lunges forward a few feet. Those pushing
regroup themselves and start exerting pressure again, until—boom!—again it
moves.

In dramatic terms, the beat is the moment of yielding when emotional pressures overcome emotional resistance and compel a moment of changed awareness. From this definition it is apparent that each character must have a conception
of what the conflict is, like two wrestlers who must make contact in order to
compete. Finding beats, therefore, means findings the important moves in the
match, and defining the strategy, from each protagonist's point of view, leading
to each meaningful strike and counterstrike.

There may be one beat or there may be several in a scene. All the beats may
belong to one character, or there may be beats for both, some even simultaneous
and mutual. Either may remain unconscious of the other's change of consciousness, though the audience should be able to read the changes in both.

Discussion: In rehearsal agree where the beats are, and what causes them.

EXERCISE 23: IMPROVISING AN INTERIOR MONOLOGUE

Useful When: A text refuses to come alive, and you need a powerful method
of getting actors to externalize their understanding. Also useful when you are
far along in rehearsals and still have intransigent trouble spots. Asking a cast
member for his inner monologue at such a trouble spot usually reveals immediately what the problem is.

Purpose: What an actor says and does is only the surface of his character's
existence. In real life, we have a rich inner life going on all the time, and no
fictional character can be interesting or complete without the same. This exercise
compels actors to fill the space between the lines and actions with the character's
private thoughts and feelings, and therefore to make what is externally observ-
able into the product of a genuine inner life.

Activity: Before each line or action, the actor improvises his character's thoughts
voice or interior monologue. This hard work is often habitually evaded, but
having to do it out loud invariably yields a deeper understanding because a high
degree of commitment is unavoidable. It is evident when an actor has failed to
make sense of what his partner means, or to link up with his own previous
utterances. Here the director can be of great help. Demanding that an inner
monologue be kept up is a sure way of immediately upgrading a so-so performance. It also stabilizes a performance by supplying a reliable process to link
each forward step of a character's visible process.

Discussion: Do the inner monologues show that your actors are on the same
wavelength and sharing the same interpretation? What did you (the director)
learn from the actors?

EXERCISE 24: CHARACTERIZING THE BEATS

Useful When: You need to clarify and energize a scene or a passage that is muddy and lifeless.

Purpose: To give each phase of the buildup to the beat a clear intention and identity, which in turn sharpens the turning point, the beat itself. To focus attention on subtext, and on the actor's body language, movement, and voice range.

Activity:
1. Ask the actors to devise a brief tag line for each phase of the pressure that builds toward each perceived beat. So far as possible, phrase these tags in a way that always expresses volition (examples: "Leave me alone!"; "I need you to notice me"; "You're not going to hoodwink me again." Be sure each tag is in the active, not passive voice ("Let me go to sleep" instead of "I am being kept awake") so that each tag line expresses active will even when the character is being victimized. Each tag line should contain an element of "I want . . ."

2. Now get the actors to approximate the scene from memory, but speaking to each other using only the tags in place of dialogue. In order to build up pressure for the beat, the actors will have to vary and intensify the pressure each applies. Where pressure in the text may seem to be applied through logic, here it can only be applied emotionally by action, using the voice and body as instruments. This necessity causes interesting developments in the actors' range of expression, shifting it from verbal/logical to physical/emotional, with a corresponding increase in power.

3. Now have the actors play the scene as scripted, and marvel at the difference.

Discussion: What did you learn about the movements the actors used this time? About their emotional range? About their communion when the exercise forced it into continuous existence?

EXERCISE 25: ACTIONS AT BEAT POINTS

Useful When: A scene seems monotonous, wordy, and cerebral. This technique can return the spotlight to the turning points.

Purpose: To focus and physicalize the beats and to behaviorally demarcate the phases of the scene.

Activity: When the beat points are located and tagged, ask the actors to devise several actions that develop out of their character's change of awareness. These can start out multiple and exaggerated in order for the director to choose which feels best. The chosen action can be brought down to an appropriate level of subtlety.

Discussion: What is really at stake for each character at each beat? Is there interpretational leeway? What is the range of options in terms of behavior that could be appropriate? Which is the freshest?

EXERCISE 26: GIVE ME TOO MUCH!

Useful When: One or more of your actors is under an emotional constraint, and the scene is stuck in low gear.

Purpose: To release actors temporarily from restrictive judgments they are imposing, and give them permission to overact.

Activity: Tell actors you feel that the scene is bottled up and that you want them to reach for the same emotions but exaggerate them. Exaggeration brings clarity, and it also licenses actors to go to emotional limits that they fear would look absurd if produced under normal conditions.

Discussion: You can now tell your cast what to change and at what new levels to pitch their energy and emotions. Frequently exaggeration on its own clears a blockade. Ask actors how it felt to go so far beyond their previous levels. When actors switch from dabbling fearfully in the shallows to leaping with abandon off the top diving board, they often find they can now do the elegant dive. Frequently they will report letting go of a specific fear.

EXERCISE 27: LET'S BE BRITISH

Useful When: A scene has become overprojected, artificial, and out of hand. Actors have begun to feel it will never work, that it is jinxed.

Purpose: To return the actors to playing from character instead of striving for an elusive effect.

Activity: Ask your actors to play the scene in a monotone, with emotion barely evident, but fully experiencing their character's emotion underneath the reticence.

Discussion: It is generally true that repressing emotion heightens it; for a scene that has turned into sound and fury, this may lead back to basics. Did it? What did the actors feel?

EXERCISE 28: SPOT CHECK

Useful When: A line or an action repeatedly does not ring true.

Purpose: To put a probe into an actor's process at a particular moment.

Activity: Simply stop a reading or an off-book rehearsal at the problem point and ask the actors what their characters' thoughts, fears, mental images, etcetera were at that moment.

Discussion: Often you will find that someone has a misconception or is forcing an emotional connection and falsifying it. At worst, doing this acts as a sort of breathalyzer test, jolting the actors into keeping up the inner lives of their characters for fear you will pull them over. Use sparingly.

EXERCISE 29: SWITCHING CHARACTERS

Useful When: Two actors seem stalemated and not properly aware of each other's character. Can arise when a defensive actor's over-preparation precludes him or her from adapting to nuances in a partner's playing. May also be because your actors distrust each other or feel incompatible.

Purpose: To place each actor temporarily in the opposite role so later he or she empathizes with another character's predicament and achieves an interesting duality.

Activity: Simply ask actors to exchange parts, without regard for sex, age, or anything else.

Discussion: Ask each to say in a few words what he or she discovered about the scene when he or she carried the other role, and if they had any revelations about their original parts.

EXERCISE 30: TRANSLATING A SCENE INTO AN IMPROVISATION

Useful When: The cast seems unable to generate the emotion the scene calls for.

Purpose: To free the actors from the letter of the scene in order to recreate its spirit.

Activity: Take the main issue in the scene, the one that is causing a problem, and translate it into two or three analogous scene subjects for improvisation. For example, if you have a scene about a conflict between a daughter and her suspicious and restrictive father, you might assign improvs on

1. a scene between an officious nurse and a patient who wants to leave the hospital

2. a bus driver and a rider who wants to get off the bus before the next stop

3. two customers in a supermarket checkout line, the younger of whom wants to jump the line because she only has three items.

Each of these situations has a built-in conflict over rights and authority, and tackling them rapidly one after another will generate a wider emotional vocabulary that can be reimported into the original scene. At the very least, this exercise can ground the static electricity that builds up over repeated failures with the formal text.

Discussion: This either works or it does not, and there is not much to argue about. Try to keep improv equivalencies up your sleeve for any scene that may give trouble. Actors may initially resist your request, but usually come to enjoy the refreshment that improv brings when a scene has become oppressive and immobile. Most will be impressed that you are able to quickly provide an alternative approach like this.

P·A·R·T V·I·I

FILM PROJECTS

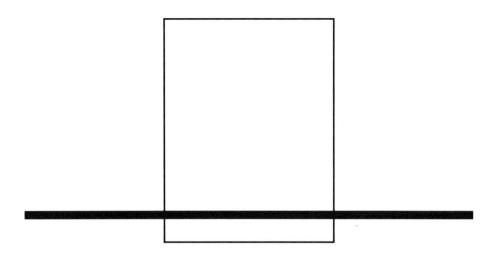

C·H·A·P·T·E·R 3·3

LEARNING TO SEE WITH A MOVIEMAKER'S EYE

The four study projects in this chapter are all designed to familiarize the student director with some essentials of composition, editing, script analysis, and lighting. Collectively they yield the basics of seeing from a cinematic perspective, and will help you recognize what will work and what will not.

PROJECT 1: PICTURE COMPOSITION ANALYSIS

Equipment Required: Video player, preferably with freeze-frame and variable-speed scan functions. Note that four-head players have better scan and freeze-frame capability than two-head, which usually break up a static picture unrecognizably. Your monitor set can be a domestic TV receiver, but it is best to connect VCR sound (usually labeled "line out") to the auxiliary input (or "line in") socket of a hi-fi. Reproduction is better, and you are less likely to get an annoying waterfall roar each time you stop the player. A slide projector and/or an overhead projector to enlarge graphics under study is useful but not indispensable.

Object: To study first how the eye reacts to a static composition and then how it handles dynamic composition, in order to compose visual elements more consciously.

Study Materials: For static composition, a book of figurative painting reproductions (best used under an overhead projector so you have a big image to scan), or better, a dozen or more 35mm art slides, also projected as large images. Slides of Impressionist paintings are ideal, but the more eclectic your collection the better. For dynamic composition use any visually interesting sequences from a favorite movie on videotape, though an Eisenstein movie would be ideal (see titles suggested under Project 2: Editing Analysis).

ANALYSIS FORMAT

I haven't found a need for any formal way of logging one's reactions, though if you are working alone, notes or sketches would be a good way of keeping a log of what you discover. Unfortunately, help from books on composition is not easily gained, as many texts make the whole business seem intimidating or formulaic. The uninitiated come away feeling there must be rules. In my experience such rules prevent seeing instead of promoting it. Trust your eye to see what is really there and use your own nonspecialist vocabulary to describe it.

A stimulating and highly productive way to investigate composition is to do so with several other people. Though what follows is written for a study group, it can be undertaken solo if circumstances so dictate.

STRATEGY FOR STUDY

If you are working with a group, you will need to explain what is wanted more or less as follows:

> I'll put a picture up on the screen. Notice what point your eye goes to in the composition first, and after that, remember the course it takes as you examine the rest of the picture. After the image has been on the screen for about thirty seconds, I'll ask someone to describe the sequence of movements his eye followed. You don't need any special jargon because your responses come from the specifics of each picture. Please avoid the temptation to try and find a story in the picture, or to guess what the picture is "about," even if it suggests a story. We're doing this solely to discover how each person's visual perception actually worked.

Each time you project a still frame, pick a new person to comment. Not everyone's eye responds the same way, and there will be some interesting discussion about the variations. However, there is usually a good deal of agreement, so people are led to formulate ideas about visual reflexes, and about what compositional components the eye finds attractive and engrossing. After they have seen enough pictures, encourage your group to formulate some compositional guidelines.

When the group has formed some ideas and gained confidence from analyzing paintings, I usually show both good and bad photos. Photography is less visibly contrived and tends to be accepted less critically because artistic choices other than subject are less evident in realism. This is a good way to discover just how many classical elements can be found in what appears to be a straight record. You can graduate to more abstract images, even to completely abstract ones, and find a lot of pleasure in seeing the same principles at work. Many people, relieved of the burden of deciding a picture's "subject," can begin to enjoy a Kandinsky, a Mondrian, or a Pollock for itself, without fuming over whether or not it is really art.

Here are some questions to help you formulate ways of seeing more critically. They can be applied after seeing a number of paintings or photos, or you could direct the group's attention to each question's area as it becomes relevant.

STATIC COMPOSITION

1. After your eye has taken in the whole, review its starting point. Why did it go to that point in the picture? (Common reasons: brightest point in composition, darkest place in an otherwise light composition, single area of an arresting color, significant junction of lines creating a focal point.)

2. When your eye moved away from its point of first attraction, what did it follow? (Commonly: lines, perhaps actual ones like the line of a fence or an outstretched arm, or inferred lines such as the sightline from one character looking at another. Sometimes the eye simply moves to another significant area in the composition, going from one organized area to another and jumping skittishly across the intervening disorganization.)

3. How much movement did your eye make before returning to its starting point?

4. What specifically drew your eye to each new place?

5. If you trace an imaginary line over the painting to show the route your eye took, what shape do you have? (Sometimes a circular pattern, sometimes a triangle or ellipse, but can be many shapes. Any shape at all can reveal an alternative organization that helps one see beyond the wretched and dominating idea that every picture tells a story.)

6. Are there any places along your imaginary line that seem specially charged with energy? (Often sightlines: between a Virgin's eyes and the baby's, between a guitarist's and his hand on the strings, between two field workers, one of whom is facing away.)

7. How would you characterize the compositional movement? (I.e., geometrical, repetitive textures, swirling, falling inwards, symmetrically divided down the middle, flowing diagonally, etc. Making a translation from one medium to another—in this case from the visual to the verbal—always helps one discover what is truly there.)

8. What parts, if any, do the following play in a particular picture:

a. repetition	f. straight lines	j. textures
b. parallels	g. strong verticals	k. nonnaturalistic
c. convergence	h. strong horizontals	coloring
d. divergence	i. strong diagonals	l. light and shade
e. curves		m. human figures

9. How is depth suggested? (This is an ever-present problem for the director of photography who, if inexperienced, is liable to take what I call the firing squad approach: to place his human subjects against a flat background and shoot. Unless there is something to create different planes, like a wall angling away from the foreground to suggest a receding space, the screen is like a painter's canvas and looks like it is—two dimensional.)

10. How is the individuality and mood of the human subjects expressed? (This is commonly through facial expression and body language, of course. But more interesting is the juxtapositions the painter makes of person to person, of person to surroundings, or of people inside a total design.)

11. How is space arranged on either side of a human subject, particularly in portraits? (Usually in profiles there is lead space, that is, more space in front of the person than behind them, as if in response to our need to see what the person sees.)

12. How much headroom is given above a person, particularly in a closeup? (Sometimes the edge of a frame cuts off the top of a head, or may not show one head at all in a group shot.)

13. How often and how deliberately are people and objects placed at the margins of the picture so you have to imagine what is cut off? (By demonstrating the frame's restriction one can make the viewer's imagination supply what is beyond the edges of the "window.")

VISUAL RHYTHM: HOW DURATION AFFECTS PERCEPTION

I have stressed the idea of an immediate, instinctual response to the organization of an image; unless shots are held to an unusual length, this is how an audience must deal with each new shot in a film. Unlike responding to a photograph or painting, which can be studied thoughtfully and at leisure, the filmgoer must interpret within an unremitting and preordained forward movement in time. It is like reading a poster on the side of a moving bus: if the words and images cannot be assimilated in the given time, the inscription goes past without being understood. If, however, the bus is crawling in a traffic jam, you have time to absorb, become critical, and even rejecting of the poster.

My analogy illustrates how there is an optimum duration for each shot to stay on the screen, depending upon the complexity of its content and form, and the accessibility of its significance (meaning, how much work the viewer must do to extract the shot's authorial meaning). That duration is also affected by an invisible third factor, that of expectation. For the audience will either work fast at interpreting each new image, or slowly, depending on how much time there was to process the shots immediately preceding.

This principle, in which a shot's duration is determined by content, form, significance and inherited expectation, is called visual rhythm. As you would expect from such a musical term, a filmmaker, like a musician, can either relax or intensify a visual rhythm. There are consequences in this for both the rate of cutting, and for the tempo of camera movements.

Ideal films for the study of compositional relationships in film and visual rhythm are the classics by the Russian Sergei Eisenstein, such as *The Battleship Potemkin* (1925), *Que Viva Mexico* (1931–32), *Alexander Nevsky* (1938), and *Ivan the Terrible* (1944–1946). His origins as a theatre designer made him very aware of the impact upon an audience of musical and visual design. His sketchbooks show how carefully he designed everything in each shot, down to the costumes.

Designer's sketches and the comic strip are perhaps the progenitors of the storyboard (see Figure 10–3B). It is much used by ad agencies and conservative elements in the film industry to lock down what each new frame will convey. Storyboarding is helpful for the inexperienced, even when one's artistry only runs to drawing stick figures.

DYNAMIC COMPOSITION

With moving images, more compositional principles are at work. When the components of a composition move, it is called a dynamic composition and a new problem emerges, for a balanced composition can become disturbingly unbalanced should someone move across frame, or leave the frame altogether. Even the movement of a figure's head in the foreground may posit a new eyeline, which in turn demands a compositional rebalancing. Then again, a zoom in from a static camera position demands reframing since compositionally there is a drastic change, even though the subject is the same. To study this, find a visually interesting film sequence, such as the chase in John Ford's *Stagecoach* (1939) or that in William Friedkin's *The French Connection* (1971). The slow-scan facility on your VCR is useful. See how many of these aspects you can find:

1. Reframing because the subject moved (look for a variety of camera adjustments)
2. Reframing as a consequence of something or someone entering the frame
3. Reframing in anticipation of something or something entering the frame
4. A change in the point of focus to move attention from background to foreground, or vice versa (This changes the texture of significant areas of the composition from hard focus to soft.)
5. Strong movement within an otherwise static composition. (How many can you find? Across frame, diagonally, from background to foreground, from foreground to background, up frame, down frame, etc.)
6. How much does one feel identified with each kind of subject movement? (This is a tricky one, but in general the nearer one is to the axis of a movement, the more subjective is one's sense of involvement.)
7. How quickly does the camera adjust to a figure who gets up and moves to another place in frame? (Usually subject movement and the camera's compositional change are synchronous. The camera move becomes clumsy if it either anticipates or lags behind the movement.)
8. How often are the camera or the characters blocked (that is, choreographed) to isolate one character? What is the dramatic justification?
9. How often is the camera moved or the characters blocked so as to bring two characters back into frame? (Good camerawork is always trying to show relatedness.)
10. How often is composition more or less angled down sightlines, and how often do sightlines cross the screen? (Here there is often a shifting of point of view from subjective to objective.)

11. What does the change of angle and change of composition make you feel toward the characters? (Probably more involved, then more objective.)

12. Find several compositions that successfully create depth and define what visual element is responsible. (An obvious one is where the camera is next to a railroad line as a train rushes up and past. Both the perspective revealed by the rails and the movement of the train create depth.)

13. How many shots can you find where camera position changes to include more or different background detail in order to comment upon foreground subject?

INTERNAL AND EXTERNAL COMPOSITION

So far we have been looking at composition internal to each shot. But another form of compositional relationship is the momentary relationship between an outgoing shot and the next or incoming shot. This, called external composition, is a hidden part of film language; hidden because we are unaware that it influences our judgments and expectations.

A common usage is when, for example, a character exiting the frame in shot A leads the spectator's eye at the cutting point to the very place in shot B where an assassin will emerge from a large and restless crowd. Here the eye is conducted to the right place in a busy composition.

Another example might be the framing of two complementary close shots in which two characters have an intense conversation. The compositions are similar but symmetrically opposed. In Figure 33–1 a two-shot (a) gives a good overall feel of the scene, but man and child are too far away. The close shots, (b) and (c), retain the feel of the scene but effectively cut out the dead space between them. Note that the heads are not centered: each person has lead space in front of his face, and this mimics their framing in the two-shot. The man is high in the frame and looking downwards, and the child lower in the frame and looking up—just as in the matching two-shot.

Other aspects will emerge if you apply the questions below to your sequences under review. Use the slow-scan facility to examine compositional relationships at the cutting point, and go backwards and forwards several times over each cut to be sure you miss nothing. Try finding these for yourself:

1. Where was your point of concentration at the end of the shot? (You can trace where your eye goes by moving your finger around the face of the monitor. Your last point in the outgoing shot is where your eye enters the composition of the incoming shot. Notice how shot duration determines the distance the eye travels in exploring the shot. This means that shot length is a factor in external composition.)

2. What kinds of symmetry are there between complementary shots (that is, between shots designed to be intercut)?

3. What is the relationship between two different-sized shots of the same subject that are designed to be cut together? (This is a revealing one; the inexperienced camera operator will often produce medium shots and close shots of the same scene that cut together poorly because proportions and compositional placing of the subject are incompatible.)

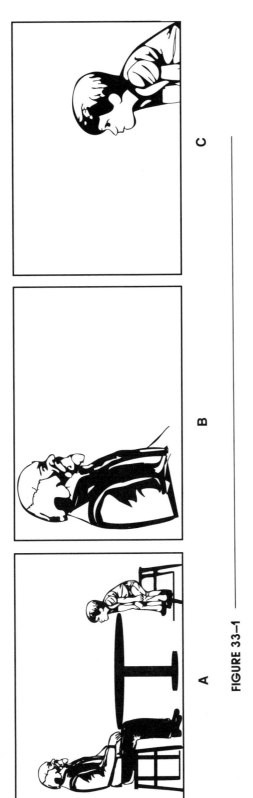

C

B

A

FIGURE 33–1

Wide shot and two complementary closeups. Notice lead space in front of each CU character, and how the height and placing in the frame of each mirrors the composition of the master shot.

4. Examine a match-cut very slowly and see if there is any overlap. (Especially where there is relatively fast action, a match cut, to look smooth, needs two or three frames of the action repeated on the incoming shot. This is because the eye does not register the first two or three frames of any new image. We can think of this as a built-in perceptual lag. The only way to cut to music on the beat is to make the cuts two or three frames before the actual beat point.)

5. Find visual comparisons in external composition that make a storyteller's comment (for instance, cut from a pair of eyes to car headlights approaching at night, from a dockside crane to a man feeding birds with arm outstretched, etc.).

COMPOSITION, FORM, AND FUNCTION

If form is the manner in which content is presented, then visual composition is not just embellishment but a vital element in communication. While it interests the eye and even delights it, good composition is an organizing force used to dramatize relativity and relationship, and to project ideas. Superior composition not only makes the subject (content) accessible, it heightens the viewer's perceptions and stimulates his imaginative involvement, like language from the pen of a good poet.

My own persuasion is that one should first involve oneself with a subject, and then find an appropriate form in which to best communicate that subject. Another way of working, which comes from being primarily interested in language rather than subject, is to decide on a form and then look for an appropriate subject. The difference is one of purpose and temperament. Content, form, structure, and style are analyzed in much greater detail in Part IV: Aesthetics and Authorship.

While this project has been devoted to pictorial composition, I would be remiss not to point out how much a film's sound track is also a composition, and one critically important to a film's overall impact. The study of sound is included below in the editing study project.

PROJECT 2: EDITING ANALYSIS

Equipment Required: VCR as in Project 1.

Object: To produce a detailed analysis of a portion of film using standard abbreviations and terminology; to analyze the way a film is constructed; to learn the conventions of film language so they can be used confidently.

Study Materials: Any well made feature film will do, but I particularly recommend Nicholas Roeg's *Don't Look Now* (1973). Adapted from a Daphne du Maurier short story, the film is set in Venice and fully exploits its exotic location. The narrative style is admirably compact and allusive, relying heavily upon editing to telescope each event into a brief montage of essential moments. Roeg's background is in camerawork, so not only does he value the visual above the spoken, but his composition and camera use are masterly. The film also has a dense and highly evocative sound track. The narrative, which develops out of the trauma a couple suffer at the loss of their child, moves freely backwards and forwards in time, and this is particularly evident in the lovemaking scene.

Other feature films I would recommend for study are Terence Malick's *Days of Heaven* (1978) for its evocative cinematography and its unusual and effective pacing; Peter Weir's *Witness* (1985) for the superb Amish work sequences and for the ways it defines urban and Amish lifestyles; and Martin Scorsese's *King of Comedy* (1982) for the wide variety of material and moods it encompasses.

For an adaptation of a classic Ambrose Bierce short story there is Robert Enrico's *Occurrence At Owl Creek Bridge* (1962), which tells its complex story with virtually no dialogue and uses the camera with great subtlety. The film is a especially useful for the way it uses rhythms and sound effects, for its creative distortion of time, and for its agile camera with many matching angles, each contributing a piece of revelation to the whole.

FIRST VIEWING

Whatever film you choose, first see the whole film without stopping, and then see it a second time before you attempt any analysis. Write down any strong feelings the film evoked in you, paying no attention to order. Note from memory which sequences sparked those feelings. You may have an additional sequence or two that intrigued you as a piece of virtuoso storytelling. Note these down too, but whatever you study should be something that hit you at an emotional rather than a merely intellectual level.

ANALYSIS FORMAT

What you write down is going to be displayed in split-page format, where all visuals are placed in the left half of the page, and all sound occupies the right half (see Figure 2–2 and accompanying text). First you should transcribe the picture and dialogue, shot by shot and word by word, as they relate to each other. Once this basic information is on paper, you can turn to such things as shot transitions, internal and external composition of shots, screen direction, camera movements, opticals, sound effects, and the use of music.

You will need to make a number of shot-by-shot passes through your chosen sequence, dealing with one or two aspects of the content and form at a time. Your draft transcript should be written with wide line spacing on numerous sheets of paper so you can insert additional information on subsequent passes.

It is better to do a short sequence (two to four minutes) very thoroughly than a long one more superficially, since your object is to extract the maximum information about an interesting passage of film language. Some of your notes, (for example, on the mood a shot evokes) will not fit into the script format, which must show only what can be seen and heard. Keep notes on what you felt as a separate entity.

MAKING AND USING A FLOOR PLAN

For a sequence containing a dialogue exchange, make a floor plan sketch as in Figure 33–2, where character Eric enters, stands in front of William, goes to the phone, picks up a book from the table, looks out the window, and then sits

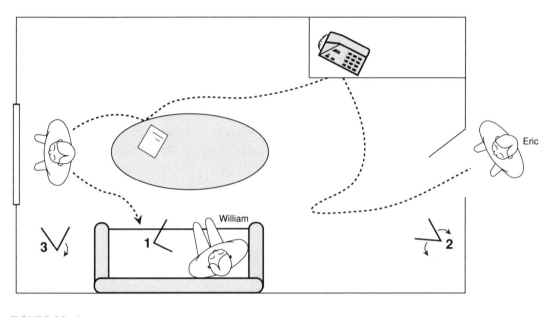

FIGURE 33–2

Floor plan showing entry and movements of character Eric, and the camera positions to cover the action.

down on the couch. The whole action has been covered by three camera positions. In analyzing a film, a floor plan allows you to recreate what the room or location looked like in its entirety, and record how the characters moved around and how the camera was placed to show this. This will help you decide in future where to place your camera. It can also show how little of an environment need be shown for the audience to infer the whole.

STRATEGY FOR STUDY

Your split page log should contain action-side descriptions of each shot and its action as well as sound-side notes detailing the content and positioning of dialogue, music start/stopping points, and featured sound effects (that is, other than sync or diagetic sound).

Scrutinize the sequence by categories. I have listed them in a logical order for inquiry, but do not hesitate to reorder my list if you prefer.

Very important: read from film rather than read into it. Film is a complex and deceptive medium; like a glib and clever acquaintance, it can make you uneasy about your perceptions and too ready to accept what should be seen or should be felt. Recognize what you felt and connect your impressions with what can actually be seen and heard in the film.

To avoid overload, concentrate on a few of the given aspects at a time and try to find at least one example of everything so you understand the concept at work.

First Impressions: What was the progression of feeling you had watching the sequence?

Definition and Statistics: What determines the beginning and ending points of the sequence? Is its span determined by

- being at one location?
- being a continuous segment of time?
- a particular mood?
- the stages of a process?
- something else?

How long is the sequence (minutes and seconds)?

How many picture cuts does it contain? The duration of each shot and how often the camera angle is changed are aspects of a director's style but are just as likely to be derived from the sequence's content. Try to decide whether the content or its treatment are determining the number of cuts.

Use of Camera: How many different motivations can you find for the camera to make a movement?

- Does the camera follow the movement of a character?
- Does a car or other moving object permit the camera to pan the length of a street so that camera movement seems to arise from action in the frame?
- Does it lay out a landscape or a scene geography for the audience?
- Is the move one which goes closer, and intensifies our relationship with someone or something?
- Does the camera move away from someone or something so we see more objectively?
- Does the camera reveal significant information by moving?
- Is the move really a reframing to accommodate a rearrangement of characters?
- Is the move a reaction, panning to a new speaker, for instance?
- What else might be responsible for motivating this particular camera move?

  When is the camera used subjectively?

- When do we directly experience a character's point of view?
- Are there special signs that the camera is seeing subjectively (for example, an unsteady handheld camera in *Owl Creek* for a running man's point of view)?
- What is the dramatic justification?

  Are there changes of camera height?

- To accommodate subject matter?
- To make you see in a certain way?
- For other reasons?

Use of Sound: What are the sound perspectives used?

- Complementing camera position (near mike for close shots, far from mike for longer shots, replicating camera perspective)?
- Counterpointing camera perspective? (Altman films are fond of giving us the intimate conversation of two characters distantly traversing a large landscape.)
- Uniformly intimate (as with a narration, or with voice-over and "thoughts voices" that function as a character's interior monologue)
- Other situations

How are particular sound effects used?

- To build atmosphere and mood?
- As punctuation?
- To motivate a cut? (next sequence's sound rises until we cut to it)
- As a narrative device? (horn honks so woman gets up and goes to window where she discovers her sister is making a surprise visit)
- To build, sustain, or defuse tension?
- To provide rhythm? (meal prepared in a montage of brief shots to the rhythmic sound of a man splitting logs; last shot, man and woman sit down to meal)
- To create uncertainty?
- Other situations?

Editing: What motivates each cut?

- Is there an action match to carry the cut?
- Is there a compositional relationship between the two shots that makes the cut interesting and worthwhile? (*Don't Look Now* is obsessed with these.)
- Is there a movement relationship that carries the cut (for example, cut from car moving left-to-right to boat moving left-to-right)?
- Does someone or something leave the frame (making us want to see a new frame)?
- Does someone or something fill the frame, blanking it out and permitting a cut to another frame that starts blanked and then clears?
- Does someone or something enter the frame and demand closer attention?
- Are we cutting to follow someone's eyeline, to see what they see?
- Is there a sound, or a line, that demands that we see the source?
- Are we cutting to show the effect upon a listener and what defines the right moment to cut?

- Are we cutting to a speaker at a particular moment that is visually revealing? What defines that moment?
- If the cut intensifies our attention, what justifies that?
- If the cut relaxes and objectifies our attention, what justifies that?
- Is the cut to a parallel activity (that is, something going on simultaneously)?
- Is there some sort of comparison or irony being set up through juxtaposition?
- Are we cutting to a rhythm (perhaps of an effect, music, or the cadences of speech)?
- Other reasons?

What is the relationship of words to images?

- Does what is shown illustrate what is said?
- Is there a difference and therefore a counterpoint between what is shown and what is heard?
- Is there a meaningful contradiction between what is said and what is shown?
- Does what is said come from another time frame (for example, a memory of one of the characters or a comment on something in the past)?
- Is there a point at which words are used to move us forward or backward in time? (That is, can you pinpoint a change of tense in the film's grammar? This might be done visually, as in the old cliché of autumn leaves falling after we have seen summer scenes.)
- Any others?

When a line overlaps a cut, what is the impact of the first strong word on the new image?

- Does it help identify the new image?
- Does it give it a particular emphasis or interpretation?
- Is the effect expected (satisfying perhaps) or unexpected (maybe a shock)?
- Is there a deliberate contradiction?
- Other effects?

Where and how is music used?

- How is it initiated? (often when characters or story begin some kind of motion)
- What does the music suggest by its texture, instrumentation, etc.?
- How is it finished? (often when characters or story arrive at new location)
- What comment is it making? (ironic? sympathetic? lyrical? revealing the inner state of a character or situation? other?)
- From what other sound (if any) does it emerge (segue)?
- What other sound does it merge or segue into at its close?

Point of View and Blocking: Blocking is a theatrical term meaning the way the actors and camera are moved in relation to the set. Point of view means more than just literally whose eyeline the audience shares. Point of view refers to whose reality the viewer most identifies with at any given time. This turns out to be a much more complicated and interesting issue than it first seems, for a film like a novel can present a main point of view (probably through a point-of-view character) or it can present multiple, conflicting points of view. The author's statement is largely through the handling of point of view, yet the work's appearances can be deceptive unless you look very carefully.

Sometimes there is one central character, and one point of view, like Travis Bickle's in Scorsese's *Taxi Driver* (1975). Or there may be a couple whose relationship is at issue, as in Woody Allen's *Annie Hall* (1977). Successive scenes may be devoted to establishing alternate characters' dilemmas and conflicts. Altman's *Nashville* (1975) has nearly two dozen central characters, and the film's focus is the idea of the music town as their point of convergence and confrontation with change. Here, evidently, we find the characters are part of a pattern, and the pattern itself is surely an authorial point of view that questions the way people subscribe to their own destiny.

Here are some practical ways of digging into a sequence to establish how it covertly structures the way we see and react to the characters. A word of caution, though. Point of view is a complex notion that can only be specified confidently after considering the aims and tone of the whole work. Taking a magnifying glass to one sequence is therefore a way of verifying your overall hypothesis. The way the camera is used, the frequency with which one character's feelings are revealed, the amount of development he or she goes through, the vibrancy of the acting—all these factors play a part in enlisting our sympathy and interest.

To whom is the dialogue or narration addressed?

- By one character to another?
- To himself (thinking aloud, reading diary or letter)?
- To audience (narration, interview, prepared statement)?
- Other situations?

How many camera positions were used? (Use your floor plan.)

- Show basic camera positions and label them A, B, C, etc.
- Show camera dollying movements with dotted line leading to new position.
- Mark shots in your log with the appropriate A, B, C camera angles.
- Notice how camera stays to one side of subject-to-subject axis (an imaginary line that the camera avoids crossing) to keep characters facing in same screen direction from shot to shot. When this principle is broken, it is called *crossing the line,* and has the effect of disrupting the audience's sense of spatial relationships.
- How often is the camera close to the crucial axis between characters?
- How often does the camera subjectively share a character's eyeline?

• When and why does it take an objective stance to the situation (that is, either a distanced viewpoint, or one independent of eyelines)?

Character blocking: How did the characters and camera move in the scene? To the location and camera movement sketch you have made, add dotted lines to show the characters' movements (called blocking). You can use different colors for clarity.

What points of view did the author engage us in?

• Whose story is this sequence if you go by gut reaction?

• Taking into account the angles on each character, whose point of view were you led to sympathize with?

• How many psychological viewpoints did you share? (Some may have been momentary or fragmentary, and perhaps in contradiction to what you were seeing.)

• Are the audience's sympathies structured by camera and editing? Or are they molded independently by perhaps acting or the situation itself?

FICTION AND THE DOCUMENTARY

So many of these analytical questions apply equally to the documentary film that one realizes how much the two forms have in common. This is more than a similarity in film language, for some of the important questions cannot be applied to most nature, travelogue, industrial, or educational films. These lack precisely what distinguishes the fictional and documentary forms—authorial vision; that is, they lack a point of view and a critical perspective upon what it means to be human. At its best this gives a feeling of authorial voice, a human sensibility that unifies the events it shows, even though the making of a film is collaborative. We sense the presence of a storyteller's sympathy and intelligence, and what in lesser hands might be technical or formulaic becomes vibrantly human. This vision is the best sort of leadership, for unegotistically and by example it teaches us to see our world differently.

PROJECT 3: A SCRIPTED SCENE COMPARED WITH THE FILMED OUTCOME

Object: To study the relationship between the blueprint script and the filmed product.

Study Materials: A film script and the finished film made from it on videotape. The script must be the original screenplay and not a release script (that is, not a transcript made from a finished film). A suitable script is to be found in Pauline Kael's *The Citizen Kane Book: Raising Kane* (New York: Limelight Editions, 1984). Another is Harold Pinter's *The French Lieutenant's Woman: A Screenplay* (Boston: Little, Brown, 1981). The latter has an absorbing foreword by the author of the original novel, John Fowles, which tells not only the story of the adaptation, but speaks from a novelist's point of view about what is involved when one's novel makes the transition to the screen.

A very interesting variation, where obtaining an original script is a problem, is to use a film adaptation of a stage play, and study an obligatory scene, that is, one so dramatically necessary that it cannot be missing from the film version. Good titles are

> Arthur Miller's *Death of a Salesman*
>   (a) Laslo Benedek's 1951 film version with Fredric March.
>   (b) Wim Wenders' 1987 TV version with Dustin Hoffman. Interesting for its expressionist sets and because a theatrical flavor is retained.
>
> Edward Albee's *Who's Afraid of Virginia Wolf?*
>   Mike Nichols' 1966 film version.
>
> Peter Schaffer's *Equus*
>   Sidney Lumet's 1977 film version.
>
> Tennessee Williams' *A Streetcar Named Desire*
>   Elia Kazan's 1951 film version.

STRATEGY FOR STUDY

Phase 1. Studying the Original: If possible, select an unfamiliar work, and read the whole script (or stage play). Choose a scene of four or five pages.

1. Draw a floor plan. (See Figure 33–2 for an example.)
2. Make your own shooting script, substituting action for dialogue wherever feasible, and making use of your location environment. (See Figure 2–1 for standard script layout.)
3. Mark in characters' movements on floor plan.
4. Mark in camera positions (A, B, C, etc., and indicate camera movements). Refer to these in your shooting script.
5. Write a brief statement about (a) what major themes you think the entire script/play is dealing with, and (b) how your chosen scene functions in the whole.

Phase 2. Studying the Film Version: First see the entire film without stopping. Then run your chosen scene two or three times, stopping and rerunning sections as you wish. Carry out the following.

1. Make notes on film's choice of location (imaginative? metaphoric?).
2. Make a floor plan and mark in camera positions, movements of characters.
3. Using a photocopy of the scene, pencil in annotations to show what dialogue has been cut, added, or altered.
4. Note actions, both large and small, that add significantly to impact of the scene. Ignore those specified in the original, as the object is to find what the film version has added or substituted to the writer's vision.

5. Note camera usage as follows:
    - any abnormal perspective (that is, non-standard lens used)
    - any camera position above or below eye level
    - any camera movement (track, pan, tilt, zoom, crane). Note what you think motivated the camera movement (character's movement, eyeline, story teller's revelation, etc.).

6. Note what the thematic focus of the film seems to be, and how your chosen scene functions in the film.

Phase 3. Comparison: Compare your scripting with the film's handling and describe the following:

1. How did the film establish time and place?

2. How effectively did the film compress the original and substitute behavior for dialogue?

3. How, using camerawork and editing, is the audience drawn into identifying with one or more characters?

4. Whose scene was it, and why?

5. How were any rhythms (speech, movements, sound effects, music, etc.) used to pace out the scene, particularly to speed it up or slow it down?

6. What were the major changes of interpretation in the film and in the chosen scene?

7. Provide any further valuations of the film you think worth making (acting, characterization, use of music or sound effects, etc.).

How well did you do? What aspects of filmmaking are you least aware of, and need to develop? What did you accomplish?

PROJECT 4: LIGHTING ANALYSIS

Directors do not need to understand the technique of lighting; that is the DP's role. But they do need to know what effect each different lighting setup produces, and what the terminology is to effectively describe it.

Equipment Required: VCR as in previous projects. It is helpful when studying lighting to turn down the color control of your monitor so that initially you see a black and white picture. Adjust the monitor's brightness and contrast controls so the greatest range of gray tones are visible between video white and video black. Unless you adjust for optimum performance you simply will not see all that is present.

Object: To produce an elementary analysis of common lighting situations in order to better understand what goes into creating a lighting mood.

Study Materials: Same as in previous project, only this time it will be an advantage to search out particular lighting situations rather than sequences of special dramatic appeal. The same sequences may fulfill both purposes.

LIGHTING TERMINOLOGY

Here the task is to recognize different types and combinations of lighting situation and to apply standard terminology. Every aspect of lighting carries strong emotional associations which can be put to work in drama to great effect. Technique and the terminology to describe it are therefore powerful tools in the hands of the aware. Here are some basic terms:

Types of Lighting Style

High-key picture: The shot looks bright overall with small areas of shadow. In Figure 33–3 the shot is exterior day, and the shadow of the lamppost in the foreground shows that there is indeed deep shadow in the picture. Where shadow is sharp, as here, the light source is called *specular.* A high-key picture can be virtually shadowless so long as the frame is bright overall.

Low key picture: The shot looks dark overall with few highlight areas. These are often interiors or night shots, but in Figure 33–4 we have a backlit day interior that ends up being low key, that is, having a large area of the frame in deep shadow.

Graduated tonality: The shot has neither bright highlights nor deep shadow but consists of an even, restricted range of midtones. This might be a flat lit interior, like a supermarket, or a misty morning landscape as in Figure 33–5.

FIGURE 33–3

High-key scene, hard or specular lighting, high contrast. Notice compositional depth in this shot compared with the flatness of Figure 33–4.

FIGURE 33—4

Backlit low key scene, subject silhouetted against the flare of backlit smoke.

FIGURE 33—5

Graduated tonality scene, low contrast because key light is diffused through morning mist.

Here an overcast sky diffuses the lighting source, and the disorganized light rays scatter into every possible shadow area so there are neither highlights nor shadow.

Contrast

High-contrast picture: The shot may be lit either high or low key, but there must be a big difference in illumination level between highlight and shadow area, as in Figure 33–6, which has a shoot-and-whitewash starkness. Both Figures 33–3 and 33–4 are also high contrast images although the area of shadow in each is drastically different.

Low-contrast picture: The shot can either be high or low key, but with shadow area illumination level near that of highlight levels. Figure 33–5 is high key, low contrast.

Light Quality

Hard lighting. This is any specular light source creating hard-edged shadows; for example, sun, studio spotlight, or candle flame. These are all called effectively small light sources because a small source gives hard-edged shadows. Figure 33–3 is lit by hard light (the sun), while the shadow under the chair in 33–4 is so soft it is hardly discernible.

Soft lighting. Any light source is soft when it creates soft-edged shadows or a shadowless image as in Figure 33–5. Soft light sources are, for example, fluorescent tubes, sunlight reflecting off matte finish wall, light from overcast sky, or a studio soft light.

FIGURE 33–6

High-contrast image with very few midtones owing to back lighting and no fill.

Names of Lighting Sources

Key light: This is not necessarily an artificial source, for it can be the sun. The key is the light that creates intended shadows in the shot, and these in turn reveal the angle and position of the supposed source light, often relatively hard or specular (shadow-producing) light. In Figure 33–3 the key light is sunlight coming from rear left and above the camera. In Figure 33–4 it is streaming in toward the camera.

Fill light: This is the light used to raise illumination in shadow area. For interiors it will probably be soft light thrown from the direction of the camera, which avoids creating additional visible shadows. There are shadows, of course, but they are hidden from the camera's view by the subject. Fill light, especially in exteriors, is often provided from matte white reflectors, through diffusion material, or is derived from bounce light, that is, hard light bounced from walls or ceilings to soften it.

Back light: This is light thrown upon a subject from behind, and often from above as well as behind, as in 33–4. A favorite technique in portraiture is to put a rim of light around a subject's head and shoulders to create a separation between him and the background. Rain, fog, dust, or smoke (as in this case of garage barbecuing) all show up best when back lit.

Practical: This is any light appearing in frame as part of the scene; for example, table lamp, overhead fluorescent, or, as in Figure 33–7, the candles on a birthday cake. Usually practicals provide little or no real source of illumination. Here the candles light up the faces, but not the background.

FIGURE 33–7

Practicals are any lights seen in frame, like these birthday candles. Strong set light prevents the background from going dark.

Figure 33–7 illustrates several lighting points. The girl in the middle is lit from below, a style called "monster lighting" and rather eerie for a birthday shot. The girl on the left, having no backlight or background lighting, disappears into the shadows, while the subject on the right is outlined by set light, that is, light falling on the set. The same light source shines on her hair as a backlight source and gives it highlights and texture.

Types of Lighting Setup: Here the illustrations are of the same model lit in various ways. The effect and the mood in each portrait varies greatly as a result. The diagrams show the positioning of the key and fill lights. In a floor plan diagram such as these, one cannot show the height of the shadow-producing light sources, only the angle of throw relative to the camera-to-subject axis. Heights can be inferred from the areas of highlight and their converse, the shadow patterns.

Frontally lit: The key light in Figure 33–8 is so close to the camera-to-subject axis that shadows are thrown backwards out of the camera's view. You can see very slight shadows in the folds of the subject's shirt, which show that the key was to the right of camera. Notice how flat and lacking in dimensionality or tension this shot is compared with 33–9 and 33–10.

Broad lit: In Figure 33–9 the key light is some way to the side, so a broad area of the subject's face and body is highlighted. Key light skimming the subject lengthens his face, revealing angles and undulations. We have areas of deep shadow, especially in the eyesockets, but these could be reduced by increasing the amount of soft fill light.

Narrow lit: The key light in Figure 33–10 is to the side of the subject and beyond him, so that only a narrow portion of his face is receiving highlight. The majority of his face is in shadow. This portion of the face is lit by fill light, or we would see nothing. Measuring light reflected in the highlight area and comparing it with that reflected from the fill area gives one lighting

FIGURE 33–8

Frontal lighting: flattens the subject and removes much of a face's interest. Most flash photography is frontal and correspondingly dull.

FIGURE 33-9 ————————————————————————————

Broad lighting: illuminates a broad area of the face and shows the head as round and having angularities. Revelation becomes interesting because lighting is selective.

ratio. Remember when taking measurements that fill light reaches the highlight area but not vice versa, so you can only take accurate readings with all the lights on.

Silhouette: Here in Figure 33–11 the subject reflects no light at all, and shows up only as an outline against raw light. This lighting is sometimes used in documentaries when the subject's identity is being withheld. Here it produces the ominous effect of someone unknown confronting us through a bright doorway.

STRATEGY FOR STUDY

Locate two or three sequences with quite different lighting moods, and using the definitions above, classify them as follows:

FIGURE 33-10 ————————————————————————————

Narrow lighting: illuminates only a narrow area of the face. More fill used here than in Figure 33–9. The effect is decidedly dramatic.

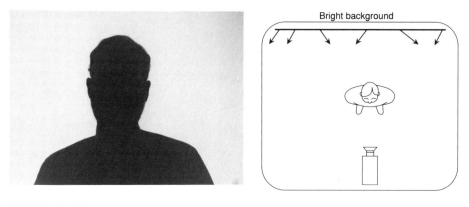

FIGURE 33–11

Silhouette: all light is from the background and none reaches the subject's face.

1. Style: high key / low key / graduated tonality?
2. Contrast: high or low contrast?
3. Scene: intended to look like natural light or artificial lighting?
4. Setup: frontal / broad / narrow / back lighting setup?
5. Angles: high / low angle of key light?
6. Quality: hard / soft edges to shadows?
7. Source: source in scene is intended to be _____
8. Practicals: practicals in the scene are _____
9. Time: day for day/night for night/dusk for night/day for night?
10. Mood: mood conveyed by lighting is _____
11. Continuity: any differences of lighting to show that wide and close shots can, within limits, be handled differently?

After you have analyzed several different sequences, see if you can spot patterns emerging that suggest how directors of photography set about translating the emotional associations of the location and situation through lighting. You should also find that predominant colors have a good deal to do with a scene's effect on the viewer. For instance, Hitchcock's *The Trouble with Harry* (1955) places its unwanted, unburied corpse in the serene beauty of autumnal New England. In Louis Malle's *Pretty Baby* (1978) the director of photography Sven Nykvist produces with great economy of means the ruby-shaded opulence of 1917 New Orleans bordellos. Scorsese's *After Hours* (1985) has many threatening night exteriors in New York City, and a lot of dark, "cold" colors.

Two classically lit black-and-white films are Welles' *Citizen Kane* (1941) with cinematography by the revolutionary Gregg Toland, and Cocteau's *Beauty and the Beast* (1946) whose lighting Henri Alekan modeled after Dutch painting, especially its interiors.

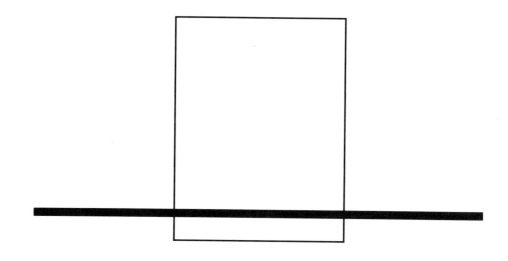

C·H·A·P·T·E·R 3·4

SHOOTING PROJECTS

These exercises alone constitute a long and fairly complete course in filmmaking. You can if you wish enter the book here, start production, and use the rest of the book as a resource to solve problems and stimulate your ideas. I have included relevant questions after each assignment to help you measure your work's strengths and weaknesses.

FILM OR VIDEOTAPE?

You can shoot these projects on film or videotape. On the whole, basic training with tape has most of the advantages, being cheap and requiring no turnaround time for processing. Video's low cost permits one to shoot enough takes to achieve a level of performance and camera control that would be prohibitively expensive in film. Because videotape equipment is semiautomated and the results immediately visible, you can concentrate on directing rather than upon the imponderables of film exposure, latitude, depth of focus, lighting, and so on. Another big advantage is that videotape allows multiple versions to be edited experimentally from the same camera original—an important facility since learning narrative compression is so important. Though film also permits this, reconstituting a workprint is time consuming and a heavily spliced print ceases to be projectable.

ON DEVELOPING YOUR TECHNIQUE

The projects are designed to develop a broad and representative repertoire of directing and editing skills. Technique should not become an end in itself. Speaking of painting, the novelist Thomas Hardy said that "Art is the secret of how to produce by a false thing the effect of a true." This holds good for all the artifice that goes into filmmaking. In the end, good technique is whatever goes unnoticed by the audience because of the film's credibility and grip on the viewer's imagination. Poor technique or technique misapplied is anything else that draws attention to itself and fails to serve the film's purpose.

The first projects are basic technique and embody modest subject matter. Their simplicity is deceptive. Please resist the beginner's fatal attraction to reach for big themes and neglect screen grammar and basic storytelling skills. Where a project requires lighting, keep it basic and simple, so you do not get sidetracked into the absorbing joys of cinematography.

I have supplied requirements, procedures, and hints, leaving much of the problem-solving—the richest and most enjoyable area of learning—to your ingenuity and resourcefulness. When in need of information, go to the table of contents at the front of the appropriate production phase for which you want information. You can also use the general index at the back of the book.

Most of these assignments are best criticized by a group reaction, so the filmmaker becomes accustomed to working with an audience reaction. Some of the projects have a great number of critical assessments, too many to monitor while watching a cut. In a group, individuals can specialize by watching out for one or two particular facets. This ensures a discussion of depth and breadth from which everyone, particularly the maker, can learn much.

PROJECT 5: BASIC TECHNIQUES: GOING AND RETURNING

Skills:
1. Controlling screen direction
2. Panning and tilting to follow action
3. Composition
4. Editing: action match cutting
5. Editing: cutting together different sizes of similar image
6. Telling a story through action and without sound
7. Compression of real-time situation into shorthand version
8. Editing to music

ASSIGNMENT 5A: PLAN, SHOOT, AND EDIT LONG VERSION

A car draws up. Mary, the car's occupant, approaches a house looking up at a window in pleased anticipation. She mounts a flight of steps to the front door. There she discovers she does not have her keys. Perplexed, she returns to her car, which she expects to be open. Finding the door locked, she curses, thinking her keys are locked in. Looking inside, she sees that the ignition lock is empty. Patting her pockets and looking around in consternation, she spots her keys lying in the gutter. She picks them up, relieved, and returns toward the house.

Figure 34–1 is a specimen ground plan. Adapt yours to your location (mine is a one-way street to allow the driver to drop her keys in the nearside gutter). The ground plan shows Mary's walk and the basic camera positions to cover the various parts of the action. No sound is necessary.

Figure 34–2 is a storyboard with representative frames from each camera position. In your coverage incorporate

1. establishing shot of locale with car arriving (Figure 34–2/A),

2. medium shot (MS) Mary turning corner in path thus changing her screen direction (Figure 34–2/B),

3. close shot (CS) feet walking right-to-left (R-L) and left-to-right (L-R) to match Figure 34–2/B (Figure 34–2/D1),

4. closeup (CU) panning telephoto shot of Mary walking, looking up at window (Figure 34–2/D2),

5. feet enter shot descending steps, camera tilts to follow action (Figure 34–2/G),

6. point of view (POV) shot of empty ignition lock (over-shoulder Figure 34–2/F1, CU 34–2/F2), and

7. big closeup (BCU) keys in gutter, hand reaches into frame and takes them (Figure 34–2/F3).

The sequence edited in its simplest form might look something like this:

Camera Position	Shot Number	Action
A	1	Car arrives, Mary gets out, slams door, exits bottom right of frame.
B	2a	Mary enters L-R, begins crossing frame.
D2	3	CU of Mary smiling up at window.
B	2b	This is the rest of shot 2a. Mary continues L-R, turns corner of path, walks R-L toward steps and up them.
C	3	Mary rises into frame from R-L, fumbles for keys, can't find, looks back at car, turns back out of frame.
B	4	Mary descending steps, across frame L-R, turns corner, crosses R-L.
E	5a	Mary arrives from right of camera, walking screen R-L at car, fails to open door, curses.
F1	6	She crosses frame, repositions herself looking R-L to see ignition, peers inside.
F2	7	CU her POV of empty ignition lock.
E	5b	Mary straightens up, pats pockets, sees something on the ground.
F3	8a	CU keys lying in gutter, Mary's POV.
E	5c	Mary reacts, stoops down.
F3	8b	CU of keys, hand comes in, takes them.
E	5d	Mary straightens up looking relieved and exits into camera, her body blacking out the frame. End sequence.

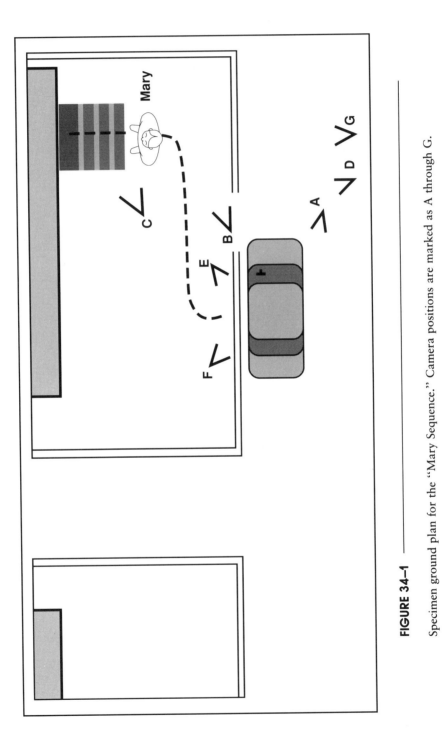

FIGURE 34–1

Specimen ground plan for the "Mary Sequence." Camera positions are marked as A through G.

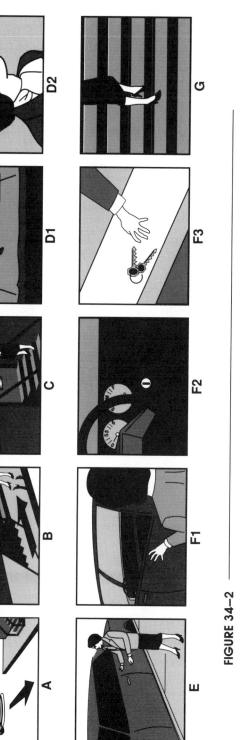

FIGURE 34–2

Storyboard frames showing setup for the various camera angles in Figure 34–1.

Notice that shot 2 is intercut with a CU, while the action in shot 5 has been intercut three times. When directing for this kind of double-cutting it is inadvisable to shoot such short individual pieces to exactly fit a script concept. More consistent, and easier on the actors, is to shoot a large section or even the whole action, afterwards selecting the fragments you require from the continuous take during editing.

Notice at the end of shot 5, when Mary returns with the keys, that her movement is used to black out the screen by walking right up to the camera lens. To start out another shot in the same way, have the actor walk away from the lens, so the screen goes from black to action. This device is among many called transitional devices. If you overuse them, you run the risk of being considered tricksy.

Cut this version together, taking into account

- cutting from shot 2a to 3, make sure Mary's walking rhythm is maintained and that you do not inadvertently make her take two steps on the same foot. A rhythm match will be required for other walking shots, too.
- cutting from 5a to 6, there will probably be an action match. Following is one of the few rules in filmmaking.

Action Match Rule: (a) for best match establish start of action in the outgoing shot, then use incoming shot to complete the majority of the action; and (b) if the action flowing across the cut is at all fast, you must repeat three frames of the action at the head of the incoming shot because the eye does not register the first two or three frames of any new image. A frame by frame analysis would show a slight overlap of the action, but at normal speed it appears smooth and continuous.

- cutting from 5c to 8b, same principle. Let Mary just begin to stoop and then cut to keys with hand entering at top of frame shortly afterwards. If you leave too much footage before the incoming hand appears, you will imply that Mary is eight feet tall.

Discussion: Run your cut version. How long is it; two or three minutes? Try applying these criteria:

1. Are the action matches smooth and logical, or do they jump?
2. Are the pans and tilts smooth and motivated by Mary's movements?
3. Do pans and tilts anticipate the motivating action, or lag behind?
4. Did you vary the camera height to create interesting angles?
5. Did you compose to create the maximum perspective and depth?
6. How is the framing and composition on static shots?
7. On the CU pan did you remember to leave compositional space ahead of her feet?
8. Where you cut from two sizes of the same shot (between camera positions B and D1) was there a radical enough change of image size to allow a natural-looking cut? Too small a difference gives the impression of a jump cut.

9. Did you keep screen directions logical, or did you "cross the line"? If you did, you may be able to use safety coverage (close shots of feet walking) to space out and therefore camouflage the mismatched shots.

ASSIGNMENT 5B: EDITING A MORE COMPRESSED VERSION

Run your cut and consider which pieces of action are vital, and which are links. Surely a lot of the walking is of secondary importance. If, for instance, Mary turns and looks back in the direction of the car, we don't need to see her cover every inch of ground in returning to it. Let us amend the first cut and do a compressed version. Here's where the unused bridging closeups come in, signified in the new abbreviated list with an asterisk:

Camera Position	Shot Number	Action
A	1	Car arrives, but cut before it comes to complete halt.
B	2a	Mary enters L-R, begins crossing frame.
D2	3	CU of Mary smiling up at window.
D1	*	Her feet L-R.
B	2b	Mary arrives at corner of path, turns R-L; cut immediately to:
C	3	Mary almost at door, fumbles for keys, can't find, looks back at car, turns.
G	*	Feet descending a couple of steps.
D1	*	CS feet walking R-L.
E	5a	Mary almost at car, fails to open door, curses.
F2	7	CU her POV of empty ignition lock.
E	5b	Mary straightens up, pats pockets, sees something on the ground.
F3	8a	CU keys lying in gutter, Mary's POV, her hand comes into frame and removes them.
E	5d	Mary straightens up looking relieved and exits into camera, her body blacking out the frame. End sequence.

Discussion: How long is the sequence this time? It should be thirty to fifty percent shorter, yet have lost nothing of narrative importance. See if you can cut it down further, to perhaps as little as thirty to sixty seconds overall. You will find shots or parts of shots that can be eliminated. If you set the audience up to infer what is not literally visible, they will. Doing this, you allow the audience to actively participate, to use imagination rather than passively witness something that requires no interpretation. That would be dull.

ASSIGNMENT 5C: EDITING TO MUSIC

Having discovered how much leeway there is to the length of many of the shots, you can now turn Mary into a musical star. Find a piece of music with a strong beat than enhances the mood of the sequence. Reedit the materials placing your cuts and major pieces of action on the beat or on the music's instrumental changes. Be aware that for a cut to appear on the beat, it must occur three frames before the actual beat point because of the perceptual lag mentioned above. The only nonnegotiable aspects of your earlier cut are the action match cuts. There is only one way to make them look right.

Discussion:

1. How tightly does the action fit the music?
2. Does cutting on the beat become predictable? If so, try cutting on a musical subdivision.
3. How much compromise did you have to make with the tight version to adjust the action to fit the music?
4. What does the music add to the earlier version's impact?

PROJECT 6: CHARACTER STUDY

Skills:

1. Revealing a character through action
2. Using mobile, *cinema verité* coverage
3. Blocking camera and actor for mutual accommodation
4. Developing counterpoint between words and action
5. Imposing a second point of view.

ASSIGNMENT 6A: PLAN, REHEARSE, AND SHOOT CHARACTER-REVEALING ACTION

Alan, alone, makes breakfast in his own way.

In your coverage incorporate

1. action of about four minutes that is emotionally revealing of Alan's basic character, particular mood, and immediate past and future,
2. revealing interaction with objects (no people, no phone conversations),
3. a single, nonstop handheld take using wide-angle lens only,
4. camera movement (pan, tilt, handheld tracking shot, etc.) to follow or reveal as necessary,
5. close and long shots produced by blocking subject-to-camera distance as necessary,
6. thorough exploitation of location,
7. lots of rehearsal with camera to make all the above look smooth and natural, and
8. safety cutaways, point of view shots, inserts.

Discussion: In rehearsal you will discover that you need to organize things in stages. First you will need to determine Alan's character and situation, then figure out how to externalize these for the audience. Camera coverage will develop first out of what the actor does, and then out of compromises made by camera and actor for each other. For instance, some actions will have to be slowed down to look normal on the screen. You will probably need to have the actor turn some actions around so they are visible by the camera without it having to traverse the room to see from the other angle, and so on. You will probably need lighting; if you can, place lighting stands in a tight group against the least interesting wall, so your camera has maximum freedom to move without shooting telltale stands and supply wiring.

Looking at your results, apply these criteria:

1. Is the piece interesting to watch?
2. Is the setting used to best advantage?
3. Does the audience learn something about Alan from everything he does?
4. Is he natural?
5. Does one have a sense of his previous day or night?
6. Can one guess something about the day he anticipates?
7. Is there variation of mood and rhythm in what he does?
8. Is there a built-in sense of development in the piece?
9. Does it keep within the four-minute time requirement?
10. Does the camera work feel natural and generally unobtrusive?
11. What makes camera work seem intrusive or even objectionable?
12. Does the camera depart from Alan, take its own initiative, and make its own revelations (showing for instance that while Alan is searching for the butter, the frying pan is smoking ominously)?
13. Are there motivated variations in camera height?
14. Does the camera seek to relate Alan to everything he is doing? (For instance, shoot over the toaster at Alan's face waiting for toast to pop up, rather than show toaster, then pan to Alan waiting—here they would be separated instead of related.)
15. How does Alan's movement look onscreen? (If too close too much of the time, the audience may feel seasick. Composition can also go out of control. Too wide, and one feels distanced as if watching a stage performance.)
16. Are Alan's movements predominantly contrived to happen across the frame or within the depth of the frame? What is the difference in feel?
17. Do you ever feel that the camera is caught by surprise (when can that be legitimate?) or knows in advance what will happen next? (Is this permissible?)
18. Does the audience feel it is spying on Alan unawares, or is there guidance, a feeling that the camera has its own ideas about him and is deliberately showing particular aspects of him? What should determine which storytelling mode you should use?
19. How much of the take is dramatically interesting and how much is dead or link material?

ASSIGNMENT 6B: INTERIOR MONOLOGUE

Add an interior monologue track as a voice-over (VO) in which we hear Alan's thought process. In planning this you will need to consider the following:

1. Which actions does a person do automatically from long habit?
2. Which of them require thought?
3. Upon what grounds is each decision made?
4. At what points are a character's thoughts in the present?
5. At what points do they fly away elsewhere, and why?

Do not forget to shoot room tone as necessary "spacer" should you want to extend pauses in the VO. When you have completed the assignment, try to assess whether

- the interior monologue voice is anywhere over- or under-informing the audience,
- the loss of suspense in knowing (rather than inferring) what is going on inside your character is offset by other dramatic advantages, and
- you have, overall, used too much or too little VO.

ASSIGNMENT 6C: VOCAL COUNTERPOINT AND POINT OF VIEW

Now write and record a different VO track to contrast revealingly with what one sees. Action should suggest one meaning, sound another, and the conjunction of the two should yield a third, more complex set of possibilities. The aim here is to develop tensions between picture and sound, a series of deliberate ambiguities or even contradictions that nudge each audience member toward drawing his or her own conclusions about the discrepancies. Here you are impelling the audience to actively develop ideas about Alan's character. Suggested voices are

- Alan telling his psychiatrist that his compulsions are going away,
- Alan describing his efficiency and foresight in a job interview,
- Alan's mother telling him how to eat well now that he is on his own,
- Alan's wife telling a friend how difficult he is to live with, and
- Alan's wife describing to her friend the qualities that make her love him.

Discussion: There is, of course, ample scope for comedy here, but you might like to try creating sympathy for your central character. The VO will have to be carefully written, timed against picture, and rehearsed. Be aware that the first two suggestions above are both apparently Alan's view of himself, though they allow the audience to develop an independent sense of Alan that might correspond with that of the psychiatrist and job interviewer. The remaining suggestions are perspectives of Alan that also serve to profile the speaker.

Do not forget to shoot room tone as necessary sound spacer should you want to extend pauses in the VO.

When you have completed your first version, ask

1. Is there a narrative development in the VO?
2. Does the VO sound natural, or does it sound like reading? (To avoid this, show the actor the lines, then have him or her improvise them. Afterwards

edit them to the action. This is not a certain procedure, but the results will have a spontaneity that is difficult to achieve any other way.)

3. Have you left spaces in the VO to allow us to look and interpret for ourselves? (Wall-to-wall VO would suffocate the audience's own developing perceptions.)

4. What are the most telling juxtapositions, and why?

5. Have you varied the juxtapositions' implications, sometimes adding to, sometimes contradicting what we see? (This keeps the audience guessing and therefore actively involved in decision-making.)

6. Through using VO were you able to lift the link actions to the interest level of the best action? (If you were wise, you wrote VO to raise the dull parts and left the eloquent actions to speak for themselves.)

7. Did you leave interesting sound effects in the clear? (To do this you will need to lay VO as a second track, then mix the two, raising the level of snyc original track in the spaces between VO blocks.)

PROJECT 7: EXPLOITING A LOCATION

Skills:
1. Developing a mood
2. Making the mood move from objective to subjective
3. Making use of cause and effect
4. Capitalizing upon inherent rhythms
5. Implying both a point of view and a state of mind
6. Suggesting a development
7. Using sync sound as effects
8. Using music to heighten or interpret the environment

ASSIGNMENT 7A: MOOD SEQUENCE

Select an interesting location and without using any main characters develop a mood sequence of about two minutes that changes and intensifies. In film terms, a location can be any interior or exterior setting; it might be a harbor, motorcyclists's cafe, farmyard, teenager's bedroom, stock exchange, fairground, bookshop, airport, or anything else that is mainly a physical entity rather than a human event. In planning your sequence, consider

1. What is present to structure the sequence? (Time progression? Increasing complexity? Forward exploratory movement of camera?)

2. What cause-and-effect shots you can group together into subsequences? (Within a winter forest scene, you establish icicles melting, drops of water falling past window, drops falling in pool, rivulet of water flowing through ice, etc.)

3. Are there any inherent rhythms to be exploited (water dripping, cars passing, a street vendor's repeated cry, dog barking, etc.)?

4. Do the sequences move from micro to macro view, or the reverse? (Start with BCU water droplets and develop to view of entire forest; or conversely, start with aerial view of the city and end on a single overfilled trash can.)

5. Can you create a turning point that marks the onset of a heightened or altered sensibility? (For instance, in a deserted sandy cove the camera discovers a single smoking cigarette butt. Thereafter, coverage suggests the uneasiness of wondering if one is being watched by a lurking human presence.)

Discussion: Since the sequence is dependent on the impressions each image and activity suggests rather than upon the movements and words of a central human subject, you must be responsive to the inherent rhythms in the material, and the natural duration of each shot in its context. You will need to define a beginning, a middle, and an end, just as if you were writing a dramatic scene, but they must come from the setting itself.

Here fiction filmmaking merges with the documentary; the environment has become a character under study by the storyteller. We ask that the environment grow and change just as in a character study, and we want the audience to react and be involved. As always in character study, the contradictions are the richest source of awareness. In a seaside scene it is juxtaposing frenetic game players with corpulent sun-worshippers that provides the astringent comparisons, or the waves compared with the stillness of the rocks. Every setting like every character contains dialectical tensions, those unreconciled and coexisting opposites that define the subject's scope and subjective meaning to the observer.

Depending on who the observer might be (a child, an old man, a foreigner, a thief, an explorer, someone revisiting his past, etc.), the environment can be interpreted very differently and even suggest the observing consciousness of a particular person in a particular mood, even though that person is never seen.

When you have edited your sequence together, consider

1. What are the phases of your sequence and where does each end?
2. What is the overall rhythmic movement of your sequence?
3. Where does the turning point(s) come? Is it decisive?
4. Is the sequence too long (usually because of lack of development)?
5. Does the sequence flow or does it seem fragmented (lack of subsequences each with its own beginning, middle, and end)?
6. Does it feel rhythmically right and inevitable throughout or are there some stumbles?
7. What mood is actually established (compared with that intended)?
8. What is the nature of the observing consciousness (anger, fear, lethargy, hedonism, etc.) and how does this change (development)?
9. What part did natural sound play in your organization (a lot, a little, or none at all, sound being simply diagetic accompaniment)?

ASSIGNMENT 7B: ADDING MUSIC

Now add music to your sequence, choosing it carefully (no songs; the aim is to work with emotional associations, not verbal, narrative ones). By taking a cassette of several possible pieces of music into the editing room you can try each against your scene before deciding which works best.

Music can augment what has been created pictorially, or, more interestingly, it can suggest something underlyingly different; for example, a peaceful harvest scene accompanied by an ominous marching tune, or abandoned houses in a blighted urban area seen against an impassioned Bach chorale. Antiphony leads the observer to invent the hidden meaning of the scene, and suggests that it may either be subjective to a character in the film or to the storyteller—that young farmworkers go off to die on foreign battlefields, or that poverty and failure are somehow part of God's plan for mankind.

Run your scene and ask

1. What is the music's contribution?
2. Did it feel valid, or was it a facile imposition?
3. Were there places for the natural effects to "bleed through?" (Your choice of music may be affected by wanting to be sure that particular effects are not drowned.)
4. Did you reposition certain cuts or pieces of screen movement so they fit the rhythmic dictates of the music?
5. Did you find a natural starting point for music in the sequence, and a natural ending point? (The start and stop of some kind of movement can motivate music in- and out-points, as can the ending or beginning of a strong diagetic sound effect. Study feature film practice for further guidance.

PROJECT 8: EDITED TWO-CHARACTER DIALOGUE SCENE

Skills:

1. Planning and shooting dialogue exchanges.
2. Camera placement.
3. Editing using verbal rhythms and operative words.
4. Controlling the scene's point of view.

ASSIGNMENT 8A: MULTIPLE COVERAGE

Take a short scene (approximately three minutes) that includes some sort of game and prepare to shoot as follows:

1. Cast the actors.
2. Decide the location.
3. Make several copies of the script and mark up one with the beats.
4. Rehearse the scene.
5. Develop the accompanying action, going beyond what the script calls for.
6. Make a floor plan of the location showing characters' moves and intended camera positions (see Figure 33–2, for example).

7. Define what you want the scene to accomplish and whose point of view the audience is to (a) mainly and (b) partially share and understand.

8. Using another copy of the script and colored pens for each camera position, mark up the script with your intended editing plan. Plan to cut between angles at times of major subject movement so cuts will look motivated, and be sure to shoot generous overlap at intended cutting points or you will not have choices in making the action match cut.

9. Shoot, playing the whole scene through in each major angle, thus allowing yourself to experiment widely during the editing.

10. Edit strictly according to your plan.

11. Solicit audience critique.

12. Reedit according to what you now feel should be done.

13. Solicit new audience critique.

14. After the fine cut, write yourself some directorial guidelines based on what you have learned.

Discussion: This project covers a huge amount of ground even though it is very short. It will take a fair amount of effort and organization. Do not shortchange yourself on the planning stage; there is much to be learned from first theorizing what you intend to do; doing it, and afterwards assessing where your planning went awry. The coverage I recommend allows you to both carry out what you intended, and to reedit it in other ways.

I should make clear that in a professional situation, shooting full-length multiple angles for long, intricate scenes is decisionless coverage that wastes actors' energies, crew time, and filmstock. It indicates a lack of vision about the scene's final form, and an ominous willingness to delay decision-making until editing.

However, at first when you lack experience and confidence, and particularly if the scene is short, it may be counterproductive to shoot any other way. Limiting coverage to short segments would mean not only risking an inflexible coverage but the stop-start nature of your shooting will probably prevent the cast from ever getting into its stride.

Long takes make consistent success hard to achieve throughout, but you can allow imperfect sections when the shooting script—marked up with your intended cut—shows that an inadequacy falls in the part of an angle you do not intend to use. Having this information at hand helps you decide immediately whether to call for another take.

A word on the placing of a scene: comedy should be fast paced, about thirty percent faster than life if it is to look right on the screen. Serious scenes often need to be temporarily slowed so that pauses, silences, eyeline shifts, or an exchange of glances can be fully exploited. The experienced director knows that these are truly the high points of the scene for which dialogue was merely a preparation. Beginners often reverse these priorities and strive to ensure that no silence, or silent action, ever threatens to bore the audience.

Once you are in the cutting room, it is heartening to see that wise coverage will let you double a pregnant pause; by cutting to a different angle you can add together the pauses from both. Conversely, if the moment was held overlong, you can abbreviate it through making the same cut between matching angles.

Although the editor cannot speed up or slow down the way words emerge, he or she does effectively control the rhythm and balance of action and reaction, which is a very large part of any performance. Surefooted editing can make a huge difference to the degree of thought and feeling the audience attributes to each character, and this can greatly improve the sense of integration and consistency in the acting.

When assessing your edited version, ask the following:

1. Do action match cuts flow smoothly?
2. Is screen direction maintained?
3. Have you revealed the room geography as necessary, or is the locale confusing to a first-time viewer?
4. Is the environment fully utilized by the characters and thus made active in the drama?
5. Is it apparent onscreen when a character changes body position (crosses his legs, for example), or does he move offscreen and reappear looking confusingly different? (An interesting way to get around this is to hear him move, and "see" the move through the changing eyelines of someone watching.)
6. Are convincing dialogue rhythms maintained, even when a cut takes place in the middle of a sentence?
7. Have you fully exploited eyeline shifts? (The most natural of all cutting points occurs when a character shifts his eyeline; we want a cut that shows us what he now sees.)
8. Have you fully expanded moments of significant action and charged silences?
9. Do changes of scene rhythm occur convincingly with changes in the characters' perceptions, thought patterns, and actions?
10. Does the scene breathe (either moving us close or distancing us where psychologically necessary, switching us between subjective and objective camera positions for variety)?
11. Does the way you have shot and cut the material convey a point of view (that is, effectively reveal the state of mind of the main character)?
12. Is the game (or other shared activity) used to reveal psychological changes in the characters?
13. Does the game develop convincingly?
14. Are there any redundancies (of dialogue, action, angle, etc.)?
15. Does the scene feel right in length (better to feel a little short than too long)?
16. What does the scene imply about back-story and what might come after?

ASSIGNMENT 8B: EDITING FOR AN ALTERNATIVE POINT OF VIEW

Reedit your scene to see if you can make the audience identify with a different point of view, such as the secondary character's point of view or an omniscient storyteller's point of view.

Discussion: Apply the same criteria as in Assignment 8A, but also ask what additional coverage you would need to make the audience more fully sympathize with the new point of view.

PROJECT 9: AUTHORSHIP THROUGH IMPROVISATION

Skills:
1. Involving actors in script idea development.
2. Spontaneous and creative interaction between actors and director.
3. Directing an event for direct cinema coverage, useful where actors must merge, for example, with a large and uncontrollable public event.
4. Editing documentary-style coverage.
5. Script development from taped improvisations.
6. Stylistic decision-making.
7. Working intuitively and thinking on one's feet.

ASSIGNMENT 9A: DEVELOPING A SHORT SCENE

Follow the instructions for Chapter 31, Exercise 15: Bridging Emotions to develop a three- to four-minute scene between two characters. Then, once the scene is reasonably stable and secure, use a handheld camera to cover the complete scene in three different angles: character A, character B, and two-shot.

The goal is sufficient coverage to allow considerable freedom in cutting the scene together, and to be able to cope with the unavoidable variations inherent in multiple takes of an improvised piece. You will have to rely upon your camera operator for the quality of the coverage, so it is best to bring him or her in early to shoot rehearsals.

Cut together a complete version, and ask yourself the questions in Project 8A. In addition, consider:

1. When was mobile, handheld footage stylistically appropriate and when not? What conclusions can you draw to help you make up guidelines for yourself?
2. How acceptable is the dialogue track? (You will need to checkerboard your dialogue tracks in editing, and do a mix to get the best out of them.)
3. Was the coverage adequate or does it show on the screen that the operator was sometimes caught by surprise? What effect do these moments have upon the audience?
4. How much does the unpredictability of the characters' movements prevent you from more deliberately showing their environment? (If, for instance, the philosophy of the piece is that "we are all figures in a landscape" yet the figures dominate to the exclusion of their surroundings, the improvisational form would be completely counterproductive.)
5. How much does your coverage convey an integrated point of view? Whose is it, and does it arise more from the performance than from the camera treatment? (This is extremely hard to pinpoint, but nevertheless, too important to neglect.)

6. Did you have enough close detail (closeups, inserts, and eyeline cutaways that have to be grabbed by panning to the thing or person seen)?

7. Does the composition succeed in showing a revealing relationship between

   - people? (crestfallen son, for instance, in foreground, angry mother in background)

   - objects? (miner grandfather's tombstone in foreground, the coal mine that killed him in background)

   - people and some aspect of their environment? (forlorn, withdrawn child standing in a playground that looks like a concentration camp)

Discussion: The mobility of handheld coverage generally projects the feeling of spontaneous human observation, as opposed to the godlike omniscience accompanying perfect composition and steadiness. It injects an interesting sense of fallibility and subjectivity into the coverage. Sometimes, of course, this is intrusively wrong—for instance, during a sequence of misty mountain landscape shots at daybreak when nobody is supposed to be about. Here rock-steady tripod shots are a must.

In "direct cinema" coverage where the director cannot line up each shot, the creative initiative passes to the camera operator, who must have the mind of a dramatist, not just that of a technician or still photographer. You quickly find out whether your operator sees only composition through the viewfinder, or whether he or she is finding dramatic meaning and focus within a scene. Some do, some can learn, many will remain detached visual designers.

Sound coverage here is catch as catch can (something your sound recordist will probably hate). While the camera must adapt to the action, the mike operator must try to pick up good sound in a swiftly changing, unpredictable situation and stay out of frame. You will need to do a rough mix before you show your work to an audience, or the sound discrepancies will cause them to misread the piece's inherent qualities.

Time your first cut for comparison with the next assignment.

ASSIGNMENT 9B: EDITING A SHORTER VERSION

Now edit your initial cut down, trying to make it tighter and more functional by eliminating verbal and behavioral padding. To do this you will have to debate with your editor the dramatic function of much that is said and done on the screen, and to devise methods of eliminating without trace whatever does not deserve to be there.

1. What percentage of the original length did you eliminate?

2. In what ways is the new cut more effective?

3. How consistent is the pace of dramatic development?

4. Was all expository detail included by the actors?

5. Was each new piece of necessary information artfully enough concealed?

6. Did it come too early or too late?

7. What did you feel about the acting?

Discussion: The strength of improvisation is usually the spontaneity and realism of the acting and the conviction of the characters, while the biggest problems usually lie with achieving a satisfying development. Improvisation often suffers from inconsistent dramatic growth, with long plateaux during which both actors and audience feel the pressure for something to "happen." This predicament tempts the actors to desperate acts of manipulation to get the piece moving again. Another related problem is the difficulty of burying exposition in a series of ongoing events. You do not want your audience to feel the presence of an editorializing hand during verbal exchanges, feeding such giveaway lines as, "Isn't it rough being out of work for three months, Ted?" and, "The last time we met—you remember, it was at the supermarket. You got mad because I couldn't give you back the money you lent me back in September."

Even if no clumsy authorial hand crashes through the backdrop like this in your piece, the probability is high that you will be dissatisfied with it. At times it is overcompressed, at times unavoidably flaccid. Editing removes a lot of padding, but also reveals inadequate joints and structural problems. However, if things go reasonably well, you end up with interestingly developed characters and a story line to work with, and this can take you to the next stage.

ASSIGNMENT 9C: SCRIPTING AND SHOOTING FROM AN IMPROV ORIGINAL

Transcribe the scene onto paper and rewrite it, aiming to keep the words the actors used, but compressing verbiage into pithy lines. Distribute and camouflage any expository information, and make all possible dialogue into actions that do not require accompanying words. This way characters can show their feelings instead of telling them to each other. Now, using the same cast and location, rehearse and shoot the scene as in Project 8.

Discussion: Compare the two versions of the same scene.

1. What was lost by turning an improvised performance, shot documentary-style, into a scripted and more formally controlled scene?
2. What was gained?
3. What else did you specifically discover through doing this and what did you learn about authorship and directing through doing it?

PROJECT 10: PARALLEL STORYTELLING

Skills:
1. Intercutting two narrative lines
2. Counterpointing two moods or activities to imply a storytelling commentary
3. Advancing two story lines concurrently so each acts as a cutaway for the other, and both are kept to brief essentials
4. Showing separate, concurrent events developing toward a time of eventual convergency

ASSIGNMENT 10A: SEEING THE SCENES AS SEPARATE ENTITIES

Either write or improvise two whole scenes whose content will intercut meaningfully and provoke the audience to see a connection. Suggested subjects:

Man getting ready for a date
Woman getting ready for the same date

Burglars getting ready to rob a house
Detectives making preparations to trap them

Man rehearsing how he will ask for a raise
Two managers discussing how they will fire him

Write each as a complete scene, then make photocopies and scissor them into sections that can be experimentally interleaved as a "paper cut" version of the eventual parallel storytelling. Before we intercut the scenes, however, we want to see each as a separate entity first.

Now cast, shoot, and edit each scene separately and assemble them so that one whole scene follows the other.

Discussion: Do a reasonably tight edit on each sequence and then assess them as follows:

1. What change in implications are there when you run them in reverse order? (The detectives, for example, may have arrived too late, and the firing may follow the request for a raise, instead of precede it.)

2. How long is each sequence?

3. What do you gain in dramatic buildup by staying with each unbroken sequence?

ASSIGNMENT 10B: LONG INTERCUT VERSION

Now intercut the two sequences according to your paper cut, losing nothing of the original material.

Discussion: Assess as follows:

1. What ironies are you able to create? (Perhaps you counterpoint that the woman preparing for the date has bought a new dress while the man forgets to clean his shoes.)

2. What meaningful comparisons do you create? (Both the man asking for a raise and his managers think he is underpaid.)

3. What causes and effects does the audience link together? (Both detectives and burglars have radios.)

4. Do both sequences appear to be happening at the same time, or is one retrospective in comparison with the other? (For instance, a son from abroad searching for his parents finds that his father is already dead. His father's death is intercut with his mother's account of it, which is softened to spare the son's feelings.)

5. Does one sequence foretell the outcome of the other? (In Roeg's *Don't Look Now* (1973) the famous lovemaking scene is intercut with the couple getting dressed.)

ASSIGNMENT 10C: SHORT VERSION

Now reassess the cut. Because it is no longer necessary to maintain the illusion of continuous time, you can pare away anything that the audience could infer, and which is now nonessential. You will probably see a number of new or different points at which to cut across to the parallel story.

Discussion: Now consider the new version as follows:

1. How much shorter is the new version compared with the two original sequences?
2. How many of the ideas for your new cut arose out of the shooting, blocking, and playing of the scene?
3. How much more information did you get from repeatedly watching the interplay of the two scenes?
4. What kind of dramatic capital has been gained and what lost through intercutting?
5. Knowing what you know now, how should a writer plan the raw materials for such sequences?

ASSIGNMENT 10D: USING JUMP CUTS

Now experimentally reassemble the two sequences in chronological order, but using only the pieces you chose for the intercut version, using jump cuts.

Discussion: Eliminating the slack material between the high points does two things: it moves the story along faster, and it accentuates an authorial attitude or voice by discarding objective time and openly espousing only the pieces of time that matter. Flat-footed realism and its linear, continuous time has given way to something more challengingly subjective.

If you hate this version of your sequences, it is probably because the jump cuts themselves make ugly visual leaps. This would not be true had you had an opportunity to design them.

> *Similarity of Frame:* For instance, you might cut from a bed with two people reading, to the same bed with them asleep, to a morning shot with one still there and the other dressing in the background. Older convention would dictate a long, slow dissolve between the three set ups (which should be taken with the camera locked down in the exact same position so each composition is exactly the same) but the same narrative content can be done in a fraction of the time and at a fraction of the cost by jump cutting. In this usage, the jump cut becomes not a mistake or something unavoidable, but a formal storytelling device of great agility.

Difference of Frame: With a bold difference of composition you can simply jump cut forward in time. During a wide shot of people preparing to fire a piece of pottery you can cut to a close shot of the oven, somebody opens it, and the pot is already fired. We understand that a piece of insignificant time has been eliminated, even though dialogue continues with an unbroken sentence across the cut into the new time plane. The TV commercial has familiarized audiences with these cinematic shorthand devices.

There is a wealth of implications here for a more personal, staccato storytelling style, one freed from the literalness of present-tense realism. Alain Resnais has pioneered the cinema's greater freedom in time and tense. His *Providence* (1977) sets up the fascinating labyrinth of a dying novelist's mind as he spends a night of pain anticipating a visit by his family the next day. As in his earlier *Last Year at Marienbad* (1961), Resnais is able to depart from the present not only to plumb his point-of-view character's memory, but his tortured imagination, too. These developments have great significance for writers, directors and editors alike who wish to address the audience's imagination using a cinematic language of greater rhetorical flexibility.

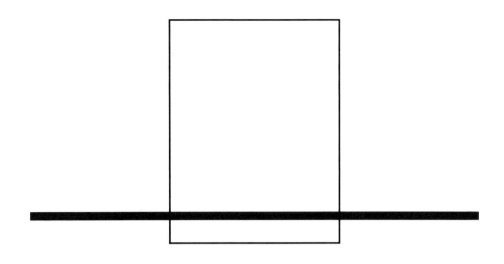

G·L·O·S·S·A·R·Y

More information on these terms may be found by looking in the index.

A & B rolls Two or more rolls of film camera-original from which release prints are struck.

Acetate sheet Clear plastic sheet used in making titles or animation cels.

Action match cut Cut made between two different angles of the same action using the subject's movement as the transition.

AD Assistant director.

Adaptation The unique way each character adapts to the changing obstacles that prevent him or her from gaining his ends and a prime component in externalizing his or her conflicts.

ADR Automatic dialogue replacement. *See* Postsynchronization.

Aerial shot Shot taken from the air.

AFI American Film Institute.

Ambient sound Sound naturally occurring in any location. Even an empty, quiet room has its own special atmosphere since no space is truly silent.

Angle of acceptance The height and width of the subject filmed by a particular lens at a given distance expressed in a lens table either in degrees or as measurements. Photographed image also depends on aspect ratio of the format in use. Wide-screen format will have longer horizontal measurement.

Anticipating Term used to describe when an actor speaks or acts in advance of the appropriate moment.

Anticipatory sound Sound brought in ahead of its accompanying picture.

Aspect ratio The size of a screen format expressed as the ratio of the width in relation to the height. Films made for television are photographed at a ratio of 1.33:1. *See also* Angle of acceptance.

Atmosphere track Sound track providing a particular atmosphere (cafe, railroad, beach, rain, for example).

Attack (sound) The beginning portion of any sound.

Audio sweetening The level and equalization adjustment process that accompanies sound mixing.

Auteur theory   The concept that one mind controls the creative identity of a film
Axis   *See* Scene axis.

Baby legs   A miniature tripod for low angle shots.
Back lighting   Lighting from behind the subject.
Back story   The events stated or implied to have happened prior to the period covered in the screenplay.
Bars   Standard color bars generated in video systems, usually by the camera.
BCU   Big close up.
Beat   Point in a scene where a buildup of dramatic pressure effects a noticeable change in one or more characters' consciousness.
BFI   British Film Institute.
BG   Background.
Blocking   Choreographic arrangement of movements by actors and camera in relation to the set.
Body copy   Nondialogue descriptive portion of screenplay, usually consisting of stage directions and physical description.
Book, the   Actors' name for the script.
Boom   Support pole suspending the microphone close to the speakers but just out of shot.
Boxcar cutting   Crude method of assembling sound and action segments as level-cut segments for speed and convenience.
Broad lighting   Lighting that produces a broad band of highlight on a face or other three-dimensional object.
Business   The in-character activity generated by actors to fill out their characters' behavior.
Butt splice   Taped film splice made without the overlap necessary to cement splicing.
Buzz track   *See* presence.

Call back   Calling back actors who have successfully passed the first round of auditioning for a second round.
Camera left/right   Method of specifying movement or the placement of objects in relation to the camera: "Davy turns away from camera and walks off camera left." Also expressed as screen right or left.
Camera motivation   A shot or a camera movement must be motivated within the terms of the scene or story if it is not to look alien and imposed. Camera motivation is often answered by asking, "What is the point of view here?"
Camera-to-subject axis   The invisible line drawn between the camera and the subject in the composition. *See also* Scene axis.
Cattle call   The call for a number of actors to try out, often simultaneously, for parts.
Cement splice   A film splice made by cementing two overlapping portions of film together.
Chalk marks   Temporary marks made on the floor to ensure that actor or camera stops at a precise place.

Character biography   The biographical portrait an actor invents as background to the character he or she is to play.

Character generator   An electronic device for producing video titles.

Checkerboarding   The practice during conforming of alternating film scenes with black leader in each A & B roll of camera original. Sound tracks prior to mixing are likewise alternated between two channels, with silence separating sound segments. Both black frame and silence allow the operator a grace period in which to adjust printer or sound channel settings before the arrival of the next segment.

Cinema verité   Documentary shooting method in which the camera is subservient to an actuality that is sometimes instigated by the director.

Clapper board   Marker board used at the beginning of takes whose bar closing permits separate sound to be synchronized. Also called the slate.

Climax   The dramatic apex of a scene.

Coincidence   Dramatists in a tight spot make things happen or people meet "by coincidence," a crutch overused at the dramatist's peril.

Color bars   Standard electronic video color test, usually generated by the camera.

Color chart   Chart attached to film slate board as color reference for laboratory processing technicians.

Color temperature   Light color quality is measured in degrees Kelvin. Common light sources in moviemaking contain a different mix of colors. The eye compensates effortlessly, but film and video cameras (or lighting itself) must be adjusted to prevailing color temperature if white objects are to be rendered as white onscreen. Mixing daylight (around 5,400°K) and studio lights (3,200°K) in the same scene leads to an unnatural lighting effect. One source must be filtered to make its output match the other, and the camera must likewise be filtered or electronically color balanced for all scene colors to be rendered faithfully.

Comm   Commentary.

Communion.   The principle by which actors react to the unforeseeable nuances in each other's performances in order to regain the spontaneity of real life during a rehearsed performance.

Complementary shot   A shot compositionally designed to intercut with another.

Composite print   A film print combining sound and picture.

Compression   Sound with a wide dynamic range can be proportionately compressed so that loudest and softest sounds are closer in volume. All TV transmissions and most radio transmissions, with the exception of high-fidelity music stations, are compressed. Cinemas usually give you the authentic range between whispers and the roar of battle.

Concept   The dramatic *raison d'être* underlying the whole screenplay.

Conforming   The process in which the film camera original is edited in conformity with the fine-cut workprint prior to making release prints.

Confrontation   Bringing into final collision those people or forces representing the dramatic piece's main conflict.

Contingency percentage   A percentage usually between ten and fifteen percent superadded to a budget to provide for the unforseeable.

Contingency planning   Scheduling alternative shooting for any scenes threatened by weather or other imponderables.

Continuity   Consistency of physical detail between shots intended to match.

Continuity script Script made after postproduction as record of film contents. Useful in proving piracy or censorship.

Contrast Difference in brightness between highlight and deep shadow areas in an image.

Contrast ratio Ratio of lightest to darkest areas in an image.

Controlling point of view The psychological perspective (a character's or the storyteller's) from which a particular scene is shown.

Counterpoint The juxtaposing of antithetical elements, perhaps between sound and picture, to create a conflict of impressions for the audience to resolve.

Coverage The different angles from which a given scene is covered in order to allow variations of viewpoint in editing.

Crab dolly Wheeled camera support platform that can roll in any direction.

Craning A boom supporting the camera which can be raised or lowered during the shot.

Crash zoom Very fast zoom in or zoom out.

Crib notes Director's notes listing intentions and "don't forgets" for a scene.

Crossing the line Moving the camera across the scene axis. Can be problematical.

CS Close shot.

CU Closeup.

Cutaway A shot, often a character's physical point of view, that allows us to cut away momentarily from the main action.

Dailies The film unit's daily output, processed and ready to be viewed. Also called rushes because of the rush involved in readying them.

Day for night Special photography that allows a sunlit day shot to pass as moonlit night.

Decay The tapering away of a concluding sound.

Deep focus Photography that holds objects both near and far in sharp focus.

Degradation A picture, either video or photo, becomes degraded when it passes through several generations of copying.

Depth of field The depth of the picture that is in acceptably sharp focus. Varies widely according to lens and f-stop in use.

Deus ex machina The improbable event imported into a story to make it turn out right.

Diagetic sound Sound that belongs naturally with what we see in picture.

Diffused light Light composed of disorganized rays that casts an indistinct shadow.

Direct cinema A low-profile documentary style of shooting that disallows any directorial intrusion to shape or instigate incidents.

Dissolve Transitional device in which one image cross-fades into another. Also called a lap dissolve. One sound can dissolve into another.

DOF Depth of field.

Dolby A proprietary electronic recording system that produces low-noise sound recording, that is, having a lowered systemic hiss.

Dolly shot Any shot on a wheeled camera support.

Double-system recording Camera and sound recorder are separate instruments.

DP Director of photography.

Dramatic dynamics   The ebb and flow of dramatic pressure through the length of a scene or of a whole piece.

Dramatic interpretation   The selection of a dominant meaning for a particular text.

Dub   To copy from one electronic medium to another. Can be sound or video picture.

Dutch angle   Shot made with camera deliberately tilted out of horizontal.

Dynamic character definition   Defining a dramatic character by what he or she wants and is trying to accomplish.

Dynamic composition   Pictorial composition as it changes within a moving shot.

Echo   Sound reflections that return after a constant delay time.

Edge numbers   Code numbers imprinted on the edge of camera original film and printing through to the work print.

Effects   Sounds specially laid to augment the sound track of a film.

Emotional memory   An actor who carefully devises specific actions to fit a particular mood of his character finds, when he performs, that he spontaneously experiences the character's emotions.

Emotional transition   Emotional change during a scene. Scripts often challenge actors by calling for leaps from one mood to another in a shorter time than is normal in life.

Energy level   Both scenes and performances have their own energy levels. A director will often call for a change in energy level when a scene is not working out, or when actors are getting tired.

EQ   Equalizing.

Equalizing   Using sound filters to reduce the discrepancy between sound tracks that are supposed to match and sound seamless.

Establishing shot   A shot that establishes a scene's geographical and human contents.

Exposition   The part of a scene or a story in which basic information is relayed to the audience. Good exposition is buried within action and goes unnoticed.

Expressionism   A mode in art in which verisimilitude is laid aside in favor of techniques that evoke the subjective vision either of a character or of the storyteller.

Ext   Exterior.

External composition   The compositional relationship between two images at the point of cutting between them.

Eye light   Small wattage light mounted on camera to put a liquid sparkle in actors' eyes.

Eyeline   The visual trajectory of a character in a scene.

Fade down   Lower sound level.

Fade to white   Fade an image to white instead of to black.

Fade up   Raise sound level.

Falling action   *See* Resolution.

FG   Foreground.

FI   Fade in.

Fill light   Diffused light used to raise light level in shadows cast by key light.

Flash forward   Moving temporarily forward in time, the cinematic equivalent of the future tense. This quickly becomes a new form of present.

Flashback   Moving temporarily backwards in time; a cinematic past tense that soon becomes an ongoing present.

Floor plan   *See* Ground plan.

FO   Fade out.

Focal distance   Distance between camera and subject.

Focus (acting)   Seeing, hearing, thinking in character. When an actor loses focus he or she becomes self-conscious and aware of participating in a make-believe world.

Foley   Generic name for a stage where sound is recreated to picture.

Foreshadowing   A somewhat fatalistic narrative technique by which an outcome is hinted at in advance. Helps to raise expectant tension in the audience.

Form   The means and arrangement chosen to present a story's content.

Freeze frame   A single frame arrested and held as a still picture.

Frontal lighting   Key light coming from the direction of the camera and showing the subject virtually without shadows.

FTs   Footsteps. Often must be recreated.

FX   Effects

Generation   Camera original (in film or video) is the first generation, and copies become subsequent numbered generations, each showing increased degradation of the original's fidelity.

Genre   A kind or type of film (horror, sitcom, cowboy, domestic drama, etcetera).

Givens   Whatever is nonnegotiably specified in a text.

Grading   *See* Timing.

Graduated tonality   An image composed of mid tones and having neither very bright nor very dark areas.

Gray scale   Test chart useful to camera and lab technicians that shows the range of gray tones and includes absolute black and white.

Grip   Location technician expert in handling lighting and set construction equipment.

Ground plan   Diagram showing placement of objects and movements of actors on a floor plan. Also called floor plan.

Gun/rifle mike   Ultradirectional microphone useful for minimizing the intrusiveness of ambient noise.

Hard light   *See* Specular light.

Headroom   Compositional space left above heads.

High angle   Camera mounted high, looking down.

High contrast   Image with large range of brightnesses.

High down   Camera mounted high, looking down.

High-key picture   Image that is overall bright with few areas of shadow.

Highlight   Brightest areas in picture.

Hi-hat   Ultralow camera support resembling a metal top hat.

Improv   Improvisation. A dramatic interaction that deliberately permits an outcome to emerge spontaneously. Improvs can involve different degrees of structure, or may set a goal to be reached by an undetermined path.

Insert   A close shot of detail to be inserted in a shot containing more comprehensive action.

Int   Interior.

Interior monologue   The interior thoughts voice an actor will sustain to help himself or herself stay in character and in focus.

Internal composition   Composition internal to the frame as opposed to the compositional relationship existing between adjacent shots, called external composition.

Irony   The revelation of a reality different from that initially apparent.

Jump cut   Transitional device in which two similar images taken at different times are cut together so that the elision of intervening time is apparent. From this the audience infers that time has passed.

Juxtaposition   The placing together of different pictorial or sound elements to invite comparison, inference, and heightened thematic awareness on the part of the audience.

Key light   A scene's apparent source of illumination, and the one creating the intended shadow pattern.

Key numbers   *See* Edge numbers.

Keystone distortion   The distortion of parallel lines that results from photographing an object from an off-axis position.

LA   Low angle

Lap dissolve   *See* Dissolve.

Lavalier mike   Any neck or chest microphone.

Lead space   The additional compositional space allowed in front of a figure or moving object photographed in profile.

Legal release   A legally binding release form signed by a participant in a film that gives permission to use footage taken.

Leitmotiv   Intentionally repeated element (sound, shot, dialogue, music, etcetera) that helps unify a film by reminding the viewer of its earlier appearance.

Lens speed   How fast a lens is depends on its maximum aperture.

Level   Sound volume.

Lighting ratio   The ratio of highlight brightness to shadow illumination.

Limiter   Electronically applied upper limit, useful for preventing momentary transient sounds like a door slamming from distortion through overrecording.

Line of tension   Invisible dramatic axis, or line of awareness, that can be drawn between protagonists and important elements in a scene.

Lip sync   Recreated speech that is in complete sync with the speaker. Singers often lip sync to their recordings and fake a singing performance on television.

Looping   *See* ADR.

Lose focus   *See* Focus.

Low angle   Camera looking up at subject.

Low-contrast image   Small differences of brightness between highlight areas and shadow.

Low-key picture   A scene that may have high contrast but which is predominantly dark overall.

LS   Long shot.

Magazine   Removable light proof film container for a film camera.

Mannerisms   An actor's idiosyncratic and repeated details of behavior. Very hard to change or suppress.

Master mix   Final mixed sound, first generation.

Master shot   Shot that shows most or all of the scene and most or all of the characters.

Match cut   *See* Action match cut.

MCS   Medium close shot

Metaphor   A verbal or visually implied analogy that ascribes to one thing the qualities associated with another.

Midtones   The intermediate shades of gray lying between the extremes of black and white.

Mimesis   Action that imitates the actuality of life.

Mise-en-scène   The totality of lighting, blocking, camera use, and composition that produces the dramatic image on film.

Mix   The mixing together of sound tracks.

Mix chart   Cue chart that functions like a musician's score to assist in the sound mix.

MLS   Medium long shot.

Montage   Originally meant editing in general, but now refers to the kind of sequence that shows a process or the passage of time.

Montage sequence   *See* Montage.

MOS   Short for "Mit out sound," which is what the German directors in Hollywood called for when they intended to shoot silent. In Britain this shot is called mute.

Motif   Any formal element repeated from film history or from the film itself whose repetition draws attention to an unfolding thematic statement. *See also* Leitmotiv.

Motivation   Whatever plot logic impels a character to act or react in a particular way, usually a combination of psychological makeup and external events.

MS   Medium shot.

Murphy's Law   "Whatever can go wrong will go wrong." Applies also to people.

Mus   Music.

Music sync points   Places in a film's action where music must exactly fit. Also called picture-pointing and can be overdone.

Mute shot   *See* MOS.

Narr   Narration.

Narrow lighting   Lighting which in portraiture produces a narrow band of highlight on a face.

Negative cutting   *See* Conforming.

Noise   Noise inherent in a sound recording system itself.

Noise reduction   Recording and playback technique that minimizes system noise. *See also* Dolby.

Normal lens   A lens of a focal length that, in the format being used, renders distances between foreground and background as recognizably normal.

Obligatory moment   The moment of maximum dramatic intensity in a scene and for which the whole scene exists.

Off-line edit   Manual, noncomputerized video editing. *See also* On-line edit.

Omniscient point of view   A storytelling mode in which the audience is exposed to the author's capacity to see or know anything going on in the story, to move at will in time and space, and to freely comment upon meanings or themes.

On-line edit   Video editing assisted by a computer that can locate and line up specific time-coded frames in the process of assembling a final cut.

Optical   Any visual device like a fade, dissolve, wipe, iris wipe, ripple dissolve, matte, superimposition, etcetera.

Optical house   A company specializing in visual special effects.

Optical track   A sound track photographically recorded.

OS   Offscreen.

Over the top   Expression signifying a performance carried out with a surfeit of emotion.

Overlap cut   Any cut in which picture and sound transitions are staggered instead of level-cut.

Pan   Short for panorama. Horizontal camera movement.

Perspective   The size differential between foreground and background objects that causes us to infer receding space. Obviously distorted perspective makes us attribute subjective distortion in the point of view being expressed.

Picture pointing   Making music fit picture events. Walt Disney films used the device so much that its overuse is called "Mickey Mousing."

Picture texture   This can be hard or soft. A hard image has large areas in sharp focus and tends toward contrastiness, while a soft image has areas out of focus and lacks contrast.

Playwriting   One actor's tendency to take control of a scene, particularly in improv work, and to manipulate other actors into a passive relationship.

Plot   The arrangement of incidents and the logic of causality in a story. Plot should create a sense of momentum and credibility, and act as a vehicle for the thematic intention of the piece.

PM   Production manager.

Point of view   Sometimes literally what a character sees (a clock approaching midnight, for instance) but more usually signifies the outlook and sensations of a character within a particular environment. This can be the momentary consciousness of an unimportant character, or that of a main character (*See* Controlling point of view). It can also be the storyteller's point of view (*See* Omniscient point of view).

Postsynchronization   Dialogue or effects shot in sync with existing action.

POV   Point of view. When abbreviated thus it nearly always means a shot reproducing a character's eyeline view.

Practical   Any light source visible in the frame as part of the set.

Premise   *See* Concept.

Premix   A preliminary pass in which subsidiary sound elements are mixed together in preparation for the final mix.

Preroll   The amount of time a video editing rig needs to get up to speed prior to making a cut.

Presence   Specially recorded location atmosphere to authentically augment "silent" portions of track. Every space has its own unique presence.

Prop   Property.

Property Physical object handled by actors or present for authenticity in a set. A term also used of a script to which someone has secured the rights.

Rack focus Altering focus between foreground and background during a shot. Prompts or accommodates an attention shift (a figure enters a door at the back of the room, for instance).

Radio microphone A microphone system that transmits its signal by radio to the recorder and is therefore wireless. Famous for picking up taxis and CB enthusiasts at inopportune moments.

Reader's script Transcript of a finished film presented in a publisher's format that makes maximum use of the page.

Reconnaissance Careful examination of locations prior to shooting.

Release print Final print destined for audience consumption.

Research Library work and observation of real life in search of authentic detail to fill out fictional characters and situations.

Resistance Human evasion mechanisms that show up in actors under different kinds of stress.

Resolution The wind-down events following the plot's climax that form the final phase of the plot's development. Also called falling action.

Reverberation Sound reflections returning in a disorganized pattern of delay.

Rising action The plot developments, including complication and conflict, that lead to a plot's climax.

Room tone *See* Presence.

Rushes Unedited raw footage as it appears after shooting.

Rushes book Log of important first reactions to performances in rushes footage.

Scene axis The invisible line in a scene representing the scene's dramatic polarization. In a labor dispute scene this might be drawn between the main protagonists, the plant manager and the union negotiator. Coverage is shot from one side of this line to preserve consistent screen directions for all participants. Complex scenes involving multiple characters and physical regrouping may have more than one axis. *See also* Crossing the line.

Scene breakdown A crossplot that displays the locations, characters, and script pages necessary to each scene.

Scene dialectics The forces in opposition in a scene which usually require externalizing through acting, blocking, composition, visual and aural metaphors, etcetera.

Scene geography The physical layout of the location and the placing of the characters when they are first encountered. *See also* Master shot.

Screen direction The orientation or movement of characters and objects relative to the screen (screen left, screen right, upscreen, downscreen).

Screen left/right Movement or direction specifications. *See* Screen direction.

Screenplay Standard script format showing dialogue and stage direction but no camera or editing instructions.

Segue (pronounced "seg-way") Sound transition, often a dissolve.

Set light A light whose function is to illuminate the set.

Setup The combination of particular lens, camera placement, and composition to produce a particular shot.

SFX Sound effects.

Shooting ratio The ratio of material shot for a scene in relation to its eventual edited length. 8:1 is a not unusual ratio for dramatic film.

Shooting script Screenplay with scenes numbered and amended to show intended camera coverage and editing.

Sidecoaching During breaks in a scene's dialogue the director can quietly feed directions to the actors, who incorporate these instructions without breaking character. Most often used when shooting reaction shots.

Sightlines Lines that can be drawn along each character's main lines of vision that influence the pattern of coverage so it reproduces the feeling of each main character's consciousness.

Silhouette lighting Lighting in which the subject is a dark outline against a light background.

Single shot A shot containing only one character.

Single-system recording Sound recording made on film or video that also carries the picture. *See* Double-system recording.

Slate *See* Clapper board.

Slate number Setup and take number shown on the slate, or clapper, which identifies a particular take.

Soft light Light that does not produce hard-edged shadows.

Sound dissolve One sound track dissolving into another.

Sound effects Nondialogue recordings of sounds intended either to intensify a scene's realism or to give it a subjective heightening.

Sound mix The mixing together of sound elements into a sound composition that becomes the film's sound track.

Sound perspective Apparent distance of sound source from the microphone. Lavalier mikes, for instance, give no change of perspective when characters move or turn because they remain in a fixed relationship to the wearer.

Specular light Light composed of parallel rays that casts a comparatively hard-edged shadow.

Split page format A script format that places action on the left hand side of the page and its accompanying sound on the right.

Stage directions Nondialogue screenplay instructions, also known as body copy.

Stand in Someone who takes the place of an actor during setup time or for shots that involve special skills, such as horse-riding, fights, etcetera.

Static character definition Giving a character static attributes instead of defining him in terms of dynamic volition.

Static composition The composition elements in a static image.

Step outline Synopsis of a screenplay expressed as a series of numbered steps, and preferably including a definition of each step's function in the whole.

Sting Musical accent to heighten a dramatic moment.

Storyboard Series of key images sketched to suggest what a series of shots will look like.

Strobing The unnatural result onscreen resulting from the interaction of camera shutter speed with a patterned subject such as the rotating spokes of a wheel or panning across a picket fence.

Structure The formal organization of the elements of a story, principally the handling of time, and their arrangement into a dramatically satisfying development that includes a climax and resolution.

Style An individual stamp on a film, the elements in a film that issue from its makers' own artistic identity.

Subjective camera angle An angle that implies the physical point of view of one of the characters.

Subtext The hidden, underlying meaning to the text. It is supremely important and actors and director must often search for it.

Superobjective The overarching thematic purpose of the director's dramatic interpretation.

Surrealism Also a movement in art and literature. Concerned with the free movement of the imagination particularly as expressed in dreams, where the dreamer has no conscious control over events. Often associated with helplessness.

Sync coding Code marks to help an editor keep sound and action in sync.

Tag An irreducibly brief description useful for its focus upon essentials.

Take One filmed attempt from one setup. Each setup may have several takes.

Telephoto lens Long or telescopic lens that foreshortens the apparent distance between foreground and background objects.

Tense, change of Temporary change from present to either past, future, or conditional tenses in a film's narrative flow. Whatever tense a film invokes speedily becomes a new, ongoing present. For this reason screenwriting is always in the present tense.

Thematic purpose The overall interpretation of a complete work that is ultimately decided by the director. *See* Superobjective.

Theme A dominant idea made concrete through its representation by the characters, action, and imagery of the film.

Three-shot/3S Shot containing three people.

Thumbnail character sketch Brief character description useful either in screenwriting or in recruiting actors.

Tilt Camera swiveling in a vertical arc, tilting up and down to show the height of a flagpole, for instance.

Time code Electronic code number unique to each video frame.

Timebase correction Electronic stabilization of the video image, particularly necessary to make it compatible with the sensitive circuitry used in transmission over the air.

Timing The process of examining and grading a negative for color quality and exposure prior to printing. Also called grading.

Tracking shot Moving camera shot in which the camera dolly often runs on tracks like a miniature railroad.

Transitional device Any visual, sound, or dramatic screen device that signals a jump to another time or place.

Treatment Usually a synopsis in present tense, short story form of a screenplay summarizing dialogue and describing only what an audience would see and hear. Can also be a puff piece designed to sell the script rather than give comprehensive information about content.

Trucking shot Moving camera shot that was originally shot from a truck. The term is used interchangeably with tracking.

Two-shot/2S Shot containing two people.

Unit   The whole group of people shooting a film.

VCR   Videocassette recorder.

Verbal action   Words conceived and delivered so as to act upon the listener and instigate a result.

Visual rhythm   Each image according to its action and compositional complexity requires a different duration onscreen to look right and to occupy the same audience concentration as its predecessor. A succession of images when sensitively edited exhibits a rhythmic constancy that can be slowed or accelerated like any other kind of rhythm.

VO   Voice over.

Volition   The will of a character to accomplish something. This leads to constant struggle of one form or another, a concept vital in making dramatic characters come to life.

VT   Videotape.

WA   Wide angle.

Whip pan   Very fast panning movement.

White balance   Video camera setup procedure in which circuitry is adjusted to the color temperature of the lighting source so that a white object is rendered as white onscreen.

Wide-angle lens   A lens with a wide angle of acceptance. Its effect is to increase the apparent distance between foreground and background objects.

Wild   Non sync.

Wild track   A sound track shot alone and with no synchronous picture.

Window dub   A transfer made from a time-coded video camera original that displays each frame's time code number in a window near the bottom of frame.

Wipe   Optical transition between two scenes that appears on screen as a line moving across the screen. An iris wipe makes the new scene appear as a dot that enlarges to fill the screen. These effects are overused on the TV screen.

Wireless mike   See radio microphone.

WS   Wide shot.

WT   Wild track.

XLS   Extra long shot.

Zoom lens   A lens whose focal length is infinitely variable between two extremes.

Zoom ratio   The ratio of the longest to the widest focal lengths. A 10 to 100mm zoom would be a 10:1 zoom.

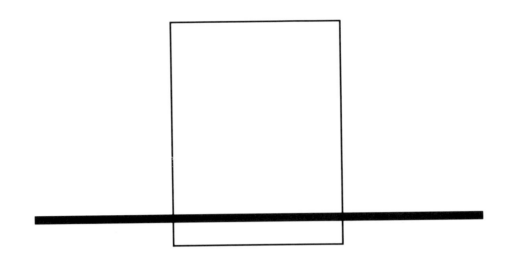

A·N·N·O·T·A·T·E·D B·I·B·L·I·O·G·R·A·P·H·Y

ACTING

Barr, Tony. *Acting for the Camera*. New York: Harper and Row, 1982. Excellent and comprehensive. Best advice: "Learn the role—not the lines."

Blum, Richard. *Working Actors: The Craft of Television, Film, and Stage Performance*. Boston: Focal Press, 1989.

Hodgson, John and Ernest Richards. *Improvisation*. New York: Grove Press, 1974. Comprehensive approach to drama that emphasizes the connection between acting and living.

Marowtiz, Charles. *The Art of Being: Towards a Theory of Acting*. New York: Taplinger, 1978. Intelligent and stimulating, full of ideas about the function of drama in the theatre.

Moore, Sonia. *The Stanislavski System*. New York: Viking Press, 1965. The master's ideas made accessible, something his voluminous writings do not. Later revisions available, but I like this version best.

Morris, Eric and Joan Hotchkis. *No Acting Please*. Los Angeles: Spelling Publications, 1979. Very practical. Concentrates on the emotional honesty that is so important to the film performance.

Spolin, Viola. *Improvisation for the Theatre*. Evanston: Northwestern University Press, 1963. Huge amount of source material for acting experimenters with much useful rationale, but dauntingly systematized.

SCREENWRITING

Bergman, Ingmar. *Four Stories by Ingmar Berman*. Garden City: Anchor Press, 1977. Four documents that were the starting point for films in Bergman's nontraditional screenwriting process.

Blacker, Irwin R. *The Elements of Screenwriting*. New York: Macmillan, 1986. Brief and very much to the point.

Dmytryk, Edward. *On Screenwriting*. Boston: Focal Press, 1985. Conversational, good examples but conceptual and not procedural.

Edmonds, Robert. *Scriptwriting for the Audio-Visual Media*. New York: Teachers College Press, 1978. Survey of screenwriting forms and their applications.

Field, Syd. *Screenplay: The Foundations of Screenwriting*. New York: Dell, 1982. A favorite.

Rubenstein, Paul Max and Martin J. Maloney. *Writing for the Media*. 2d ed. Englewood Cliffs, NJ: Prentice Hall, 1988. All aspects of screenwriting.

Swain, Dwight and Joye Swain. *Film Scriptwriting: A Practical Manual*. 2nd ed. Boston: Focal Press, 1988.

Vale, Eugene. *The Technique of Screen and TV Writing*. New York: Simon and Schuster, 1982. Extended and analytic; usefully compares film, theatre, and novel forms.

ADAPTATION

Bluestone, George. *Novels into Film*. Berkeley, CA: University of California Press, 1957. Discusses formal limits and specific films.

McDougal, Stuart Y. *Made into Movies: From Literature to Film*. New York: Holt Rinehart and Winston, 1985. Theory, texts, and case studies.

Richardson, Robert. *Literature and Film*. Bloomington, IN: Indiana University Press, 1969. Intelligent discussion of the relationship between the two forms.

DIRECTING

Bresson, Robert. *Notes on Cinematography*. New York: Urizen, 1977. Tantalizingly brief entries from the notebook of the French veteran director tackling many fascinating issues.

Dmytryk, Edward: *On Directing*. Boston: Focal Press, 1984. Chatty and full of well founded advice, but hard for the beginner to apply.

Rabiger, Michael. *Directing The Documentary*. Boston: Focal Press, 1987. The documentary equivalent to this book.

Sherman, Eric. *Directing the Film: Film Directors on their Art*. Boston: Little, Brown, 1976. Stellar cast of directors talking about all aspects of their craft. Still the job remains remote.

LIGHTING

Carlson, Verne and Sylvia Carlson. *Professional Lighting Handbook*. Boston: Focal Press, 1985. Professional lighting methods and hardware.

Millerson, Gerald. *The Technique of Lighting for Television and Motion Pictures*. Boston: Focal Press, 1982. Thorough but good for beginners.

Ritsko, Alan J. *Lighting for Location Motion Pictures*. New York: Van Nostrand Reinhold, 1979. Covers every aspect of the lighting and rigging problems that beset films made on location. Presumes no prior knowledge.

Samuelson, David W. *Motion Picture Camera and Lighting Equipment: Choice and Technique*. Boston: Focal Press, 1986. Specifics and use of a wide range of equipment; discusses special situations.

Sylvania Corp. *Lighting Handbook for Television, Theatre and Professional Photography.* Danvers, MA: GTE Sylvania, 1984. Manufacturer's handbook detailing many lamp types but also containing articles on light, light measurement, electricity, and lighting setups.

VIDEO CAMERAS AND RECORDING

Caiati, Carl. *Video Production the Professional Way.* Blue Ridge Summit, PA: Tab Books, 1985. Compendium of tech information but in a cramped format.

Cheshire, David. *The Video Manual.* New York: Van Nostrand, 1982. Good for explaining principles to beginners.

Costello, Marjorie and Michael Heiss. *The Video Camcorder Handbook.* Los Angeles: HP Books, 1987. Working concepts, brands, hookups.

Fuller, B., et al. *Single-Camera Video Production.* Englewood Cliffs, NJ: Prentice-Hall, 1982. Comprehensive production techniques manual that also explains principles.

Mathias, Harry and Richard Patterson. *Electronic Cinematography: Achieving Photographic Control over the Video Image.* Belmont, CA: Wadsworth, 1985. Advanced video techniques.

Millerson, Gerald. *Video Camera Techniques.* Boston: Focal Press, 1983. Handling, operation, and use of video cameras.

Robinson, J.F. and P.H. Beards. *Using Videotape.* Boston: Focal Press, 1981. Operation, principles, and care of videotape recording machines.

Robinson, Richard. *The Video Primer.* New York: Perigee, 1983. Field production techniques and concepts of video, both in overview and later in depth.

MOTION PICTURE TECHNIQUES

Adams, William B. *The Handbook of Motion Picture Production.* New York: John Wiley & Sons, 1977. Encyclopedic, fully illustrated.

Arijon, Daniel. *Grammar of the Film Language.* Boston: Focal Press, 1976. Useful for understanding the mysteries of camera placement and framing to ensure smooth editing. Quantities of inexplicably nude figures.

Clarke, Charles G., ed. *American Cinematographer's Handbook.* Hollywood: American Society of Cinematographers. New issues regularly, this is the cinematographer's bible and contains an incredible breadth of professional-level information compactly presented. Surprisingly accessible to the beginner.

Eastman Kodak Co. *Cinematographer's Field Guide.* Rochester, NY: Eastman Kodak Co., 1978. Hip pocket guide to using Kodak motion picture products.

Happe, L. Bernard. *Basic Motion Picture Technology.* Boston: Focal Press, 1978. Good at explaining working principles.

Malkiewicz, J. Kris. *Cinematography: A Guide for Film Makers and Film Teachers.* New York: Van Nostrand Reinhold, 1973. A preferred text for intermediate filmmaking that extends from cameras, filters, lighting, and sound recording through editing and production.

Pincus, Edward and Steven Ascher. *The Filmmakers Handbook.* New York: Plume, 1984. Accessible to the beginner, lots of information both technical and conceptual. Good for the experimental filmmaker.

Samuelson, David W. *Motion Picture Camera Techniques*. Boston: Focal Press, 1979. Information on a wide range of camera-related topics clearly presented.

MICROPHONE, RECORDING, AND SOUND MIXING TECHNIQUES

Clifford, Martin. *Microphones: How They Work and How to Use Them*. Blue Ridge Summit, PA: Tab Books, 1977. Thorough and user-friendly for a relatively technical work.

Hubatka, Milton C., Frederick Hull, and Richard W. Sanders. *Audio Sweetening for Film and TV*. Blue Ridge Summit, PA: Tab Books, 1985. Techniques and equipment rather than applied artistry.

Nisbett, Alec. *The Technique of the Sound Studio*. Boston: Focal Press, 1979. Useful for understanding possibilities of sound mixing.

——*The Use of Microphones*. Boston: Focal Press, 1983. Well presented audio engineer theory and practice.

EDITING

Anderson, Gary H. *Video Taping and Post Production: A Professional Guide*. White Plains, NY: Knowledge Industry Publications, 1984. Totally technical.

Burder, John. *The Technique of Editing 16mm Films*. Boston: Focal Press, 1979. Practical introduction to tools and concepts.

Dmytryk, Edward. *On Film Editing*. Boston: Focal Press, 1984. Anecdotal and conceptual more than a guide to procedure.

Hollyn, Norman. *The Film Editing Handbook*. New York: Arco, 1984. Deals with feature film editing. Very good on organization and method in the cutting room.

Reisz, Karel and Gavin Millar. *The Technique of Film Editing*. Boston: Focal Press, 1968. Still the standard work for the concepts of editing, full of good information, but cramped in layout and with oppressively dated examples.

Rosenblum, Ralph. *When the Shooting Stops . . . the Cutting Begins*. New York. Penguin, 1980. Personal and funny account of the professional editor's way of life.

Walter, Ernest. *The Technique of the Film Cutting Room*. Boston: Focal Press, 1982. An A to Z of the physical process of the cutting room.

FINANCE, PRODUCTION, AND DISTRIBUTION

Goodell, Gregory. *Independent Feature Film Production: A Complete Guide from Concept Through Distribution*. New York: St. Martin's Press, 1982. Legal, business, facilities, services, distribution, and a lot of production aspects, too.

Gregory, Mollie. *Making Films Your Business*. New York: Schocken, 1979. Survival qualities, writing skills, budgeting, the law, financing, distribution, contracts.

Singleton, Ralph S. *The Film Scheduling/Film Budgeting Workbook*. Beverly Hills: Lone Eagle, 1984. A must for your production manager. As a bonus, contains original screenplay to Coppola's *The Conversation* (1974).

Wiese, Michael. *The Independent Film and Videomaker's Guide*. Boston: Focal Press, 1984. Finding investors, preparing the prospectus, researching the market, producing, and distributing. Specifically for short and documentary films.

————*Home Video: Producing for the Home Market*. Westport, CT: Michael Weise Film/Video, 1986. Good for the independent producer wishing to penetrate a variety of markets.

EDUCATION AND CAREER POSSIBILITIES

American Film Institute Guide to College Courses in Film and Television. Princeton, NJ: Peterson's Guides, (perodically published). Comprehensive listing of institutions, their faculty, philosophy, equipment, and core courses.

Bone, Jan. *Opportunities in Film*. Lincolnwood, IL: VGM Career Horizons, 1983. Organization of the film industry, workshops, seminars, conventions, unions, job hunting, and schooling abroad. Feature film oriented.

London, Mel. *Getting Into Film*. New York: Ballantyne, 1977. Cheerfully irreverant but realistic survey of what it takes to work in film.

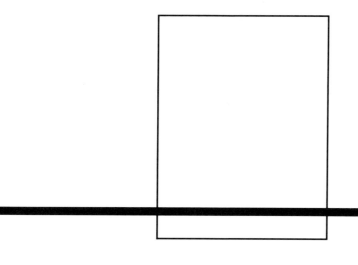

I·N·D·E·X